Karen

Karen

A Brother Remembers

Kelsey Grammer

Harper Select

SUMMON PUBLISHING

Published by Harper Select, an imprint of HarperCollins Focus LLC.

Any internet addresses, phone numbers, or company or product information printed in this book are offered as a resource and are not intended in any way to be or to imply an endorsement by Harper Select, nor does Harper Select vouch for the existence, content, or services of these sites, phone numbers, companies, or products beyond the life of this book.

ISBN 978-1-4002-5282-4 (eBook)
ISBN 978-1-4002-5281-7 (HC)

Library of Congress Control Number: 2024948682

Printed in the United States of America

25 26 27 28 29 LBC 5 4 3 2 1

A Note to the Reader

Karen is a visceral, saturated, honest, ecstatic recounting of my sister's days until her final desecration. It is a Life book—a celebration of Karen's life. I wanted to tell Karen's story while including a bit of my own, the story of our life together, and most importantly, the love we shared. It is an unflinching account, raw and punctuated with horror. The words spilled from my mind to my fingers to the pages of this book. It poured from days long past. Fresh and alive. Fifty years hence, I learned that love, our love, is forever. It also brought me great Joy. To see her smile again, that was really something. And in hopes it might bring solace to those who have suffered like horrors— that's in there, too. From a loving brother, I invite you to meet Karen, to know her and to remember her with me. Karen.

Kelsey Grammer

I stood outside a door in the hallway of a mortuary. I placed my hand on the doorknob and stepped inside. The room was filled with a harsh light. I closed my eyes tight.

Why am I here?

Karen Elisa Grammer was born on July 15th, 1956, in Perth Amboy, New Jersey. Her father was Allen Grammer, and her mother was Sally Grammer.

She died on July 1st, 1975—two weeks before her nineteenth birthday.

She was my sister.

This is her story.

Murder. The word is simple. It is not simple to understand. Short of it being a life sentence for a loved one and for those who love them, it is almost inexplicably difficult to understand through their eyes. The people who love those who have been taken struggle with the idea of what they must have felt and seen and suffered. The dynamics of murder are savage and surreal as we contemplate the nature of the death—its cuts and fissures and blood—its cruelty and finality. So the story of Karen's life will be told backwards. Starting with her final moments, Karen will come to life for the reader with her husk before us and her life extinguished.

It may perhaps flash across the course of her story as it does in memory . . . fondest moments are often dashed by the image, distorted by it, because of the sheer horror it invokes, the questions it asks over and over of what it must have been like for her. And there is a guilt that comes along as well, regretting that that worst of all nights in her life gets so much attention, so much more than the wonderful memories of her as a child and her days as such an extraordinary person. And such a light. Karen was a wonderful woman, child, sister, friend, granddaughter, daughter. She was definitively alive and excellent in her love, her insights, and her compassion. She was decidedly brave in her choices and her passion. She was artistic and sensitive and genuine. She was kind and caring, and at no time in her story is her victimhood of more value than her life.

I am standing at the threshold of our bathroom door. I am seven years old. Karen is five. Teeth have been brushed. Time for bed. As I reach to turn out the light, I ask her if she had the same trouble seeing in the dark just after turning off a light switch as I did. I was not able to see until my eyes adjusted, which took quite a while. I was reluctant to step down the hall until they had adjusted. She told me to close my eyes before turning off the light. Close them tight, turn off the light, wait a

2

second, open them, and then step forward into the darkness. You can see. And I could see.

In the mortuary, moments later, I eased my eyes open and the trick still worked. Only in reverse. Karen is with me now. Chastising me. A fifth rewrite of a single sentence is completely unnecessary: ***"They get it."*** I counter that words are very important to me. The right phrase or collection of words is even more so. She already knows this about me. ***"Suit yourself."***

And so it goes. This back and forth between us, as we lived. It goes on. Always. It does not corrupt the intention nor soften the impact of the story . . . it is an exchange that continues between us consciously and subconsciously at all times.

I could see . . . blinding light became bearable after my eyelids, closed for a time, allowed my pupils to adjust. Then I could see.

Okay, that should do it.

"Yes, indeed, it should. Continue."

I could see. The saddest thing I had ever seen: Karen hollowed out. She was not as she had been; she was on a gurney, covered with a white sheet. The light was from a large window on a Colorado morning that seemed desolate and more like winter than a warm day in July—bleak and barren. The bridge of her nose looked filled in with putty, or mortician's wax, in an attempt to hide a prominent ridge of cartilage exposed by dehydration. And at her feet, the sheet was pierced by toes that looked like sharp bones protruding through it. She had been dead for some time and her once vivacious body was a desiccated husk, nothing more. No longer Karen but an empty vessel. Lifeless.

"That's Karen," I said.

But it was not Karen. There was an almost comforting lack of Karen in what remained of her body. She was not in there, I thought. What was unmistakably alive and vital in her, that which had animated the features and the eyes and the intellect of my darling sister, was no longer; the laughter, the joy were elsewhere. Perhaps my heart—with me, in me. There was hope and there was hurt, indescribable hurt. But I felt she was indeed with me, watching me, regretting that I was forced

3

to see her that way, sorry that she could not hold me when I wept. I felt her with me. And I swore to keep her in my heart forever.

I will remember you forever, I told her.

And in my heart, I almost heard her say, "But, please, not like this."

I am sorry, Karen, that it has been so hard for me. This last image of you was impossible to shake for years and years—it haunted me in quiet moments and down dark streets, ambushing the joy of a cherry blossom day, crushing it without warning. And today, even to this very day, it has the power to make me shake with grief. But—it will not be as I remember you . . . I promise!

"Once we establish a motive, we will be close to catching these guys." The detective who met me at the airport told me that along the way. He was a wonderful guy. He cared about what had happened, what was happening. Six dead . . . so far. There would be a seventh. Someone was murdering people in Colorado Springs. Why? No one knew at that point. The killings were brutal and rocked the community—Karen's particularly brutal. Unidentified for several days, her picture was actually published in the local papers: Do you know this girl? Traces of her torture lingered in the photo.

Her roommate had circled the eyes with a doodle of glasses like the ones Karen wore. She did not call the police.

It was a call from me to the Colorado Springs Police Department that finally got the ball rolling, knowing who she was. Karen and I had spoken on July 1st. I was at home in Pompano Beach at the time. She was coming home after the Fourth of July weekend to visit and celebrate her nineteenth birthday on the 15th of July. It was a wonderful conversation. I hadn't seen her since Christmas. I wanted to introduce her to Jill, my girlfriend, and even "fiancée.

There were some clouds on the horizon though.

By way of context, I feel it's important to know who I was, what I was, a few short weeks before Karen died. We had both left home two years earlier. What had I become in that time? Who was I?

I had been "let go" from Juilliard. There was a rather messy process at school. The freshman class of acting students had been winnowed down at the end of the school year, and the same fate awaited a few of us as the sophomore year came to its conclusion. We were all keenly aware that a visit to the upstairs offices was likely not very good news. Jill was aware of that, too.

Liz Smith, Robert Williams, and Gene, whose last name I will not include here because of something I will share momentarily. The three of them greeted me. There were kindnesses exchanged and some encouraging words, but then the final assessment was that I would be better served in a different environment. I thanked them for their time and shared a real appreciation for them and the things they had taught me. I admired them so, was actually a little scared of them as they were the very best in their professions, and I was deeply grateful for the time I had been there. I did wish that I could stay but it seemed their minds were made up; so, I cheerfully accepted the news and resolved to step boldly into the abyss of a future without Juilliard . . . a future elsewhere.

I want to take a minute to sing the praises of Liz Smith and Robert Williams. Liz was a magnificent woman. Please remember these are the recollections of an eighteen-year-old boy with very little knowledge of the world and a surging amount of testosterone; so that when speaking with Liz or receiving instruction from her, her more-than-ample bustline was a distraction of sorts. A passive infatuation, if you will. I was also very impressed with her knowledge and skill at helping us achieve a "rib swing"—a method of breathing meant to support the voice. There was no one more helpful in my life when it comes to the speaking voice. She taught me how to find it and keep it. She was very imposing and inspired a many faceted admiration—professional and profound with a dash of youthful foolishness, I confess. She wore a lot of sweaters. They looked great. We worked together years later, exchanged many kind words, and I related how thankful I was for her instruction—it had proven invaluable throughout my career. I never told her of my secret "crush" on her. I like to think she would have gotten a kick out of it. It was harmless enough. She was a woman of note in more ways than one, and I hold her in high esteem to this day.

Robert Williams specialized in text work and diction, as well as voice production. I would marvel at his skill with a piece of text and his ability to unlock the meaning of a complicated passage with a single word's inflection. A remarkable storyteller. My fellow students and I mused how lucky his children were to have him bedside when being told a story. Years after I left the school, it was Robert who would show up at the backstage door of every show I did, no matter how humble a production, and congratulate me on the performance. It was no small feat to find these productions; no small feat to get there and attend them from uptown. He taught at Columbia as well as Juilliard. A remarkable man and even a friend in my mind, as he showed support well beyond any expectation. Those visits backstage were amazing. They helped me and buoyed me more than I can say. I wish I had told him, but I think he knew. The smile and surprise on my face must have told him. I was so grateful.

Gene was an important influence in my young life and even a profound influence in my work today. I did not think so at the time. In fact, I had a low tolerance for his class—my acting class, incidentally, because he seemed very interested in the young women in it, very interested. I will not suggest that there was anything more than an interest; but it did seem "lopsided" to me, for want of a better word, and my attendance waned considerably. To his credit, he did end up in a relationship that lasted for several years with one of the young women in my group—a wonderful actress who has gone on to a great career in the theater and in film. She and I have worked together since and I think she is a substantial talent, even a treasure in our profession. I will spare her name here as I do not wish to cause any harm.

Gene taught me two things…two things that have proven invaluable throughout my career. Once, while walking out of school, Gene followed up on a point of confusion I'd had in class. I was not certain of myself or my worth or my abilities, and my tentative nature in entering a scene was starting to hobble me. He asked if I had any answers for him. I told him I didn't even have the right questions. Hence, I was almost paralyzed in a scene, uncomfortable to make myself seen or to call attention to myself.

As we walked from the elevator, Gene suggested that "seduction" was one of the key elements to success on stage. He elaborated

6

seduction exists in all interaction—that moment when we get another's attention and they become interested in us. To illustrate, he turned midsentence, offered his hand to one of the security guards at the front desk, and said, "How are you today?" "Wonderful," said the guard. They exchanged a smile and shared the moment, affable and anonymous but connected. Point well taken.

I would recall years later that to seduce the audience would be a very important part of success. To make that contact, to offer a wink of the eye, to charm an audience into the circle of the performance—this was a lifeline, courtesy of Gene. He probably wouldn't remember.

Another occasion took place in class. An emotional recall exercise is commonplace in acting school. I was dealing with Gordon and his death, attempting to access our connection and having some difficulty as he had been dead for many years at that point. The class was watching as Gene turned his attention to me and asked what I was working on or who. I answered, "Gordon, my grandfather. He died when I was twelve." "Did you love him?" Gene asked. "Yes." "Then tell him." *Then tell him*—and that was when the floodgates opened. I wept and wept as I bleated out what I had never told him before. I Love You. I love you, Gordon. And the channel of my emotions opened up, mourning the loss of the man who meant everything; and I connected with something I had suppressed for seven years. That openness has been a great tool in my work since that day.

Karen's murder, just weeks later, would throw me into a spiral of conflict between emotional surrender and restraint. Both, at the same time, was impossible. And so I wrestled between despair and resolve as arrangements were made to ship Karen home. The business of death is comforting in a way—it distances the grief with tasks and planning, distracting from the hole that has been left by the loss of a loved one.

I chose a coffin and paid for the flight. The friendly detective was as sympathetic and informative as he thought appropriate. The inevitable question came: Had Karen been raped?

The detective said, "No." He was a very kind man, and though I learned later that she had indeed been raped and tortured, I do not blame him for keeping it from me during that sad car ride to a Ramada

Inn to spend the night. With a person in pain perhaps the entire truth is not necessary. To know more than I had already seen might bludgeon me unnecessarily. Perhaps that was his thinking.

Each paragraph leads me to a recollection that may seem a departure from Karen, but they are equally relevant because they are the story . . . so as I write, the kindness of that detective leads me to my grandmother, Gam, as she was called. His discretion was a departure from my grandmother's directness.

A knock came at the door of our home in Pompano Beach, Florida. Two local detectives asked if there was anyone in the home with a heart condition. And my own heart began to race. I answered that my grandmother had had some medical difficulties lately and they asked if I would step outside with them.

"Is this about my sister?" I asked, knowing it was. We walked around the front of the house to their car. On the hood of the car, they laid out a looseleaf folder and opened it to a page on which they'd written "Karen Elisa Grammer."

"We have a Jane Doe in Colorado Springs that is feared to be your sister," said one of the police detectives. They discussed the need to fly out to make an identification. They asked for dental records. I referred them to our dentist and said I would make plans to fly out the following day. Their manner was impeccable. I thanked them. Then, I turned and searched my heart for the tears I knew would come but there was a delay. So much would have to be done. Everything had changed.

I entered the house and went directly to my grandmother's bedroom. She was seated in her chair beside the bed. I told her gently that the police had identified Karen's body in Colorado.

Gam just said, "I knew it."

Karen had been dead for more than a week. She had died in the early morning hours of July 1st. No more than six hours after I spoke with her. We had no cell phones then and Karen had always been a very free spirit. Her plans to be home around July 7th were not set in stone, but a phone call from one of her roommates alerted us that something was up—but even then, we waited one more day. I believe it was around July 9th when I called the local police and then connected with the

Colorado Springs Police Department. The following day, the detectives from the Pompano Beach Police Department came to the door.

My mother was not home when I broke the news to Gam but she was due back from work an hour or so later. My grandmother and I waited. When she arrived, I had no idea what to say. I greeted her and asked her to join me and Gam in her bedroom. I asked her to sit down and said we had some bad news.

"She's dead!" my grandmother blurted out, "Karen's dead!"

And that was that. My mother's reaction was like nothing I've ever seen.

Karen is telling me to stop now, so I shall. I have written of it before. I only went down this path to illustrate the difference between the detective who met me at the airport and the crustiness of my grandmother. She had lived a much harder life than most and I suppose her delivery reflected a kind of weary disenchantment with the world and its affairs . . . she was equally devastated by Karen's death; she just buried it in a bottle and a rough disposition, a hardened heart. It broke her, though. Gordon's death took her great Love, and Karen's took her hope of the future. I was still her "little man," but this was devastating beyond all measure.

Gam lived another four years or so and saw me begin a career as an actor, but she lost so much with Karen and would never be the same.

Between

My first attempt at a chapter heading. *Between.* I like the way it looks. I like the suggestion of a doorway. But I am not sure it's necessary. Not trying to be flippant here. Just honest. I might do chapters. I might not.

Anyway, I stepped away from this for a couple of days. I was thinking of Henry Fielding and how he commented on his own writing throughout his classic novel, *Tom Jones.* I have been tasked by my sister to tell her story. While working through a medium named Esther, a truly gifted one, we had a session where she brought Karen's wishes to me. Write my story. This is how I am going about it. I mention Fielding because I want people to know why I might jump in and make comments on my own writing as we go along. I liked it. Liked it when he did it. So, I am borrowing it. It's Henry's fault.

It is all about me!

In conversation, when my wife asked me if I was doing my writing for my sister or myself, I responded it was impossible for me to tell the story of Karen's life without what that story means to me. I suppose it is possible to simply do a chronological recounting of Karen from birth to death and that is certainly an element of this exercise, but Karen's life story hasn't ended. She has been with me every day of my life. Sometimes not in the waking moment to moment of my days but every day she is in my heart and mind. Even as I write, she is here. So, I suppose, it is all about me *and* Karen when I tell Karen's story. Recounting her history and the events that landmark her story is part of what is going on here. Another part is how she continues in me . . . or . . . how I have imprisoned her with my inability to let her go. That idea haunts me. And maybe the point of it all. I do not know. I do intend to share every recollection and every connection I can to bring her story to anyone who might be interested. And I believe there are many who would be interested in knowing more about the greatest girl ever! Hyperbole for most . . . Truth for me. If you care to continue, I will show you. The "ME" of it will do its best to honor her completely with insights and invocations, instances when Karen's story is my story and those when it is not.

Jill.

Jill stood at the cafeteria entrance at school. Her eyes anxious and hopeful. I shrugged my shoulders and told her, "I'm out." I had been let go from Juilliard. And I convinced myself what happened upstairs at the Drama Department was not tragic. Until I saw the look on Jill's face. She seemed crushed by the news—more crushed than I felt. In an instant, I took her look to mean she no longer saw me as her future. In an instant. That look was a rejection, a judgment of me and my worth and I watched the love drain from her eyes. It broke my heart. I tried to convince her this might prove good news in time. I took her in my arms hoping for some consolation and instead felt something gone from her.

Worse than being kicked out of school, Jill was finished with me.

Maybe I should not have taken it so seriously. We'd been having so much fun together. Our love was so perfect. Our future so bright. Perhaps her look was nothing more than the realization that we'd no longer be having lunch together at the world's greatest school of the arts. Perhaps, the dream of another two years together as shiny, new talents in the rarified air of the Juilliard School might be worth a little sadness. I did not give her enough credit. I wish I had.

I'd like to take a moment to thank Karen here. Kayte, too. I am certain now that Karen had this kind of journey and "coming clean" in mind. I am also certain that Kayte, whether she is aware of it or not, is acting in concert with Karen to help point out a couple of things along the way. It was Kayte who suggested maybe Jill was just sad and

12

I'd misread her reaction. Maybe so. She had every right to be sad. A month later, Karen died and upon reflection, to Jill's credit, she stayed with me for another year. We rented an apartment together. We still made plans for our future. I auditioned almost every day. She went to school. I waited tables. She gave it a good try. And honestly, I didn't make it easy on her. I was desolated. Drowning in grief. And I almost took Jill with me.

I checked in at the Ramada Inn. I think I tried to sleep a little and then went downstairs for some food. I ordered a steak and hoped the waitress might take pity on me and sit down for a time. I fantasized her asking me why I was so sad and finally inviting me to refuge with her that night. I was aching for a refuge. There would be none. I ate my dinner in silence and played out the scene of a beautiful girl of virtue so moved by the pain of a strange young man that she would give herself to him, just for a night, and take that pain away. Karen knows this is true even as she points out my great flair for self-indulgence and excess. Nice story, though: two sad people giving solace to each other on a night when the air itself was impossible to breathe. I went to my room to call Jill.

Jill was in Texas. Houston. Her family was in the process of moving there as her dad had been recently promoted. When we met, her family lived in West Hartford, Connecticut, the capital of insurance companies, and sure enough, her dad was pretty high up at Aetna. The move to Texas was an advancement but maybe a little challenging for her mom. I don't really know. I think I recall her telling me how she was warming to Houston when I visited there on the way to my first acting job in San Diego.

I liked Jill's parents. Jill warned me never to let them know I rode a motorcycle but as I was on my way cross country on my motorcycle—a Honda 750, one of the best bikes on the road at the time—and as I roared up to their beautiful suburban home at sunset, I am afraid the proverbial cat was out of the bag. This was a year after Karen died. It was the first time I met her dad. I had met Jill's sister, Sarah, in New York, and her mom after we started seeing each other. My memory is not quite clear on this, but I think we told them we wanted to get married. They seemed okay with it.

Jill and I had actually chosen the kind of dog we would get after the blessed event, a Samoyed we were going to name Sarka, a mix of our sisters' names, Sarah and Karen. Years later, as I adopted a white shepherd puppy, the name fell to her. Out of a sentimentality perhaps or just because it was perfect for a big white dog, I gave it to her. Sarka was a great name for one of the great dogs—a remnant perhaps, or an echo, of a once-great young love.

Sarka under her favorite olive tree in Van Nuys. A cool spot of earth in the California sun. She was a lovely girl.

I sat at dinner with Jill's folks and obviously the "bike" came up. Her dad was squarely against motorcycles. I am not sure how I tackled the conversation as it has been some time since, but the young man they assumed was a somewhat mad, impetuous renegade, managed to leave the impression, on his departure, of a reasoned and responsible suitor to their beloved daughter. I won them over and left the house feeling deeply fond of them.

A week later, I would have a phone call with Jill that was a good-bye call.

But on the call with Jill now, from the Ramada Inn, she consoled me and asked about Karen, what I knew, how I was holding up. I spoke about the kind detective and what we knew of Karen's final hours. My flight to Colorado was fine and I told her about a gentleman seated beside me who was very pleasant and apologized for prying when I told him why I was flying that day. I think he bought me a Bloody Mary—I was old enough to drink back then as the legal age was eighteen. He wished me luck and offered a sympathetic handshake with a feeble word of encouragement when the flight ended. A nice man. His company had made the flight easier. I thanked him for his kindness then and I thank him now. Jill and I cried together on the phone and made plans for her to visit Florida. She would come for a good chunk of the summer, and, in the fall, we would move together back to New York City. But first, I would return home with Karen's body—to her funeral and to my mother and grandmother.

I would like to take a second here to sort out something. This is not a story about Jill, but telling Karen's story has helped me understand what it meant to lose Jill as well. I have not really allowed myself to be honest about who we were to each other, how much she meant to me. I never realized how grateful I was that she chose to love me, and I have never realized until now how wrong I was about her. Kayte, my wife, helped me with that. She restored my faith in Jill. I was willing to let that single look of disappointment or confusion dismiss her love for me, fearing she had dismissed me. The truth is, Jill stood by me through some impossibly painful days and was driven away. I could not see how hard she was trying. I couldn't see at all. She stayed because she hoped the pain would pass. She hoped to salvage the life we'd planned and believed our Love was strong enough to do it. I never realized that until now. God Bless Her. Who knows what might have been, but my pain was absolute—a few things yet to tell, but we ended.

Jill died fourteen years ago. Her sister, Sarah, reached out at the time, but we never connected. I always wondered why. Why she reached out to me. Perhaps it was to let me know Jill's love had been authentic—as real as mine, perhaps. I am sorry I doubted it. I wish I'd thanked her—wish it hadn't taken me until this very moment to know the truth. My apology is late, Jill. I regret that.

The morning of Karen's funeral. Most of the day is a blur. I don't remember crying at all. I remember being pissed off. I had requested the coffin be closed. I told my mom that Karen didn't really look like Karen anymore; seeing her would not be a comfort in any way. She seemed content with that. Gam agreed.

What upset me most was that those who spoke at the funeral service did not really know Karen. They had no personal knowledge of her. The words could have applied to anyone. I wished I had spoken but thought I would never get through it. I was probably right but the whole service left a bad taste in my mouth, as the words Karen deserved at her funeral were not spoken. They did not touch how funny she was and how brave she had been in life. They did not hint at the depth of love she had achieved or how much we loved her. She was the love of my life. A constant. It was Karen who finally insisted our family start saying we loved each other out loud. She was the voice of it, the keeper of love and guardian of the sacred in our family. And I was her protector, her big brother.

Once, when one of the neighborhood kids had ambushed her with a brutal snowball attack, I sculpted an "ice ball" to exact a dreadful retribution upon the offender. I am not proud of it necessarily, but it was a perfectly executed affair. From a considerable distance, and with Karen out of danger, I took aim and hoisted my rock-hard projectile directly at the head of this awful young man. It was a bull's-eye. Fit for a bully! And it sent him home, crying, more shocked and embarrassed than hurt. This had been the dynamic of our childhood together. I looked after my little sister. There was no one closer to me. Mess with her, you were messing with me!

Boy, was I knocked for a loop with all that when Karen was killed. There is no delicate way to say it. Recounting her funeral and the events of her death has made me realize how mad I was at myself and how angry that the one thing I had always done, I didn't do. I felt emasculated and empty. All my big brother "protector" bullshit was just that.

No.

Karen. Get back to Karen.

Okay.

It is important to remember the tragedy of her death belongs to her. Not entirely true, perhaps; because, you see, I have often said that to dismiss my own feelings about it. "The tragedy belongs to her"—as if I had no right to view it as my tragedy. But it belongs to me too. Her death belongs to her; the consequence belongs to me and to the men who killed her. And to me because I couldn't stop them. I didn't stop them. That was my issue with it all and I felt like I failed her. I felt I should have stopped it. I felt I abandoned her. None of this was logical. It was just true. I wasn't mad at the speakers at her funeral, I was mad at me. I should have stopped them even if I couldn't stop them. Her killers. I should have killed them. Karen was not to be hurt . . . not on my watch.

It took twenty years to forgive myself. Well, that is not exactly true, either—to *almost* forgive myself. If it had been possible, I would have killed them. I would still kill them, if it were possible. If it were possible, I would have given myself in place of Karen. At least, I think I would have. If it were possible. If it were possible Karen would call me on a weekend and our kids would visit. We would celebrate birthdays and graduations and see each other grow old.

Or maybe I am just full of it. I have spent years pretending I had found some lofty reserve about Karen but a little scratch on the surface and the rage and anger and devastation erupt. They had no right to touch her.

Freddie Glenn is up for parole again in thirty-eight days. The fucking nerve of this asshole to expect some kind of reprieve or release because "he has served long enough."

Freddie Glenn.

Shadow. Of Shadow. From Shadow. I do not know. But he is the last of her murderers—rather, the first in her murder, the last left alive. Up for parole again . . . and again . . . and again.

Also, the very last to see Karen alive. To know her. I envy him that. Hard to explain, but I do. More in time.

An apology. For profanity. I leave the offensive language in because it's how I felt as I was writing. And to acknowledge this is something seething within me. Rage. At the same time, however, it makes me small and reduces a righteous anger to a base and commonplace expression. I am capable of pettiness and crassness—I leave the language in to illustrate that point. And though almost anyone would forgive me for it, I still wish to apologize. There is a passage similar well into the book that I will now remove. A single indulgence in the profane is enough. Freddie deserves nothing from me. Certainly not obscenity. It diminishes me. It diminishes Karen. I will not yield to that.

Freddie once said at a hearing, "I was a good kid." Really? A good kid? I intend to see you rot in jail. I do not get released from my prison because it seems like it's been long enough. I find you a miserable, detestable creature, but I will not abdicate my dignity because of you. I forgive you because we are all forgiven. I cannot embrace your release or grant you the freedom to hurt someone ever again. Seven murdered people is enough! Find a way to do the world some good from prison and I will sing your praises at the gates. More than that I will not accept. It is possible you were a good kid, and something swept you up that swept up the life of my sister and my mother and my family, other families and your family, and no time is sufficient or "enough" to wipe away that damage. For the pain they have suffered, I do indeed forgive you. Your poor mother, your poor family! I have never felt them like this—felt their broken hearts as mine. God Bless Them. So much suffering. Let it be.

The things I have said here, I have never said. So. We share a prison, Freddie. A prison you made. Our prison. It need not be Karen's. She is free. You and I may share it forever, but now? Telling her story releases me. Karen lives beyond your savagery, as she always has. And finally, my unending grief yields to the memory of my beloved sister shining and alive. We are free to love one another beyond your reach. Melt into the shadows, Freddie. I will not tarry with you there. Not anymore.

But there is more to tell. As a man who has lived through many curses and self-afflictions, I know the "prison" has more than one cell. One and then another. Karen's life. Our family. Her brief history. Her lasting impact. These call me to another page. To go deeper, honestly and with an open heart, toward the promise of an even greater freedom. I am blessed to have many with me. To hold my hand. I have you now. And I have Karen.

I am wrangling with something. Something Esther told me. You remember Esther. Esther is a medium.

A clarification. An explanation.

Esther's "channeling." A friend asked how it works. Esther is recognized in certain circles as a woman of great talent. She can access messages from the other side. She has skill in diagnosing health issues and past lives issues, and many revere her as a medium of great insight. It was during a simple phone call when she passed along Karen's request. I do not know how it works. There was a shaking of sticks or rattles on the other end of the line. Some incantations. I heard a soft singing. Shamanic entreaties, I suppose. And then . . . information. Useful hopefully. In my case, yes. It has become a prescription. Filled by my writing. A prescription to heal my soul. And Karen.

And what I am wrangling with is a suggestion Esther made: *Karen may be ready to come again to take another life on this plane.* I don't like it. I am reacting selfishly. The thought of losing her a second time is very hard, very hard indeed. It's all so confusing. You see, I believe she is with me forever. She is forever. But this is all a bit much for me. I am new to this dimension of past lives and "contracts" before we come. Contracts with whom? I have a raft of new friends, dozens of fellow seekers who share this journey; they throw these ideas around like confetti. They ask who they are, why they are and what it all means. And it seems they find answers. At least part of the time. Me? I am lost. I do not know.

"Continue the story."

Continue. Right. Fill the prescription.

Write.

So, we must return to the day of Karen's funeral because it begins so many things. There was a flower arrangement sent by Larry Pedicord and the Pine Crest Day Camp that did dissolve me into tears. Remember, I said I did not cry that day but it's not true—I cried when I saw those flowers. I forgot.

Spencer was there. My friend, Spencer. I named my first daughter after him and my sister: Spencer Karen Grammer. A medium once told me Karen was honored I included her in the naming of my first child. As if I would do anything else! The middle name seemed appropriate as Spencer was a new being. She could not be Karen; she would be her own person. And she is. The naming of a child is something parents usually take pretty seriously, hoping to give them a strong, unique name that will serve them well in life. Biblical names are easy, as are famous artists, family friends, and ancestors. The name Spencer came from a lifelong friend; the Karen, from her aunt. The original Karen and Spencer had known each other in life. They were friends too. To see them joined this way, together in the name of my first child is pleasing, a great comfort. A legacy that honors them both.

My grandmother once said that you know your true friends by their actions. When someone says, "I'll be there for you if you need me, let me know," it's not such a big thing. A friend knows when you need them. A friend shows up. Like Spencer did. That is how you know the friendship is true.

I called Spence after my mom had come home that afternoon. He had known that we'd started to look for Karen. Maybe he even called me; I don't remember. "Heard anything?" he may have asked. I told him, "Karen's dead. She was murdered." No. I called him. Spencer walked through the door forty minutes later and we talked through the night, trying to figure out what had happened. We mourned Karen and celebrated her in alternate turns of remembrance and disbelief. His being there was everything.

We don't really connect anymore. I am not sure what became of him. I hope he's okay. His name did serve my daughter well, I think. I miss him.

Outside the funeral home, I recovered myself a bit and Mario Peña appeared at my side. Mario had been Karen's sixth grade teacher at Pine Crest School in Ft. Lauderdale, Florida. Karen and I started attending school there in 1967 after Gordon died, after he had moved his wife and family from New Jersey to Florida.

Mario was a special one. Karen's sixth-grade teacher. We became great friends and remained great friends for years and years until his death. I see him now as the page unfolds: a happy memory. And in seeing him, I am reminded to include some happiness in this book—the happiness in Karen's life. There is an abundance of it. And she is guiding me. I feel her.

Mario Peña is relevant. He was a kind man and a great teacher who shepherded the two of us in that first very difficult year without Gordon. For me, Mario was a friendly face with a wry smile but for Karen he was the chief male figure in her sixth-grade education after the loss of the most important man in her life. As far as Gordon was concerned, Karen was the center of the Universe! Princess Coca-Cola.

It was a presumptive joy to spend even a minute with Gordon. He was the light of the world and that light always shone on Karen. They would play Monopoly, which Gordon pronounced invitingly, "MO-NO-PO-LY." "How about a game of Mo-no-po-ly?" he would say as he walked into the house and invited Karen to come for some fun before dinner. "Come on, Princess Coca-Cola!" It is as vivid as any memory I have of him: Gordon, striding toward the kitchen door from the front yard and waving his joy to join him. I had forgotten how clear a memory this was for me. I did not feel slighted. I think I envied them the bond they had. This is not to tarnish the bond we had but you could tell the love between them was effortless and pristine and beautiful beyond any other . . . there was no effort, it was like their lungs filled and fell at the same moment, always. It was a perfect love. Once again, I tell you I have never said these things before—surely, I must have seen them and felt them, but until now, I have never known or been able to comprehend what Karen and Gordon meant to each other. I would like to think I'm jealous but that would not be right. I didn't envy them this bond—I basked in it. How magnificent their love. I have a remarkable joy and inexplicable gladness. I am watching that towering man and his little girl step from the yard that night into Heaven. Together. Forever.

I never realized when Gordon died that Karen lost Gordon, too. Our world ended. We would have to build another.

To start, Gordon's love for Karen was so rich, I cannot imagine how lost she felt when he was suddenly missing. Karen was ten, I was twelve. I would be a poor replacement for him as the "man of the house." The path before us was uncharted and there had been no preparation for it. I am struggling here to find the next piece to share. In all honesty, if I surrender to the uncertainty I feel now in writing, I find myself exactly where I was in the days after Gordon left us: uncertain, uncertain of everything.

Gordon died of cancer in mid-June of 1967. He was sixty-three. The bottom dropped out. There was nothing.

Just months ago, while in deep meditation, I transported back in time to a night with Gordon sitting on our terrace in Atlantic Highlands, New Jersey. I was eleven years old. I sat alongside Gordon after dinner, as was our custom, gazing out at the night sky and the fog rolling in off the Atlantic into our small harbor. There was the faint slap of halyards on masts, bells on buoys, fog horns. Naval Ammunition Depot Earle stood, an ominous shadow looming on the horizon in the outline of an aircraft carrier—"The Wasp," my grandfather would whisper with a sense of awe.

To the right, more distant on the horizon was the shining skyline of Manhattan. We were on the Jersey side of New York Harbor, near Sandy Hook. Just below sat the Atlantic Highlands Yacht Club. The yacht club was the nightly destination for our walk along the docks. There were fishing boats and hearty year-round sailors moored there in winter; in summer it was a thriving little dockage and where I first learned to sail. We would stroll right to the end of one dock and then turn back, make our way up the next and as we reached the end of the second dock, we concluded our review of the day's challenges and insights. Then Gordon would walk up the stairs to the promise of a warm reception, a scotch and some friendly conversation with the regulars and he would hand me a cluster of quarters and tell me to play a few racks. It was there I became a pretty good pool player.

"Sign of a misspent youth," he would chuckle and then dare some of his pals to try me. I never disappointed him. I don't play pool anymore, but I was the closest thing to an underage shark the club had ever known.

A drink or two at the bar with the usual crowd. Wanda and Ollie were often there. They lived in our building and Wanda was Doug Peterson's mom; Dougie became a great friend and is a great friend. Suzie Barnes was there sometimes, and I have no idea how it so happened that Suzie gave me my first driving lesson in her blue VW Beetle along our street in Pompano Beach when I was fourteen years old. I would fly past the house and Suzie would scream at the top of her lungs, "Kelsey, just hit the clutch and the brake at the same time and *stop!*" I suppose a proper time to explore that memory may emerge, but I have no idea how the hell she got there. I sure did like her, though; we all did. And I remember a psychotherapist who drank as much as any of them, a woman who held her liquor and was obviously a bon vivant.

Gordon was a bit of a bon vivant himself. He enjoyed good company. I guess I did too. I would approach the bar for a refill on my Coke (kids were not allowed to sit at the bar in New Jersey) and drink in the gossip. I love that bar to this day. I loved the gathering of people and the small talk and the general goodwill that refracted off the faces as they stared out at the harbor. They lifted their glasses for another drink from the bartender; their glass placed at arm's length, slid forward, a tap of the forefinger on the place it had been, and another drink appeared in an instant. It was a good place.

Gordon and I would make our way home after an hour or so, maybe just a bit more than an hour, and ride the elevator up to dinner at apartment 7D.

"We're moving to Florida," came the announcement a year earlier, after Gam and Gordon returned from Ft. Lauderdale. They had paid cash for a house there. We would be moving to a small place for a year or so and then off to Pompano Beach where Gordon would retire, and we would live in the sunshine and tropical splendor of South Florida. We were ecstatic. The entire family had taken the train to Hollywood, Florida, two years earlier. We swam every day. The sun was magnificent and wooed us all with its warming rays. So, when our grandparents announced the move in our kitchen, we jumped about the room in hoots and howls of delight. The apartment in Atlantic Highlands was the stopover. Gordon had actually bought two apartments next to each other to provide an extra bedroom for my mom. It was not far from Perth Amboy—yes, Karen's birthplace, and where Gordon worked the last few years of his career with Chevron Oil Company. The plan was to spend a year or two at most. Gordon would retire early. Karen and I could attend Atlantic Highlands Elementary School, just a few blocks and a short walk from our apartment. As it turned out, we were new kids in a fairly tough town. I hear good things about Atlantic Highlands now, but then it was not the nicest place to live and certainly not the nicest place to go to the local public school. As a temporary home, though, it would do. We had privileges at Fort Hancock so we could go to the beach right out at the end of Sandy Hook—beautiful. And we shopped at Fort Monmouth and had our special dinners at the officers' club because Gordon was a retired colonel in the Army Corps of Engineers. I was extremely proud of that fact. He had served in World War II. Pacific Theater. Army Corps of Engineers. Guadalcanal. He was my hero. I am pretty sure Karen felt the same way.

My wife, Kayte, and I do ceremonial meditations at home. It was during one of these when I had my vision of Gordon. After dinner. Gazing out on the harbor and the city lights, as I told you before, the night I sat with Gordon on the terrace. Gordon nursed his third or fourth Haig & Haig scotch. We sat in silence mostly while enjoying the night air and one another's company . . . I was twelve years old. We would be leaving for Florida soon.

I finally realized what I saw that night. I saw him dying. His body was convulsing at irregular intervals, belches and spasms. I could hear them as he choked down acid and burped up air. He looked extremely uncomfortable, and I was unable to help him or even speak. The spell passed after a while, but my vision showed me that in that moment I knew the man I worshipped would be leaving. Life would be changing. A life I loved and the man I loved as my father was dying. And I cried just last spring, the tears of that boy a lifetime ago, whose life was ending too.

Ahead from there, back from here.

Karen was dead. I walked out of the funeral home with Mario Peña. The sun was bright. The world was rolling by out on Federal Highway just as it always had. A burger drive-through was buzzing with activity. Just another day. It was a hard day. The Grammers were one fewer . . . and the Cranmers. My mom's maiden name was Cranmer. Gordon and Evangeline were her parents. She married Allen Grammer which everyone remarked was very close to the same name. Sally Cranmer Grammer, as my mom was sometimes called, walked ahead of me. I believe she wore a dress or suit that was not black, but flowered. Fitting for Florida.

I turned and shook Mario's hand and flashed back to the moment we met. Mario was more than just Karen's sixth-grade teacher. He was well known and well liked around the school. A bit of a star. Karen loved him and boasted that he was the greatest teacher she ever had. The Pine Crest Preparatory School was a kindergarten through twelfth grade affair and was situated on a large campus in Ft. Lauderdale that was split into two sides. Elementary school and high school were divided with sixth grade being the final year before students transitioned to the other side of the school for seventh through twelfth. The sides did not interact very often but one day, probably a month into our first year at Pine Crest, I happened to be at the main office. I do not remember why but I was not in trouble which would normally have been the customary reason. I have to cry foul on myself here—truthfully, I was not in trouble and rarely was. I was standing at the main desk there and possibly confirming our phone number for the head office . . . something like that, when Mario Peña walked in. He did carry himself like a man of importance and I liked him instantly.

I approached him and introduced myself. "I am Kelsey Grammer, Karen's brother, and I am very good!"

I have no idea why I said such a thing, but Karen had told me what a wonderful guy he was and I wanted him to like me. I guess he did. We enjoyed a great friendship until he died thirty years later. He was one of the main influences in my life and even had a chance to see that his "fears" for me were not realized. As several of the faculty at Pine Crest had warned, a career as an actor was not an easy path and I might be wiser to seek another. "Something to fall back on" was the common phrase but I always thought that if I had something to fall back on, I probably would. So, I chose acting. Mario did support the decision and it pleased me that, in time, I was on my way. As we said goodbye that day, however, the news was not so good. I was kicked out of Juilliard. Two years earlier, I was the first Pine Crest student to be accepted there. Ah, how I had fallen! But this was not the death sentence some believed it to be—Karen had been given a death sentence and nothing would ever be so final and devastating. My future as an actor or what have you, would be fine. I had a future.

I caught up to my mother and we walked to the car. I believe Gam was waiting there as well. We talked on the drive home about how the service did not seem particularly inspired or helpful, but my mom thanked me for deciding on a closed casket. Grateful, I think, that she did not see Karen lifeless and altered. My poor mom.

We got home and received a surprise call from our family doctor. He asked if I had slept. I had not. Not for three days or so. He said he was calling in a prescription for Valium and to take one so I could get some rest.

Another call came. It was Wandi. Wandi had been the golden girl of my school and someone—well, I was absolutely in awe of her . . . to the point that even when it seemed she might be interested in me, I was incapable of accepting it. So far out of reach she was, and I so

▲ An early picnic.

▼ Karen did make me smile. There's that joy. Look at my face.

▲ Easter Sunday, dressed up. Most of our shots with Karen and me in blazers and such are taken on Easter Sunday. We did dress up from time to time but always at Easter.

◀ Karen and the famous candy jar.

I always thought she was pillaging ▶
candy while standing on a
chair. I was on the chair.

◀ With Mom.

▼ Looks like the same day. Bucket on the head. Good look.

▼ Prison Yard. It was here my mom told me that Paul's mother from across the street would sometimes drop him and disappear for a few hours. We didn't mind. I think my mom did. ▼ Prison Yard pool.

▲ Sand box. One rain kind of destroyed it but I thought it was cool.

▼ Together. It was profoundly
together we lived. Every day.

This was the title card for a Super ▶
8 movie Gordon shot of us. Karen
in a tutu. She was great.

▲ Another Easter Sunday.

▲ Same day as the cover. Yup, Easter Sun

▲ Walking in the back door in Colonia.

▲ And the same day as the cover again. I am doing a somewhat tortured impression of Louis Armstrong singing "Hello Dolly!" It was my favorite back then.

▲ Same day as the cover once more. Another Easter Sunday.

unworthy. In my own eyes. I felt equally intimidated by her older sister Alix—it is a long story filled with the foolish imaginings of a lovelorn adolescent with even a bit of a crush on their mother. I will leave it at that. Anyway, Wandi called and in her attempts to comfort me she broke down and sobbed. It was the most comforting thing that happened that day. I am not sure I ever told her. We stayed friends for years afterward and I regret that we have not seen each other for a very long time. But Wandi will always hold a singular place in my heart. I sense she knows that. I hope she knows that.

I drove to the drugstore and picked up some Valium. I took one that night and as I lay down, the drowsiness consumed me.

That night I slept.

Then

Karen approached three men entering the back of a Red Lobster in Colorado Springs. She had come to pick up her paycheck before heading out to the mountains for the Fourth of July weekend. The three men had come to rob the place.

There had been several murders in Colorado Springs that summer—these men were responsible. Karen had no idea who they were as she asked them what they were up to, but I am fairly certain she discerned quickly what suddenly faced her: destruction. The story I was told by the district attorney and others involved in the arrest of these men has never really been clear. I think they hoped to spare my feelings and keep the horror of what had actually happened from me. I appreciate that and I accept their reasons for being vague. The specific details of her suffering were kept from me, but some information had to be offered. Conjecture of what she suffered is probably just as brutal as the reality; my imaginings likely paint the worst picture. But this is Karen's tragedy, not mine. Yes, I offered that perspective earlier, but this tragedy is Karen's triumph, as well. Her strength that evening is unfathomable. Her dignity stands forever an inspiration to me. What I have endured is nothing by comparison, but it was enough for me—enough to hobble me in the journey of Life and Love and Joy for a long time. I could not forgive myself. I will address that more. For now, that evening only.

The men abducted Karen. They held her hostage for several hours. The district attorney told me Karen negotiated with them for her life. She would do whatever they asked if they spared her. I am not sure she laid it out like that. Perhaps she implied she hoped they would spare her. I am sure that by the time they took her to the apartment where she was raped and tortured by them, Karen understood that her life was at stake. I have thought for years about her heart in that moment. How it must have been beating. Not like a rabbit's, frozen in terror before a wolf, but increased and urgent and calculating as she tried to offer them a way out of killing her.

Karen was always the brave one. Karen could even stand up to my grandmother. She had a heightened sense of right and wrong. And was willing to go to bat for herself in the onslaught of what she believed to be unfair. I could follow this path for pages about her character and courage. But I will force myself back to that night. I am tempted to take a convenient off-ramp when the table is set with something I would rather not remember or recount—but the table is set. I see her on her knees. I see her violated. Slapped, punched, knocked to the floor. I see her blindfolded by the blue scarf that was never found. I hear Freddie as he takes her glasses from her and ties her hands.

"You won't be needing these."

They never found her glasses. I see her entered by these animals. Sodomized by these animals. And let me say right now they are nothing more than animals. If you wish to take offense at my characterization of them that is your right, but may I suggest you check your humanity? Or your brain? You clearly have no heart. I am tempted to rail that cruelty is considered commonplace in today's society and with those who seem to take joy in another's suffering. I will not. It dishonors Karen. Suffice to say that good people are horrified by what happened to my sister. And there are plenty of good people left. Enough said. I am detouring from the facts of that night. Easy to understand why but this passage from Shakespeare's *Richard II* came to me last night as I lay in bed planning this next day of writing. Or dreading it:

29

I have been studying how I may compare
This prison where I live, unto the world.
And for because the world is populous
and here is not a creature but myself,
I cannot do it; yet I'll hammer it out.

It reminds me how I have lived in a prison with this night since that night. This particular prison is fashioned by own mind. I have played it over and over in my head for forty-nine years. That night. My prison. No self-pity implied and no sympathy required. The door has swung open.

After they had taken their turns, the discussion fell to what they would have to do with Karen. Perhaps, it was their game to boast of all the people they had killed, but for now, it seemed they were concerned that leaving anyone alive could lead to their arrest. Knowing the same fate awaited Karen, their most recent conquest, they openly discussed killing her . . . she could identify them. I become paralyzed when I imagine it. The callous discussion of her death while she still breathed, while she still hoped to live. Unfathomable.

I took a few days away from writing. This section is difficult. Yes, I intuitively knew it would have to be "hammered out"—hence the quotation. But I did not realize how difficult.

A digression.

I have known several mediums in the past. Spoken with dozens. I even produced a show called *Medium*. Hoping to connect with Karen is what fueled it. My interest. Members of the trade would often meet with me and offer readings. Some were good, some not so good. I did meet several I would characterize as gifted. One of them, in fact more than one, suggested that Karen had been taken out of her circumstance before her execution. This idea is hard for me. Has been for years. Is it possible? I am looking for the words to express it. I do not even comprehend it. So how can I explain it? This morning I stumbled upon something. Or it was given me. A way in.

When I was sixteen, I took my then-girlfriend, Liz, "up coast," as we called it. We'd start the day surfing and then head down to school. We took Brett's car, a white Cougar with super-wide rear tires—something we all thought was really cool back then. Honestly, I still think it's cool. Maybe a little silly. Still cool. Anyway.

We paddled out at Fort Pierce and enjoyed a pretty nice swell that day. A couple of hours and we had to get back. Brett asked me to drive. Going "up coast" meant we had to get up pretty early and people would share driving because of how tired we could get; it was like starting the day before the day. Glassy swells about six feet, some good rides and then back we'd go. It had been drizzling which made the waves indescribably smooth . . . a great day. The drizzle turned to a substantial rain as we were cruising down the turnpike. Now, along the Sunshine Highway, giant loads of goods and merchandise, barreling down toward Miami, tended to leave a kind of waviness in the road itself. It can lead to a pooling of water along the highway that is hard to discern, especially in a heavy rain.

Surrender! That may be the point. We surrender to the circumstance before the outcome, uncertain of what will be. Maybe that's it.

So, as we drove, the Mickey Thompson "slicks" lost traction and we began to spin. I desperately tried to alter the outcome, downshifting, accelerating, turning into the direction of the skid but we just kept going round and round in circles . . . nothing would get us back to traction, so I let go of the steering wheel and surrendered. I watched the car and Liz and Brett, he in the back, now awake, as we spun around at least seven times. The Cougar slid off the shoulder down a slight incline toward one of the canals that cross the Florida landscape. I was not certain that the stanchion at the head of the canal would slow our progress, but we were considerably less a hurtling projectile at that time, likely to stop any minute once the skidding was done. I tried the wheel. No traction whatsoever, so that even at five miles an hour, there was nothing to do but wait. I waited, quite removed from the experience, until the outcome. The stanchion stopped our progress.

Here then is a possible window into understanding what the medium had said. Karen had been taken out of the experience. Maybe it is something we all have hard-wired. Something so overwhelming tends to slow things down. Or speed up, rather. I remember as I saw the car spinning around and around, it seemed impossibly slow, as if my mind was taking pictures at three or four times the natural speed. More pictures in the same space of time: slow motion. Perhaps, too, in slowness we can discern a possible escape . . . the shutter of our minds is in overdrive, processing thousands more images than usual to find a way out. Maybe. It may be there is something in this idea. Something. Something more. I don't know.

Right now, Karen is in my mind and the last hours of her life are calling.

Karen escaped, but not for long. I do not know how, but this is what I imagine. She was back in the car with only two of her abductors. I believe this is true. Michael Corbett, who was the "ringleader," so to speak, was not there. This is my understanding. At some point, Karen jumped from the car, or when stopped, was able to wrest her way clear of the car and them. I believe she thought she might get help from one of the mobile homes she could see from the car. This is the idea I have held loosely since her death. In one sudden moment that presented itself, Karen escaped and hoped to make her way to the trailer park where she might rouse someone's attention and stop her imminent execution. There are other possibilities, of course, but this scenario is fed by something one of the investigators told me—"She escaped them, briefly."

The problem with all these imaginings is that there were forty-two stab wounds. When did they stab her? And that many times? Seven wounds were enough to kill her. Or rather, seven of the wounds would have been sufficient to take her life—each of them enough to kill her. So, when did she get them? As I write, I envision she was stabbed at their apartment. Hypothesize, rather. Stabbed for fun or to terrify her. Or just for their greater pleasure.

And it is here I have to stop myself. I promised I would not extend too far beyond the facts as I know them. The police and the DA told me that they were still unclear as to how Karen escaped them, but that she got away from them for a time. There are so many questions I cannot answer, but to theorize is not helpful. I do not know the full story. There must have been so much blood. She escaped them some-how; they pursued and it was Freddie Glenn who slashed her throat, almost decapitating her. They left her for dead. Even after that, she was able to crawl to a nearby trailer and seek help. She was so strong, my sister. My God, I wish I could have stopped this! I wish I could have helped her. The man who lived in the trailer found her. I regret I never apologized to him. No, that's wrong, it was not for me to apologize but to thank him. I wish I had thanked him. In the final moments of her life someone had been kind. Paramedics tried to revive her but could not. Karen is dead.

As I am sitting in the screening room with my kids, my mind replays an earlier conversation I had with an agent about this book. Then James Taylor pops into my mind. We named our son after him. James Taylor and Karen. They are connected in a way I will explain before long. I have started writing a book about my sister, I had told the agent. A book. I think. Is it a Grief book? No. It is a Life book. There is Grief along the road, surely, but this is about Life and about Karen and about my life and about the life we have lived together before and after her human experience.

But now, my kids and I are watching a film. So, I may as well men-tion the title—*Sing 2*. Fun. Celebratory. All the characters giving their all. Joined together in song and vision. Striving for the best they can do.

Suddenly, a voice in my head says: ***"If it's not worth everything, it's not worth anything!"*** The voice is Karen's. Or mine. I don't know. But I realize this is something she taught me. Something never said. Something I knew but never said out loud. Until now.

Her death did teach me—how precious life is. Life, in the time we have. There can be only one choice. To live fully. And in blinding clarity, in that very moment, it coupled itself with every memory I have. Last night. Extraordinary how she lives within me. In my Heart. Karen showed me what had to be done throughout my life since the day she died. And she has lived in me and with me ever since.

I am riding down an Alabama afternoon, dark as midnight, storming through a violent downpour at 100 miles an hour . . . on my motorcycle. The speed serves two purposes. One, I am resolute to reach my destination—San Diego—in four days. And two, I am able to see better in the rain at that speed than a slower one. The beads of water spend a split second on my helmet shield at that speed and the road is visible in the midst of a downpour, illuminated by my solitary headlight as I throttle toward Dallas, Texas.

I have told this story before but never with this set of eyes. So many things had taken me to this point in time. So much of my future lay ahead of me. As if this was a single measure in $4/4$ time, four notes of a symphony just beginning. Four days. And into those four days, so much was baked; so much was poised.

I was absolutely alone, speeding toward the unknown in a kind of purposeful surrender, certain that though nothing was promised, this was the next amazing gift of my life. It was indeed worth "everything" to discover if it would be worth "anything" at all. I did not know then, as I know now, that though it seemed I was completely alone, she was with me.

As the storm raged on, a sudden bright light blinded me for a second and I felt a surge of energy run through my entire body. It quite literally lit me up. Lightning. It was like the Sistine Chapel. It was like Buddha when the Earth spoke, "I bear you witness." The entire Universe, as I knew it, was guiding me along the way, lighting me the way to a new life. And Karen was there, and affirmation, and God. And we were all smiling.

A few hours later, I pulled into a gas station to fill up and stretch my legs. I must have looked like, I don't know, a half-drowned rat, but something was working, because as I headed around to the men's room, a rather attractive woman sitting on the hood of a tricked-out pickup truck, satin hot pants and all, smiled at me and asked where I was headed.

"Dallas," I told her.

"Dallas? Why don't you just spend the night with me, and you can get an early start in the morning?"

This was possibly the best offer I had ever had. I'd certainly never had one like it before. A night to shelter in the arms of a magnificent stranger! Tempting, indeed, as it brings back memories of a darker time not long before. I thanked her anyway and headed back to my bike on my way to Dallas. It was nice to be noticed. I believe she sensed, and I hope she knew it was not that easy to walk away. I did look back a few times . . . and smiled. She smiled, too.

"Thanks," I said; and then, "Sorry."

"That's okay, honey, you drive safe."

I can hear that lilting Southern charm as I write. Irresistible! Well, not quite, obviously; but I can still hear it. A wonderful memory.

Back to Karen's funeral.

I am looking at my mom now as I open the car door for her. I let her in the front. Gam was fine to sit in the back. Not her custom, but in this case, fine. I drove the 1972 brown metallic T-bird home. It was a great car.

Moments before, Mario and I had noticed the lunch crowd bustling about and discussed how the world hadn't taken notice who it was missing. Just not the way it works. I think of Christ. The world gave Him so much Hate and He gave them so much Love. God Bless Him. God Bless Karen. God Bless Mom. God Bless Evangeline (Gam). My God, even as His body distorted in the grimace of inhumane torture, Jesus beseeched, "Father forgive them, for they know not what they do." Their Hate and their Fear killed Love. Imagine that. How could that happen?

God Bless Gordon. Gordon grew up on a horse ranch in California near Fresno. Black Mountain Ranch in the Kettleman Hills. His dad's place. His mom died when he was six months old, and his brother blamed him. Gordon did not believe in God.

When I began writing this evening, I thought it was time to talk about Gordon. Get to that porch one night so long ago in Atlantic Highlands. I am blocked a bit. I realize that as I write many of the memories that jog into place and reveal a connection to some feeling or shame that I have carried, I am suddenly clear of them. As if writing about them has taken their teeth. The exercise is meant to free me for the next chapters in my life, unencumbered by doubt and fear.

The prison door swings open. Again. Karen is telling me I do not lose myself when I let these things go. I think I used to believe I did and that is perhaps why I waited so long to tell her story. She knows this frees me, *is* freeing me. It may also free her.

That night sitting on the porch with Gordon, we were basically silent except I could see and hear him belching, even as he tried to choke down the sound. It was very violent. It made me uncomfortable. And in the vision that took me to that night, I learned something else.

Waypoints.

Like navigational markers, there are events that I will circle again. Some more than once. To help us know where we are and where we are going. On the terrace that night. It was then I knew for the first time that Gordon was dying. My eleven-year-old self knew he was dying. I wasn't aware of it at the time; I am aware of it now. A question I had never asked was answered and through this window into the past, I saw that innocent boy and his grandfather keeping company before an approaching storm they didn't know was coming. Immersed in the vision of that night, I wept for them both. And it showed me something else. It showed me Gordon's fear that we would perish as a family if we did not leave New Jersey; if he didn't get us out of Jersey and down to Florida. So, in returning there, I am now allowed to thank him. For the first time. Congratulate him on a job well done. We had made so many plans together. Spring training camp, a deep-sea fishing yacht he meant to buy . . . we had driven to Egg Harbor, to the boat manufacturer at the Jersey Shore to "kick the tires," so to speak. Just spending time with him. We were going to have so much fun. It was not meant to be, but it was his dying act to get us to a place we could thrive and grow up safe. That was his goal. That's what he had been up to in his final days. He did a beautiful job.

And I never knew. A flood of gratitude swamped my heart. And Admiration. Still does. He did it! Thanks, Gordon. Thanks so much. What a man you were and what a great example. I can still mourn Gordon, but now I know everything I didn't know when I was just a boy who had lost his soul. I am so proud of him as I miss him and from some distance, finally, I can comfort that boy and honor that man.

And thank you, Karen.

Waypoints. I repeat them because they have more to tell. Others? Well, some things just bear repeating.

There was a night in Virginia Beach. We stopped at a familiar little motel near a golf course where we stayed when visiting Florence and Stanley Hodges, Gordon's best friend. They were also Karen's and my Godparents. I loved that place. I loved them. It was always such fun visiting them. Anyway, this was one stop on our way to Florida . . . the last time we would ever see it. We were joining Florence and Stanley for dinner and as we waited for the "girls" to get ready, Gordon and I sat outside enjoying the setting sun. He had never once spoken to me about the war. He started with a tale about a dance called the "Shag." Apparently, it was pretty popular in the early years of World War II. Gordon recounted the story of a young, innocent American recruit who approached one of the nurses from Australia at a USO social.

"Would you like to 'shag'?" he had asked her, and she slapped him.

Apparently, to shag meant to have sex. It was the first ribald exchange between us. It was amusing. I was awkwardly appreciative of the joke.

Then he turned to Guadalcanal. "Me smell Jap"—this was how his Philippine trackers would tell him of enemy soldiers in the jungle ahead. Please, accept my apology for any perceived wrong in expressing this phrase as it was in the day. It was a very simple way for two people who spoke different languages to identify the presence of an enemy who was determined to kill them. In such a situation, people rarely have the time to speak of said enemy in any but the most immediate and possibly least honorific way. Hence, what his Philippine guides and trackers would always say was some quick assessment of "Jap" presence, status and the likelihood of danger extremely near. Gordon's admiration for their skill and his gratitude for their friendship was apparent whenever he spoke of them. I assume there was a life debt of some sort that was shared between them. Or maybe it was just a true friendship: love, good men in a bad place, respect.

In any case, sitting there that night, after we shared a little laugh about the soldier and the "Shag," Gordon's eyes grew melancholy and distant. He said, "They killed four of my boys. They cut their heads off and their dicks, stuck their dicks in their mouths, and put their heads where their dicks had been." He also mentioned the night two boys who had just shipped in stood watching the glorious tropical sky. Gordon warned them they should keep an eye out and stay down. Moments later a Mitsubishi Zero, an infamous aircraft of the Imperial Japanese Navy, suddenly appeared over the mountain at the end of the runway, strafed it and killed the two boys instantly.

It was the only time Gordon spoke to me of what he saw there, what he experienced. He was speaking to me as a man that night. A sign of respect and of trust, I think, that I was up to the job ahead.

He stood and said: "Let's go get some dinner." Gordon Savage Cranmer. He stood with the stature of a mountain—majestic and regal. He passed by me. And I felt, as I always felt with Gordon, a kind of awe.

Dinner was fun. We laughed and were joined by several of Gordon and Gam's friends. I was not aware other people would be there. There was Lee Bonney and his wife, I forget her name right now…no, Thelma!— that was it—Florence and Hodges, Gordon and Gam, my mom, Karen, and me. I am a little shaky here, but I think even Jack and Adelaide were there, friends my grandparents had met on one of their many cruises, though I do not remember their last name. I liked them, too. I liked them all.

Karen and I spent most of the evening together as the grown-ups laughed well into the night, moving the party back to the motel where they drank heartily and laughed even harder into the wee hours.

I really liked those people. They knew how to have fun.

On the occasion of Michael Corbett's first parole hearing, the arresting officer picked me up at the airport, just as he had done all those years before. It was equally surreal as the first time we met. Only this time, the government was considering releasing men who killed seven people.

The community still echoed the scars of that summer, when their brutality served up a series of deaths beyond imagination. Colorado Springs looked just as bleak. Its fence of mountains seemed just as barren and cruel. I don't mean to trash Colorado Springs. It seems a nice community, and the people with the criminal justice system I have met there through the years have all seemed dedicated and thoughtful. I'm sure folks understand why I might have an uneasy time with it. I have returned there twice since Karen was murdered. I hope I don't have to go back.

Michael Corbett died in prison a few years back now. Good. In prison. I know he left behind a wife who advocated for him to be released. She has my condolences. I am sorry for her loss. When I met Michael, I sat quite close to him as he spoke of his time in prison and how well he was regarded by fellow inmates and officers alike. He had been on dialysis for some time so the vigor of the man who towered in my imagination with all the virulence of an epic villain actually looked quite weak and sheepish. I suspect this was part theater, part sincerity and part fiction. I remember saying there was little he could do to convince me he should die anywhere but in prison. And then it was Kathy's turn. Kathy had been the young wife of one of their victims. A soldier, PFC Winford Proffitt. What a great name. Winford. Like a man crossing the sky, surfing the wind.

Backstage at a Frasier *filming and at Winford's funeral.*

I imagine Kathy reading this line one day. I think she'll like it. Kathy had a bit more experience with Mr. Corbett. She shared with me something that happened during the trial. I had not been asked to be there. But Kathy had been in court, and she recounted a moment when Michael mouthed a threat to kill her while he was sitting in the courtroom. Her father had seen it, as well. This guy was dirt through and through. We can spend years of self-incrimination and guilt that somehow the society we helped create did a disservice to this animal. It is not true. No matter how much we would like to blame ourselves for savagery against our loved ones, there is no truth to it.

And Kathy, in the moment when the hearing turned to her sentiments about Michael Corbett and his request for parole, was breathtakingly simple. Without apology, she questioned what he had thought his "little killing spree" (her words) was all about; but she would do everything in her power to make sure he died in jail. I wished at the time, I had had the balls to be so honest and brutal—not half again as brutal as the murders they dished out to our loved ones.

I admire Kathy so much. I admire her for remembering. She has lived a good life after she lost her young husband, but she has always honored the life these three destroyed and took from her. We share a pain we would never have chosen but we have a love and a bond that is unbreakable. Those three men did break our hearts but never our resolve. And so, Michael Corbett died in jail. I spent an afternoon sorting through a myriad of emotions and anger and then realized that his being gone was exactly as it should be. He is no more. He is gone. His Soul is back in the foundry where perhaps he can be shaped by good and God. We need not carry him any longer.

The night of Winford's death, Kathy and her husband were out on an evening with a friend. They thought it might be fun to track down a little marijuana. The friend said he knew where they might find some and they headed off to an area near a park in Colorado Springs. Lured away to a site some distance from public view, Michael Corbett lunged a large knife (bayonet) into Winford that pierced his liver and went through him. His reaction was to run immediately to his wife. Winford was given a fifty-fifty chance of survival. Hours later, Kathy was told her young husband had died. Kathy had moved from Florida to join Winford and sought to start a career as a nurse in the Army. He was buried with full military honors, and a young bride no older than my sister would now face life without him. Kathy told me she has never spent a day without thinking of him. I know how she feels. She would be there when Freddie Glenn came up for parole, as well, to offer her support. Ironically, Kathy and Winford had dinner at the Red Lobster where Karen worked just two weeks before he died.

At Freddie Glenn's parole hearing, Kathy was there. As good as her word.

Karen's best friend, Momo, got in touch a few days after the funeral. I do not remember if she had been there for it or came back to Ft. Lauderdale afterward. It would be nice to spend some time together. I had known Momo since we moved to Florida. She was in sixth grade with Karen and Mario Peña. That is where they became best friends. I always thought of her as my friend, too. I wish we were still in touch. I think she and my mom remained pen pals even if they did not see each other. Momo had an older sister, Claudia, and an older brother whose name I forget right now. I barely remember their mother and father, but I liked the siblings, each and every one of them.

I drove down to Momo's house and we spent the night together. Now, being the red-blooded American boy I was, the thought of actually "spending" the night together did cross my mind, but the idea was dismissed. We were both reeling from Karen's death, and I was still in love with Jill, of course. So, we spent the evening holding each other and spoke of the love we had for Karen. What we knew and did not know about the past year of her life; how she got to Colorado and why. We reminisced about her. I realized then I loved Momo, had loved her all that time since we'd all been kids together. I was completely at ease and because she was beside me, I felt closer to Karen than I could have imagined.

I think her brother's name was Craig—it just hit me. I hope they are still well. Life has thrown me many a surprise the past couple of decades ... some folks I still envision as young and vibrant are gone. The traffic of life, I suppose, but I will always see them as the young people I

41

once knew. Even when I do catch up to some of the friends of my youth, I notice that time may have worked some magic on them but cannot erase the beautiful young woman I knew, or the bold innocent optimism of the young man I once called friend. They are still in there as electric and magnificent as they were in their youth.

So it is with Momo. Dorothy was her given name but "Momo" stuck, apparently, because it was how she asked for more milk as a little girl. Cute. We talked through the night sharing many great memories. We cried a bit. We laughed a lot. I remembered the night my mom woke me saying to get up and go get Karen—she was in the Ft. Lauderdale jail. Momo and possibly Jan were with her. I am not that sure about Jan but there were more than just the two of them, that much I knew. They were accused of breaking into Momo's home. They were found there having a small party, a pot party . . . highly illegal and very juvenile. Hence, the police were not really intent on charging the teens . . . they were just a gaggle of girls being a little silly at a friend's house while her parents were away for a few days. This was the key to their downfall—Momo's parents had told the security people who patrolled their private community that the house would be empty and to keep an eye on it. So, when they saw some lights on and noticed a bit of activity, they approached the house.

At this point, the group of girls all went quiet and hid in a closet, sealing their collective fate. This was when I finally realized Karen and her friends were more involved in the "counterculture" than I was. They weren't exactly potheads, and they weren't hippies; they were just young people who understood image was important and that the desired image was not the image of their parents or even an older brother. So, I went down to get Karen. I suppose Momo's brother got her; I never saw her that night. Karen was brought into a room to sit with me for a time and one of the arresting officers came in to give her a very benign lecture and release her.

"You may go," he said.

Then Karen turned and said, "Pig!"

Absolutely ridiculous. He shrugged his shoulders wearily and left the room. Obviously, this was something he was hearing a lot of in those days. I felt bad. He was a nice guy.

We were free to go. I got to the car with Karen and really lit into her. "It was unnecessary and certainly uncool to call that man a pig. Do you understand what that man could have done instead of let you go?" Nothing from Karen. I was so upset with her but we kept quiet during the ride home. I finally said to her that the trick is not trying things that might get you into trouble. The trick is to try them and make sure you don't get caught. Hiding in the closet?! Mom was so upset. Anyway, Karen was not a bad kid. She was just a kid. But maybe it was Karen's job to stir things up. It was Karen who first pointed out that our family did not say we loved each other. She stood toe-to-toe with my grandmother and asked her why we were not a family that was close or comfortable with closeness and why we would never, no matter what the circumstance, mention that we loved each other. She challenged us to say it out loud.

"Come on, Mom. Say it. Say I love you."

"Oh, don't be silly."

"Then say it."

"All right, I love you."

Karen managed to make it a fun game and then turned her attention to Gam. After considerably more prodding came Gam's reluctant surrender: "All right, I love you, too." But, and this is important, we did say it to one another after that. Not all the time but we did. I suppose Gam and Sally and Gordon all came from a time when it was not as common to speak that way within a family. It was understood that we loved each other. It was also a little too exuberant for a family who survived the depression and fought in the war to say things that should just be evident. Of course, they loved us and we loved them! It did not require a great deal of chatter. Even I did not go around saying it a great deal. But we all got a little better at it, thanks to Karen.

I had a wonderful teacher, Ron Krikac, who persuaded me to try acting. I will speak more about him in a bit, but he shared a story with me about one of his great friends who had several kids. According to Ron, her kids were the most wonderful children he had ever met, wonderful people, as they were in college at the time. He asked her if there was any one thing to which she could attribute their substantial character and decency. She told him that she always said she loved them... out loud. Every day. No matter what. She loved them. And told them. So, in my life today it is probably the one phrase I say more than any other. I thank Karen for making it a household word in a household that was not that comfortable expressing it. I think she'd be proud of me today. Mom got better at it, too. Karen would surely have been proud of the love and the goodness and dignity Mom carried through the loss of her little girl and her life afterward. She carried heartache in every moment and yet stood tall. My inspiration.

Karen's first boyfriend was Danny. Danny Eng. He was the son of a Chinese father and a Seminole mother. He was a lovely guy. His race was a challenge to the family... to my mom and Grandmother. It was a "background" thing. A "what kind of future could you have with him?" thing.

"We all know what's going on here," I told them in a rage of indignation and disappointment. "You are better than this!"

I liked Danny. And we had been taught that color or creed or any of those other qualifiers were non-existent... now, it seemed that they were being a little hypocritical, to say the least. Karen and I both called them on it. Gordon had taught us never to regard another person as anything but an opportunity to know someone new and learn something we did not know. They rose to the occasion. Their concerns vanished. They were indeed better than that. I remember my mom just saying, "You're right."

And at that moment, I admired my mom and Gam. They were as good as they had taught us to be. From then on, Danny was part of the family. Danny and my mom remained friends until she died. Remarkable people. Once again, I find myself saying I wish I could see Danny and his wife. I don't do social media stuff, for obvious reasons, but I think I will have to reach out to several of the folks I have mentioned here because I have missed them. I have had the good fortune to know some wonderful people and to have known so much love in my life. Yes, there has been the other stuff. But the important days are the ones where goodness and light were evident in spite of the darkness. Such a night was the night with Momo. I am so grateful to her. It was during that night she told me of Karen's prediction for me. Kelsey is going to do it all. I promised her that night that I would try. I think part of the reason Karen came to me recently was to remind me of that promise. Maybe even a little kick in the ass.

And something funny happened as I am writing. There is a show called *Phineas and Ferb*... the kids watch it. It is on in the background, and the theme song has these words: Phineas and Ferb—"Are gonna do it all!" And the song ends. Another reminder that this may very well be a cause-and-effect place, more tuned to us and our imagination than we are aware.

And another reason. In the regression I did with Esther, she led me down a series of steps toward a cave. At the entrance of the cave, she said I would meet two young people and I did. They were a pair of lovely Asian children who took me by the hand and led me toward the mouth of the cave. As we reached the opening, the children morphed into me and Karen. They still held me by the hand as we went deeper inside the cave into a sort of tunnel that led to a great room.

At that point, Esther said the young girl was going to give me something. She waited a bit as I searched my thoughts and just as something came to mind, Esther asked me what it was. It was a surfboard, which brought a smile to my face. A surfboard was a direct link to my understanding of God and my relationship with Him. It was on a surfboard that I saw Heaven and realized I was safe no matter what, forever. With a wink, I promise to elaborate in the very near or not too distant future about the surfboard and such.

But suddenly the surfboard changed into a brown slalom ski—a water ski. I remembered it. I had bought it at Sears once I felt confident enough about skiing to get one for myself. I loved that ski.

And then, the vision shifted to an irreplaceable day when Karen and I, with our neighborhood friend, Luanne, had gone skiing in the late afternoon. The truth is neither of them was a skier, so I guess they came to let me ski as it was not legal to ski with fewer than three in the boat. Luanne had the wheel, Karen watched facing the stern of the boat ready to give Luanne a heads-up if I wiped out. She would give the signal and then Luanne would turn the boat to retrieve me or start up again if I was not yet ready to quit. This was all pretty standard. We had several friends who would do this with us, and I had taken years to try it. Glad to handle the boat until one day I decided I should know how to ski. Turned out pretty well. I was good at it. It took me one day to go from skiing with two to dropping one and then just starting out with a slalom ski. I was goofy-footed for skiing but surfed regular. I still don't know why.

On this particular day, we decided to head up the Intracoastal to Deerfield Beach. There is a canal there that cuts deep into the middle of the state. It is one of the canals that is used as a lock of sorts to control water depths and flows. The canal is no wider than thirty feet. And it is probably fifteen miles long, which means if you are traveling at or about thirty-three miles per hour, then you have half an hour of skiing in and half an hour out. It is too narrow a cut to make a turn with a skier, so you have to drop and then restart. The water is like glass along the cut and makes for some of the most ideal skiing near our home in Pompano Beach.

Some people may find it annoying switching tenses as I am bouncing around from present day to Karen, to me, to yesterday, to fifty years ago; but this is how time and memory work. It is not static or locked into chronological progression. It is always and at once flowing from one moment to the next, one memory to another, one time into all time. Hence, if this journey seems haphazard, so be it. You have not lived as I have. You do not live as I live.

After we made the turn and started back toward the Intracoastal, the sun began to set and the water became even more still as the wind had vanished with the change in temperature. The long light of sunset cast even longer shadows at that time of day. The sun was setting directly behind me as I cut back and forth across the boat's wake and edged into a deep turn sending twenty feet of water into the sun's rays. I was not aware of the visual effect but the sensation and the warmth on my back and the spray on my body were one of the greatest experiences I have ever known.

Karen began to wave her hands in the air as if to signal something magnificent was happening. And on we went for another twenty minutes as the sun dipped deeper into the hollow of the canal. Mangrove swamps on either side fenced what finally looked like fairytale wings. And so, I flew along, Karen and Luanne both looking back at the spectacle and reveling in it.

As the canal ended, I dropped the tow rope and waited for the girls to swing around to fetch me. They were both transported by how beautiful it had been. They spoke of it with emotion and even gratitude that such a thing could exist in this world. I had been no more than a messenger; a looming shadow of a boy immersed in God's beauty.

The three of us had shared something we would never know again; and I was completely unaware of its impact until fifty years later when I took a guided regression into my youth, and for the first time saw what Karen saw. She wanted me to see it. And then, Esther said Karen wanted to tell me something: "Remember." Karen wanted me to remember—this day and the thousands of others when love was all we knew, and Creation's great light filled us with wonder. Remember. Remember this and not the things that do not serve you. Or us. This love we had—*have!* Correction. Nothing can tarnish the days of splendor we shared. Nothing. Remember.

And so, I emerged from my session calling throughout the house that I finally knew who I was: "I am a water angel!" I bellowed. "Karen just showed me and told me to remember." Admittedly, I have a flair for exaggeration and entertainment but what I was saying was entirely true even as I allowed the moment to be a bit inflated in my delivery. That is the kind of hairpin I am. And the family seems to enjoy it. Now, when times are a little hard or challenging, I may rear back and proclaim there is nothing to worry about because I am a water angel! It helps. And . . . it's true.

People often ask what another's favorite word is. Mine is "remember." It has been for a long time, and I remember when it became so. Back during college when one of Jill's classmates had a choreography assignment. She had approached me with an idea to put movement to music that was no more than the spoken word; a short piece based on a poem

47

that was read aloud by me. The cadence, rhythm and melody were basically provided by the intonation, delivery, and pitch of my voice. I do not remember the name of the poem, but I do know for certain it was the use of the word "remember" that made it seem more meaningful. To be remembered. To have been once a part of something or someone and then lose them, leave them, means we lose membership. To be remembered means to be brought back to the family, the fold, the love that was taken from us and to live in it again, fully. Of course, I extrapolated that death is only disaster if we are not remembered.

And so, remember became my favorite word—just about six months before Karen died. A few months ago, she asked me to tell her story. I will. I am. And I will remember her.

W. H. Auden wrote a wonderful line about his aunt, speaking of her in the "pomp and sumpture of her heyday." Karen's life was so short that it barely had anything other than a heyday! She lived it full. I am proud of her for that. It might be appropriate to break things down along the line of Gordon's death: before and after. In Titusville near Cape Canaveral, as it was called before John Kennedy was shot, changed to Cape Kennedy afterward, we had stopped at a hotel—or motel, rather. It would be our last stop on the drive to our new home in Florida.

I remember Karen washing her face and how Gam and Mom both remarked how grown up she looked as she cupped the water in her hands and splashed the soap away. Her hair was pinned back, and she did look like one of those commercials for Ponds or some such cleanser with the beautiful model making a simple task of washing up look unbelievably glamorous. I think that simple moment redefined Karen for us all—as if she were poised on the verge of womanhood. It is hard to say it any other way. She was ten years old and honestly not very far from womanhood, at that. Even so, moments later, Karen and I were chasing our cat Nanci around the motel room and wrapping her in our arms asking if she would like some protection. I have no idea how or why this particular torture was devised for Nanci during our trip, but my sister and I would track her around the furniture and spring ourselves upon her. Snuggling into her, Karen and I would ask, "Do you want some protection?" in a sort of strange middle-European accent. We had the best time and the most patient cat in history, tolerating the absurd attacks with style and even a little purring. She was a great cat! She'd been with the family since just before I was born. And Karen, half-woman, half-little girl, was the best person. She was funny and free and spontaneous. The day before we had stopped in Jacksonville at an aquarium for a couple of hours. Karen and I were sitting in the back and Gam was driving, or rather parking the car, when there came a loud bang.

"What the hell did you hit now?" said Gordon.

I think Gam had actually run over a parking sign, but Karen and I exchanged the silliest look, filled with knowing and a kind of glee at how funny Gam and Gordon could be together. It was a priceless look... God, she could make me laugh. Of course, we never laughed out loud in such situations—that would have been rude and we were not rude children. We were good kids. We always prefaced a request with "May I...?" instead of "Can I....?" Should we slip up, Gordon would remind us that of course we can but it was not the way to ask. I have encouraged this in my own children, as well. Yes, we do pass things along from generation to generation and I am always pleased when someone mentions how polite they are. I understand that many take issue with this convention but when a young person says, "May I please have this or that?" it is impressive and connotes good character. I would like to add that I took great pleasure in pleasing my grandfather. If he said it was time to jump, I was crouched in readiness awaiting further instruction.

It was raining the morning we planned to leave Titusville. We let "Nanci-cat" out (I just remembered we called her that sometimes) and started packing the car. An hour or so later, Nanci was not back. It was decided Gordon and Gam should press ahead, so Karen rode with them. Mom and I would wait till we found Nanci and head down once she showed up. We waited for most the day. Finally, Mom thought we should consider moving along. We shouted a few more pleas and just as we climbed in the car, Nanci-cat came sheepishly from beneath a bush, wet and shivering, but finally ready to take the last leg to our new home. I wrapped her in a towel and held her till she warmed up, falling asleep on my lap.

Ron Krikac, whom I mentioned was instrumental in pointing me toward acting, became a friend throughout the rest of high school and beyond. We were eating oysters one night at one of the local joints along Federal Highway when somehow the conversation turned to family pets. I told him that I grew up with a cat named Nanci. "Nanci with an 'i'," as my grandmother always said. And for some reason this just sent him into gales of laughter. I guess it was kind of funny and so like Gam to add a twist. She was a very funny person with a wry sense of humor herself. It is nice to look back on her with that in mind. Not far up the road from where we were eating was the first place we stayed in Pompano Beach. Mom and I arrived near darkness at a tiny little motel. Karen and Gam and Gordon were there, and it was clear Gordon was not doing well.

As I am discovering this story as I tell it, stumbling into forgotten moments and falling into holes that I feebly try to fill, one of those holes is the moment Gordon went to the hospital. I think it was the next morning. I believe that Gam took him to see a doctor at Broward General Hospital. They ran some tests? I really don't know. But that morning or the next, Gordon was admitted to the hospital. His body was riddled with cancer.

I stepped away from writing for about ten days and had a number of thoughts while visiting upstate New York with the family. Bill and Claire Carvell were numbered among Gordon and Gam's best friends. They lived in upstate New York, near Kingston. On several Thanksgivings we would drive up from our home in Colonia, New Jersey, to visit them and celebrate the holiday in the country. They lived on a piece of land they called Copper Head Mountain. It was very cool.

Bill had a riding mower that thrilled me no end and I always volunteered to mow the whole property. I think now he was probably ecstatic when I arrived and always asked if I could mow the lawn. I would spend hours making those neat, overlapping rows of freshly mown grass that gave an apron of geometry to their lovely home. It was truly fun for me. After that, we would often spend a morning doing some shooting. Bill was an avid gun collector. He even had some rather exotic guns that we would try—target shooting only. I imagine they had hunted in their lives, certainly Gordon, as he had been raised on a ranch in California at the turn of the century. But hunting was never on the agenda. We would set up some targets and even take aim at a moving target Bill had rigged to a wire with a pulley and try a shot as it whisked past. This taught me to "lead the target" in a practical exercise, depending on the gun. There was an old .45 revolver, like the Wild West, a snub-nose detective special, an actual Derringer, like the gun that killed Abraham Lincoln, that had a huge kick; and a semi-automatic pistol, as well as a small caliber shotgun. All were unique and offered insights into the world in which they were made, the history of the time and in the case of the snub-nose, a sense of what it might be like to work the streets of Manhattan as a cop in the 1920s.

I suppose imaginings of this kind might have been an indication of where I would settle in life—a career of imaginings and lending myself to lives I would never live but could pretend to live. An actor. Then again, any boy in my place would probably have pictured himself as a gunslinger or protector of the streets, a champion of the people—grand ideas of being useful in adulthood, of doing the world some good. That was the hope. It is still my chief hope and aspiration—to do the world some good. And make a living. It was these trips to Bill and Claire's that seeded the dream that finally brought me just forty-five minutes from there to my favorite home in upstate New York. It is the birthplace of my latest venture, Faith American Brewing Company, and it is the continuing cradle of my well-being and connection to the Source.

It was Bill and Claire who taught me that friends show up. The minute we were told Gordon was sick, they got on a plane and were at the door of that sad little motel within hours. They held our hand and took the journey with us as Gordon made his exit.

It was our second day in Pompano Beach, Florida. The next morning, Gam got up and announced that cots could be rented and there was no reason we shouldn't be sleeping in the house we meant to make our home. So, later that day, we moved in.

Bill was a terrific guy. As I write, I remember a few gems he shared with me. He was missing half of his index finger. This was apparently from an "accident" when opening a taxi door for a woman who thought he was trying to grab it for himself. She brusquely pushed her way past him and into the cab and then slammed the car door shut, his finger sadly lopped off at the second knuckle now inside the cab as it sped off—the clearest example I have ever known of "no good deed goes unpunished!" Probably not something that could happen today unless we could recreate the scene with an original yellow cab. Their doors were extremely heavy, metal slamming on a dried out, minimal strip of rubber to make a seal against the rain and weather. Bill's finger didn't stand a chance! I believe he told me he was in uniform that day. He escaped the war only to have his hand mangled by a hurried stranger on the West Side of Manhattan. He wrapped his handkerchief around his remnant of a digit and made his way to Roosevelt Hospital for a stitch.

Notwithstanding that his left hand was missing part of a finger, Bill was a pretty strong swimmer. Or so he told me one afternoon at the apartment building community pool in New Jersey. We were all settled around a couple of tables. Suzie Barnes was there (the gal whose VW I commandeered years later for my driving lessons), Doug Peterson, his mom Wanda and her husband, Ollie, Gordon and Gam, my mom, Sally, and sister, Karen, possibly Joanne Venore (I'll get to her in a minute) and I seem to remember there was a pigeon who had adopted us for the afternoon and everyone kept calling him Walter Pigeon, after the famous actor. Everyone was drinking. Well, all the adults were drinking.

The men were thrilled Joanne was there, as was I. Joanne was a perfect sixteen-year-old girl. Her brother, Bobby was my friend, in no small part because Joanne was his sister. I was eleven years old and at dinner one night at Bobby's, Joanne casually announced they'd had their measurements taken in gym class that day at school and hers were 36-24-36. I stopped eating. I am not sure I thought of anything else for almost a month. Joanne had a sister, Nancy, who was fourteen and pretty easy on the eyes, as well. It was a stupefied adolescence spent in awe of women. I realize some may attack it as a gender ignorant romp through a toxic male environment, but I was just a kid who believed there was nothing more beautiful than a girl. Sorry. I did not want to harm or control or dominate any women—I just wanted to be near them and marvel at them. Their attention made me feel like a million bucks; their scorn like I was dirt and nothing more.

So, on this day around the pool, Joanne's shining young womanhood refracting through the minds of the men and women alike, Bill suddenly issued a challenge. I was swimming a series of laps in the pool and I was pretty good. Bill stood at the edge of the pool and said he would bet me five dollars that he could beat me in a race to the end and back, a lap and back.

I turned to Gordon and said, "What do you think?"

"You can take him," he said.

I looked to Karen, who nodded in agreement and then my eyes made their way to Joanne. She seemed supportive and disinterested at the same time . . . she was, after all, just a person who lived in perfect beauty always and therefore never bothered with such silliness. Back to Karen and there was a steady look of confidence in her. I said, "Okay!"

But standing at the edge of the pool about to start, I suddenly chickened out. I did not believe I could beat a grown man to the end of the pool and back—I thought I would get my butt kicked. I was eleven, Bill was fifty plus, in great shape and his mind had beaten me already. He had baited me and he had a confidence that was unsettling. I announced we did not have to do this, and Bill agreed it was probably a good idea not to go through with the race. I stood humiliated. Finally, I asked if we could just do the swim for fun, no money involved. Bill said okay. We took our positions and Bill got a good jump at the start. About halfway through the first lap, I realized I was passing Bill. Then I realized on the way back he never got farther than that half lap anyway. You see, his bluster had convinced me there was no way to beat him—a two-pack-a-day smoking, middle-aged man who did not swim every day as I did. It was absurd to think he could beat me. He sputtered to an end after a tortured half lap and took some time to make it back at all.

I remain uncertain of the lesson involved except to never underestimate oneself. Believe in yourself. And if you don't believe in yourself have the nerve to bluff your way to victory. Bill had won that day. I could easily outswim him, but he clearly outplayed me. That has not happened much since.

From Claire I learned what a loving woman could be. It was her style to be open and honest with her emotions and never criticize. When she and Bill came, it felt as if our family was whole even as the hole in our hearts was being driven home. She was patient and kind and creative. I never understood why she and Bill did not have children because she was so good with me and Karen. She remained interested in us and listened. It was with Claire we had our best conversations. Seeing her and seeing Bill always felt like family. In writing about them here, I am welling up, seeing their faces, feeling that love. It really is their "Upstate NY" that sent me back twenty years later to find my own.

One Thanksgiving when I was six, I had mowed the lawn and put the tractor back in the barn, filled it with gas and then presented myself to Claire for breakfast. She had cooked a pound of bacon and stood at the stove. She told me to help myself and I wolfed down the entire pound. With a slightly exasperated look she gave me a task— run around the house four times and then come in for breakfast. I did so. Two minutes later I presented myself once more to an equally exasperated Claire, who finally asked if I ever slowed down. I told her no, of course. Claire told me to sit down and wait while she prepared a full breakfast for everyone, and I was quite content to watch her masterfully make up some more bacon and French toast and scrambled eggs and stewed tomatoes. I just loved being there with her.

It was Claire who came back from their first visit with Gordon and described how he opened his eyes when she said hello. "Claire?" he had said at the sound of her voice and his big blues just made her light up. I could see she loved him. These were real friends—friends for life. No death, no tragedy, no distance can ever change that. My goodness, those were sad days. Beautiful days.

Writing about these days has been challenging. It has been cathartic and revealed many things I had forgotten, many things I was unaware of consciously that have been brought forward into conscious knowledge. By this voyage into the unknown, or the undiscovered, there has been healing. And it has opened new avenues of grief. Karen's story is our story—the family story. Our story is hers. What I know of it I can only suppose but this feels true as I step forward, word by word, into her life and mine and all our lives, not one is written without the sudden realization of a truth beneath it. The story has been left until now, stowed away as if to be released in bits at a later time . . . a time when it is ripe for telling. Karen asked me to tell her story. But not until now. I wonder why? I will ask this question several times. The experiences we shared, I only know through my own recollections and not through her eyes, so I will try to serve her as though I am her vision. I am wrestling with a bit of guilt that what's unfolding is more mine than Karen's, in that I am an observer of her life and did not actually live it. This shortcoming is something to acknowledge and let be, I am afraid. There is no way to correct this aspect, my aspect of her life mingled with knowledge I have directly of her and information I imagine she wishes to impart to me now. Or communicate to others.

The lesson of cherishing a life and not lingering on the loss is universal. The question remains: Why now? Are there things Karen knows that she wants me to know? Are there things I know that I do not know I know? Are there things I simply don't know, and God knows it's time I did? No matter what, there are things I am learning that have given me a much deeper comprehension of who I am and how I got here—who Karen and I were and who we became. And there are questions I thought I knew when this started and where to look for answers. But perhaps, more importantly, I am meant to know innocence once more as I did with her. As we did together. Before so much of what we knew and loved together was taken from us by the traffic of life. By inimical energies tilted against us. Innocence. Love. Joy.

To know Joy. Again. That Joy.

The last time I saw Gordon alive was during a visit to his hospital room three or four days into his stay. Karen was there. Mom and Gam. Gordon and me. Gordon was the fulcrum of my life . . . I knew nothing but him. The highs and the lows of my days were anchored always to him. And they were always shared with my sister. Chief cook and bottle washer, top kick or drill sergeant—these were my mom and Gam. These were words Gam used to describe herself. The "top kick" kept the show running. The Commanding Officer was Gordon, but she was the nuts and bolts of the home and she was damn good at it. Mom made sure there was order and love and as much peace as possible between all parties. She was a balance, a different kind of fulcrum to which her children, Karen and I, were tethered and tended. Mom did the Christmas tree and wrapped a lot of the presents. Gordon was the spirit of Christmas, the giver of all, our provider. And Gordon and his daughter, Sally, loved each other as only a father and daughter can. She was the real apple of his eye, and I never knew it until just now. We thought he loved us. And he did. But the love he gave my mother was something. It is why she took us home to Gordon when my dad missed the mark, so to speak.

I will not slander my father. There was something missing between my mom and dad. That's all. In defense and admiration of my mom, she never said a bad word about him to us. He was always given respect even as we knew there were rarely birthday greetings or Christmas packages throughout the years. Enough said. I really do want to offer him the same respect my mother taught us, and I was thrilled to meet him and his family after Gordon died. My mother was a daddy's girl. He looked after her and she worshipped him. He deserved it. And my mom needed the warmth of home and the love of her father. I believe the only way she could face the reality of being a single mom with two kids in the late 1950s was to get home where she was safe and we would be, too.

There was always a bit of tension between my mom and Gam. I do not know all the intimacies and intricacies of it, but they had been together during the war. In Texas. Sally, her daughter, was getting her first taste of womanhood as a thirteen- or fourteen-year-old and Gam, barely a woman herself, was at the edge of her patience a good deal of the time. I do not think my mom would have gone back if Gordon were not there to offer his support and affirmation throughout. Also, my mom knew what a great man he was—loyal, responsible, strong—fairly good qualities to shepherd two children without a dad.

My grandmother was not blameless in all this, but she had a very complex childhood of her own and probably more than a just explanation for the complexities of her relationship with her own daughter. More to follow on that.

Be assured, there was no lack of love in the family. There was a lack of ease expressing it, a mountain of undercurrents and subtext that made it quite difficult for them. But honestly, until Gordon died, not difficult for Karen and me. They gave us a wonderful home, the three of them. I cherish what they did. I am grateful to them for the splendid days I spent in that home.

I have devoted a good deal of time building a reflection of that family in my own life. Some woeful miscalculations and some wrong turns, surely, but today there is something I can proudly claim—I have a fantastic family. They are loved beyond imagining. Yes, some stray pieces remain to be rounded up and brought back to the heart of us but there is Love, and where there is Love there is always a way.

I claim my family. Not sure I have ever said that out loud or known it so deeply as I do now. Again, thank you, Karen. To the reader, don't be alarmed or put off by what may seem a glib expression of gratitude. I am comfortable with it now. I am comfortable with the idea that Karen is here and the architect of an unfolding path through our past and into our future. She is here. She is Love. She is Courage and Comfort. She is unyielding and unending. Karen is my sister. Forever.

So, where to now, Karen?

"Manhattan. There is something you need to purge. Jill. Start there, just after my funeral. Leave us with Gordon for the time being."

I feel as if I should explain something, almost parenthetically. I have written that Karen has always been in my head. From the moment she died. Been with me.

I offer this, an idea that is taking shape as I try to explain it: one can choose whatever version of afterlife they like. I like the idea that there is a soul that never dies. And I like the idea that after death, a soul can still manifest itself in some form or other, making itself known on this plane. I like these ideas. But . . . I have no tangible knowledge that they are true. What is true is that I hear her sometimes—sometimes clear as a bell. I have never "seen" her, but I see her every day in my imagining.

I wish I could feel her, but I remember every time we touched. We were kids sharing a bed on a winter's night, laughing and giggling about whatever silliness the mischief before slumber had conjured. The noise had finally driven our mother from her bed, threatening the dreaded hairbrush spanking as she charged down the hall with her weapon held aloft. "I told you kids to be quiet!" she chastised, as it was customarily her third trip down the hall. Our giggling only increased as she "beat the bed" in a mock spanking as she entreated, "Now, get to sleep!" We would huddle together under the covers and continue to talk in whispers until we did finally slip off to sleep. I have held her in my arms as she cried, I have wrestled with her as she kicked at me for some perceived wrong when she was little. I can see the scissors I used to even her hair in a perfect straight line at the middle of her back. I will never forget the softness of her soul as we rocked together on the hammock whispering our memories of Gordon that first summer after he died. She was a beautiful girl and a beautiful sister. She was the love of my life. Yeah, I said that already. It bears repeating. I felt closer to no one. I love her still and I hear her still and I talk to her still—and forevermore.

And forevermore, I blame myself for not defending her that night. I could not save her. I did not save her.

Jill stepped off the plane in Ft. Lauderdale. My, she was a magnificent young woman. I felt my heart flutter and my spirits rise the moment I saw her. I loved her so much. She was the most beautiful thing I had ever seen. And in that moment, Jill was everything. Just seeing her there saved me. It was love, surely. The future was Jill, and it was shiny and perfect. She was perfect.

◀ Karen with Gordon on the
Boardwalk, Atlantic City.
Gam in the background.

Seashells at Atlantic ▼
City. That's the Dennis
Hotel in the background.
Our favorite spot.

▼ Standing by the pool with Gordon.
If only I could be like him.

◀ Outdoor art exhibit in Atlantic City. Mom and Karen.

Some of Karen's early poetry. ▶ She was always a good writer.

▼ Atlantic City. My, we did love it there.

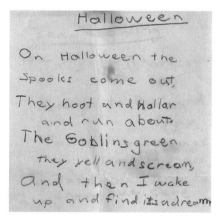

The Christmas Tree

The Christmas Tree
    it shines so bright,
It gives off a most
    heavenly light.
We trim it bright we
    trim it gays,
And sit around it
    on Christmas Day.

▲ At a camp we both attended...I don't remember much about it. I like this shot of the two of them.

Halloween

On Halloween the
Spooks come out,
They hoot and hallar
    and run about.
The Goblins green
    they yell and scream,
And then I wake
up and find its a dream

▼ Karen and Mom out front of the Colonia home.　　　▲ Atlantic City after the big hurricane in '62.

LIKE A SHIP THAT'S LEFT ITS MOORINGS
   AND SAILS BRAVELY OUT TO SEA,
SO SOMEONE DEAR HAS SAILED AWAY
   IN CALM SERENITY:
BUT THERE'S PROMISE OF A GREATER JOY
   THAN EARTH COULD HAVE IN STORE,
FOR GOD HAS PLANNED A RICHER LIFE
   BEYOND THE UNSEEN SHORE.

▲ The cover page on Karen's Memorial book. I
hated this. I am okay with it now. But not really.

▼ This was my notepaper during a call with Esther when
she told me Karen wanted me to tell her story.

I suggested that I would have to look but I thought
there were very few pictures I could use.

Esther said Karen was saying there were plenty.

The dining room table after I realized there were indeed plenty of photos. There are Army documents as well that speak of Gordon's service. Letters from his father from 1907 and a pamphlet that describes Gordon's earlier years up to his graduation from Berkeley.

Karen's keepsakes on an open page of her memorial book. The list beneath—names of those who sent floral remembrances. I wept again at this page. So many who cared enough that day and had the courage to offer comfort.

Her hair is here. A little box with a pink ribbon. Gordon's handwriting, 1966. A year before he died.

Her graduation tassel is here. A ring, a Girl Scout pin, a monogrammed "K" for sealing wax she used in her correspondence.

▲ We send off Gordon and Gam on one of their many cruises. That's Gordon's hat I'm wearing.

Looking very sixties and grown up as their ship embarks. I think that is Ron standing at the right. ▼

As I write, I am drawn to the drive to my home that day, the first Jill ever took. Jill saw things she had never seen . . . she saw where I came from. I had always hoped, when we spoke of our sisters, that we would all meet one day. So much had been broken by Karen's death, so many hopes and dreams and assumptions about how life was going to go. I asked Jill to step aboard a boat on a very rocky sea indeed. Add to that the idea that I had already failed her at Juilliard. Now she was seeing me in the light of my youth without the joy. This was a tough row to hoe. She saw the young man she loved, but a failure and a tortured one at that, suffering from a loss that could barely be expressed. I was not an easy person to love at this time . . . of course, I was still worth loving; that is not the point. It was just very challenging for a twenty-one -year-old woman to align herself with a once fearless and, dare I say, charming young man who had lost his confidence and his charm.

Freddie Glenn said he was a good kid. So, I wonder what happened to him that somewhere in his life he had the effrontery and self-loathing to plunge a knife forty-two times into Karen's body. Over and over again his hatred stabbed into her after he and his friends had raped her. More than once. And there was more. Some good kid! And now, whenever he appears for parole, his protestations are never about how he longs to do something good for the world or how he wishes he could take it all back. According to Mr. Glenn, as far as I can tell, he has been in jail long enough; just a good kid who somehow ended up in prison for a murder that doesn't quite merit the rest of his life incarcerated. So, he tore apart an innocent girl . . . ruthlessly, mercilessly, violently.

To think of his days concurrent with mine and Jill's that first few months after Karen died is the source of diabolical confusion and anger and regret. We were the good kids. Karen was the good kid. This man was an executioner without any law to guide him, no decency at all and no humanity. As I spent the next months and years trying to figure out how to go on, he spent them hoping he could get out, not be held accountable. He and his friend actually pleaded "Not Guilty" and would have us believe to this day that it was just a slip-up when it was actually a vicious, premeditated assassination and destruction of my eighteen-year-old sister. Letting her live would have threatened the freedom of his friends and himself. So, they happily performed desecration of an innocent girl for what was to be an extra month of freedom before they were sent to die in prison.

Freddie Glenn received the death penalty for his crime. During the Carter administration, the Colorado Supreme Court agreed to review all death penalty cases and so his sentence was commuted to life in prison. He owes his life for what he did. He owes forty-two lifetimes for every stab wound he punched into my sister. My opinion.

This kind of outburst is not uncommon in my life. Not frequently, but often without warning, my emotions still gather and my rage still burns for what these men did. Remembering Jill and now realizing we were as good as dead, too, has kicked them back into my thoughts. There were yet some good days for us, but the veil had been cast over our lives and was drifting down, slowly choking our love.

Jill and I made love the minute we got home. She was the refuge. She helped. I think it gave us both a renewed sense that our life together was meant to be. She was there for me. I believe the weeks we had been apart had shaken us both. Karen's death impacted everything we knew. There were already questions about our future because of my dismissal from school and now the plans we had made would have to shift. My, it was good to see her, though. Our love was true. That meant everything.

We spent three weeks luxuriating in our young love and the beauty of Florida. We would take the boat out to the Atlantic, shut down the engines, and just drift for hours as we dove into the blueness of the Gulf and sunned ourselves between intimacies on the deck, sweating so much we would slide right off one another and jump back into the ocean! It was magnificent. And so was she.

I am still grateful we had that time together and grateful to her for her love. Looking back, I do know she loved me and that is a realization that releases years of self-doubt and self-loathing. Looking at it from this distance, I realize Jill and I did our best in a very difficult time. And we almost pulled it off. I was no longer the shiny promise she had met in our early days, but she did not yield to doubt. She came to be my support with the belief and faith that our love would see us through. My grief would not allow it.

I was also wrestling with my new status as a "failure," not so much in Jill's eyes as in my own. I remember driving in my old Maverick with her and sniping at her about her lack of faith in me—I was sniping at myself—but as the conversation heated up, I forced the notion that she would leave me one day and then regret it when she saw how successful I had become. I think I said something about being on Johnny Carson. So, where in creation did I get the self-confidence to believe such a thing while also believing I was worthless? Why was I barking at the woman sitting right beside me? I was just afraid she didn't want me. Maybe she didn't want me—but—there she was! Crazy. We suffer mostly at our own hand and perception, or at least, I do. I am sorry.

"Forgive yourself."

Forgive myself?—that is still hard for me to do. Another reason to write Karen's story. Karen's story told frees me from mine . . . or frees me *in* mine.

Free in my own story. Now isn't that something?

I need to repeat an earlier confession. Or rather, expand on it. I am afraid of losing Karen. I am afraid telling her story sets her free and I will lose her again. It is extraordinarily selfish of me. I have already admitted that.

But, in addition, I have liked her nearby, close when I want her close and all but forgotten in other moments of my life. And I am not proud of that. They were moments when I was running from myself. It turned out I was also running from her at the time and perhaps this idea of being free in my own story is actually false. Freedom comes from living in every story that intersects my own. But then, that raises an entirely different question.

"You can't stop on every corner." That is what an old friend, Doc Grant, used to say. Doc Grant was a man I knew in San Diego during my time there. He deserves some respect and more than a simple mention here, so I am expanding the tale. Commensurate with my regard for him. Doc owned a little pub where the young actors would gather to shoot pool and share a beer. Great burgers. And it was not the most expensive place in town. Perfect for a gaggle of underpaid apprentice actors. I was playing a pinball machine when a looming shadow appeared over my left shoulder. Doc. I still don't know his first name. Nor do I know if he was a doctor of any sort. I continued to play until my ball finally drained and I turned to greet him.

"I'm Doc. I own the place."

He was a mountain of a man, midthirties, with a winning smile and a way of peering into a person. He gave me his best inquisitive look and then explained he had seen me in the place the last several weeks. What was my story? Actor. Shakespeare Festival. I relayed only the bare minimum. We sat down and shared a meal. A burger. A great burger. Like I said. Doc was an entrepreneurial guy, making a footprint for himself in the business community of San Diego. He was enjoying some considerable success. He volunteered a great deal and also shepherded a number of young men, high school students and underprivileged kids mostly helping them become young men of accomplishment and self-respect. I was impressed. He would take young men under his wing and help to guide them toward excellence. He offered to do the same for me. I suggested it might be better if we try "friends" instead. I was a bit beyond being sponsored. And there was another thing about this circle. He called its members "Juniors." I explained I would never agree to be called junior. Gam's little man would never be anybody's junior! Friends it would be. Friends it would have to be. Nothing more. Okay.

So, is it a casualty to destiny if we do stop at every corner? Every corner that presents itself along the way? Maybe so. Doc seemed to think so. Still. I did stop for a time and share a corner with him. There was a football game and an introduction to the United Way—a charity arm of the NFL. A couple of graduations to attend. An ROTC ceremony for one of his juniors. Doc was doing some good things. He was a member of his community and he taught me what that means. Showing up. Getting involved. A good lesson. But Doc had been a man trying to do the world some good for a long time. He did three tours in Vietnam. Service was in his DNA. His habit.

I value the time I spent with him. "You can't stop on every corner." Well, of course you can. But maybe not the best idea.

I invited a guy from the acting company to join me and Doc for one
of his events. It may have been a Rotary Club thing, but something
to do with San Diego and networking. All the things Doc was good
at. My pal excused himself. And Doc took that opportunity to utter
the now-famous phrase. The point being this: Stop where you have
the greatest likelihood of growth. Familiarize oneself with excellent
people. Seek the greatest potential in all human interaction. Do not
stop for everyone or every corner.

Discernment! We are allowed to learn and choose our first, best
destiny. Discernment gives us the tools to stop and not stop, to go,
to linger for a time but always to move along, should that be necessary; and even decide to stay on a path of our choosing, should that
be desirable. I tend to repeat experiences, even several times, before
learning from them. I replicate them . . . go back to a familiar corner
willfully. Even when I know I have stopped there before; even though I
know it holds no new lesson. Even as I recognize it is not a lesson that
is "good for me." Honestly, I have been drawn to them again because it
feels good, even as I already know it will not feel good for long. Thanks,
Doc. Thanks for bringing it up and pointing it out to me, even though I
am still working on it.

The point being? We *are* free in our own story. Free to choose how
long to stay wherever and with whomever we wish to tarry. And we
are free to move on. The decision is always ours. Doc called years later
after seeing me on *Cheers*. "You did okay," he told me. Looking back. So
did you, Doc.

Back to Karen.

There you go. I didn't stop for very long, did I? I don't mean to be
too cute here. This all started with the idea that I was free in my own
story. That we can go down these alleyways and detours at will. But
not all of them. I want to keep Karen in my life, not lose her. And to my
fears about freeing her? Freeing her does not lose her. Karen's story
will be told. Honestly. I will honor her and honor our family. Many
corners yet to visit. Many. I may stumble as I go . . . but I will choose

wisely. I will stop for a time at one or another. Some Karen's. Some mine. But not every corner. And then move on. You're going to have to trust me on this. I'll get you through it. And honestly, Karen won't let me linger too long where we needn't be.

I struggled with the last few paragraphs. Clarity. Relevance. These are important. Struggling is okay, though. Hammer it out! Right. I have struggled with life many times. Struggled with many things. People. Experiences. Is it worth it? My desire to discover things I do not know—this is strong in me. I believe life experience is the life's blood of my work. Is it worth stopping on every corner? Gathering "grist for the mill?" Maybe. Worth stopping again and again at a familiar corner that counterfeits itself as different one? Probably not. Knowing the difference. Spotting it. That's the tricky part. Like I said. Discernment.

Gordon.

Gordon handed me his electric razor to clean the whiskers out of it. I pulled the screen off the mechanism and looked inside it at all the gray hairs, stubble from his face and it put me off. I feel guilty about that still. I banged the screen on the edge of the wastebasket and returned it to the shaver. I was scared. It made me feel bad to see his hair. This has me confused. It confused me then. What was I seeing? Fifty-five years later, I am asking that little boy, who was about to become a man before his time, why he was scared? Why was he repulsed as he was? What was I seeing? I felt helpless. Perhaps, that has something to do with it. I felt empty. I felt alone. Makes sense but even now I feel a deficiency in myself that I was repulsed, that that was what I felt.

How can I stand up?

Again—*"Forgive yourself."*

People who know me know I have trouble with my feet and ankles. I have trouble standing and walking. It was not always the case. There is a circumstantial case that points to vaccine damage from the polio vaccine. It may have had an impact. But it grew worse when I was twelve. Not really sure how it happened or why, but it feels possible that my shame about my grandfather's razor would bring me to my knees. That is what my gut is telling me. "How can I stand up?" I know why I asked the question. It seemed natural at the time. Life started to compress me. The weight of it. Forgive yourself. Maybe there is wisdom in the answer. You took on so much it broke your ankles. Time to let it go. Put it down.

I did the right thing. Something I put in my notes a while ago: to carry Karen any longer probably burdens her. That day in the hospital, I took upon my shoulders the weight of my mother, my grandmother and my sister. I wanted to. I was willing. Gordon died the next day and now I would carry them for a time. It wasn't so heavy. It was my job. But here's the thing. I still want to carry Karen. Yet, ironically, she has carried me all these years. Karen's death, that's what really broke my ankles. And now, I don't want to break hers. She has carried me long enough. Even lifted me up when I couldn't stand. If I forgive myself, maybe I make things a little bit easier for her? I don't lose her; I free her by forgiving myself. Huh. Maybe.

I slept beside my daughter last night, my daughter, Faith. Faith Evangeline Elisa Grammer. Elisa is my sister's middle name. My aunt, Elisa, was my dad's half-sister. Faith in turn shares Karen's Elisa; and her grandmother's Evangeline. We all carry each other. My son Jude's middle name is Gordon. James, my youngest, carries the name of his great-grandfather, Ellis, in Auden James Ellis Grammer. And my son Gabriel carries mine—Kelsey Gabriel Elias Grammer. My daughter Mason carries the name of a dream I dreamed of great civilizations and those who built them, Mason Olivia Grammer. Kandace Greer Grammer, another KG, a name picked by her mom knowing the men in my family went by middle names. A great tip of the hat for Greer. And my first child, Spencer Karen Grammer. My old friend and my sister joined in her name. I repeat myself here, but this does bear repeating. It suits her. A unique and magnificent young woman, it connects her to magnificent people she will never know. But they are connected. We are all connected to each other in this time—and in this time, to echoes of a former time. Connected. Echoes of generations past. With us, of us.

There was a Thomas Dimmick, relative of my grandmother. He died when he was twenty-one. Cholera. Crossing the country on horseback with his family and perished after drinking tainted water while hunting Buffalo. He died in the night after hours of agony. I called my grandfather, Frank, my father's dad, when Karen was killed and all he could say was, "This family is cursed." I am not sure I believe that, but he saw his son gunned down at the age of thirty-eight and his first wife die in distress at an early age. I am not sure I understand what happened to her, but his feelings about the family may well have been a response to all the pain he had known in love. I learned later in life that he and his brother never spoke again after their mother's death. "Cursed" may have been his way of explaining away the difficulty, the challenges that jump out on life and our loved ones without warning. He had a giant nose. Quite remarkable, honestly. And his daughter, by his second wife, Wilma, my Aunt Elisa, has a tiny nose. Isn't that something? And isn't it remarkable to see this in the context of a tortured family and still attest to the proboscises that grace that family? Silly. Yes, you're right. But there it is! I didn't know Frank very well, but I liked him, and it broke my heart to tell him about Karen that day. And to hear his broken heart break again.

My point is that we carry them, generations of them. We carry their tragedies and misfortunes, perhaps unaware that they are there with us. But we also carry their triumphs and their bravery and courage. These magnificent men and women who risked everything to build a better life for themselves and their children. We carry that too. And that is glorious! These ancestors who rose to the height of their time or sank to the depths of their failings—all are within us and lifting us up or passing their challenges to us.

Ellis Dimmick was my grandmother's dad. He was dishonorably discharged from the Marine Corps. I gave James his name in hopes that it might find a better end. Bring it some joy. And it has. Ellis had a tough run of drunkenness and tragedy . . . his brother had overdosed on drugs that were used to sedate dental patients at the turn of the last century. It was a horrible death at a young age. It was passed to Ellis who probably blamed himself. Gordon's mother, Cora—my great-grandmother—died six months after his birth. No one knew why. Years later, one of her great-grandsons, a specialist in rare diseases, suspected it was Valley Fever. Gordon's older brother, Lee, always blamed him. And Gordon became the commanding officer of a battalion in the Army Corps of Engineers who spent two years on Guadalcanal. I have mentioned it before. He rarely spoke of it, but he did reveal some of the horrors he witnessed a week before he died. He spent his whole life carrying the death of his mother and then all the boys who died in his care. Or I believe that is what he felt. Of course, I do not know these things. I do not channel or have the "gift," so to speak. But lately, I live in pentimento. Through the thinning veil of time, images and people of the past reveal themselves in the present. Sometimes merely insinuating through a whisper or a shadow, yet often with greater clarity, stepping into this life from worlds and lifetimes ago—passing from one to the next and back again throughout perceived time, thus defeating time. So it is for me with my loved ones and especially Karen, especially now as I write about her. So many things come up. Many good. One recurring horror. I have stood a thousand times beside a dumpster near the back of the Red Lobster as Karen faced her killers. She knew. I see her now, seeing them. She knew.

I also see that there are many piggybacking with us. The collective story of our several and shared lifetimes is revealing itself. The buried treasure. And I confess I feel lighter. It has brought me great joy to feel close to her. Close to Karen again. And it has helped heal me to some degree. Of course, as this unfolds, I find more. So, we have more to go.

"I have promises to keep and miles to go before I sleep."

Jill flew home and then to New York. I followed later, after painting Mrs. McDaniel's roof. I needed a little cash before renting an apartment and the few hundred dollars Helen paid me really helped and I thanked her. I thank her now. She was a neighbor two doors down. Stan, the airline pilot, lived next door to her, and between us was a guy who was rarely in his home. It was a nice neighborhood. Sue lived down the street and had always been a friend. We never got together—the "girl next door" thing was not a thing, as it turned out. I think we doubled-dated a couple of times when she had a friend visiting. She was a nice person. It was her family's hedge that offered refuge to my sister's runaway rabbit, Gideon. Gideon was a large (no, giant) white rabbit with red eyes, straight out of a song from the 1960s. Gideon was a bit of a character. He would escape his enclosure from time to time and I think he thought he was running away and securing his freedom by hiding under Sue's bush. Or shrubbery, more appropriately. And as I went looking for him, it was a fairly easy task to spot a giant white rabbit with red eyes beneath a small hedge just feet from the driveway. Anyway, Gideon was convinced he was hiding effectively at the edge of the lawn just at the base of the hibiscus. He was not. He was clearly visible. And yet, as I approached, giggling that he was so silly and ridiculously in plain sight, he would hunker down just a bit more and get very still, as if he was trying to make himself less visible, smaller even, eyes closed tight and frozen in his imagined hiding place. You could sense his crushing disappointment as I walked right up to him, lifted him into my arms and made the short hop back to our yard. Wonderful to have known so many wonderful things. That crazy rabbit. He makes me laugh.

Stan, the airline pilot, is a fond memory. Stan and his wife worked for an airline of which she was cabin crew and he a hotshot pilot. They fell in love in the friendly skies; extremely friendly if I am to believe Stan. I do not remember his wife's name, but I remember she was quite a looker. Shapely and sultry, she had a way of looking through a young man that was kind of scary and kind of enjoyable at the same time. No, I did not do the "young man and the neglected wife down the road" thing, but she was a fine woman, and Stan surprised me when he talked about how he was always unfaithful to her. He called it "sport f . . . ing." He also had a great boat on which I did go "sport fishing" with him. His sex life did not cross into my life other than my disbelief his wife was not a part of it. Or maybe she had her own secrets and "training sessions." Or maybe Stan was just a big talker. They were fun, though. He had a handlebar moustache that he said "tickled" the ladies. I had no idea what he was talking about at the time, but I get it now. He was quite a character. Cocktail hour seemed to start pretty early with them. They laughed a lot and enjoyed each other a great deal. I looked at them as an ideal couple, honestly. The philandering and loose nature of their sex life did confuse me a bit, but I admired how close they were and how dedicated to one another. Not sure if I could ever live as they lived but I did long to find that one who completed me. They were good people. It was a blessing to know them.

Anyway, after the summer of '75, I returned to New York City to begin my life with Jill. Karen would be with me. I could not, or would not, let her go. It was not an easy year. New York was not in the greatest shape either. I think the city had recently defaulted on a bond issue that meant the city was bankrupt. Real estate values plummeted, rental properties were paying tenants a bonus, or the rental agencies were paid a fee by landlords to find occupants. I checked out an apartment on Eighty-First Street between Columbus and Amsterdam. It was a one-bedroom affair with a little kitchen, a smallish living room and a view of the next building's brick wall about ten feet from our window. It would be home until June of 1976. I shopped for furniture at the Salvation Army Store a few blocks from us, found an okay bed and bought a new mattress and box spring from a cheap bed place on Broadway. It was very spartan, but Jill and I set up housekeeping together. She kept her eye drops in the fridge. I thought that was really cute. Something not so cute was that she would not tell her parents we were living together. I am not sure where they thought she was living—I guess with her roommates from before—but it made me feel pretty bad that I was a secret or that we were a secret, rather. I just felt nonexistent and asked her to allow her parents to grow up with her. We were serious about each other; we had taken this step toward a life together, but to keep it a secret made it wrong. And we were lying to her family. As I write this, I feel small and young and just like I did back then. The only difference now is I am willing to acknowledge it. I tried to understand it when I was with Jill and persuade her to tell her parents that they should surely know how we felt about each other, but maybe Jill and I weren't exactly on the same page. That look in her eyes outside the cafeteria at school still haunts me.

Something else, or someone else, who still haunts me is our son. Jill and I conceived a son the September or October the year before I was dismissed from Juilliard.

We aborted him.

I know that many people do not have a problem with abortion, and though I have supported it in the past, it eats away at my soul. We agreed to meet back in New York a few days before the end of Christmas break, to keep it a secret and to kill him. I was not happy about it and told Jill that I was willing to keep him. I never wanted her to accuse me of being unwilling to have the child, but I also did not plead with her to save his life. I supported the idea that a woman has the right to do what she wants with her own body. I still do. But it was hard for me. Still is. Hard to see how anyone has the right to do as they wish with another person's body. A baby's body. But I didn't even have the nerve to ask. Maybe if I'd asked, I would shake my forty-something son's hand every holiday. Kiss my grandkids. I said I'd be willing to keep him, but I left it up to her. I did not ask. Seems to me his life was worth that, at least. But there is the whole mess in a nutshell. A woman's right to choose? Of course. A child's right to exist? Of course. Life. We wrestle with it to this day. Or rather . . . some do.

Six months before my sister was slaughtered, I volunteered to have my son's body vacuumed out of his mother's. I regret it. That's all I meant to say. God, forgive me. *Forgive yourself.* Forgive myself. Okay. On this one, not sure I can. It did occur to me that Karen's death was a tit for tat, but God does not work that way. I know that now. That was part of my issue with blaming myself. But I was not responsible for Karen's death. I was not there to stop it. That was not my fault either. Karen died. I had nothing to do with it. The death of my son—that remains at my feet. Society forgives me for it, but it lingers in my heart as a failure of conscience, a selfish theft of an innocent life.

I do not wish to harm Jill's family by this admission. I want to apologize to my son. I wish I had met him and raised him. The doctors, or so-called doctors, who have executed generations of children in this manner—I have no idea how they call themselves doctors. Something about the "first, do no harm" thing. But I offer no controversy. I wish to offer comfort. To all. My heart goes out to any who has known the pain of losing a child. Or of losing a loved one. I write for them and for those who still hope to find solace in the midst of a mad world. I just wanted to say I was sorry about my boy. I will leave it at that.

What happened in New York that year was consequential in many ways. I had not lost Jill yet . . . but I was on the path to losing her. I had already told her I expected her to leave me. Truth be told, I left her. I left her alone in that apartment at night. Almost every night. I found work at several places. But at night, except for one job in a very upscale restaurant for a couple of months, I would walk the streets. From midnight to dawn, I paced up and down the streets of Manhattan. I was angry. Spot a shadowy figure in a dark alley, I would walk right toward it. I wanted to hurt someone. I wanted to hurt anyone who had the nerve to touch me or threaten me in any way. I was ready to tear them apart. And in this way, I walked for months. I wanted to kill someone. I wanted to kill myself. I felt I was fit for a violent end and so, I went seeking it.

But it was not to be. As I skulked from block to block, strangers crossed the street at my approach. In the wee hours of the city night, none of its denizens would grant me anything but a wide berth. Maybe they just thought, *Why risk it?* Or maybe I was protected by Karen—and God, though I wasn't really speaking with God at the time. Whatever the reason, my nightly strolls left me more alone than ever. Returning home, I would apologize to Jill and say I couldn't sleep. It was a bad recipe for a young couple.

I found work enough to pay the bills and she continued at school. We did manage that. But these were hard days. I would open the fridge on a morning, searching for something to eat. Then I would close the door minutes later and realize I had been staring blankly into it for more than an hour. I was not worth knowing, let alone loving.

It was during this time that the Colorado Police had captured the men who killed Karen and built a case against them. There was no need for me to attend the trial, the prosecutor told me. This was a slam-dunk conviction and living through the horrors of Karen's death over and over again as the trial proceeded was not something they wanted to inflict upon me or the family. Of course, I was doing that anyway. I know my mom was doing the same and Gam was lost in her own almost comatose state of blame and despair. I can't say how she felt but I can imagine. Same goes for my mom. Each of us probably blamed ourselves knowing it wasn't the truth, but still felt like truth anyway. That's where I was, at least.

So, when I'd come home from my nights prowling the streets, it would be close to dawn. I would whisper my apologies to Jill, still slumbering, and an hour or two later she would make her way to school. I can't remember if I made her breakfast or even a piece of toast, but I think I did some of the time. I hope I did. I really did love her. I remember every morning she would take her eyedrops out of the fridge and describe to me the delight she took in keeping her eyes open as she administered the drops. She said how she liked to watch the drop form and then slip from the bottle and land on her open eyeball. This explains why the fridge and the aforementioned fact I thought it was really cute. I even trained myself to do the same so I could understand and share her pleasure. I do it to this day. It really is fun. And keeping the drops in the fridge means that splash in the eye is chilled, adding an extra blast of refreshing, cleansing hydration. So, off Jill would go to her shiny world and I would retreat to waiting tables a few times a week, haunting the streets at night, spending the rest of my time in bed to sleep for a couple of hours or to watch the old movies on Channel 5 or Channel 11. I lost the waiting job at the restaurant one afternoon, I don't really remember why ... I did think it was unfair ... but, yeah, that's right, Life is unfair sometimes. These then, were the days I might never leave the bed at all until Jill came home.

One afternoon, I was watching a movie about a mother and daughter and how they found each other and forgave each other, and it wasn't a good movie or a bad movie. It was a run-of-the-mill tearjerker movie that was the perfect film to turn me inside out. I began to cry and then cry out in anguish about Karen and everything that had happened, the desolation and despair retching out of me uncontrollably. Jill entered the apartment. I did not know she was there. I was aware my grief had become something of an issue for her. Understandably so—it stood between us. She came into the bedroom and tried to console me for a moment but could not. My entire core was aching and once opened, the purging could not be stopped. She couldn't help; she couldn't help me at all. She held me and tried to tell me it would be alright, as she had done so many times before, but after a while she just broke. She begged me to stop, that she could not go on any longer with me in this kind of pain. She screamed in pain herself that our love was not enough, she was not enough, her devotion was not enough to stop this agony. And the agony was hers, as well. All that we had been, and all our hoped-for future, was shattered.

"You have to stop," she pleaded. "We cannot go on like this. I can't go on like this!"

She was right. And it may be that afternoon did start me down a path that helped. I have never thought of it before, but I believe it was after that I began to search more earnestly for an acting job. Hazy here, but I think it was about mid-November. The time from late September seemed interminable but it was probably no more than eight weeks. Jill was not wrong. I did need to stop. And it was killing us. It did kill us. But it was this particular afternoon that set me on a new course. Not away from Jill but toward Life—it just turned out that the life we had planned together would not survive. Jill went home for Thanksgiving. I stayed in the apartment that year. No turkey. I was the turkey. Ha! The almost eternal descriptor of someone hopelessly inept. A Turkey! Apt, at the time, I'd say. I don't really remember going home for Christmas but I know I did—home for the first Christmas without Karen. Jill went to her new home in Texas. I do remember asking if she'd told her parents we were living together. She had not. It didn't help. I didn't like being a secret. It made me feel even more like a turkey.

So, starting that January, I determined to do some auditions and get myself in gear. This began a season of great frustration. I had no sense of what was too much or too little, so this was the stretch of one hundred auditions in one hundred days that did not yield a single job . . . except the last two. I think Jill was actually in shock that I had finally been offered an acting job. We had grown apart that spring and she was clearly enjoying the attentions of another young man in the acting school. I noticed a look between them one night in our apartment that was pretty clear. We were all friends, sort of... Michael and Jill were just poised to take it a bit further. I noticed it but I didn't say anything. Gone were the days of fighting for her; I honestly couldn't make a convincing case to choose me over Michael. Except for some menial jobs and some remodeling work, I hadn't amounted to much. Auditions were, as I said, pretty shaky. I was asked to do an all-male production of Shaw's *Lady Windermere's Fan*—funny, we rehearsed just a few days and then the director—Bill Gammon, I think his name was—got another job. Three days later, he asked if I would want to do some painting and construction work at a theatre company, APA, Ellis Rabb's company that was reinventing itself. Jack McQuigan (could be MacQuigan, I am not sure) was a producing partner, and he basically pointed me to some odd jobs around their new office space, while he spent the morning moving papers from one side of the desk to the other. After lunch, he would move them all back. I answered the phone once and took a message from Robert DeNiro. Pretty cool. Even cooler that I ended up working with him years later. Amazing journey.

Anyway, at APA, there was a man named Joel Martin who was going to be casting productions for the company, presumably at the Lyceum Theatre on Broadway, where Jack and Ellis had enjoyed many successes in their previous collaboration. I was removing a dropped ceiling one morning when Joel walked in and took a long look at me up on the ladder. I am not sure what prompted him to ask me if I was an actor, but I said hello and after a time he said simply, "Are you an actor?" I told him I was and then he asked me my name. "Kelsey Grammer," I told him. Then, to my surprise, he asked if I would be interested in auditioning for The San Diego Shakespeare Festival. I said yes. Two days later, I did Macbeth and Nick Bottom, my "set pieces" for Jack O'Brien who was directing Shakespeare's *As You Like It* that summer. They requested that I wait outside and moments later, Joel emerged, invited me back inside and Jack asked if I'd like to join the apprentice program that season. There was one hitch. They would not be providing transportation. I would have to get there on my own and the job started—in one week.

Funny. I am writing this as I sit in a hotel room in Alabama. There was a violent storm last night. Tornadoes ripped through parts of the countryside. It was a night much like that darkened day almost a life-time ago in Alabama. A thunderbolt and the promise it brought me. A sign then; a sign now, perhaps—I am on the right track. It was four days after the audition in New York. Alive again tonight in Alabama. I love this world.

I made my way back to our apartment to tell Jill the good news: I finally had a job. An acting job! Back then, we used to have answering services where living people took messages and then relayed them back to the intended recipient. It was very efficient and worked very simply. I would call the service number. They would ask what mailbox I was checking and then they would tell me what the message was. Please, call [the name I do not remember] at the Matunuck Theater. I had auditioned there a couple of days before. I checked in with the name who left the message and he explained they wanted me to play Candide in their upcoming production of the Bernstein opera. Wow! Two job offers on the same day. So, suddenly, my stock was rising. Not enough to win Jill back but enough to get her attention and probably force Michael's hand. Jill and I discussed the offers, and I was drawn more to the Shakespeare of it, convinced that I did not have the singing voice or sufficient command of my voice to play such a demanding role as Candide. But also, I was always drawn to Shakespeare. San Diego it would be. I think we discussed that Jill might join me in San Diego, at least for a visit, after I settled in. She was excited for me, I think. At least, the year of auditions and the difficulties might have a silver lining. I still believed that Jill might actually be my girl for a bit longer but there were visions in my head of a new life and possibly a new "someone" in the future. We did make love the night before I left and I was happy about that. I guess it was a kind of good-bye kiss. Not quite closed, yet, our life together, though our love had been spent by events beyond our control. Sad because how we deal with events beyond our control never steals our right to deal with them as we choose, to rise above them or to endure in spite of them. I say this now from the lux-ury of an acquired wisdom that I did not possess back then. Jill was brave and courageous—we both were. It just got the better of us. No one's fault. I loved her. I love the memory of that love. It was a good thing. We gave it a good try.

The next morning, I flew to Ft. Lauderdale to get my motorcycle. I had spoken to my grandmother and told her I had good news. "You got an acting job," she said. She was pretty sharp. I asked if she could spare me some cash for the flight home to grab the bike and get me on my way to San Diego.

I believe it's time to devote a significant chunk of praise to that motorcycle. It carried me unfailingly through adventure after adventure, tale after tale, journey upon journey. My goodness, what an amazing machine and what an amazing part of my youth! I had that bike for ten years and thousands of miles, countless miles. There's more to flesh out down the road but this part of the story starts one year before. Semester's end and the very end of Juilliard for me.

My next destination was Rhode Island. I drove the bike there after Jill and I left school and left behind the disappointing news I'd had. She went to West Hartford, where she had been raised, and I left for Narragansett to spend the summer in a friendly place for me. When I was sixteen, I had gone there to spend a month at my dear friend, Jay's house. I hoped to get a job down at Point Judith on a fishing boat, perhaps. I ended up unloading fish from the hold of a large tuna boat. Never went out to catch any but standing in waders, knee-deep in almost frozen fish, pitchforking them from the boat on their way to be processed, I made more money in a single day than ever before. I drove one weekend to see Jill, and we spent a lovely afternoon in Connecticut. A lunch at a restaurant called the Mill and a visit to the Hill-Stead Museum, where the famous Japanese watercolor *Under the Wave of Kanagawa (The Great Wave)* resides. I was a little surprised how small it was in person, as it had loomed in my imagination as a quintessential expression of the culture and the medium too. My imagination made it bigger in proportion to my respect for it. I did not lose a fraction of my respect for it, though; I just had to rescale expectation to the reality. Honestly, it was even cooler once I had sorted out the whole size issue. It was mounted above a window in the company of several other paintings; it sat center, just below the crown molding and was no more than eight by ten inches. It really did occupy an enormous space in my head. I thought it was magical. And I still did. Oops! I feel another diversion coming on. It is relevant, though.

I was surfing in a fairly significant southern chop near one of the small jetties in Palm Beach, Florida. It was kind of blown out but there were some nice, quick rides and fairly big for that break. I was sixteen. And it was great. I was truly one with the waves and the experience and the sun and my breathing, exaggerated and exercised but not shallow, almost as if the rhythm of my breathing mirrored the breaking of the waves. The rides just kept coming one after the other as I would kick out of one and begin another almost an instant later. A paddle or two, spin and drop in again. It was a hot day, so hot I was actually sweating in the water; the water was warmer than the air itself.

And suddenly, a perfect wave. I turned, dropped in instantly, and was covered up as it broke above my head and cocooned me in a cascading tunnel of ocean. A glance above me, the sun through the water, and I disappeared. I became a drop of water in eternity, a light in the light of God, an illuminated being in a realm of illumination—I was immortal and free, in the ether and the full blossom of Life itself, eternal life and beauty. I whispered to myself I no longer had anything to fear, not Death, not anything. It was the greatest experience of my life. And then the wave ended, and I launched myself into the air, dropping moments later into the bath of natal sea from whence we came! This is the light I see when people describe The Light! It is the light I carry in me. It is perhaps the light that carried me through so much darkness. My God. My God, I am so grateful for all I have known. All you have shown me.

That watercolor must have some serious magic that it could take me tonight, in memory, to the wave that took me to the face of God. Or maybe it is God's magic. Maybe it's all God. Maybe we all are. This Journey...this Life...God. Magic.

Karen brought me here. Karen knew what was in my heart. Karen is here with me. In every moment, she is here. And God is here.

Karen's story. The telling of the tale widens it. Mom is here, and Gam and Gordon, too. Their lives spilling in from memory as every word and every thought brings them back to life. I just didn't know—I didn't know they were there and always had been. Hoped they were, I suppose, as I have spent years speaking out loud to all of them. But now, as never before, I write their names and feel them; I speak to them and hear their answer. There will be more of them, from them . . . and from others. Others, now willing to show themselves, after so long a time forgotten.

Widening.

Now, I am in Rhode Island forty-nine years ago. It is 1975. Things take a dramatic turn a few days after unloading that fishing boat. I had just moved into a house with a couple of other roommates. I had a decent bedroom and anticipated visits from Jill. Money was going to be good and the summer seemed promising. Then my mom called from Florida and told me Gam was not well. She had been taken to the hospital after finding her just sitting in her room unresponsive and barely breathing. "I am not sure she's going to make it," said Mom. So, I jumped on the bike and drove straight through to Pompano from Narragansett. It took me thirty-one hours, several rainstorms slowed things down and I was wet and dry six or seven times along the way. Pretty much the toughest trip I had ever made. I was exhausted and put myself straight to bed when I arrived. Gam was already home and honestly looked a lot healthier than I did. Whatever had stricken her had passed; she was spry, I was wretched. Maybe she just needed a good rest. Exactly what I needed after the drive. So, suddenly, I was in Florida and thought I should stay as Karen would be turning nineteen in a few weeks. I was home, she would come home as well, spend some time, possibly spend the summer and Jill would come to visit. I was anxious for them to meet. It was shaping up to be the perfect summer. This was the gist of my last phone call with Karen.

This takes me to other summers. Two summers before, I was

working a couple of jobs before heading up to NYC to start school. Gam and Bob were married by then. My mom was dating a boat captain named Kenny. Bob was a boat captain too. I guess the women in my family liked some combination of a man in uniform and in a stupor because both these boys were big drinkers.

Gordon's bedside, years before, is calling me back to my sister and me. Leave us with Gordon for a time, as Karen said. Or as I think she said. And so, I left us with Gordon as instructed, and return now to us, beside him for the last time...the last time we would see him. My sweet sister, so innocent and pure. My grandfather. Our grandfather. Gam and Mom, Bill and Claire. And I, frozen beside him as he handed me his razor to clean the screen. I knew how to do it. I had done it before. But I was frozen.

How can I stand?

Why did I ask that question?

Settling on something. I think I know now. Triggered. Triggered shame. Gordon's gray stubble triggered me into a memory of shame. And I wondered if anyone knew what was happening. I didn't. But something was wrong. Did anyone notice? I think Karen did. I see her sitting there in a chair at the foot of Gordon's bed and her eyes are wide and kind—watching me struggling with something I could not explain. I finally tapped the screen on the edge of a wastebasket beside his bed and handed him back the razor with the screen in its place and clean for the next day's shave.

"I came to bring you Joy." This was a statement from Karen as channeled in a session with her and several others. It was addressed to me. I do not know exactly what was meant but I will say with certainty and gratitude that she did bring me great joy. Was it about our childhood or was it about right now? Did she come to bring me Joy or asked her story be told so that there would be joy? Are both true? It requires honest self-examination. And recollection of a time I do not recall. But I am learning this exercise reveals truth. Whether consciously or not, memories from before memory are coming to light. And it has brought great joy indeed. But the question persists, rather questions persist: how is it she came to bring me joy?—was there no joy before Karen? I

think it is possible she brought me lightness. I needed to lighten my perspective and my perception to realize I was surrounded by joy. Karen offered me some tools to happiness, and she continues to do so with this. What follows is heavy on guesswork and speculation, but . . .

I think the little boy I was, and the baby I was, knew his father did not want him. It is not uncommon. I was lucky Gordon was there. *He* wanted me. In fact, when I was born, his brother Lee called him and said, "Congratulations, you finally have the son you've always wanted!" Something comes to me as I stand with my younger self, standing in that room with his razor in hand. Gordon was my grandfather, not my father. And it is here I recount something that shamed me, shame I felt one afternoon in sixth grade. It was football season. We were a team of Lilliputians. There were a few of us visibly closer to manhood than the others, but we were a small bunch overall. It was the first time Gordon had ever attended a game and it came down to a goal line stand to stop the opposing team and seal the victory. A draw play, I saw the runner coming straight at me and I met him head-on, stopping the drive and winning the game. It is the only time in my life I have made such an impact in a sporting event. Gordon saw me do that. I ran to him moments later and received a prideful hug from the man who meant the world to me. I went in to change, higher than high that I had pleased him and made him proud. One of my peers came up to me and asked, "Who was that old guy I saw you with?"

"My grandad, Gordon," I told him.

"What, don't you have a dad?"

I had a dad who didn't want me. I had a grandfather who did. But suddenly I was ashamed of Gordon and ashamed of myself. And when I saw the gray hair in his razor screen, it reminded me of the shame I felt that day. I didn't know that then, but that is what rattled me. I didn't know having a man of Gordon's stature to love me and shelter me and guide me was the greatest gift I could have had. I'd like to apologize to Gordon and I already know it is accepted. I was young and foolish and conscious that my life was not the same as the boys whose dads were around. So, my dad didn't want me. So what? I had a grandad, a war hero, a pillar of achievement, who did. I was proud of him. I have confessed a smallness brought on by some rotten kid. I am able to stand "a tiptoe" that I was loved by such an extraordinary man and chosen by him. Thanks, Gordon. I love you. Gordon was my "Dad."

Funny, I remembered the shame but not why I'd felt it. It was all still in there. Undiscovered till now. So was the pain about my dad. It explains a lot of things. I've always had trouble believing I was wanted. It's okay. I was just a kid. Let it go.

Let it be.

The morning after our visit to his hospital room, Gordon died. My mom was with him. She had been sitting beside him reading, just keeping him company, when she noticed his breathing had stopped. The nursing staff responded quickly and quickly knew he was no more. Mom took care of the hospital protocols for the death of a patient. Then she drove home. On the radio, a song came on: "Would I make the same mistakes if he walked into my life today?" The lyrics are from the musical *Mame*. She broke down on the way home and sobbed, wishing, wondering if things might have been different or even should have been.

Mom shared that Gordon was gone. Gordon was dead. Nothing can describe how that felt. Nothing left of Gordon but the husk—and at the risk of seeming indelicate, it was a handsome husk to be sure. Gam said so. He had not looked so good in twenty years—her words. That was after his funeral. He had probably lost twenty-five pounds, possibly more, during his last few months. He looked good, apparently; Karen and I were not allowed at the funeral. Truth is, I think Gam took some solace in the fact that he was still a handsome man. She had married well. She had married young, married for love and she stayed with the man she loved; his being handsome was still important to her. And seeing him then and seeing him through the eyes of her youth, simultaneously; Gordon was still the man, her man! He looked good. It was important. And pleasing.

Karen. How did it feel for Karen? I am not sure Karen had the same difficulty about our dad as I did. She came home to Gordon and Gam, me and our mom, straight from the hospital. She was the one adored by Gordon. I was given lessons by him about manhood and propriety. I knew he loved me, but Karen was flat-out "adored."

I am trying to place myself inside the childhood mind of my sister and feel what she felt. Oh, my, what a gift she was—to me, Gordon, the whole family. There was absolute joy that she had come and regardless of a few likely sideways glances from me, the two-year-old former apple of the family eye, Karen was greeted with delight. She must have felt it, and it must have felt good. I am so happy she came to the home that wanted her. It was a good childhood. We were loved. Karen and I lived well, ate well, were well dressed and given everything a young girl and boy could want. She was a good student. She was a great card player. Better than me. A great artist. I was her protector and the toughest kid on the block. I looked after her. That was my job. Gordon was her champion and admirer in chief. It was wonderful to see them together.

Gordon filmed her with his 8mm camera on the day of her first dance recital. It was adorable. She wore a little lavender tutu. I'll never forget it. She was so cute. Karen wore her hair in a "pixie"—that was the style then. I see her in an instant. In a hundred different ways, I see her. I see her from the early days of my recollection to the teenage girl I chided for not using her head. "Use your head," I would say. I say it to this day to my young children and even to my not-so-young children. I even say it to my dogs. "Use your brains!" And they never do. Once in a while the kids surprise me, and they seem to get it: the dogs . . . never!

When Gordon died, Karen may have felt more alone than any of us. I don't know for sure. By then, she was very close to being a woman herself, living in a home with three generations of women and knowing her position in the home now was likely more challenging. The history books are full of stories of mothers and daughters in conflict, and here now was a home with two mothers and two daughters, one granddaughter but one a daughter also, still with a mother who was not the easiest to live with and all of a sudden, all these factors probably made it a little tough on Karen—all of a sudden. And all of a sudden, I was the only man in the family. But it did give me a certain stature, a certain station, by the simple nature of being the only one. Each of the women in the home turned to me for support and assistance. And I did the best I could to help them all. One sister, one mother and one grandmother—and as the only man now, a kind of husband/son/brother/head of the family dynamic was my inheritance and my new job description. Pretty likely to fail under such circumstances, but for choice, there was only to put one foot in front of the other and to endure. We actually did a damn sight better than just "endure" but the orders of the day were tall, indeed. Oh, yes, I had to be a kind of Keeper of the Peace and Minister of Justice, as well. There was a lot of "girl-on-girl" crime going on and I was woefully unprepared for it. But I did okay. I think all three of them would probably say the same under the circumstances. Gordon left a big hole.

Understanding women or understanding the needs of the women in my life became extremely important. I fell short. It would have been impossible to do otherwise. But I did my best. Gam announced after a couple of weeks that she had spent forty years cooking every day and she was no longer cooking at all. I made a deal with her: if she would cover the groceries, then I would be willing to cook. Thus began my career as a gourmet chef. Truth is, I didn't cook every meal. I did cook dinners, mostly the meats or main courses. I would steam some vegetables and throw together a salad and my mom did a lot of prep and cooking, as well. I was great at steaks and burgers, I perfected escargots. That had been one of Gordon's favorites and when we had dinner at the Fort Monmouth Officer's Club, it was always our mutual selection. Escargots...I daresay mine were pretty good, even the best. I rarely hazard boastfulness and I submit this to assure you my best was the best. I will stand by it.

Another favorite of Gordon's was a Beefeater Gibson. This is where I acquired my liking for cocktail onions. I enjoy them to this day and that is why. I enjoy even more a Gibson. Imagine my delight when one afternoon on a trip to Chicago, I sat down and ordered a Gibson at Gibson's—the drink had been born there and it was served as a signature drink should be served—to perfection. I had two. I almost always have two when I visit Chicago and I am happy to say, I have visited there and worked there many times.

I have sung the seventh-inning stretch at Wrigley Field and I have thrown out the first pitch at Comiskey Park for the Sox. I even cut the cake at Chicago's 150th birthday. The mayor was out of town. In *Boss*, I was playing the fictional mayor, Tom Kane, at the time, so they asked me to do it. It is a great town. The Windy City. It does blow a lot. Polit ics? Weather? Probably a little of both. The City of Big Shoulders. An apt nickname, as it looms large in the middle of the country, swaggering with buildings broad and tall as man's imagination. The architectural tour there is majestic and illustrates what visionaries and mavericks have accomplished there on the canvas of Chicago—they even made the Chicago River run in the opposite direction. Amazing.

Karen would have liked it and if what I am selling is true, then she has liked it when I have been there. She has been with me. Why would I always feel her only when I am mournful and self-pitying? Today, I embrace the idea that she would be more likely along for the ride when riding high or celebrating life. She wouldn't want to miss the good stuff. And she would just as likely rather keep my eye on the joy than on the anguish. She did come to bring me Joy, after all. I suppose the same is so on either side of the veil. I am grateful. I hear her. I didn't always hear her . . . my grief drowned her out, even as she was screaming. I must be one stubborn cuss to have missed her pleas to live my life and relish it. I hear her now. Joy.

At no time do I wish to say what happened to Karen is not horrible. It is horrible. It is the worst nightmare I have known. It is amazing she has found a way to give me this. Light! Renewed and alive, my love for Karen is breathing and filling my heart. Lifting me. Maybe it was always there but until now, I could not know it. I had closed my eyes in darkness, blocking out the light. She opened them. And now I see.

Things haven't changed much between us, have they? I love her. I am grateful.

I miss my mom. Our mom. Almost time to talk about Mom.

There is another page for the motorcycle. One last page for Jill. Another for Gam. Okay, several. And many more for Mom. And Karen. And the almost fifty years since Karen died, many pages and revelations and recollections to come. All part of Karen's story. And there are others. To be discovered, uncovered.

Time to rest.

Time to have a drink and relax a bit. The Alabama air is mild tonight. The lapping waters of the bay have yielded many a truth and insight.

Earth's rhythm cradles me.

A Letter to the Reader:

I realize it may seem odd that I invoke things like Earth and Channels, Recollections and Intuition. I regret any derision it might invite in response to what is an honest tale, told as honestly as I can. I come to this moment in time with no affectation or filter. What I write is what I feel and remember. I edit as I go based upon a desire to be precise and expressive. And I write to honor my sister, the past, my family and the truth that has been revealed to me during this excursion, this journey. Many things have been revealed. I have tried to relay them here with as little flourish and self-indulgence as possible. These words are the best reflection of my intention. They are unembellished. Occasionally, I will and have attempted to entertain, because "that is the kind of hairpin I am." Forgive me or do not forgive me. It may comfort you to know, I forgive myself, at least for attempting to entertain—full scale self-forgiveness, well, not quite there yet but it is a stated goal of this exercise and possibly its purpose. Stick around for the ride, if you like; set it down if not.

Cheers!

Kelsey Grammer

P. S. Thank you for your indulgence thus far. I appreciate it. If you choose to stay with us to the end?—thanks for that, too.

Karen was almost eleven years old when Gordon died. I have no idea how she felt about it. We discussed it, but what I knew of her heart and her soul at the time was very limited. I barely knew what I was feeling. If I am to be honest, I knew nothing of anyone's feelings but my own. I was also uncertain if anything I was feeling was appropriate. My whole world ended. That is pretty much all I knew. The future was over except I kept waking up each morning, enduring another day that ended as the one before. Loss and emptiness.

One night, I gazed at my beautiful sister on the hammock with me. Together we would talk of Gordon. And together, mourn him. I have never been closer to anyone than Karen, and never closer to Karen than on that night. Together we kissed our Gordon good-bye. Underneath the mango tree, Karen and I embraced and buried our grandfather. It was a night of gentle breeze and starlight and we spoke of how we loved him. We were kept from the funeral, I think, because Gam hoped to spare us the devastation of seeing him. Or perhaps, to spare herself the sight of us in more distress than she could bear. A tough exterior. Soft inside. So this was our farewell to Gordon, our ceremony to say good-bye. The rhythm of the night sky and the wind in the trees echoed our farewell to him. Hours later, after a night of mourning and gentle remembrance, we never really spoke of him again. It was the end of something. Gordon had ended. Our lives had ended with him. Not our lives, per se, but the lives we had known. It was the end of our childhood.

Release the fear; embrace the feeling.

I folded myself into bed after writing this last line. As I return to it this morning, I like it but am trying to discern the next point I wanted to make. I am drawing a blank. I do know what the sentence means, I think. It is a recognition of a simple truth. Feel an emotion and release the fear attached to it that may or may not be coming along for the ride. My wife, Kayte, and I spoke by phone moments ago and she had a revelation last night: it is not "fear *of* dying" but rather "fear *is* dying." That seems right. The moments when fear has disabled me from action have stopped my life. There have been instances I stopped going forward with something that might have taken me to a better life, perhaps; but fear stopped me. What might have happened—who knows? It is dead to me. Yeah, that is right.

Something else is stirring.

Bubbling up is the first Christmas without Gordon and concurrently the first Christmas without Karen; they are a mirror, one to the other. One down. Two down. The slow dwindling of our family marked by these twin days only eight years apart.

I have said we did not speak of Gordon. I don't really remember. Karen and I didn't discuss him much after that night, but that Christmas was all about him. About his absence. He had been the keeper of Christmas, its chief progenitor ... well, after Christ and God, of course, but he may very well have been its "Holy Ghost" because Gordon brought Christmas alive in our home as no other.

Mom used to trim the tree and we would help. Gordon would add ornaments. Tinsel. Lights outside. Gam was less keen as she disliked the mess of Christmas. Gam was the only person I've ever known who was given coal in her stocking, but this is for a later passage, a tale to come. She did like fruitcake! If I remember rightly, there was a September, or early fall delivery of a fruitcake every year. It would promptly go to the back of the fridge and once a week, Gam would pour in a healthy dose of brandy. Come Christmas, that puppy was soaked. Pieces of it would be placed on a plate and the booze just ran out of it, hemorrhaging alcohol—just the way Gam liked it! I have never really enjoyed fruitcake but it sure was popular with the grown-ups. Anyway, that first Christmas without Gordon, there was still fruitcake.

There was also a beautiful tree. Mom had trimmed it with her customary brilliance and Gam helped place the tinsel. In this, it turns out she was quite an artist, insisting each strand be placed one at a time and gently draped near another, each branch shining with "icicles"—we had all the trappings. But we were missing something—a little bit of heart. It was hard to muster the presumptive joy of our Christmases past. Honestly, it was a hard year without Gordon. Something about Christmas still came shining through, though: Love. The renewed spirit.

The birth of man, the birth of the new man in each of us and the Son of God, all in one. And our remembrance of Gordon. How he loved that day—he was the picture of cheer, the very spirit of Christmas. Presents always spilled out ten feet or more from the tree. Wrappings were always elaborate and colorful. Tags on dozens of gifts said "Karen" or "Kelsey" and we spent weeks before the blessed day identifying them and memorizing their location beneath the tree so that on Christmas morning, we could beeline to our respective bounties.

The last few sentences of the previous paragraph were written partly to entertain you and to ease a persistent, personal gloominess for me. About that day. There had been so much joy in the past. We had to try, didn't we? A twelve-year-old in full voice attempting Gordon's bellowing holiday baritone to raise the family spirits. I did my damnedest. We all gave it our best shot and kept the tears at bay until the day was ending, and the simple sadness of our family over-came us. We drifted off to bed with our broken hearts, exhausted with grieving and rejoicing. There could not be a better day. And not a sad-der one. That day. That Christmas.

Snow was falling on Christmas Eve. My bedroom window was open, and a gentle breeze billowed a blanket of winter upon our rooftop. I leaned out the window with a ruler to measure the accumulated snow outside; it was three inches deep. I still don't know if that is how precipi-tation, specifically snowfall, is measured but at the age of seven, it was a good indication of a terrific Christmas Morning to come. Karen, now six, was ecstatic. As I was. The massive flakes melted on our tongues and the falling snow gently tickled our faces. Magic. Absolute magic. And Santa, we could sense, was nearby. I swore I heard the printing of rein-deer hooves on the roof. Swore I heard bells jingling. Faintly, but clear and unmistakable. With that I turned and asked Karen if she'd heard them too. It didn't matter because I raced down the stairs with Karen hot behind, jumped the last several steps and landed squarely facing the fireplace of the living room. In it was a roaring fire and beside it the tree but in the middle of the room, where things had not been when we went to bed, were suddenly a go-cart and a dollhouse. Santa had been and gone in the blink of an eye. There were some other surprises strewn about the room unwrapped and our eyes were wide with wonder that he could come and go so quickly but we were transported by the notion we had been so close to a glimpse of Santa! We would never be closer to a face to face with the man in red again.

Dear God, I miss her. I miss my sister. She was so full of joy. She was such a wonderful girl. I loved her so much. That face shining and alive, so innocent and so fun. That was irreplaceable. Thanks for being my sister, Karen. Thanks for sticking with me too. I know you have. I feel you near me and within me. I will stick with you forever. We almost met Santa together! Amazing.

So, Christmas without Karen that first year was difficult. Every time I thought of her, I thought about how she died and not how she lived. I am grateful for this assignment because as I write about Karen, I am blessed to feel her alive as before—all ages, all our shared experience. Pentimento. I am brought back to it here. I think it is possible to gaze at one picture in memory as another image from the past presents itself beneath, then pass through that image into a third that suddenly lives again. And, if unencumbered by doubt, step into the world of that image and remain fully immersed in it while simultaneously immersed in a fourth and fifth. All at the same time. Innumerable memories coinciding like fingers on the same hand. All there. And each need only be pulled into focus for a moment, briefly obscuring the others, full and palpable, while another and another stand side by side on the other side of time just as vivid. Living. Breathing. In the exact same moment. At the exact same time.

Karen lives again; the young Kelsey is there beside her. Karen graduates high school, Kelsey is there applauding. That magic day as a water angel, the memory engendered by Esther's guided tour, is a moment now alive and forever alive in me and in Karen and even in Luanne, who drove the boat that day. I have no idea what became of her. But I remember now, we kissed that day. I liked Luanne. And she will forevermore be that lovely girl a blushing boy folded fondly in his arms. Shy. Unimaginably shy he was. I wish Luanne well and thank her for an indelible experience. It makes me smile and it ignites the imagination. There is no part of this that is unreal or distant. It

89

is now. And why "remember" is my favorite word. All things can be brought back to the now if we simply remember. Every memory resides on the same canvas to be brought into focus or returned to the background at the whim of a scent or a sunrise or the lyrics of a song. So many more wonderful memories than those that crush the spirit; and those few that can, persistent and potent, have taken much too much of my time since Karen died. They are dwarfed now by the sheer volume of magnificent memories unearthed on this journey. I had thought they were essential to preserve Karen's memory—the facts of her demise and destruction; but honestly, the best moments of our life lived together—these are the ones that preserve her and revivify her and restore us. I see her again fresh and young, breathing and smiling beside me, looking me right in the eye. I gaze back at those beautiful hazel eyes and that sardonic smile and we laugh together. And it is as real as the very day we were there—in fact, we are there, and here and in all the other times we shared. Now and forever.

Thank you, Karen. And God. And thank you, Esther. I could not have done this without any of you. Oh, and I should thank Loretta. She introduced me to Esther. I have to thank Phil, as well, who introduced me to Loretta. And Kayte, my wife—Phil is her brother. I thank her and I would like to thank Phil, especially. His earnest search for Truth has brought so many engines of enlightenment into our lives. My goodness, the list goes on and on!

And there is this book.

In speaking with Kayte yesterday, I fell back in time to Liz. I wrote of her before. My girlfriend who was along for the ride when we had an accident after a day of surfing. There was something I needed to get off my chest about how she hurt me. We had been seeing each other for only a week or so and we were quite enamored of one another but the following weekend she slept with another guy. I thought maybe there was an issue with the accident and feeling unsafe, perhaps. I do remember when she told me, and I was devastated and said I would not be able to see her anymore. I surprised myself. It hurt so much. But yesterday, when speaking with Kayte, I remembered a moment stepping into the cafeteria with Liz a few days before the weekend. A teacher, Ron,

The fourth terrace down. Where I sat with Gordon on many a night.

Around back is the pool where Bill issued his swimming challenge.

▲ The apartment building. #7D, our two-year stopover before we moved to Florida.

This is the parking lot where Eleanor was legs akimbo on the hood of her Lincoln convertible. Yes, they were a beautiful pair. The car and Eleanor, I mean.

Karen. Nice posture. ▼
Same terrace.

Atlantic Highlands Yacht Club.
Looking pretty much the same.

Nothing but warm memories here.
A little bittersweet, I suppose.
The evenings I spent there were
the closest I ever felt to Gordon.

The docks at the marina. These days soaked
into my conscience. Those walks. The small
talk. The warmth of the club waiting.

Bill Carvel. ▼   ▼ And Claire.

Gam, in Colonia, not long before the move to Atlantic Highlands.

Florence and Stanley Hodges. Our godparents. In Atlantic City, you guessed it. Gam and Gordon's best friends. We would stop to see them in Virginia Beach on our way to our new home in Florida.

Gam and Florence. Some sort of party.

Karen, top row, left. ▶
This was the girl
whose face seemed
so mature as we made
our way to Florida. My
grandmother marveled
at how she washed
her face one night in
a hotel. Like a proper
beauty, she said.

▼ The motel with the two of us swimming.
We stopped for a couple of nights
there. Our last visit ever. Gordon
spoke of the war outside our room.

▼ The Virginia Beach motel where we always
stayed when visiting Florence and Hodges.

Our Florida Home. Gordon never had a
chance to live there. He got us there, though.
Bless him. Our life begins in Florida.

Football at Pine Crest. I'm in there somewhere.

▲ Karen's sixth grade class.

▲ I wrote my first song at this piano. A song about Gordon. This was around Thanksgiving that first year without him.

Our little boat. One year later. The house is behind me on my left. Port side. Karen took this picture. We would sit this way together for years but almost every day and night that first year.

◄ Gordon at Berkeley. Captain of the crew.

▼ You can tell she adored Gordon. He loved to hammer out a tune with a single finger. They did love life. And each other.

▲ Gordon at 14, in repose on the corral fence, Black Mountain Ranch.

The 20s. The decade and their ▲ ages. Their early years together seemed pretty fun. Living in San Francisco, where my mom was born.

Gam and Gordon around 1960. ► Gam always said that on her gravestone, she would like to have this inscription: Just a second, I haven't finished my drink yet.

▼ Gam. Evangeline Lucille Dimmick. This might be her senior year at Miss Head's School for Girls. A little sadness in those eyes?

Gam with her cousin, Torance. ▲ The scribblings below and on a few of the other pictures throughout are authored by my mom. I would not have known otherwise.

▲ And then came Sally.

Mom in Texas, 14 years old. ▶

Gordon in uniform. Lt. Col. Cranmer. I think this is just after the war. ▶ They lived in Hollywood for a year before moving to Colonia, NJ. Gordon was in uniform a good deal of the time. Still working for the government. The business of the war not quite done.

▼ Gam and Sally shopping in Texas during the war. Men in uniform behind them.

▲ Texas again with Aunt Lela standing. Gordon is overseas at this point. The other girl, the dog—no idea. Lela lived with them for a long time but I have no real knowledge of her life with them. She was a wonderful artist.

Gordon at work. All these shots because of this book and once again Mom and Gam pictured on his desk.

▲ Gordon on Guadalcanal. Outside his barracks. Twenty-eight months overseas. I may be the last of a grateful generation, but I am proud of Gordon beyond words. And proud of my mother and grandmother.

▲ I had these two pictures in my possession for years. Lovely shots of Gam and Sally at age thirteen or so.

▲ Sally (Mom) did look very mature here but still just a girl.

▲ Then the move to Jersey. Breaking ground on Surrey Lane.

▲ The completed home. The home where I lived until I was ten.

the same Ron, asked at the door if I was in love. "No," I scoffed. "Love is down the road!" Well, Liz heard that and a couple of days later she was with someone else. And, yesterday, I imagined it must have hurt her. And I am sorry. Maybe I was in love. Maybe it was my first love. I was just being careful and foolish and didn't want to jump to conclusions, but it did feel like love. It scared me to suddenly feel there was someone I wanted around all the time. And maybe that is why I said what I said. Maybe we weren't going to end up together, but she did make me feel like a million bucks and I should have had the stones to say so. Anyway, thanks to you, too, Liz. I am sorry if I hurt you that day.

This leads me back to the phone call I made to Jill after I got to San Diego on the motorcycle. We hadn't spoken for a few days. I had been sleeping in the park behind the theatre but would manage to find a little apartment the next week. Rehearsal ended one afternoon and I finally called Jill. We exchanged a couple of niceties and I finally blurted out, "So, who you sleeping with?"

"Michael," she said.

And then, I said, "I figured." And a moment later, a long moment, I said, "I guess this is it then."

So, that was it. And I felt the ache I had anticipated for almost a year anyway. The ache of being worthless and a failure and of knowing we were not the shiny couple of my youth, but a spent one, languishing in a habit of losing. We lost so many things: a child, a love, hope, respect for one another and finally our passion. All had been killed along with Karen that awful day in July. It was sad. It was also sad when I learned Jill died. Jill. I'd hoped she was okay. She was fifty-five. Still young. I still remember that first time she locked eyes with me on a walk through Manhattan. A chill was in the air and the night was clear. Without thinking much of it, we agreed a stroll around the park might be nice and at a corner along the way, Sixtieth and Fifth Avenue, she caught my eyes on her as they took her in and then she smiled a smile at me I had never seen. I knew then we had a story together. It ended badly for reasons beyond both of us. Farewell, Jill. We gave it a good try. I think well of you. Continue in Peace.

Funny that some time ago in the page count, I said it was time to praise that motorcycle. Jill and Liz are both a part of that story. Jill and I rode that bike around Manhattan the second year at Julliard. I picked it up from Leslie's house in Jersey after the winter had passed. Leslie was Spencer's sister and agreed it could slumber there in her garage until things warmed up. So, after that it became a chief companion for our adventures that spring. We drove down to the Jersey Shore together or around the city on a warm evening. I think there was a bit of mischief in Jill that enjoyed riding on it, knowing her dad was firmly set against them. Who knows? Like I said, her parents had no idea I rode a motorcycle till I roared up that night in Texas on my way to San Diego. Another fond memory from an easier time. Liz rode on the back of my bike the summer before when it was brand new. The circumstances of her visit are long forgotten but I recall the sensation as she sat behind me and held me. We stopped at a traffic light and she leaned forward and whispered how she remembered I'd always said I would get a motorcycle. She went on to tell me how it impressed her that I was one of those people who could say something and then do it. I think we had lunch and then she went off to visit a girlfriend or something; that was all. I enjoyed seeing her. Had I understood then what had happened with us, I might have apologized on the spot, rather than waiting almost fifty years and fifty pages to tell her now.

But that motorcycle was the central character, or rather trusted steed, in my life's journey from eighteen to twenty-six years of age. I think that's about right. Here goes. I am going to generate a list of names who connect with that bike. I am bound to miss a few but in no order of importance, they are: Gam, Bob, Mom, Karen, Brian, Stanley, Pamela, Jill, Carl, Spencer, Brad, Liz, Dean, Karen, Agnes, Debbie, Debby, Kim, Danny, Nate, Ellen, Pam, GW, another Pam and Robert. Off the top of my head that's about it. I am sure others will insinuate themselves into memory as it has been with every tale. And, of course, (how could I forget her?)—there was one who comes to mind suddenly and emphatically: Goose. Not a person but the greatest dog ever!

Let's start with the three Pams. There had been another Pam in my life but she was not "motorcycle-centric," if that is a word, though she did know Karen. And, the moment I write that, another Pam springs to mind—also not part of the motorcycle story, nor of Karen, so probably not destined for a mention here. Ridiculous and wonderful how the brain flies about from person to person and presents these characters, long ago forgotten, who once participated in my life. Obviously, not forgotten but rather "stowed out of conscience"—Auden wrote that. His observation was based on a regret. Mine is more pleasant: they are still in there—every one—and I am glad to see them again. It feels like that.

As I have promised not to use last names, save those who are gone or past concern if identified, I may decide to use an initial or two to differentiate the Pams. The first is Pam M. who was a lovely young woman of a particularly diminutive height—four ten. I liked her. We met one night at the beach in Ft. Lauderdale when I was sixteen. I do not remember how we planned things back then, but I think it was as quaint as simply committing to memory someone's phone number and then calling them. So it was with this Pam. I called her home a day or two later and spoke with her father. I even introduced myself and asked politely if I could speak with his daughter after I explained how we had met, and I was asking his permission if I could take her on a date. He explained it would be necessary for me to come in and say hello to her mother and him on the night, but should I pass muster at that point, he would permit her to go out for a movie or some such as long as she was back home by ten. Fair enough, I thought. He put me on the phone with Pam.

I suddenly remember, I think he was a mailman. An ironic fact, that will be ironic only to me, him and his daughter, but fun to recall at this point so many years later. Obviously, I will say no more in an abundance of discretion—as promised. I called her on the day and had to explain why we could not take my car—or rather my mother's car—because something had come up. But we could borrow my friend Danny's motorcycle. Yes, that Danny, Karen's boyfriend and my friend, too.

Danny had bought a Honda 750 recently and because we grew up on motorcycles together, he was quite happy to let me drive it sometimes. This was the beginning of my love affair with the Honda 750. Pam told me her father would kill me. So, she offered a solution: Park down the street from her house, far enough away to be out of earshot. Ring the doorbell and explain I had found parking some distance from her home and walked there. Seemed like a good plan and certainly more devious than I could have concocted. In fact, she came up with it in a matter of seconds. Girls! I know we are not supposed to credit the sexes with specific gifts but in my day, (and yes, I am aware of how that sounds), but "in my day," it was fine to consider women far more intelligent and craftier than us men! I still think it but am loathe to mention it for obvious reasons—any empirical and axiomatic truth stated in print or spoken out loud these days, is grounds for cancellation and instant banishment from society.

Anyway, things went off without a hitch and Pam was the first girl I ever had on the back of a motorcycle. It was a wonderful evening. We drove down to the beach and parked behind the Swimming Hall of Fame. We walked together and held hands and that was about it. I think Danny and Karen met up with us and we all spent a couple of hours just talking and watching the souped-up cars drive along the "Strip" as we called it then.

I took Pam home and kissed her goodnight near the house, terrified that a hostile father lurked in the shadows about to pounce. It was a lovely kiss but fraught with stress on my part. I pulled away and Pam pulled me back in for another, doubling my terror. And then, I walked her to the door. It was a great night. I want to enter into the record that this memory may be full of inaccuracies but not many, I think. We were good kids on the precipice of adulthood and excited about it. She was great. We went out a few more times but never did more than kiss; maybe more but not much. I feel good about that. She was a nice girl and a girl I treated nicely. I look back on that proudly. And honestly, I didn't know how else to treat a girl at the time. I was nice too.

Again, I am pulled to another revelation about Karen. This is her story wrapped in mine and vice versa. Karen was a nice kid, too. She was a bit earlier than I was to the whole intimacy thing. I was ashamed of myself and scared of rejection whereas Karen, perhaps through the persuasion of Danny, was comfortable with sex well before I was.

This was how it was with Danny and Karen. Karen was certainly willing, though, and I think Danny loved her, so it was natural for them to have a relationship much like that of a more mature couple.

Karen seemed to be the subject of Danny's affections and student to his attentions, but as I recall Karen's sophistication and intelligence, it may have been she who was in charge of the whole affair. And as I look back on it, it was her destiny to get there early, as she had so little time left. We did not know that then, nor did she, but I think of it that way. Karen was ready. So, when she "became a woman" as the saying goes, she was ready to behave as a woman and enjoy it. She didn't wait very long. And I am happy she had the experiences she had before her death. She lived fully. Not a second wasted. I lived timidly.

Karen and Danny were together for almost four years. Karen was discovering life without question or doubt, and I admire her for it—to this day. I was not ready; Karen was. To think that she would die just a few years later is a reminder to celebrate that she enjoyed life as she did, as early as she did.

Something in me feels a need to explain more. I do not wish to cast Karen in a light that is negative in any way. She matured early, earlier than some, later than others at the time. At that time, late 1960s, early '70s, there was an awakening among young people. It was considered natural to explore our bodies, to "drop in." We were awake to the idea of love and lust and open to the idea that both could coexist or exist without one another ... lust was fine, love was a bonus but not necessary, we did not need to justify attraction with the lie of love. Not anymore. I was a bit of a square. Karen was not. She didn't have to be. I did.

I was swimming upstream in a complexity of job descriptions—son, husband (kind of) and father of sorts, all at the same time. Beginning at the age of twelve and standing tall in the saddle until eighteen, I was responsible. Possibly delusion or illusion, but as I see it still—my responsibility. This was not my choice; it was the only choice within my reach. I dispatched my duties. I think to my credit. I was a stick in the mud, a royal pain in the ass to my sister and at the same time, a loyal servant to her ... to her, my mother and my grandmother. All at once.

Karen had her story. I had mine. Much of mine is being told in telling hers. They come together. I love her more than words can say. She is my sister. We remain together. The story unfolds. Not sure what comes next. Her days. My days. And days we shared. Ours to tell.

Unfolding.

Pamela was an actress. The third Pamela. I'd like to clear something up right now . . . the fourth Pam was actually "Pat," Patricia (also called Trish), Pam's roommate and long-time friend. I was wrong. So, three Pams only. Pam and Patricia were in San Diego. It was the night after I spoke with Jill. There was a party. I was just an apprentice but the whole company was invited so I thought I should claim my place there—it was, after all, my first. And, after all, I had endured great hardship to get there. Tallahassee to San Diego in just four days on the back of a motorcycle, hurtling through thunderstorms, lightning and freezing cold. Just one phone call ago, I had even said good-bye to my one-time fiancée. I deserved this invitation. Physical sacrifice, determination and great personal cost had earned it!

So, in I walked and said hello to many of the actors. I said hello to the Equity actors and my fellow apprentices alike. I measured my insignificance by their glances and vacant acknowledgements, but I was there. And proud to be. After a time, I sat down and was approached by Pamela. She was the lead actress in the company, she and Trish (Patricia—the presumed Pam), and as I engaged in conversation with them both, I realized I was worth this conversation with them. I liked them and after a time I also realized I was not less than them; I was someone among many, worthy as any.

As the evening wore on, I grew tired and Pamela said she was ready to go. Trish was not, so I volunteered to run Pamela home on my bike. Was she comfortable on the back of a motorcycle? She wasn't sure. She had never been on one. So, I told her I would drive her home and she would be safe. I was very good on a motorcycle, I explained. That was true. I was very good. So, my cockiness was not at all cockiness, not at all. It was confidence. Pamela accepted the ride. Trish told me where they were staying and how to get there and off we went.

This is where the story turned to something I had not anticipated. Pamela was pretty. I did not think for a minute that she was interested in me. We climbed aboard the bike. And we started up the road. On the freeway, I "opened her up" (meaning the motorcycle), and the surge of power and speed scared Pamela and she grabbed me in a kind of panic. I had told her to wrap her arms around my waist, of course, but she held me with her entire body pressed against mine in a kind of active surrender. It was honestly very exciting, almost as if her soul was clinging to mine, entering mine . . . I had never felt anything like it. She was that rare creature who could simply yield to something without restraint. Perhaps, why she was such a wonderful actress. Something else—once the newness of being on the bike subsided, her fear relaxed but not her grip. I had certainly never felt anything like that! It went right through me. A week or so later, we started seeing each other. I liked her. She was a lovely woman and a splendid talent. I was flattered to be with her, and, though I took a great deal of flak from the apprentice company and others, I enjoyed her. I claimed her for all to know.

There was a bit of a fly in the ointment, though. Pamela had lost her dog a few months before coming to San Diego. I would hold her as she cried about him. She was absolutely devastated and I admired her for that too. She could surrender to her emotions and almost lose herself in them. This is where I started to distance myself. Karen's death was still raw for me. I had grown fairly stoic about it except when pangs of grief would overcome me; pangs that Pamela suffered just as I did, only I kept mine to myself. And though her pain was genuine, and I did my best to comfort her, I could not help my feeling that something was out of balance, perhaps? Yes, I saw it as a similar grief but . . . not really. It finally drove me to seek some solitude.

As I have been writing, I have been searching in my head for the place where I found it. Sure enough, it rushes back in in the nick of time. Carl and his family were leaving town for a bit, and he offered me his place in trade for house-sitting. It was a blessing. And they had a great stereo system. I played James Taylor till the grooves wore out. "Grooves wore out" meant something back then. Not so much

97

now. "I Was a Fool to Care" and "Lighthouse" were my two favorite songs that summer, and I wept and wept as I listened to them in my solitude. Jill and Karen, so many things lost . . . and it was in that time I allowed myself to mourn . . . self-indulgently, unguarded. Unashamed. On show days, I would make my way to the theater early and play the piano in the rehearsal room for hours. This was my first time without a schedule of duties in care of others. It was a time of solace. A time of healing. I was twenty-one.

Pinning down the chronology of the motorcycle in my life is elusive. But I'll get it. It is connected to many of the people who are connected to me and to Karen, and to many stories that, in turn, connect to us both. Serving as a vehicle, if you will. See what I did there? But as recollections spill into my fingers, I find it hard to reconcile the dates. One summer is confused with another and then another. One winter at school has two or three distinct memories that seem to overlap.

Now, I know the first day I arrived at Juilliard, I rode that motorcycle. I began to question if I had it before the first year at school or the second, but I know it was the first because I have the testimony of one Stanley P. Wilson. I did promise to refrain from using last names except in certain cases—this is one. In Stanley's case, it honors him and our lifelong friendship. Stanley has been along for some of the best days of this ride, meaning my life, and he also witnessed some of the worst. But we met as I pulled up on that motorcycle to the facade of The Juilliard School to begin my first day.

I powered the bike over the curb and onto the sidewalk right in front of the building and put it on the kickstand. The first young man who walked by was Stanley and I asked him if I was indeed at the entrance to the Juilliard School. He answered I was. Then he asked where I was headed and I told him the acting school. "I will take you there!" said Stanley, in a jovial tone. "I'm in group four."

I was joining group six. It was the first day of a friendship that would start and stop a good deal but would finally blossom in earnest years later. Karen was starting school at Berry College in Georgia. A couple of bright young lights seeking their destiny in the halls of academe. I will return to Stanley in the pages to come but for now I want to visit Karen and me in the final year of high school and just a bit before.

We had settled into our different roles as young people at school. Karen was recognized as a very bright person . . . me, not so much. Although Mario noted that my SAT scores were considerably higher than anyone might have expected. I'd maintained good grades except for Spanish, and I had begun a career as singer/actor/whatever at the school. I am not trying to run myself down with that characterization. It was a bit improvisational. Most of the teachers allowed me some accommodation as I was singing with a group called The Singing Pines quite a bit. It meant I was often not in class. The arrangement was that as long as I could pass the tests, I could do as many off-campus activities as I liked.

Karen hung with a slightly different crowd but one that overlapped with mine in some key instances. She was chiefly different in her fondness for marijuana. It was not really my "thing," but I have a page from her yearbook where it mentions "shotguns" as one of her favorite things to give. So, I am now turning to some of my source material by reviewing that very book. I will also share how we came to be at the same school, Pine Crest, for most of our education but for her final year, she attended Palm Cove.

At Palm Cove, Karen had proven to be well ahead of the Junior Class she entered and was advanced to Senior so that we would both graduate in 1973. Phenomenal. I think she was the Valedictorian that year, and I remember hearing her speech at the Palm Cove graduation ceremony. She was an impressive young woman. I am still at a bit of a loss as to how it all transpired. My mom told me Karen was tired of living in my shadow. I am not sure I buy that but maybe. My shadow was not much to speak of then. I could be wrong. Maybe that is how Karen saw it and she was striking out to have her own singular station and identity apart from being my sister. I just don't buy it, but it is worth mentioning here. She excelled at Palm Cove.

I intend to ask a few of our friends still living for some insight. One is Jan, possibly Momo and I am trying to track down Danny. Bob, Brian and Ronnie were others we both knew. In fact, Bob was my best friend back then and he had a special relationship with Karen. Like I said, we were very open in those days and theirs was not a boyfriend, girlfriend thing but they were close and would spend an evening or two together from time to time. This is what I know. It may have been more but Bob never told me. Neither did Karen.

Karen and I even double-dated a few times and shared intimacies with each other's friends. It wasn't creepy or weird . . . it was natural. She was my sister and my friends, if they fancied her, were welcome to spend time with her. It didn't bother me. The same went for me and some of Karen's friends. These were very good days and innocent days. We were just exploring ourselves and our minds and our bodies together. It was a nice group of young people, and I think we navigated it pretty well. I have already mentioned how I look back on Karen's life and am glad it was so rich in experience and exploration. What we all thought would be a lifetime together was an all-too-brief visit with an extraordinary girl. I felt fortunate to know her. I think my friends felt that way, too. I still do.

An email just came in. Freddie Glenn is refusing his parole hearing in May. The next is scheduled for November of 2022. This is good news. Corbett died in prison two years ago. That was good news, too. But not enough. Not good, just good news. If I am meant to release this, it is not proving easy. I guess it's one step up, two steps back on days like these.

A surging anguish is in my heart right now. Honesty. I promise honesty in this. I am split in two. I watch myself and think how self-indulgent of me. Then the other half tells me to sod off, that getting over this is not something that'll ever happen. Getting through it is all.

True. But I do get through it. Did. Do.

I have turned to the very first page of Karen's yearbook. There on the cover page is something I have been missing. I do not have first-hand eyes on parts of my sister's life, especially her last year of high school. Here, from one of her classmates:

Karen, it was fun being in your geometry class and it was funny how you would never say anything unless it is right and that's the way it should be. Have fun at college and maybe I'll see you again.

Bill

There are others:

Karen, it was nice knowing you this year and I know you will have a very *high* time in college next year. Have a summer full of shotguns and Good Luck.

Grey

Dear Karen, can you believe we're out of here? Never forget Disney World, Kar. Stay the same and best of luck.

Always,

Betsy '73

Well, obviously, there were several things going on back then. Karen's senior year was very colorful, to say the least. I do remember Karen saying how much she enjoyed Disney World and I know she went back a few times after high school with some friends. That is pretty much all I know. She said it was great. I have no idea. And I would never guess in this instance. Karen's life was her business. You may recall how I told her a few years before that trying things was fine but getting caught was out of the question. She didn't get caught.

I am sitting with Jude, my son. I have just read him a few of the previous paragraphs. He never met Karen, of course, so, I hope he gets to know her a bit, as I read to him now. I have been sharing my progress with him as I write. Also, with Kayte. It helps and I sense that Karen is helping me too. She was wonderful. I want them to know that. I want everyone to know that. I never knew she was so good in Geometry. I was pretty good at it myself but there are mentions throughout the yearbook of her prowess in that particular subject. She did have a great mind. And, honestly, I am treading water here a bit and hoping she comes along any minute to help me with this paragraph . . .

And there she is!

Her yearbook picture. I have this same picture framed and sitting on a bench in our bedroom. And at the very second the name crosses my mind; I turn a few pages in Karen's yearbook to Lauren S. The first time I saw Lauren, she took my breath away. I had a big crush on her. Maybe she had a big crush on me too! I don't know for sure, but I do know why I did absolutely nothing about it.

And now, we head down one of those wormholes to another time in my life. I was driving the McKee Craft, our little boat that took me water-skiing down a sunset years before. It was in a little bay in Lighthouse Point a few miles from our home. I was cruising along with Jay, my old pal whose house was in that little bay—a very impressive house with a giant boat tied up at its dock. Jay's dad was very wealthy; in fact, I think his granddad was wealthy, too, so it was a very impressive home on the water. For some reason, a girl in a Boston Whaler slowly drifted by and exchanged a look with me. Wow, what a girl!—I thought. All other memory about that moment has gone from me but someone told me her name. Who is that? "Lauren S.," came the answer and I thought, *I wish a girl like that could like a boy like me.* I never saw her again or heard a whisper about her until Karen went to Palm Cove.

Then one day Karen came home and told me, "Lauren S. is thinking of asking you to the prom. She found out you're my brother." Huh? So, I guess on that fateful day, she may have thought exactly what I was thinking, only I didn't think such a thing was possible at the time— that a girl might notice me as I had noticed her. She may have asked someone, just as I had, who I was; maybe they even told her my name as someone told me hers. What a world!

She did not ask me to the prom. I never spoke to her, in fact. Ever. Maybe someone will read this, someone who knows her, maybe Lauren herself, and she will say to herself, as I said to myself when Karen told me about the prom: "Gee! Maybe I wasn't crazy." No, Lauren, you weren't crazy; maybe I was crazy not to call you right there and then. This may have been my first lesson in trusting my intuition. I did not know it at the time. I know now, as previously stated.

Throughout my life, I have nursed a feeling or feelings for someone, and as I have moved through the decades, I've begun to trust or believe that these feelings come up because that person may very well share the same feelings toward me; maybe it is their feelings I am reading? I am not sure. Doubt usually short-circuits the whole affair, and I retreat.

So it has been with me for years . . . a girl I liked may actually have liked me, but she had little chance of knowing it unless she told me. Chalk it up to shyness or just stupidity or maybe just fear. Had I deduced this earlier in life I am not sure it would have made any difference, made me any braver, but I pretty much had to be hit over the head by a girl before I could summon up the nerve to make any move at all. So, honestly, if the girl didn't make the move, there would be no move. Whatsoever. And that was that, as the saying goes. I am hoping maybe it was charming to be so shy, but . . . maybe not. Yeah, probably not.

Thank God Kayte asked if I might like to meet for a cup of coffee in London—our children's lives depended on it! Actually, I'm not sure who started talking to whom first, but we did spend the entire flight talking and enjoying each other's company. I said I would be in London for almost a week. Did she live in London? No. But she had booked an appointment to get a bob at the beauty parlor which set the hook. Just to be sure people know, "set the hook" is an expression in fishing when you know the fish has officially taken the bait, a swift tug on the rod ensures the hook is firmly lodged, and the fish is more likely to be pulled into the boat. I was hooked. "I'd like to see that," I told her. She had a great neck! Long. A bob would make it look even longer! Enough said. Kayte knows exactly what happened so I will let her tell the rest of the story some other time. It is possible my shyness subsided a bit in the thirty subsequent years between that day on the boat and that day on the plane. But I'm not sure. For the purposes of this story, I have nothing further to say. Kayte may wish to add another comment or two. That is her prerogative. I am quite comfortable, however, to declare I am still painfully shy. Nothing Kayte says can change that.

Shyness, it occurs to me, probably seems incongruent with an acting career. I always thought so, on the face of it, but there are epidemic levels of shy people in the acting profession. Why?

I am sure you guessed that I have a theory. I am quite willing to share it. I think it's simple: shy people are afraid to speak the truth. Acting is a profession or pastime in which a person can tell the truth and not get in trouble. See? Simple. And, yes, it's the easiest course in life to just tell the truth. But people do get in trouble for telling the truth. In acting, they get in trouble if they don't. Paradoxical, perhaps. No. Just ironic.

Without growing dissertational here, I will offer this. Some think acting is not a great art. I believe it is one of the greatest because it represents Truth in such a vivid manner, holding the mirror up to life, as Shakespeare tells us in Hamlet's advice to the players. Now, of course, everyone knows a mirror image is a reverse image. It isn't quite right, but it is real; it projects truth through a medium, the mirror, much as movies or the stage do. Those who master it know they are speaking truth through the fantasy of another ... the screenwriter or playwright. Their characters are brought to life by the truth of the actor who breathes life into them. Two people suddenly live in one, and the actor goes from natural being to supernatural, doubled in meaning and power. I am not writing this to impart any wisdom about art. Or acting. I believe a life in Art is a sublime and noble calling that does indeed blithe man's existence by presenting what has been called a "true lie." That is all the time I will devote to the matter.

I am writing to tell the truth about my sister and about the life she lived and the life I live with her as my constant companion. Karen has also protected me and guided me during my life, even if I don't always listen. I feel an immense irony and guilt that I was meant to protect her, yet she protected me and continues to do so. She led me to this tale and leads me in it. I try to hear her. I try to honor her, climbing to where I see her high above me. Where Karen is today is a lofty place. And I am listening as I climb. She is Legend. Maybe the whole Valhalla thing is true. Maybe our Viking blood carries it. I could drop to my knees when I think where she may dwell and in what light.

Too much? Am I overdoing it? No. The words are accurate; they are what I feel. But also, what I know. Shining in Valhalla! I see her there.

I want to go back in time to when we were very young. Karen was probably three. That makes me about five years old. It is a winter morning and I have been prepped to step outside for a day in the snow. Karen has been, too. Breakfast is finished and I rush to the door.

Mom says, "Wait for your sister."

"Aww, Mom, do I have to?" It makes me cringe to think I said that. It makes me cringe to think Karen heard me. I never wanted to make her feel unwanted or unwelcome. I also know dozens of brothers and sisters regard their siblings in this way, almost as if they are a nuisance or a burden. I know I am not a monster to have said such a thing. I am just sorry I said it. I know Karen doesn't mind but she probably did then; it probably hurt her. So sorry. Anyway, I waited for her. Karen was my constant companion and my charge—true then, true now. I was told to look after her. I was meant to look after her. Here's where I'm heading . . . my job was clear and simple and when Karen died, I felt like I failed her. I know I've said this before. I will probably say it again. It bears repeating. The ultimate irony is she has repaid the favor beyond measure. I have said that before, too. And as I write this, I see her pointing to this work as the way to release all those feelings. It is hard for me. But I am grateful. Writing is the mission; freedom is the goal. Freedom from my own sadness. Freedom from my guilt. Freedom from my shame.

"Leave that alone!"

I am trying, Karen. The shame is stubborn. Unyielding. I do see the goal in sight. It's just hard to let go of something that has lived in me all this time. Hard. Even though I know it will be a great benefice to us both. I am meant to see you in the light and not as a victim. Yes. As my companion still and sister in a life of rejoicing that is at hand. Hand in hand. And I am meant to purge any sense of myself as a victim, too. Okay. So much pain. I feel almost a traitor to release it. As if I dishonor your life to let it go. Holding onto it has made me feel closer to you. Holding onto it is what I'd thought I was supposed to do. I do not lose you by losing the sadness. I know that now. I am lighter than when the story began, and you know we have made some progress. I am better. Will I never again weep at the thought of you? I will weep buckets. You know that, too.

"There is no cause for shame, Kelsey. No cause. Shame is a second death. You are meant to be free."

Freedom does not mean free of responsibility. Freedom does not mean Karen's murderer should be released or released from consequence. If they let him go, what will I do? How can I ever be free? Guilt and shame are baked into this more than I would like. If I cannot keep him in jail. Fresh guilt, fresh shame? Consequence. If I fail, I fail her again?

Hammer it out. Right.

There are some things I must clear categorically. That night, when Karen stood before them, her killers—it has more to tell. It is as if a laser is pointing at the hardest places, those least likely to heal. The imagination is so full of horror—so sticky about that night. So difficult. And so, it must be uncovered. There is a letter. It was written by Jim Bentley, Senior District Attorney, Fourth District, Colorado, in 2018. This is years after Glenn first qualified for parole. That was several years before, but in this instance, Freddie Glenn had applied for placement in Community Corrections. A copy of Jim Bentley's letter:

106

OFFICE OF THE DISTRICT ATTORNEY
4th JUDICIAL DISTRICT

Daniel H. May District Attorney	Kim L. Kitchen Assistant District Attorney

January 8, 2018

Re: Freddie Glenn DOC#43516

Dear Community Corrections Board,

    I have been notified by the Colorado Parole Board that Freddie Glenn has applied for placement in Community Corrections. The possibility that this inmate may be released from custody causes me great concern. As a Senior Deputy District Attorney I have represented the Fourth Judicial District Attorney on Mr. Glenn's cases since 2010. Freddie Glenn and his co-defendant Michael Corbett terrorized the citizens of Colorado Springs between June 19, 1975 and July 1, 1975. Over two weeks they robbed and killed three people in three separate despicable incidents. Even forty two years later these murders stand out as examples of cruelty and depravity seldom been seen in our community or anywhere in Colorado.

    It is important to remember that Freddie Glenn is in a category of criminals that is extremely rare. Most homicides are situational. Meaning that but for the specific circumstances which occurred at the time of that one homicide, a defendant generally poses little danger to others. Freddie Glenn and his confederates deliberately targeted multiple victims in separate incidents over a period of weeks. This total lack of respect for human life puts him into a very small and unique group.

    The first murder occurred on June 19, 1975, the defendant, Michael Corbett and another individual robbed twenty nine year old Daniel Van Lone. Van Lone had just gotten off work as a cook, at the Four Seasons hotel. He was abducted and taken to a remote area. According to police reports Daniel Van Lone begged the defendants not to kill him. Van Lone pleaded "please don't kill me, please don't kill me." Mr. Van Lone's pleas fell on deaf ears as he was shot in the head. All Mr. Glenn and his cohorts got from Daniel Van Lone was fifty cents.

    On June 27, 1975, the Defendant and the others meet with a soldier, Winfred Proffitt, ostensibly to sell Mr. Proffitt some marijuana. Winfred Proffitt was stabbed in the chest with a knife. The blade lacerated Mr. Proffitt's liver. Mr. Proffitt struggled for life but died as a result of the stabbing. Michael Corbett later told investigators that he stabbed Winfred Proffitt to death because he wanted know to what it felt like to kill someone with a knife. Freddie Glenn was a co-defendant and convicted of murdering Mr. Proffitt.

    The third murder occurred after the Defendant and his co-defendants in attempted to rob a Red Lobster restaurant on July 1, 1975. They decided not to rob the restaurant because they believed they had been made. They left the restaurant but thought that nineteen year old Karen Grammer knew they had planned to rob the restaurant. Miss Grammer had been waiting at the restaurant for her boyfriend to get off work.

    Freddie Glenn and others kidnapped Miss Grammer. In a series of acts which displayed an utter lack of respect for human life and decency, they repeatedly raped Karen Grammer over a period of several hours. They

Colorado Springs Office: 105 East Vermijo Ave., Colorado Springs, CO 80903 719.520.6000
Cripple Creek Office: 112 N. A St., PO Box 958, Cripple Creek, CO 80913 719.689.9757

107

OFFICE OF THE DISTRICT ATTORNEY
4ᵗʰ JUDICIAL DISTRICT

Daniel H. May
District Attorney

Kim L. Kitchen
Assistant District Attorney

then took Miss Grammer to a mobile home park where Glenn repeatedly stabbed her. Then they dumped her out of the car to die.

Freddie Glenn was convicted in all three of these murders. When the Defendant was convicted of the murder of Karen Grammer in case, 75CR22789, he was sentenced to death. That sentence was later changed to be a life sentence when all current death penalty sentences were set aside by the Colorado Supreme Court in 1979.

Freddie Glenn's actions earned him a special status as a cold blooded and cruel killer. His actions were so extremely violent and devoid of conscience that he should not be released from custody. The defendant claims that he is remorseful for his actions but the only way we have of measuring his character is his past behavior. The defendant proved that he is extremely dangerous and that he is capable of acts of depravity that shocked the core of this community.

Freddie Glenn is in relatively good health. He is only sixty one years old. Freddie Glenn is a threat to any community he is released into if his request is granted. I question what facility is available to appropriately house the defendant if his request for relief is granted. What community corrections placement is there in Colorado that could properly supervise someone with the type of history this defendant presents? The most appropriate place for the defendant is the Colorado Department of Corrections. I ask you to deny the defendant's request for relief.

Sincerely,

_____
Jim Bentley
Senior District Attorney

Colorado Springs Office: 105 East Vermijo Ave., Colorado Springs, CO 80903 719.520.6000
Cripple Creek Office: 112 N. A St., PO Box 958, Cripple Creek, CO 80913 719.689.9757

108

Some of the details he gives do not reflect my recollection. The other murders he recounts are horrible and show a contempt for life even before getting to Karen's murder. It was Jim Bentley I believe who spoke with me back in NYC when I was living with Jill. He had explained how seven people died, Karen being the sixth and they were going to try them for only three murders . . . these three were a "slam dunk," he said. I would not be needed in Colorado to testify. The letter sent to the board reviewing Glenn's status likely condensed many of the details in an attempt not to overwhelm them. Even so, the horror was still evident and harrowing in a letter forty-three years later. As I recall the events of that evening, there are some inconsistencies in the letter contrasting what I was told. A couple of lines stand out.

On the top of page 2, the letter mentions Karen was waiting for her boyfriend at the Red Lobster, waiting for him to get off work. I don't know who he was. I wish I did. But as I recall, the detective who met me at the plane told me Karen was entering the Red Lobster from the back, saw these men and approached them. She confronted them and asked what they were doing. It was then that she was taken.

I am not sure how big a difference it makes here but to me it is important. I see her as I have seen her in my mind's eye, saying, "What do you think you're doing?" or "Where do you think you're going?" And then I see her seeing them. I feel her stomach begin to knot as they approach her. Her eyes. She knows she's in trouble. They take her. Force her into their car.

The letter mentions they thought they'd been "made" by Karen . . . the police also told me Glenn and his pals knew she could identify them . . . that was their issue and because of that, they knew there and then they would kill her. I think Karen knew too. First, they would torture her. They decided it would be sport to rape her, keep her a bit, and took her to an apartment. This is the kidnapping. They discussed killing her openly as they mercilessly took their turns. Karen negotiated with them . . . she would do what they asked if they would let her go. I hear her plead for her life. She probably made a pretty good argument; she was a smart kid. But . . . they took her some more and then finally loaded her into the car to head for the trailer park where they planned to dispose of her body . . . once she was dead. It was on the way there, as they neared the trailer park, that Karen managed to escape.

Mr. Bentley's letter said she was killed in the car. I do not believe it was possible to kill her in the manner Freddie Glenn did while they were in the car. He would not have had the leverage sufficient to be so savage and brutal. I believe she escaped and as she ran away, Freddie Glenn, furious that she had wrestled free from him, caught up to her and in a rage stabbed her over and over again, plunging his knife into her body, tearing it out of her to the full height of his reach and then plunging it in again. She was almost decapitated they told me. I mentioned it earlier but repeat it here to illustrate the savagery and the inhumanity of that "good kid." How did she feel at the first cut? And the next. And the next. Forty-two times. When did she know she would not live? She still crawled to a possible rescue at the trailer of a stranger who wasn't home. It was there she died.

If I repeat myself, it is because I have repeated this a thousand times. It has played on a loop in my mind till I have almost been complicit in her death by its remembrance. Yet, it will surely play again. They are scenes and questions with no end and no answers. I must take the images and keep them, even as I find a way to let the pain go. I mentioned the psychic who told me Karen did not suffer; God had taken her well before her execution. Is it possible she did not suffer, knowing, as I do, that she still fought for her life until the very last of it? I know in my heart I am meant to cherish her and even be joyful we had the time together we did, and I know I am no longer to carry it as I have. The story, thus far, has given me that. Also, I know now that it will always be with me, but it needn't destroy me as it almost did. It hardened my heart. I briefly spoke of this earlier but with suppositions guessed at and untrue. Nothing but truth. . . . that is imperative. Only then can it grant my heart the distance it needs to heal; and hold it, no longer to heart, but at arm's length and see her. Remember her. Forever my sister. And hold her soul, kindly. Karen. The love I carry; her life I carry. The unspeakable heartache abides elsewhere; it may never go . . . but it does not kill her anymore.

Moments ago, I was contacted by the people in Colorado. Freddie

Glenn is seeking placement in Community Corrections again. A half-way house . . . halfway to where?—I always wonder. Out, I guess. Just out. The hearing is four days from now. I will participate.

Karen's story.

It continues to the past and the days we spent there; continues in the past as it unfolds here. Remember. We live again. When we remember, when we are remembered. We are eternal.

Karen's death is not her story. Nor is it mine. Hand in hand. As it was, so it is.

"Hold your sister's hand," my mother said. We were on the subway platform outside Penn Station. We had just been to the circus. She directed us to the wall away from the tracks . . . I think I had been looking down at the third rail, the infamous third rail, where the electrical current runs that powers the trains.

"Step back, please!"

"Okay, Mom."—slightly whiny, but obedient.

Karen and I stepped back beside my mother. The train was not coming so I protested a bit and started spinning my little Charlie Chaplin cane around like the Little Tramp used to do. I dropped it several times and my mother finally lost her patience. "Drop that thing one more time and I am taking it away from you!"

Okay, I can't actually get Freddie Glenn out of my mind. So, I guess I'll run through what I'm feeling. Placement in the community translates to a step closer to freedom, to release. I do not know all the particulars, but I know the goal. I become tempted to say things that are quite flippant. Such as, "If he gets out, I get my sister back?" I know that doesn't help and I want to maintain a calm demeanor, one that is more concerned for others than solely for my own feeling. Does he have some plan to make amends? Surely, if he had one, he would have taken steps to execute it by now. I believe he could very possibly do the world some good. I don't see how his freedom makes that more likely. I believe he could resolve to do the community some good, start making his contribution from prison rather than waiting until released. His feeble justification is that he has been in jail long enough. For helping to run Kathy's husband through with a bayonet, for shooting that poor cook and stealing his fifty cents, for raping Karen again and again and finally punching forty-two holes in her body without any regard for her whatsoever—the remainder of his life in jail is a light sentence. Lighter than the one he served his victims and their families who carry his deeds to this day. When do I get out? Haven't I served long enough? Yes, flippant, perhaps, but isn't his request even more so? I think it very flippant of him to ask for Freedom, let alone believe he deserves it because he thinks the time has been long enough. Long enough for what? Your sense of right and wrong? Clearly, that's a great barometer! In your mind, everything you did was right. Until you got caught. And now, it's right for you to go? Well, I disagree. Because she is my sister, I will serve Karen and her memory—forever! Got it, Freddie? I invite you to join me.

Naturally, there is part of me that wishes to be lenient to all people who do wrong or make bad choices. My heart goes out to them. Especially when they put in the time to make amends and repent. I am neither a heartless Christian nor am I a zealot, but I believe in God, and I believe in forgiveness. But!—I also believe the State of Colorado owes my sister and the six others who died, directly or indirectly, at the hands of this man—owes them and their families, whose suffering continues to this day, to keep him away from people, keep him away from any harm he might do them and keep him away from the ability to do harm to anyone ever again. Stay in prison, Freddie, deluded that you should go free. It just isn't true. And another thing, maybe once you were, but by the time you raped my innocent sister, punched her body full of holes and slaughtered her—you were *not* a "good kid!"

I want to go back now to those good kids on the subway platform with their mom. I know it seems like one of those weird segues on the nightly news where a tragic story is followed by a bright cheerful one about a puppy or some such. But to go any further with my anger here, I could drown in it. Yes, it is all well and good to think I have tamed this part, purged it, but there it is again; at the very moment I release

112

it, Freddie Glenn rears his ugly soul. I have had enough but it asks for more. I want to retract something. I do not know if his soul is ugly. I think of him and make my own soul ugly.

Radical forgiveness. A concept.

I will speak more of it later, this concept. I believe my wife comprehends it. I am not sure I do. Later. To be sure.

Karen and I had spent the day at the circus: Ringling Brothers, Barnum & Bailey Circus. It was a bit strange, honestly. Spectacle, yes. I loved the elephants and the lion tamer. Never quite got the girl standing on a horse's back. Cute outfits, though. I always knew I liked girls. Oh, dear, a dangerous statement to make these days, I know. I am not going political here. I liked girls, okay? That's all I'm saying. Never quite understood the whole ringmaster thing, either, which is ironic as I played a retired ringmaster on a friend's show, *Modern Family*, just a few years ago. And I believe the point was made that it would be hard to follow without him. The circus, I mean. "May I direct your attention to," . . . this and that . . . Okay, I suppose a ringmaster may be indispensable. Point made and taken. I remember standing in front of the elephant cage and tossing a pathetic peanut to one of them. I felt pretty bad. I loved elephants. Not sure if I understood empathy at the time but I felt hollow and empty in some way and looked at my offering with sadness. Is that it? This is what I thought. I was standing before one of God's great creatures and threw a peanut at him. I think he may have even snaked his trunk through the bars, sniffed and picked it up. I was grateful for that, at least. But I felt bad. Not much more to say.

And this comes out of left field but born of this memory, I think. When my daughter Faith was a baby, someone gave her an elephant. A little gray, soft, stuffed, toy elephant. We named him "Peanut." The boys have elephants too. All named Peanut. All named in honor of a moment when a boy no older than my youngest, James, stood before a proud pachyderm who had the grace to honor that boy's offering by accepting—a peanut. And we return the favor to this very day. Honor him. Remember him. In our home . . . every day. Peanut. He escorts us all to Dreamland still. Almost every night.

The circus doesn't exist anymore. Not with elephants, at least. I suppose enough of us felt bad about it to put the circus out of business, except for Vegas, which is a very different animal indeed. People on display bending their bodies in the most extraordinary ways! And, yeah, I still like the girls and their pretzeled poses; the guys on the motorcycles, you can keep. To each their own.

So, Karen and I waited for the subway that day with our mom. Mom always took us into New York City. She was devoted to the idea we see things. Cultural stuff. The 21 Club, where Gordon had had a table when he worked at the Empire State Building. My grandmother used to love telling the story when Karen and I had to go into "The Twenty-One Club" to use the restroom. That is how she would say it. As if it was a truly important place. And I guess it was. Sad to think it shuttered for good just recently. Broadway! Mom took us there, too. The New York Philharmonic! Yup, we went there. Leonard Bernstein's Young People's Concerts. Fantastic stuff. We were very fortunate. Karen had a muff to keep her hands warm. Cute as the dickens in her little red overcoat and a fur muff with her hands in either side. She wore a pixie haircut at the time. Light brown hair and hazel eyes and a dear sweet person who brought me great joy.

In the session with Esther, she said Karen was meant to bring me Joy. She did. No, that she "came to bring me Joy." That was it: "I came to bring you Joy." And I wondered at the time what that meant. Was I miserable?—no, but I was sad. The whole dad thing. I didn't even know it, but I sense now that I knew it—Dad did not want me. Karen did. Mom did. Gordon and Gam . . .

Excuse me, I have to go reread a bit now to make sure I do not repeat some stuff here that needn't be. I clearly do not mind repeating important stuff. But once is enough for some of it.

I'll be right back. Just give me sixty-three pages or so to check things out.

Okay, I found it. Some pages back I spoke of the night when Kayte received a message from Karen, this was not Esther—it was Kayte, speaking for Karen, "I came to bring you Joy." I thought so. Confirmed through Esther. I will expound a bit.

114

Certainly not the only reason she came but on a soul level, Karen brought joy to a boy who was soul sick. A little boy who felt unwanted. I think that is so. And it healed him. She healed him. And she continues to do so. Remarkable. I am some tough case. I do hang on to things when maybe I should let them go. Some things that are truly important, I let go of immediately, without complaint. Maybe I needed a lesson in priorities and what is really important. There were women in my life who broke my heart . . . sitting on the dock being told there was no future. That one hurt. Probably just the traffic of a young man's life . . . the way Liz had been hurt or hurt me, the way Jill did. There were a few others. There is no place more than a mention for them here. Then, there were some good girls I left because . . . maybe they were too good. At the time. There are some things, some relationships I could have handled better, I suppose, but they do not bear mention either. This is Karen's tale. And mine as it relates to her.

Perhaps, losing Karen made me think losing was all we could count on in life. That lesson does correspond to much of what I felt when younger. And it corresponds to the night in Pompano Beach when I finally broke down about Gordon. Gordon's death came first, of course, and for a young boy, it was devastating and impossible to comprehend. It had taken me almost six weeks. Gam and I would sit out on the porch for hours at a time. Evening hours. She would nurse a cocktail and tell me stories about her and Gordon, their marriage. That sort of thing. And I would listen—just listen. It was usually after dinner and Mom would be loading the dishwasher as Karen helped her. There was a routine that fueled our days and nights and kept our heads above water. Gordon was probably there. Certainly, his energy was there— our memory of him, our different and several memories of him carried us through the nights. I do not remember how we got to bed. We just ended up there. We were numb and empty, those weeks after he died.

Karen and I did swing in the hammock together. I hung it between the mango tree and the rubber tree out back. Oh, how we loved to swing in a hammock with Gordon! I think it was my first act of trying to recreate the world he had given us when we were kids. He would flip us over sometimes and we would squeal with delight as we hung on and finally dropped to the ground. Gordon would laugh and sing us one of his silly songs. "Slue-Foot Sue" or "Big Fat Smella," "Passengers Will Please Refrain," . . . or "Pull Your Shades down, Marianne." He was so much fun. And now the fun was gone.

I tried to barbecue for the family the way he had. Cook a steak the way he did. We lived in the house he had hoped would be his final home, his retirement home where he could live out his days with his family, happily. I still don't know how Gordon couldn't have known how sick he was. Maybe he did and the last two years of his life were spent building us a future in a safer land, aware that he would no longer be able to provide for us and protect us. He was an amazing guy. And that night, on the porch with Gam, I suddenly realized that all the plans we had made together would never happen. I spoke quietly, "We were going to have so much fun together." And I wept. He did take me to see that fishing boat in Jersey. Would a man who knew he was dying go shopping for a yacht with his grandson? Maybe. Maybe not. It seemed like a cruel joke at the time. Gordon would not have done that. He wasn't cruel. So, maybe he didn't know he was leaving us so soon. Anyway, six weeks later, I remembered all we had planned together. Fishing and baseball games and boating and just enjoying my connection to an heroic and noble man. And six weeks later, I finally dissolved in tears and ran down to that dock unable to speak. I was convulsed with grief and lost in it. Sob after sob shook my body until finally it stopped. I sat with my head in my hands. Silent. After a time, a voice came—my voice. It said, "You will always be alone." And the oddest thing happened. It gave me comfort.

I just got off the phone with my son James. I am working on a film away from my family and though it probably helps me to focus on the writing, it makes me feel lonely. Jude is here with me, but the writing is taxing emotionally. And as I write the words about being comforted, I realize how much I have changed. Jude's company and James's voice both give me great comfort. Gabriel never leaves my mind or my heart for a moment. My boys! And my girls! What a miracle that life has given me so many loves.

Jude is a teenager now. There is a great deal of sleeping that goes

116

on; he has his first formal job starting in just a few days. We'll see how that works out. He keeps to himself more than I would like but I don't want to push him; a gentle hand seems best right now.

James is the baby and enjoys being the baby. The best illustration of his character came one day when his mom was on a tear about something. He sat on the couch as Mom ran off a compendium of gripes. In the middle of a convenient pause, he just looked at her and said, "Be happy!" We had no choice but to start laughing.

Gabe is a creative kid, a genius I suspect, and very athletic at the same time. A wonderful boy who admittedly changed a bit when his younger brother came along. When asked about it, "Gabe. You were so excited to have a brother, don't you remember?" His answer, "Yes, but I didn't think he would annoy me so much!" My boys! They flood my mind with images of myself at different stages of my youth. Images I know Gordon saw in me.

Mason, the college kid and Jude's sister, survived and even thrived in spite of divorce. They both did but not without some nuance of damage. We connect but not as much or as often as I'd like. Patience is a virtue. I'm around. Mason was my constant companion during her early years. I miss that.

Faith is a similar story. Her mom used to call us "Twin Flames." It felt like that and it still does, thankfully. She is the greatest light and the most beautiful child. I cannot imagine loving anyone more than I love her; except, of course, my other daughters, Spencer, Greer, and Mason. And the boys. And there is Kayte. Had I not known what I have known, perhaps, the courage to love them with all my heart would have been easy . . . but my heart, once frozen with grief, had to be thawed. They helped. There are repeatedly challenges with them, but each has my unending love, given without quarter. Of the issues that arise, some are mine, some are not. I have learned everyone has issues solely their own and then some that can only be resolved with a little help from Dad; but they are mostly theirs—the key is knowing the difference. I am a father ready to stand in the midst or on the sidelines as required. I am steady. Dad. Greer has the right to question that because we were estranged during her youth. She will learn in time that I am here for her now. She can trust that. I know one day she will. Spencer and I drift in and out. She has her life. I have mine. We intersect as often as we can, which means I miss her more than I'd like. But the love is strong and delightfully in evidence when we have time together to make up for days we've missed. We laugh a lot and sometimes cry a bit. But my love for her is a constant. Unflinching. Steadfast. Faith is still very young and when I am away from home, it can make her feel insecure and unsafe, alone. Fortunately, I can heal that with her. For them all, there is love greater than I could ever dream.

An aside.

People reading here may have a sensational interest in the challenges I mentioned. This is not a place for tabloid foolishness or airing of issues that arise for all families. Most of us are acquainted with the "challenges" of raising a child from infancy through young adulthood and beyond. With adults or parents acting badly or confrontationally. There is nothing here out of the ordinary or beyond the normal traffic of parenting with a guiding, loving hand. Also, this book is devoted to Karen. Dedicated to Karen. Not that stuff.

And an interjection.

I have never told them this, but of my older kids, all four are drawn to the same profession as their dad. If not exactly the same, then to a career adjacent to my own. I am deeply flattered by that. This is what I have not told them. To follow in a father's footsteps, as the saying goes, is deeply satisfying, and I am honored they have chosen to do so. I do not claim any responsibility for it. I have never encouraged or discouraged them. Spencer and Greer have had great success in spite of their last name. Yes, I say "in spite of" because a name that is known is often known for things good and bad. They have been visited with both as a result. I will not apologize for it, but I understand being my kid is a mixed bag. What they have accomplished they have done off their own back. I admire them for that. I applaud them for that. Mason and Jude are crafting their individual courses. Both enjoy performance and study film production in college. We shall see how it goes but I am deeply moved and pleased that they are sharing a world I love and a passion that has been my life's work. It is one of my greatest sources of pride. If they don't know any of this, which is quite possible; at least, now, they can read it here! This is praise long overdue. I am proud of them.

Tomorrow, I will return to Karen's story. My kids are a part of it. I project Karen onto them at times. With fears for their well-being. I can't help it, honestly. I try not to hinder them or color their choices with my own misgivings. Misgivings they needn't carry, but I still do. A few things yet to let go. Not sure I can or will . . . but I'll keep trying. More tomorrow. For now, I am going to watch a movie with Jude. I'm beat.

Karen and I started the next fall at Pine Crest Preparatory School. It was a good one. I entered seventh grade, she sixth. As I said before, Mario was her homeroom teacher. She pulled a great one there! I don't know if the school was aware we had lost Gordon that summer. It just occurred to me . . . maybe they did. I remember seventh grade for me was pretty much a retread of sixth grade in Rumson. It was easy for me to get good grades. Maybe too easy as I began to coast in school. It wasn't very challenging. Things at home were, so perhaps they went easy on us that first year, circumstances and all. Maybe Gam had told the school, maybe Mom did, what had happened. I wasn't aware of any special treatment but the educators at that school were the very best. Wonderful people. We got lucky. Or Gordon and Gam did, looking for the best school in town—they found it.

After Gordon died, Gam continued to do some extraordinary things on our behalf—and in one instance, something quite thoughtful on my behalf.

Ted Thurston was our gardener. One afternoon, he stayed behind after his crew left and asked if we could talk for a while. I remember sitting with him in the garage by the work bench where I had assembled a modest collection of tools and hung them on the peg board. I was kind of proud of it. I always thought it was what Gordon would have done . . . always pictured him when I would take a hammer down and make a repair in the house somewhere, install a shelf or do an odd job at Gam's request. I was pretty handy. We had Shop in sixth grade at Rumson and I'd made a set of shelves that were pretty nice and a box for keepsakes. They settled into appropriate places in our new home in Florida. I wonder what happened to them. They might still be around somewhere, maybe in my mom's stuff. I'll take a look. Might unlock some more things. Doing jobs around the house made me feel close to Gordon, like I was filling his shoes.

Ted asked me how I was doing. Okay. Like any girls in your class? The girls don't like me . . . they just call me "queer." That's because they do like you.

"It doesn't feel like that," I told him.

Ted talked me through the dynamics of girls and boys and football and keeping smart . . . said it was important to study hard and do good in school. Time would tell, he told me—there were a lot of good things ahead in life and I would find my place. He was a terrific guy. Strong guy! He had served in the army as a sergeant. Not sure which branch of the Army—like I said, Gordon had been in the Army Corps of Engineers in the Army Air Corps, which later became the Air Force. I don't know much more about it. Ted had been in the Army.

One day, he took a piece of wood in his hands. He looked at me. His arms were huge and he told me that back in the day he could tear a board like that in half with his bare hands. Wow! He gave it a try and it looked to me like it was about to rip apart but he stopped, looked up, and said, "Not wide enough." I still believed he could have done it. I loved how he shaped the idea in my head. Maybe someday I'll rip a board in half . . . why not? I think about it every time I hold piece of wood. Ted was probably the same age as Gordon would have been. I never doubted he could do it.

One day, Gam suggested I thank Ted for his time. "You enjoy your chats with him?" she asked. I did. She told me she had asked him to sit with me if he could spare the time; so many women around, maybe he could give a lost boy a taste of conversation with a grown man . . . someone he could look up to. Ted said he'd be glad to.

This amazing life. There can be such kindness in it. I want to thank Ted now. With all my heart. It made a difference. What a man!

The following year, Ted retired and told me we wouldn't be seeing each other much anymore. But I was ready. Ted helped a young boy get through the loss of his everything. He guided me back to life, pointed the way. It would be a way without Gordon, but the kindness Gordon said was in all men, Ted taught me was there. Gordon said it; Ted was the proof. Thanks again, Ted. It was an honor to know you.

My mother had an expression; Gam used it too. A little phrase to "button it up," so to speak. It goes like this: "And . . . drop your voice." Words that describe what a person actually does when they've run out of nice things to say. It comes at the end of a list when the list has been exhausted . . . when you run out of things to say, you end by saying: and "drop your voice." You get the gist.

The reason I am explaining this has to do with Ted Thurston. Ted was Black. Maybe I should have mentioned it, but it's not important. What he did was important. In fact, there could be any number of reasons he chose to help a lonely boy, but none of them was that he was Black or I was White. A person is not a color. Yes, people tend to huddle in groups. Like gravitates toward like and cultures seek a common heritage. Common experience binds them.

The world we live in today is wrestling with that and with race. Our commonality. I acknowledge that, and I also believe all people are meant to evolve toward their highest good. Based on my personal experience, my afternoons with Ted Thurston had to do with kindness. With goodness. It's what people do. Most people. And I believe most people are good. Character. Behavior. These are the things that define a person. Circumstances can and should figure, but color?— I'm just not sure it has much to do with a person's value. Their stories have value. Stories evolve by living them and situations influence stories. Situations may correspond with certain "colors" or creeds, yes, but those situations can be dealt with uncluttered by racial stereotypes and petrified presumptions. "Privilege" has entered the conversation. A breakthrough? Or just another presumption? Possibly. Not sure it helps. It is argued that those who possess it can never understand it. That's a neat trick . . .you can have it, but there's nothing you can do about it! Okay. I don't know. And I don't understand it. Maybe that's the point. I will certainly never understand how it figures as a defining qualifier in my sister's life. Or her death. Look, things were okay for us when we were kids. Life took some tough turns as it does for everyone, regardless of privilege. I have done okay since. I worked hard and had some success. And that good fortune teaches me to give back. I will say this—it was a privilege to know Ted Thurston. I think it would be a big step forward for us all to stop making presumptions about each other and get going based upon what we can fix. Do better by one another...and drop your voice. You get it.

Bound to get in trouble for this. That's okay. The price for honesty. Probably worth it. Lot of people out there making a lot of money being dishonest; taking advantage of those presumptions. Just "speaking my mind." Some are determined to get rid of that, too, these days. No thanks!

Later that year, I bought a boat. It was a little wooden boat with a small outboard engine on it. It sank the first rain we had; so, a couple days after I bought it. Karen took a ride in it. Well, the two of us took one ride in it. Hard luck for a "water angel"! But into each life a little rain must fall. And each boat, too, I suppose.

Now, I had bought that boat with money I'd saved up through the years doing odd jobs. I used to cook popcorn for parties. I saved my allowance. I cut lawns and washed cars, delivered *TV Guide* in New Jersey. In the end, I think I had a couple hundred dollars. The boat cost a couple hundred dollars, so that was it. Perfect. The engine was crap, though, so before we put her in the water, my grandmother volunteered a new Johnson, thirty-three-horsepower outboard engine. It probably cost a few dollars more than the boat, and of course, it went down with the ship on its titanic debut. The guys who sold my grandmother that engine had warned her the boat was not likely to survive very long, but we went ahead, as it was all I could buy at the time. Gam and I had made a bargain that I would buy the boat, she the engine, and that was that. After the "sinking of the *Bismarck*," not the boat's name but it felt

◀ Spencer and me at the
Empire State Building.

▼ St. John, USVI

San Diego. ▲

Disneyland. ▶

NYC before our trip to Africa. This was ▼
one of the nicest things I've ever known.

We got around a bit!

▲ Spence on the set of *Frasier*.

▲ Then came Greer. Here with
my mom and me.

With Spencer and Kayte. ▶
Again, I could not be prouder of my girls.

Not sure how I got so lucky.

Destined for dress-up. ▼

This kid loved a good pose.

With Greer. Dressed up indeed
for a night out with Dad at the
Last Tycoon premier. I couldn't
be prouder of my girls. ▶

▼ Gabe! Wonderful boy. Upstate.

▲ Alan, Kayte, Suze in the back. Gabe, Faith, and James. The tavern upstate. Home of Faith American Brewing Company.

James and Dad. Breakfast. ▶
Kitchen upstate.

Our land. Cutting hay. ▶

◀ Kayte and Gabe upstate.

▼ The last rays of the setting sun...ablaze on a thundercloud. This is a common sight up there. I loved it there as a boy. I love it still.

Upstate. View from the main house.

◀ Gabe in the snow. I love this of him. Such a smile.

▼ James! Possibly the happiest kid I have ever known.

▲ Jude joined into this shot taken in the Caribbean when we were shooting on the island of Nevis. Nice bunch.

▲ Faith, James, and Gabriel. Mom and Dad. And the two most expensive animals in history. Not what they cost; what it cost to replace all the damage they've done. White balls of love and destruction.

Jude and Mason working with Dad on ▼ the set of *Frasier* this last season. That is Jordan McMahon with us. Without him this book would not have been finished.

▲ James and a Florida sunrise. Magic. Such beauty in our lives. And to see it through the eyes of children—a gift.

▼ Kelsey is happy when his family is happy. All together. This does make me smile.

equally epic, Gam took pity on me and bought the McKee Craft from the guys at Las Olas Marine. They overhauled the engine and delivered the new, unsinkable boat to us.

My grandmother explained to Karen and me that "our" new boat was a very big responsibility, and we would have to take a Coast Guard Power Squadron Boating and Water Safety class. We were thrilled. This was the summer after Gordon died. We were both a year older. I had weathered the taunts and derision of the females in my class and Karen would be joining me at the upper school campus. Pine Crest was a kindergarten through twelfth-grade school and had separate campuses, one through sixth grade and the other starting in seventh, finishing up the senior year. They were basically two wings separated by a central Administration building. The new school year awaited us, but the Power Squadron was first!

Karen was a fresh twelve and I a mid-thirteen-year-old. We were the youngest people ever to take a Power Squadron class, and we enjoyed it. We were both sailors from our days at the Atlantic Highlands Yacht Club. We were good with boats. I remember my grandfather saying that if I wanted a boat, I could have one. "Just save your pennies!" he bellowed and laughed just loud enough to really annoy me.

Yes, Gordon did annoy me once in a while. No one could be that perfect! I think he thought it was funny how he timed the bait, got my hopes up and then slammed the door. Yes, he took great delight in lowering the boom at just the last moment. I admit it was kind of funny… just not to me at the time. But Gam helped us get a boat and that was really something. Had Gordon lived, I suspect Gam would have been the one to push him over the finish line and get us a boat anyway. Alas, we would never know. But here we were in a boating safety class with retired admirals and such, really impressive guys; and Karen and I aced the class! I was so proud!

Karen and I spent that summer together. On the boat. We saw a few of her friends. There was a girl named Jennifer who reduced me to a mumbling fool whenever we visited her. I can't imagine she was unaware of my disastrous timidity, but she rode in the boat with us and I mumbled along, she seemingly oblivious to it, as I tried to point out that flying fish were startled by our movement and flying alongside us, flying as my heart flew out of my chest and dropped to the bottom of the sea. I wonder if she ever knew. I never told her. I think I told Karen, but I swore her to secrecy. Ah, young love and how stupid it can be!

Flying fish! I just realized how cool it was that we got to see them. As I'm writing these words, I turn to Jude and ask if he has ever seen them—and suddenly dissolve again into tears of laughter at how I was quite in awe of said Jennifer. I would love to tell her now. Just to finally let it go. The laughter is almost uncontrollable. I was such a shy fool. I like him, though—my young self without the courage to tell a girl his very being hung on every breath she took. I struggled to write a single line of poetry in praise of her. Jennifer. How funny. And silly. And sweet. My goodness, it is a wonder any of us survive puberty at all!

I couldn't even look at her. "Jennifer Juniper" was a song by Donovan, very popular that summer, and I apologize for going on about it, but I am delighted to rediscover this about myself, and that precious month we all spent together on the boat. I had completely forgotten it. Bless the memory of that summer! It lifts me. A fond remembrance of a time when I was irredeemably inept and in awe of a young girl and the magic of simply being near her. I am ecstatic with the memory of being so innocent and so fond and so lost, all at the same time. Who'd have thought this journey would be so delightful, so full of joy?

Of course!

Karen did.

It's also fun to know that boy is still in there. I extend this memory and this joy and this hand to a different girl today. But it is the same hand and the same boy. Just a little altered, perhaps. Not older, no. Looks can be deceiving. But look close enough, and behind the eyes, the same unbearably shy boy extends his hand to her, the girl of his dreams. She knows who she is.

I am having fun with all this right now and I am delighted to share it with you. What does this have to do with Karen? It was her idea. It is not for me to deny her this indulgence.

I remain a grateful spectator to the days of Karen. And a grateful witness to my days with her. I watch her now as I have never watched her. I am able to see her impact on those I never knew; and as witness to the days we spent together, I embrace new knowledge of myself. I was a good kid . . . I was. I didn't know it at the time, and she has made me realize it from so far away, so long ago. But she is right here . . . time is an illusion. I am here with her. I am witness and spectator in this magic. This magic I knew. But I'd forgotten.

Not synonymous, there is a distinction between the words "witness" and "spectator." At least for me. For me, a witness is involved in the events unfolding around him; a spectator is involved but only as a distanced observer, not enfolded in the events themselves. So, whether that makes sense or not, I am both and speak as both as these pages unfold. I am a character alive in the story, as Karen is. I am an observer from some distance, a part of the story but removed. I live and speak and witness within it and, at the same time, observe from a distance, as I have for a lifetime and always will. A spectator.

That summer. 1968. It was a parade of days. Good days. A celebration of our innocence and a farewell to it—after a grieving year. A glimmer of kinder days ahead. That summer. School began in September.

But before we go back to school, we need to go back one summer.

Dad.

Time to meet him as we did then. Mom told us Dad invited us to visit him in the Virgin Islands for a few weeks. Seeing as how Gordon was dead, he thought it might be nice to see us, give us a little time away from all the sadness and all that had happened. We could meet him and his family. We could leave the grim rhythm of mourning Gordon. We could finally meet our dad and spend a little time in the imagined paradise that was his home.

"He looks like Blackbeard the Pirate," our mother told us. Oh, yeah, that'll help, Mom.

Karen and I were loaded onto the plane. I think it was a Boeing 707 . . . it was the first plane we were ever in . . . the first I remember, at least. Mom had told me that when I was two years old, we flew to New York. There was a blizzard and we would not be able to get out to New Jersey that night. Gordon called in a favor to his friend who ran the Plaza Hotel for Conrad Hilton. He was the husband of Conrad's sister, Helen, and because Gordon and "Connie," as they called him, had been friends in San Antonio, calling in this favor was not a big deal. Helen and Ed Buckley!—I remember the name now. Nice people. I remember them too. Helen came to visit us years later, just after Gordon's death. They were all friends back in Texas.

Anyway, that night in Manhattan, it was before Karen was born, just a few months before, obviously; Mom told me I pulled every plug out of the socket and she was terrified I would electrocute myself. She said it was my habit to tear everything within reach to pieces. Why should a room in The Plaza be any different? So, Mom was pregnant with Karen and I'm pretty sure we never went back to St. Thomas; not until the day when we boarded a 707 to Puerto Rico to meet our Pirate Father.

I can only surmise it from the dates I know, but at the time, the night we flew home and stayed in The Plaza, Mom and Dad were through. I feel it in my bones. Not necessarily a sad thing as I realize what a good life awaited us and how much Gordon would mean to Karen and me in those early years. I am not sure my dad could ever have matched Gordon's care and affection for us. He was a young man and wrapped up in a young man's problems. It seemed to me that he was clearly having an affair with another woman when my mom was pregnant, maybe even when she was pregnant with me. I do not mean to tar him or another, so I will check my facts and speak of it no more.

I do not wish to shame anyone in this. I have no judgment here, nor do I offer one. He was a man. They were not a match, my mom and dad, whatever the reason. I believe he married the woman he loved afterward and remained with her till his death. That is okay. It is not something I take personally. My heart goes out to him and though I did not, and do not really know him, I suspect I am his son in many ways . . . mostly the good ones, I hope. But then, I did not really know him.

Karen and I were petrified during the flight. There had been considerable turbulence. We held hands. Hand in hand. Past is prologue. We landed in Puerto Rico a few hours after we had left Ft. Lauderdale and the flight crew unloaded us and escorted us to the baggage office, much as they would handle a couple of unidentified suitcases. A lovely young woman, Spanish speaking, managed a broken English to ask us where our escort was and who it would be. I spoke not a word of Spanish but a little French. Sixth grade with Madam Chernow. No help whatsoever. I began to explain to the young woman that my dad looked just like "Blackbeard the Pirate." This sent the entire room into gales of laughter. There were several men in white shirts with wing pins in their lapels and I suppose they were managers of some sort, flight logistics, but none of them, including the young woman, were any help at all. I think they were asking us who we were and I told them our names but they had that information already. Nothing more.

I told them again that our father would be there to get us and that he looked just like Blackbeard the Pirate. More laughter. Our last name is Grammer, I continued a little louder, hoping it would make a difference. Finally, as the young woman reached for my hand and said she would take us for something to eat, the door swung open and at the end of the terminal I saw an enormous man whose black beard and waistline surely belonged to none other than Blackbeard the Pirate—or—my dad. Our dad.

Dad. We were seeing him for the very first time. He sauntered toward us and as he did, I knew he was Dad. I knew. And there was something extraordinary about that. Something magical.

Magical. Okay, I realize I use that word quite a bit. So, I want to discuss it for a second. When I use it about Karen, I am referring to the surprise of her, the loveliness of her. When I am in awe of her. Her undeniable presence and warmth, alive at the mere mention of her name. The love that exists to this day. Eternity. Magical. There is no other word. And there is God's magic... the ineffable steady pulse that is in all things... a pulse I did not feel at times, but it was always there. A magic I had lost. Lost until I opened my eyes once more; or rather, my heart. Where God's pulse echoes. The Heart. Our first organ to grow. That Magic.

But as I said, I saw my dad and knew him. I knew I was his son. I knew we were connected. I felt it though no moment together existed in memory. Until then. Yet, there it was. An inexplicable truth that had no history but was undeniable. Magical. When the truth doesn't make sense. Perhaps. Something that cannot be explained but is nonetheless. Yes.

I could not explain it. I loved him. In an instant. I loved him. That's all I'm trying to say. The minute I saw him. I do not know what Karen felt but I looked her in the eye as I held her hand and said, "That's him. That's our dad."

When he finally stood just a few feet from us, he asked if we were Kelsey and Karen. I said we were and then asked him how he knew it was us. He said, "What else would two kids twelve and eleven look like? You two are pretty much it." I wondered if he felt what I had felt. I'll never know.

We were released into his enormous hands and off we went for our short hop to St. Thomas. "Fly More with Four" was the airline's slogan. They had four engines on their prop planes; their competition had only two. Catchy. The inference being that the odds of getting to St. Thomas from Puerto Rico were twice as good if you flew with these guys. Twenty minutes later, a sunbaked runway rose from a blue, blue sea to receive us. We made it.

Karen and I rode in the jeep with our father. A complete stranger but neither of us were in any distress, honestly. It was just an adventure. And he was an adventure. We had no preconceptions about it. We had no idea where we were staying, where this man was taking us. We trusted he was our father and that he would be hosting us on his island home for a few weeks. To discover him, I guess. And that was that. "It will give you a chance to know your father." That is what our mom had said, and there was no fear. I don't remember any.

He drove along until we stopped at a jewelry store and were introduced to a woman who said she remembered when I was born. Nice to see you. We drove on to the next stop, which was where my dad and his family lived. There we met Elizabeth ("Betty"), John, Billy and Stevie. Skeets was their mom, our stepmom, I guess. We really had no idea they even existed. Betty, their eldest, was just a year younger than Karen, probably why I think they must have been together before Karen was born but I could be wrong. As I said, it isn't important now.

We settled into the routine of Dad's life. I am still sketchy on many of the details here. There was a large common room with a kitchen and a big bed, I think Skeets and Dad slept in there and the kids slept in the other room, basically, a long, large dorm with several beds and a couple of extra for me and Karen. So, six beds and a big one in the kitchen/bedroom/lounge. I believe there was a TV that faced a dining table. And a bathroom. One bathroom? I do not remember and have not tried to remember until this very moment.

Our first morning there, Betty woke Karen by banging on her head with a hairbrush; John woke me by saying Billy had peed on Pee. Pee was the cat, and Billy was just showing off, I guess. Maybe he just had a loose sense of where to relieve himself. I remember asking John what he meant . . . that's when I learned they had a cat, and that the cat's name was Pee. A few days later, I heard Stevie screaming from the bathroom. I was the eldest of the children and had been left in charge for some reason or another, and when I opened the door, I saw Stevie standing on the tank behind the toilet bowl, perched on it like some sort of hysterical bird, terrified; with his body facing the wall and his head turned face-forward, eyes locked on a giant poop in the middle of the floor, a massive dump that was clearly his, steaming, almost hissing at him, as he regarded it with horror just three inches from the toilet he had obviously missed moments before. It was a comical picture, but he was very upset. So, I stepped around the poop, cleaned him up, and took him in my arms. Once out of the room, I consoled him on the bed for a second and then cleaned up the mess in the bathroom. I remember telling John about it, and he had no particular opinion on the matter. A shrug, perhaps, as if to say it was all part of a normal day here on St. Thomas, tropical paradise, United States Virgin Islands! I never spoke of it again. Until now, of course. He was a cute kid. They were all cute kids. Skeets was a beautiful woman.

Dad had grown such a gruesome beard and expanded so dramatically from the young man whose picture is still in my home, it was hard to say he was handsome. He had been a really cute kid, too; looked a lot like his younger boys, just like them, in fact. There is a picture of him standing on a dock by a lake as a youngster. The resemblance is startling and undeniable.

Our visit there was important and eye-opening. The first time we went to his music store, Dad walked us down a series of open stairs where there were a variety of musical instruments. He stopped along the way, playing each and every one of them. He was amazing! Here was a true musician. There was nothing to say. He was good on every one of them.

He walked us along the airport terminal where the newsstand was. With a gleam in his eye, he reached in behind a display of magazines and moved his, *Virgin Island View*, to the front. He was a publisher too. Something else we didn't know about him. One night, Dad was rehearsing with his band. Karen and I looked on. It was a little later, so I guess we stayed up when the other kids had gone to bed. The drummer was missing that night. Cedrick was there, the saxophone player, I remember him best. I liked him. I would see him years later at a dinner thrown by Skeets to honor me and my dad. Honor that I had amounted to something. His firstborn. It was a lovely night. She told me I reminded her of him. "Dad." I never felt closer to him. Cedrick was there that night too. He raised orchids. Skeets, of course. Her two youngest dead by then. And I think Gus was there. Dad's best friend.

Anyway, Karen and I sat listening to the band when my dad asked if I could play the drums. Sure. "Twelve Bells at Midnight." On the downbeat of the first twelve measures, the large cymbal was to be struck signifying the musical equivalent of a clock chiming the "witching hour." I completed the twelfth measure and began just keeping time on the snare drum when my dad stopped and said I was the first guy who ever did it right. I took it with great pride. Obviously. As I still carry it with some pride. They were the first and only words of praise I ever heard from my father.

There was another of his friends who worked at a radio station. I do not remember his name but I liked him too. He had a great smile, and Dad and he laughed a good deal together. That made us feel nice. Karen and I were visiting him one morning as Dad was doing his rounds. Music shop, news stand, a little shopping at the local grocery and a stop to visit his disc jockey friend and flying pal, as it turned out.

They both had their pilot's license, and they were discussing a giant shark that had been visible from the air a few weeks before. An enormous hammerhead and the joke was it would have been a bad day to "ditch." St. Thomas had a notoriously short runway with a mountain at the end of it, water on the other side; so, many a good pilot feared ending up in the water, apparently. The shark put a dent in the frequency of water landings . . . that was the gist. Or the joke. There was not a concurrent jump in crash landings into the mountain, to my knowledge, so the story was probably more for entertainment than anything else, but it did inspire a great deal of speculation on my part. Once again, obviously. This many years later, it is still on the tip of my tongue. That day was the same day we met the rest of the family at Magens Bay. We would snorkel and enjoy the beach that day.

I found a bottle of Heineken ten feet deep or so, some distance from the sandy shore. It was unopened so I retrieved it and brought it to the surface. I had never had a beer, I told my dad, and he said we could cool it off that evening and I could have a taste. It was okay. The lesson being, I think, that he would not deny me the spoils of a successful treasure hunt—buried treasure, of a sort, treasure lost in a shallow, sandy grave. Okay, it wasn't really buried, it was just sitting on the bottom. But this was as close as I would ever come to real seafaring, pirate-tale stuff.

Dad asked me to proofread one of his editions of *Virgin Island View*. I took it very seriously. Late one night, I couldn't sleep. Dad rummaged through the fridge to make a snack . . . he salvaged some steamed spinach and some peppers and made a bunch of makeshift tacos. They were delicious. We had a good visit with him and his family—Karen and me. We did get to know him. At the end of the trip we stood atop their property and took a picture with the entire family. I always thought I looked like an idiot in it. The family idiot. I was so happy and smiled such a silly smile. Looking at it now, I see how much taller Karen was than I was at the time but besides that, I no longer see an idiot. I see a boy who was happy beyond expression that he was finally beside his dad...I didn't even know him but I worshipped him. I loved him. Little Kelsey happy at last. Karen and I headed home. She was so much more mature than I. Girls just seem to get there quicker. We headed back to Florida and to a new life.

Jumping ahead in time again. Back to the final days of the following summer. Yes, the summer of '68. The summer of mumbling and flying fish. And much more. Karen and I are entering the next year of school—eighth grade for me, seventh for her. We are standing on a launching pad, poised for what comes next. And behind us is the last summer we spent every day together, every waking minute. We'd take the boat out, walk around the mall, Fashion Square, it was called; we spent a lot of time in my room and listened to music. We swam competitively at the Lighthouse Point Yacht Club . . . that took up most mornings. I swam the IM (a swimming event that uses all four competitive strokes: butterfly, backstroke, breaststroke, and freestyle) and I do not remember what Karen swam. There's that old "all about me" syndrome. It is not really selfish, it is just self-involved...I didn't have much else to do at the time, I didn't have the breadth of mind to pay attention to much more than just putting each of my feet, one in front of the other. We would "fill up" the boat (the gas tank) at the club's dock there and spend a great deal of time just riding in it. Nights would often see us go out on the water for a cruise up the Intracoastal. Just the two of us. Water like glass, running lights shimmering red and green on either side and the stillness of the air, the hum of the engine. It was healing. Karen and I were refuge to one another.

Refuge.

Another word I have used several times already. To me a refuge is a some*one*, not a some*place*. That someone was often Karen. She sat facing me, her back to the bow, her eyes on the wake behind us, up to the moon and to me. Glistening eyes. A smile. I steered the boat with her right in front of me. The wind blew through her hair and there was a

132

softness in her, a woman in her that was emerging and would become an extraordinary person. And as I am writing, I realize it was not all about me . . . it was all about us. Some things we couldn't share, of course; but my sister and I shared a childhood together and the first tragic days of our young adulthood. She was the other part of everything. Gam and Mom. And Karen. They were my life and life was good.

I feel the boat beneath me gliding through the black water. I feel it. Right now. We are gliding along the water of life, serene and silently pressing toward our future. Time did stop for us that summer. A breath before we jumped back into challenges and bad grades, classmates and making our way through our teenage years. They would be challenging but not so bad after all. It was perfect. How I loved the air and how I loved Karen. My sister. She felt as comfortable as breathing. We were close.

And I am thrown back in time again to when I first realized I loved her. It was the day after a snow that dumped several inches in the region. Winter Wonderland for real. I was sent out with Karen in tow to play and exhaust ourselves in the drifts. Snow days were good days for moms and grandmothers.

Around the middle of the day, Mom drove up and told us we would be going to a hill nearby where she'd been told the sledding was wonderful. She had our sled and snow disc in the back of the little Falcon station wagon she drove. This was a massive hill and one we did not know. There were dozens of kids zooming down the face of it. It was probably no more than a day or two before the snow would be gone or considerably diminished but this day was epic, and the several neighborhoods from far and wide had funneled to this spot. Cars at the base of the hill were double-parked, and parents stood watching their kids fly down the slope. It was a rare sight in Jersey to have such a great dump of snow.

So, Karen and I scaled the slope and started on our way down. The little disc she took was a bit challenging to get going and she was still pretty small, too little weight to really propel her down the hill. My sled had an eagle at the cradle where you could bend the rails and steer it a bit. It didn't really carve but you could move a little to the left, a little

133

to the right. Maybe it was called an American Eagle, but it was heavy with varnished wood and real steel rails, a sled that flew down the hill at a pretty good speed. I almost slammed into one of the cars at the base; flipped myself over and off the sled in the nick of time!

As I was heading back up the hill, Karen came hopping down, spinning round and round on the little silver disc. She drifted by me sideways and at that moment, I saw her with a joy and love I did not know could exist. Suddenly, my little sister was just the most marvelous kid and I adored her. She whisked by toward the end of her ride, her little smiling face and a knit wool hat tied at the chin, the whole ensemble just made the cutest girl in the world. I was smiling from ear to ear at a passing cherub. A little cherub. I will remember that forever.

I just got off the phone to a hearing for Freddie Glenn to be released into a Community Corrections Facility. I mentioned a parole hearing when I began writing; and subsequently was informed about this different hearing after he had waived his right to the parole hearing. It is pretty interesting and an outrage, honestly, that the system can be gamed so thoroughly by the offenders while the victims have so little say. I have made dozens of statements in similar hearings, and they are never submissible twice. I stumbled today over words and sentiments and fear I may not have been as clear as I'd hoped. I have written some very honest and naked impressions of the damage this man inflicted on my sister and our family. I am forced to do it again whenever this man, who utterly decimated my sister, has the whim or desire to ask to be freed. Again. And again. I hope this time it was enough. Is it really possible that the man who chose a life a little lower than vermin can be freed? I believe he is still in there—the young man who snuffed out the lives of innocent people for the entertainment of himself and a couple of his pals. And I believe he should remain "in there" until he dies. Has it really been "long enough," as he says? Is it possible there is enough time in jail to compensate for the inhumane choices he made? Suck it up, Freddie! Take the punishment and go away. Forever!

Anyway, I hope the parole board agrees with me today. I will know later. And I haven't really thought about what to do if they release him. My own humanity is called into question as I realize I have no compassion for this man. But there is none. Maybe I will send him a copy of this book when it is finished. I have always wondered if he liked Karen . . . if after his abuses and his disgusting offenses to her, he could regard her as a human being. If he could see her as someone's sister, someone's child. He is the last person to see her alive. And, as I have said in the past, I envy him that. She was an amazing young woman. Does he have any idea what he did? Who she was? Maybe if he knew, he would agree with me about his destiny. The second he assumed he had the right to end her life, his own was forfeit. You made your choice, Freddie. Live with it. I do.

"Life is precious. Live in the moment."

I have learned over time that a moment in time can hold so many others in its measure. The very instant I am consumed with grief, a joyful memory comes and lifts my spirits. Similarly, just as I am blissfully rapt in a vision of beauty, a deflating image of Karen or the bittersweet remembrance of a squandered opportunity can hitch a ride and crash the whole affair. I am not complaining. I am content that all time collapses in the mind, in the mind's eye. The assignment has been to pull off the covers. They are off. And to remember. I do remember. Joy and Grief are walking side by side but always with an implied imperative to embrace the joy . . . any moment of joy should be given preference over the alternative. Challenging. But possible.

And so, on to the next.

Goose and the magic motorcycle. Okay. There's that word. A silly subtitle for a tale of two great loves. The bike you already know about, my magic steed of legend. And Goose is the greatest dog ever . . . I mentioned her but now seems as good a time as any to detail her claim as such. Goose was born in San Diego. She was part Malamute, part possibly Belgian Shepherd, who was a whelp out of Pamplemousse, sired by a purebred Malamute who had silver markings and was a majestic stud! I am just building up the claim, as mentioned. Pamplemousse belonged to Agnes. Pamplemousse means grapefruit in French. Agnes was very creative. A set painter and general backstage artisan at the Old Globe Theatre, where I worked for three seasons. At the end of the first season, I was asked to stick around for the winter production of *Arms and the Man,* by Shaw. Thus began my residency of sorts at the Old Globe Theater.

The Alamo.

The Alamo was a little, three-bedroom home where members of the acting company would stay during the Shakespeare Festival. Pamela, Patricia and Robert, Patricia's little girl and a curly haired nanny moved out. I moved in. Or rather, back in. I had spent most of the summer with Pamela there. Pamela, who had ridden on the back of my bike four months earlier. A lovely sojourn, but I needed a break. A couple of weeks at Carl's place. A little time. Karen. You know. I sought solace in solitude. The music. James Taylor. It helped.

Then a rapprochement of sorts with Pamela and a nice good-bye at the end of the Shakespeare Festival. We would never see each other again. And The Alamo became my home.

It was owned by Craig Noel. Dubbed "The Alamo" as it resembled the little fort with the big history, and it was a storied place with a sizeable story of its own. Craig was the Artistic Director of the Old Globe Theater. The Alamo was specifically reserved for special members of the Shakespeare company—stars flown in from New York to spend a summer in San Diego, a working vacation doing what they loved while living well. Nice. And there were plenty of famous actors who came. But at the end of the season, Craig and I made a deal. I could stay there while I was performing at the theatre. And if I was willing to do small chores around the house, as well; make some improvements during the winter. I painted the house and the kitchen. Watered the plants. I even hosted a couple of guest directors during my time there—a few weeks as they rehearsed and mounted a production. It was a great arrangement. Craig was a benefactor. My benefactor in word and deed!

He gave me a home. Where I would continue in solitude for a time. He gave me a job. Doing what I love. I played roles, significant roles in seven of Shakespeare's plays, he asked me to do Bluntshchi in *Arms and the Man*. The Soldier in Robert Patrick's *Kennedy's Children*. I won my first award for acting at the Old Globe Theatre, an Atlas Award, they called it . . . it remains on my shelf to this day. Craig afforded me countless creative opportunities in my early career. I even wrote music for two plays. It was a very good time for me. He was a wonderful man. I am grateful to him beyond measure and I was fortunate enough to tell him so a week before he died. I remain grateful for that. I got to say good-bye. And to say thank you. He provided me a remarkable final chapter to the Juilliard, Jill and Karen saga. Karen, of course, has no final chapter. She lives on.

Agnes had caught my eye by then. Creative, talented and lovely. Well, she had caught my eye before that but just after Christmas we started seeing each other. Took a couple of months to sort myself out and then to work up the nerve to approach her. One thing led to another. We were on and off for the next year or so. But mostly on.

So Goose came into my life courtesy of Agnes. Agnes and I spent some wonderful days together. Not sure I was ready to be in a relationship of any duration at that time. Well, maybe not a human relationship. The dog thing worked out fine. Agnes had bred Pamplemousse quite carefully with a pricey stud. Shortly after we met, in fact, Agnes and I drove to meet the "family." The deed was done. It took.

And a couple of weeks later, Agnes asked if I would like one of the pups. I was ready. Yes. To love again. I know it sounds a bit funny. I was ready to love again. To love a dog, at least. After Karen. And it turned out to be one of the great gifts of my young life. For that, I am deeply grateful to Agnes. I will carry her forever. There are some regrets about how things turned out with her. Not appropriate to share here. I loved her. I did. In my fashion (yes, borrowed from Baudelaire). To say more than that is not respectful at this time. She helped to raise Goose; actually, helped show me how to raise her. And in Goose I found my first great Dog Love. I would even sing of it when the Doobie Brothers came out with "Real Love." I replaced "Real" with "Dog"—*cause we both lived long enough to know that we'd quit it all right now for just one minute of "Dog Love!"* Jeanine would sing it with me. Jeanine in Minneapolis. Another forever memory. She probably deserves more mention than this, but the publishers have signaled I need to stream-line things a bit, so I will wait for the next book.

I do still sing it on occasion. An homage to Goose. And to Jeanine.

As the second season was about to begin, I asked Craig if I could get my Equity card . . . Actors' Equity Association, our union. Getting into the union can be a dizzying affair. A double-edged sword. Can't get into the union without a union job, and you can't get a union job unless you're in the union. Frustrating. So, I made a plan. I requested a formal appointment with Craig in his office. And it is here I learned a great lesson. I postulated that Craig was not likely to guess I wanted to join the union. He was busy. It wasn't his responsibility; it was mine. So, I told him. I wanted to join the actors' union for the next Festival Season. I had proven my value. I was worth it. "Wouldn't get it if I waited for you to figure it out," I told him. It was high time I asked. High time for my respectability. He turned me down. "Well, Kelsey." Without much of a pause, "No."

He was sympathetic and attentive. He was willing to give me a job in the apprentice company for another year. I would have to leave the Alamo. The leading actors would need it. So, he had been think-ing about me. Just not the way I'd hoped. I pleaded my case, certain I'd earned some respect. I wasn't overselling it or suffering from an overinflated sense of self. And Craig did listen. It wasn't that short a pause. We just didn't agree. The lesson?—know your worth. Things might not go the way you want. Not at first. Stand tall.

I rose and cordially shook his hand. Told him I would leave in a couple of days. He wished me luck. I thanked him. It had been a great year. The motorcycle could stay in the garage at the Alamo for a while. I would come back for it. Agnes helped me pack up the Fiat. Goose and I crossed the nation together on our way to Florida.

The Alamo! In San Diego! Sounds epic. Well, maybe. Epic. They were certainly great days in my life.

The Fiat! I'd forgotten the Fiat.

Okay.

One night I planned a trip to Mexico with a group of actors, I don't remember who exactly. But that night, Agnes and I drove down with some friends to the Rosarito Beach Hotel, home of a terrific margarita, great guacamole and a lovely beach. It had been built in the 1920s and was a famous, favorite spot for fabled actors of the time well into the days of Sinatra and Marilyn Monroe. The Old Globe actors also frequented it for their day-and-a-half off during the run of a play. Craig told us tales of having to bail out Prospero or Timon on a Tuesday morning and rush them back across the border for the show Tuesday night. I think our bunch was much tamer than in years past because I do not remember a single arrest during my time there.

On this particular trip, we drove in a car. I do not remember whose. I did not like taking the bike across the border, so I parked it near the theater along Balboa Avenue. Now, here is the catch. I always leave my keys with the vehicle. I do it to this day. Don't tell anyone. And though I usually put them under the seat of the motorcycle, that night I forgot and left them in the ignition. Two nights later, I returned to find the motorcycle had been stolen. I made a police report, but they were not very encouraging and since I had left the keys in the ignition, they said I was not likely to get it back. A snide look in the eye and a facetious inflection accompanied their news. Okay. Not likely. I agreed. Agnes and I went looking for a replacement vehicle and I had always fancied the Fiat 124 Sport Coupe. Not the convertible—the one with the back seat. Charlie, in high school, had one and I thought it was the coolest car in the senior parking lot that year. A lot of other guys did, too, cause when I pulled up for a visit with my old friend Spencer back in Florida, he said, "Hey, you got a 'Charlie B.' car!" It was a cool car. And it ran great. Anyway, Agnes's mom loaned me a few hundred dollars to buy a used Fiat 124 for about six hundred bucks. At the same time, she said she was going to ask her church to do a prayer circle to get the motorcycle back. I figured it was gone for good, but she assured me it might turn up. So, that Sunday, the fate of the bike was shared in church and on Monday the police called me and said they thought they had my bike. It had turned up in Mexico, been painted flat black and was seized in some sort of traffic stop by Mexican authorities, identified and marked for return to San Diego and its rightful owner—me! A miracle! I never doubted the power of prayer from that day forward.

Anyway, it was in this Fiat that Goose and I traveled back to Florida after Craig turned me down for the '77 season at the Globe. Back home in Florida, Gam and Mom were there and Bob had flown the coop. I have not really covered Bob yet, but he was a big factor and a small blip all at the same time. It may have been Bob who sent my mom and my sister packing shortly after I left for New York. This is only supposition on my part but Bob was a bit of a drunk and a tortured man, I guess. That is the most charitable characterization. He had piloted a small landing craft at Normandy Beach on D-Day. It was his great story. He told it with gusto and pride, deservedly. A Nazi plane had strafed him and he was shot in the leg. Bob played dead for a time as the plane circled back to confirm he was dead. Then he got back up and ferried several more boatloads of soldiers to the beach. It was heroic and admirable. There is a film, *The Best Years of our Lives*, in which returning soldiers from World War II reenter the world and the lives they had left behind. It is very moving and the gist of it is that the men and women who fought and served during the war sacrificed their best years. There is also a connotation and a saying that they were the "best years" because they were in service and alive as never before or since. I believe Bob's best years were those.

After the war, he had a hard time of it. He became a boat captain. He had a son, Steven. He was an aggressive guy at times, especially when drunk. And he married my grandmother sometime in late '73, I think. He had spent a year or two off and on with Gam before that. One Thanksgiving, Bob was particularly loaded and started hurling insults at Danny, Karen's guy, you remember. Well, I sat there for a time listening and finally could stomach no more. I put my napkin down, rose decisively, told him he was finished for the night and at all of sixteen years old, stood him up, grabbed him by the scruff of his neck, the back of his belt, and gave him the bum's rush out the front door. "Go Home!" That, as I slammed the door behind him. He made his way home, sobered up a bit and then started calling my grandmother. She told me he was coming back. I said he was not welcome. He could visit the next day. With that Gam huffed a bit and thought she would get herself another drink.

We had a landing at the front entrance that stepped up into the living room. Gam had a habit of grabbing the wall to assist her stepping up...this particular night, she missed the wall. And fell straight back. I saw it. I thought she had hurt her head. I checked her out. She seemed okay and then I hoisted her into my arms and told her it was time for bed. Everything would be okay in the morning. This was just another standard Thanksgiving in our home. I had dubbed Thanksgiving "Fight Night" years before, as the flow of wine and alcohol tended to open all the switches for the runaway train of the year's feelings and resentments. They would run at full throttle until the momentum either died down or crashed into blackout. This was probably the most dramatic Fight Night of them all but not truly remarkable, maybe just a bit more than run-of-the-mill. I look back at those evenings with a kind of fondness. It may seem weird, but this was our custom and our home. The life I had always known. It was also rare we exploded to the same degree during the rest of the year. Thanksgiving, it seemed, was a designated occasion for blowing off steam.

The following morning, Gam was bellowing from her bedroom. She was in pain. I made a quick assessment that the swelling on the side of her leg was not a good sign. The ambulance was called. A trip to the hospital. Gam had broken her hip. That was probably the event that accelerated her physical decline...her emotional decline would accelerate not too many years later, with Karen's murder. It broke her. And I think she may have blamed herself. As I did. Bob, apparently, had made some advances toward Karen when she came back from a semester of college. I never knew why she decided not to return but after a week or so in the house, she moved out for good into her own apartment. I have a picture on the wall of a party at her place just before Christmas of '73. Mom moved in with her boyfriend, Kenny, just after Christmas for possibly the same reason. During the winter of '73, she was in Pelham, New York, where Kenny was supervising a refit on a yacht.

I want to stop here for a moment. I am surprised as I go deeper and deeper into these days. The recall is often crystal clear. There are some spots in softer focus but as I continue, clarity comes to many of them. Just noting it here. I promised to tell the truth. I think I

141

have. There may be some embellishment for entertainment's sake. Not very much. Nothing that would not approximate the truth. Not a single lie. I am content with that. I like being open about it. I have not criticized anyone indiscreetly or unfairly. I have tried to be kind to them all. I have thanked many people I never thanked. They may never know of my gratitude. I am glad to have expressed it here, nonetheless. The Universe knows. The people who played a part in our past, mine and Karen's, are beloved, even the challenging ones. Save for those men. They deserve worse than I have served them.

Bob, or Captain Bob, as we came to call him did not mean to be such a "putz." He was a victim of whatever life had given him; not as tough as some lives, but enough for him. Enough to take him down to a place of pain and discomfort. He brought that with him into our home. The discomfort. And for a short while, everyone left except Gam. It is now 1974, spring. I am home. What was I doing there?

I have to take a break to be sure of the next few months as I recount them. Or decide which way to turn instead. Back in a bit.

Karen had not returned to the second semester at Berry College. I never knew why. She was in her apartment with a young man who may have been her boyfriend for a time but I am not sure. About the boyfriend. I remember liking him. I think I went back to my high school and gave a few lectures to the kids there; nothing formal but an impromptu visit turned into a few weeks of helping on a theater project, speaking to students about voice production. That sort of thing. I would go fishing on our boat and did some odd jobs as the spring turned into summer. Not our old McKee Craft but a Uniflite 34. A great boat. It was the same hull used for the gunboats in Vietnam. Fast. Gam had bought it for Bob but she was happy to let me use it while I was there. Fantastic fishing boat! Bob wasn't always around but I saw them kissing on the bow one evening as I had the helm. Whispered *I love you*s made me a little uncomfortable, I confess. Upon reflection, though, I was glad for Gam at the time . . . grateful she'd found a little softness after the

142

hard hand she'd been dealt. It was a tender moment. And I was actually grateful that Bob had come.

There is something a little funny I want to put into the record. There was a family who lived about three houses down. The Norths, I think. Nice kids, nice parents. Ping-pong table in the Florida room and their dad was pretty good at it. I fancied myself pretty good but I think he was better. Anyway, he had a few kids and a younger son, Carl, maybe. One night we were talking. There were three children, two boys and a girl. I don't remember their names. But one evening, they exchanged a couple of uncomfortable glances and finally said they had something to tell us. The memory is sketchy. Karen may have been there too. The youngest of them, the boy, used to fish along the sea wall of the canal. Lots of kids did. They would use a three-spiked hook and try to "snag" mullet. The canals were full of mullet.

One afternoon, he spotted a flare off a metallic object in the shallows close to the wall. Jumped down and retrieved it. It had been there for a while but probably not very long. It was not overgrown with algae or deep in the sand. It was resting on the bottom. At the water's edge, he saw there was writing on it and discovered it contained the ashes of Col. Gordon Savage Cranmer. Wasn't that your grandfather? Yes. So, what happened to it? They threw it back in at a deeper spot a bit further down the canal, assuming it was a sign of respect to those who had placed it there. I stood helplessly factoring the causes that got him there. The canal did not seem a place of honor, certainly. I do not remember if I asked my grandmother or not. But I think I did. Bob. Bob had thrown the ashes in the canal. Had she known? Yes, I think she did. And once again, as so many times already in this book, I receive a lesson. I think Gam agreed to place Gordon there. Partially, to give Bob a little room—I am sure that was part of it; but also, to give Gordon a proper resting place. Okay, we can disagree about whether it was a fitting resting place, but a proper one?—possibly. A burial at sea in front of the home where he'd hoped to spend his final days. A home that would be a place of joy in his remaining years, of tranquility and ease. I know Gam would never disrespect Gordon in any way. And I think of it now as a loving gesture, something she thought he would've wanted. An honor. That urn is still somewhere near that house in a deeper section, well beneath the silt of the canal. It is beyond my control or rescue, although a part of me would like to find it to place them all together. Maybe even spread their ashes to the winds. Together into the whirlwind! United once more on the currents of the air to settle into its loving embrace, Earth's loving embrace . . . in its seas, on its shores. And in its high places.

Sometimes the tone has a mythological grandiosity. My writing. Yes, I realize that. But! By way of explanation, I offer this. When I think of my family, I regard them as legendary. As Myth. Towering. And so they are. With my writing, and with my living!—I strive to honor their noble bones. They bear me up; I try my best.

I still have Karen's ashes and my mom's and Gam's. They are kept in a hutch at the front entrance of our home in California. I have kept them with me. It's funny. Mom kept Gam and Karen similarly in her care throughout her life. When Sally, my mom, died, I continued to house them out of sight but close by. Gam kept Gordon at home, too, until the whole "Bob" thing. Maybe we just didn't want to let each other go—not completely. I will work on this some more. For now, they will stay with me but the vision of releasing them together is quite appealing. Perhaps, I'd better find a little cash to dredge that canal? I wonder if such a thing is possible.

Let's review for a minute. I have taken you to San Diego, my time at Juilliard and I have slipped back in time to the pristine days of Karen's youth and our time together there. And now, Goose and I have just pulled up in the Fiat. Back in Florida. In 1977. Back from San Diego. Briefly. Bob is gone and my mom has come home.

I'm stuck on something. How did the bike come into my life?

I will tell you now. It was Bob. Took me a while to realize it was Bob. Now I remember. The week or so after I graduated high school, June of 1973, second week of June, in fact, Bob had asked what I had in mind for my summer before moving to New York City. I had secured a job in Palm Beach to work on an interior demo of the Sans Souci Hotel. I would beat walls and be a general laborer. It was a pretty good job. Four, count 'em, four bucks an hour! A huge step up in the world. I had been a dishwasher at Denny's for a buck eighty-three just a few years before. I dug ditches for two bucks an hour. This was heady stuff, indeed!

Bob did something lovely. He told me he was proud of how I had done in school and how I had been accepted to Juilliard. Since I would need to drive to work each morning, he wanted to give me a graduation present of a motorcycle. My Honda 750 was given me by Bob. How extraordinary a turn from so unexpected a source. What a funny world and how wonderful to see it from this perspective. I am blessed to have known them all. This man had a destiny to destroy so much I had known and yet propel me toward the unknown that would make all the difference in my future. Another one of those head-scratching moments. That is all I have—confusion and completion. From the moment this strange man walked into our world, he trampled what we knew and yet provided me the vehicle that took me from job to job, chapter to chapter in my life for a decade. He destroyed everything we had but facilitated what came next. He bestowed upon me my "trusty steed!" This journey. Mythic. As noted. All our lives are. Karen's story is no less tragic than Lavinia's, Shakespeare's tale of extraordinary human empathy, distanced by a thousand years; Karen's is a story told with personal passion, specific in memory and my experience. Both are Truth. Mine, not a timeless human grief, as Shakespeare's, but a memory only moments away from the experience itself, distanced only by a handful of days . . . my own. Remember. Karen told me. Remember. Joy, Anguish, Life, all come rushing back . . . alive as the days themselves and the nights that followed.

And just as I conclude this paragraph a rush of recognition or doubt comes over me. Bob was crafty . . . he gave me the bike to get rid of me. He drove my mother, my sister, and finally me from our home. My mother and I thought he was to blame for Karen's death . . . at least, partly to blame. I'm mad at myself. I was this close to absolving him of his crimes. Like a great wounded ogre, a malcontent, he came to thrash our family and destroy any trace of my grandfather. I prefer the more charitable description I made earlier, but either can be argued. I believe there was some reason for him to be there. All interaction pushes us toward a higher good . . . I would like to think that is true. Then, on

145

the other hand, there may be some lessons that do not merit the time they take to learn. I'm thinking about the film *Once Upon a Time...in Hollywood*. Once upon a time, it might have been really nice if Karen hadn't left, Gordon hadn't died, if her boyfriend called the cops before the men took my sister and butchered her. It might have been really something if Bob had never been. Just like in that movie, it might have been a special grace if he had strolled mistakenly into the neighboring home. But then, I would not have wished that on anyone.

Radical Forgiveness. Revisiting the idea now. It is possible, I think. But not easy. Every encounter, every person we meet, is working with us on a Soul level. Whether they know it or not, whether we realize it in the moment or years later, each person is a pathway to our highest good. I like the idea. With Bob, it remains a challenge, but I do see a window now where before had been none.

I wrote the previous few lines before speaking to Esther yesterday. Esther has been with Karen. She continues to check in with her. Perhaps, to encourage me. I am making progress. It was Karen's intention, I think, to discover the many things I have discovered, or rediscover them. Uncover them. Bob is one of them. He is uncovered now. Earlier, I wrote I had a dim memory that Karen was uncomfortable in the house with Bob there. I think when she returned from her first semester at college, Bob may have tried it on with her. She left then. And I dimly recall Karen saying something about it. No details. She didn't describe anything more than discomfort but by the time I came home for the first Christmas break in '73, Karen had her own apartment. So, it must have been a quick but not too distant retreat from home, a once wonderful home, to someplace safe. Away from Bob. The end of home for Karen. That makes me sad. She made a new one. That makes me smile. Karen was a strong one. A one of a kind.

There is a photo of me taken at her place that Christmas. There is another taken of us dancing together, Christmas of '74. It is the last photo of us together.

With Esther yesterday, she said Karen was showing her an evil man who had been very destructive. I had already mentioned I was writing about Bob. I thought that was probably who Karen meant. I am sure of it now and my natural kindness drove me to soften his impact on my family. I am always optimistic and positive. I think it comes from Christian Science. One of my memories from Sunday school was the simple phrase, "Always see God's perfect child." I took it to heart. And I have tried in all my dealings to see the perfect child in everyone . . . it has borne fruit; but it also blinded me to the idea a Soul can choose Evil. I do not believe in Evil, but people can and do choose it. I choose naivete and innocence, believing all people are good. Hard to see the good in what happened to Karen. To see any good in Freddie Glenn. But It is the good of her living I am meant to remember . . . not her end. Still hard to do sometimes.

Good.

I told Esther I'd written that Karen was the great love of my life . . . a constant. "Good," she said. And, yes, how lovely it was you were born into the same family. That was lucky, she said. In this life, you didn't have to search for one another; you arrived side by side after who knows how many lifetimes. She was the first person you loved. Consciously loved. How fortunate you were! Fortunate.

I know.

The way Karen died has made it hard to remember that sometimes. But I do remember.

Now, when I think of Karen, I smile. Recollection kicks in. One after another, episodes spring to life where before only the horror of her death had been. As predicted, the healing is evident. A smile instead of sorrow. The living eyes of Karen and not her corpse spring to mind. As promised. The episodes are funny, sometimes sad, sometimes a little scary but always a fondness is along for the ride and not a terror. Not anymore.

We'd been home from school for an hour or so. The adults trickled in from their days. Katherine left for home around three-thirty in the afternoon. Katherine worked for the family for years, looked after us when the adults were occupied. She was a lovely woman; she had an ease about her. It had been Katherine who sent the first telegram

147

of condolence when Gordon died years later. The afternoon ritual unfolded on schedule that day. Gordon arrived home just moments before Gam who had a late luncheon. Mom was home before Katherine had left. Almost three hours passed since Mom arrived and Gam had walked in the door. It had grown dark outside, just barely, but it was then I realized Karen was missing. I hadn't seen her since we got home from school. Where's Karen? No idea. We began looking, the entire family. No sign of her. We called out. Nothing. Karen was gone. Voices raised. Urgency was next and finally, panic. I think we may have called Katherine. Had she seen her? Only when we returned from school. Karen was nowhere to be found.

A digression.

We took a trip to Florida when we were young. Or younger rather. The whole family on a train bound for paradise. That's how it felt. It was an overnight journey with a club car and porters and beds that fell from the ceiling and a closeness in the family that was irreplaceable. I don't remember the trip home but I suppose it was a return ticket ten days later . . . it was not as magical, certainly, but that trip remains a wonder. I loved that trip.

I played Bridge in the club car with a group of strangers and was dealt twelve Clubs. I saw Gordon's eyes widen just a bit when he saw the hand and he gently edged me aside in the bidding. Of course, we bid a slam, but I had to know what my partner had in his hand so we started with the weak Club bid, I think, asking the longest and strongest suit in my partner's hand. Bidding four Diamonds was asking for the number of aces in his hand. And then I made the slam bid in Clubs. It turned out well. Gordon did help. I might not have been able to pull it off. There was a difficult "finesse" to be made, but it was the most amazing hand of cards I have ever seen. I think the same was true for Gordon, who had played Bridge in college since he was president of the Sigma Alpha Epsilon chapter at Berkeley. I felt like a local celebrity. The train hurtled into the night as we drifted off to sleep.

Florida was great. We stayed in one of those small motels just steps from the beach and it was the most wonderful time. We went to dinner and Gam argued with the owner of some restaurant that what he had said was Tia Maria was just Kahlua and she was not at all pleased. He ended up bringing out a bottle of Tia Maria and opening it in front of her. I am not sure even that convinced her but it was fun to watch Gam in a tussle . . . she gave no quarter and expected a lot, so the deck was always loaded in her favor. I loved her, though. Karen and I giggled. We were bright red for about three days because of all the sun and the hours we spent in the little pool at our motel; and we shivered ourselves to sleep the first couple of nights from too much exposure. It could not have been a better trip. I loved the sound of the wind in the palms. And I loved sitting in the hammock. Gordon's primary position was in the hammock. We piled on with him. Our love of hammocks was a very deep one. For the three of us, they were and would be our "magic" carpet. I won't highlight the word again in future. We have an understanding now, about that word, that needn't be flogged beyond a shared wink between us.

Time to put a hammock in the yard upstate. For the kids. So they can feel what we felt. I see her now, looking up at me with that angelic face. Karen. I rock the hammock with my feet on the ground, she stretched out, gazing skyward and we talk and talk. And we smile together.

And we still fly together.

Back now to New Jersey. Back in the old house. Back in time. Nerves are frayed and we are moments from phoning the police. I had a closet in my room that was the home of my attic monster. In fact, the closet had a direct hatch to the attic and that was the doorway to a fearful place, indeed. It also had a heavy breathing setting that played only when I was about to open the hatch and risk entry. I walked into my bedroom and thought to myself it would not be possible that Karen was in there and if so, then what might have happened to her? I risked it. Opened the door. There on the floor in a makeshift bed was Karen, asleep. Under a blanket and cozy as could be. I woke her gently and asked what she was doing. "I'm sleeping on the train to Florida." Brilliant! No one was angry. I think they all just thought, *What a wonderful idea ... what a wonderful girl.*

Florida. Let's go back there. Write the words and it happens. Just like that. It is June of '73. A day after graduation. I am lying in bed looking at my long hair ... it was an issue that I took quite seriously, the hair code at school. During my time at school. There had been some progress in tenth grade. I had run for student council and became a member. It was my only time in politics. We vowed to topple the tyranny of the hair code. Boys were meant to have haircuts that did not extend over the shirt collar. That meant short hair! We won the battle. And it may seem funny that it was such an emotional victory, but it did mean we were being taken seriously by the school and its administration. They were willing to show some regard for us as young adults and trust us to live as we promised. We were not advocating slovenly behavior or sloppiness. We were asking for a bit of Freedom. So, long hair became a staple at school. Not particularly long but for the next year and a half, all the boys let their hair go a bit. Except the football players and swimmers because long hair was seen as a handicap, especially the swimmers.

Pine Crest had a very successful swim team and it was taken very seriously. It may have been the number one team in America at the time. It was certainly in the top five and Jack Nelson coached the Women's Olympic Team in '72, I think. I think Karen may have dated a swimmer during tenth grade. But he had long hair, come to think of it; so maybe hair was not so much an issue for swimmers, as they could stuff it up under a bathing cap. It was their body hair they removed with a vengeance. Anyway, the hair code victory was short-lived and two years later, my senior year, a new headmaster arrived and reinstated it. A few of us resisted. A wig was the answer! A flag of defiance. A banner. There goes that language of legend and myth. More simply, I wanted to keep my long hair; so, I did. Went down to the local wig shop and bought myself a "Jane Fonda" wig ... similar to the hair she had in Barbarella, I think. Too long to pass the hair code, so I chopped off the bottom locks of what was a "shag" look, I guess. Stuck the wig on top of my head and packed my tresses underneath the netting. This did the trick. I looked quite ridiculous, honestly, but it was the principle of the thing. If the school didn't mind me looking this way then I didn't mind either! Karen was at Palm Cove by now but I think she regarded it as a symbol of resistance, too. It lived in the back of the car until pulling into the parking lot. I rummaged around for my wig amid the schoolbooks that also resided there, grabbed a hair tie and then curled my ponytail on top of my head where the wig was braced at the forehead and then peeled back in a haphazard affair, barely disguising the offending hair but suitably, and with a pompadour that rose about five inches above any believable height. Fun. Silly. Important! They all fit. But after the long and arduous stance, graduating in my wig, no less, I lay in my bed next morning examining my locks and decided to get a haircut. The battle had been won. Why not?

It was my friend Dean who hired me to work in Palm Beach for his dad's demolition company. He asked if I wanted a job that was pretty labor intensive but paid well. I was saving up for school so that fit the bill. And I began my daily trips up the beach road on the bike that Bob had bought me. Demolition. Beating walls was an art. I had no idea. Jimmy and Jessie were the seasoned laborers who taught me how. An eight-pound sledgehammer was sufficient to break up the side of an interior wall and then "cut" along the bottom. The wall would then drop four or five inches to the ground and topple in one direction or another . . . we tried to choose which by nudging up against the wall as it toppled. It was fairly routine, but I found it interesting, and I grew to like the boys. It was a good job. Jimmy and Jessie were pretty quiet guys. I would greet them on a morning and they would simply respond with a four-letter word. "How ya doin', Jimmy?" "Shi-!" was the grumbled response. "How's it going, Jessie?" "Shi-!" You get the picture. Well, I thought I'd landed in a very odd alternate Universe. In this world, that single word could represent the entire English language. Inflection was the key. Perhaps I'll include a sound sample to more fully illustrate what I am talking about when I record this one day. Jimmy and Jessie became pals and as the days passed they asked what I wanted to be. I told them an actor. They would laugh and laugh. Okay, so act. Act for us. Well, I did have the "Once more unto

151

the breach" speech from *Henry V* committed to memory. So, I offered up a stirring rendition and the boys seemed ready to follow me into battle. Maybe. And maybe I could act, after all.

Work at Sans Souci Hotel, interior remodel, was wonderful. Dusty, yes! Plaster dust would fill the air after a section of wall slammed to the floor. And at the end of every workday, the dust in my nostrils was stifling. A wet rag. Blow the nose a bit. Drop some water down the nostrils. It cleared up pretty quickly. Except for the caked layer of grime on my skin and hands. A rinse with the hose and a reach into the cooler for a long-neck Bud, and things were as good as gold. It was lovely.

The job drew to a close and the remodel team came in; I asked for a job with the construction company, and they hired me. It was cool to stay on the same site and participate in the rebuild. We snapped chalk lines one day. I watched the architect talk through his vision. Then one day, the foreman told me to cut out a piece of floor at the entrance. A twenty-five-pound jackhammer. Cut a floor for the staircase. I spent two hours and then the foreman came by and yelled that I had cut the wrong section and the job was ruined, it would cost thousands; you're fired! I do not know what "happened," but I did what I was told to do. Someone had made a mistake, maybe me, but I did my job.

This takes me to the next two jobs . . . and another, briefly. On the heels of losing the job in Palm Beach, I found another job at a union site. A condo development. The idea of joining a union was appealing as a construction worker because I believed it would make things better. Makes sense. So, briefly, because this ended almost as soon as it began, I worked one day and started the next morning. I was hired as a laborer, they implied that apprenticeship might earn membership, and I would sweep units before the wall board guys came in. I swept three units in the morning and two in the afternoon. I barely broke a sweat. I was good at pacing myself because I was doing demo work the month before. Harder work than this. Anyway, the next morning as I was finishing up my first unit, one of the guys came by and told me to slow down. They're not paying you to work this hard. What are they paying me for?—I thought, and I may have said that out loud. You will do two units in the morning and one in the afternoon. There would be no discussion. This was a union job and I was going to do as I was told. I finished up that unit and then I quit. I could have done six units, easily, in a day. Whatever the union was doing for its members and themselves, it just didn't sit right with me that they were asking me to do less than I could.

Yeah, I didn't care for that. Seems to me a union guarantees the employer the very best work they can do in return for respectable wages, humane work conditions and some benefits. The presumption being that no one could do the job better. The union guaranteed no one could or would, but it seemed odd to demand workers to do less than they were able. Weren't they proposing that if an employer paid them better, there'd be no one better to do the job? Anyway, I'm just beating a dead horse here.

The following week found me getting a job at a small hotel. And suddenly another rabbit hole appears to misdirect the story. It is late April in 2022. I am writing the book this very moment. I have been asking for some clarity about the summer after graduation. As I am sitting in a small hotel room at a property on Nevis, I glance at a list of flora and fauna on the island. There are several mango trees, pineapple and coconut palms, a variety of others all numbered on a page; and #19 is the Sea Grape. And boom, there it is. The Sea Grape is the name of the hotel I worked at later that summer. After I quit the construction job. The job started mid-July, I think. I worked the graveyard shift, from around 10 p.m. until 6 a.m. the following morning. I swept the tennis courts, did the hotel laundry, scrubbed the pool tile, raked the beach and tended to odd emergencies that came up, whether it was fixing an elevator or making up a room last minute that had been missed by the maids earlier that day. I read *War and Peace* during my time there. About four weeks in all. I really enjoyed that book and I am always a little prideful when I say I read *War and Peace*. Tolstoy, yes. But not in Russian. Apparently, it is an entirely different book when read in Russian. Some very prideful people have told me so moments after I whip out, "I read *War and Peace*!" "Have you read it in the original Russian?" "Well, I have always wanted to . . ."—and . . . drop your voice!

153

I befriended a couple of remarkable and unique people at the Sea Grape. One was Alex, the chef. A Scotsman who had all his teeth pulled when he was fourteen to prove he was the toughest kid in his Glasgow neighborhood…not an odd thing to the boys of Glasgow, apparently. So, Alex was about thirty years old or thereabout and he was the head chef of a fairly respectable hotel restaurant. The prime rib was amazing and the fresh fish was always a wise choice. Delicious. He was a good guy. He kept some Drambuie in the walk-in fridge. Occasionally, with a wink of an eye, Alex would ask me if I'd like a nip. Of course! We slipped into the fridge in a quiet moment, and he reached behind the chickens and produced the bottle and two shot glasses. A nice, rounded shot full and Alex would exclaim, "Ah, nectar o' the Gods!" Then he would knock it back and I followed suit.

Charles was the bookkeeper at the hotel and he always came in around 1 a.m. A great guy and he occupied the front office while I did my chores about the property. His wonderful bride brought escarole soup and some wonderful Italian food almost every evening. She was a great cook. I guess it was usually around 3 a.m. when she dutifully brought over a little picnic basket of delicacies, and they always invited me to join them. What a lovely couple. So, in between loads of sheets and towels, mostly, and chapters of *War and Peace*, I would steal half an hour with them and we would discuss the future. They were from New York and thrilled for me. I was going to Juilliard and they were so impressed. Charles told me a great story about how he came to be doing the books at a little hotel on the beach in Pompano. He was retired. Had retired about five years before and he had a passion for the horses. Charles liked to bet. He lost everything he had. Except that wonderful bride of his and his integrity. He took a job and climbed back on his feet with his wife by his side. I imagine she read him the riot act at the time, but they were a great couple and a couple of great people. I am honored to have known them. They got by.

One evening, a small group of guys came to the hotel and said they had to work on the refrigeration in the kitchen. The freezer. I opened the door for them and left them to it. A couple hours later, they waved at me in the pool scrubbing the tile on the waterline and said they were finished. All good. I didn't think to check on their work but locked up the kitchen and gave Charles the key, I'm pretty sure. I would leave around five-thirty in the morning; he stayed another half hour or a bit more until the day shift showed up. I went in the next night and got a call around ten-thirty from the manager. Could I come in tomorrow afternoon to discuss something? Of course. That night Alex told me that a dozen or so frozen butterflied lobster tails had gone missing from the freezer. Clearly those guys who worked on the freezer must have taken them, but they had been contacted and swore they knew nothing at all about frozen butterflied lobster tails. They offered a possible solution . . . maybe the kid looking after the property at night took them. So, Alex prepared me for a firing squad the next day. The owner of the hotel and the manager, I think his name was Michael, but I am not sure. The owner was a man who my mom sold Christmas cards to every year. He was a pretty good customer and I think my mom made the connection when I started working at the Sea Grape, but I did not relay it to him. We rarely saw each other and until the incident with the lobster tails, I think he was fairly impressed with my work.

In fact, when I first heard they wanted to speak to me, I thought maybe they were going to ask me to stay on and be moved up the ladder at the hotel. I even played out that scenario in my mind, feeling guilty as I explained I had to leave for school in a couple of weeks. I had enjoyed my time there. I liked the nights and the reading I did while doing laundry . . . a giant affair with two agitators on either side of an enormous spin cylinder. It was all open and when loaded out of balance, the spin cylinder could rip your arm off. It was essential to make sure it stopped completely before reaching in and adjusting the load. From the spinner to the dryers, forty-five to fifty minutes per load in the dryers and after three or four hours every night, I had managed to wash hundreds of towels and bed linens, folded it all and made it ready for the maids the following day. It was during this time I would rake the courts and hit the pool tile. The tile would always have a little layer of oil on it from the suntan lotion when people jumped in for a swim. So, every night I slipped into the water and would let myself drip-dry in between loads, conversation with Charles and his wife, Alex in the kitchen and any other tasks that might arise during the night. It was in between all these and as the dryers spun their magic (wink) that I would read—I am not going to mention what I was reading, not again. I can't face the embarrassment.

Anyway, the meeting commenced and I was fired for stealing. I told them they were wrong about me but I had to start school in a couple of weeks anyway. Why the hell would I steal lobster tails? Deaf ears. I thanked them for the time I had had there and reiterated that school was starting soon anyway but they were wrong. I think they even knew it but had decided someone had to be shown this was not acceptable. Of course, I already knew that. Maybe the show was for someone else. All behind me now, but it does bring up another little wrinkle in my memory that has to be addressed.

One of my first jobs was as a dishwasher at Denny's on Oakland Park Boulevard, the beach side just past the bridge. I had lied about my age, I admit. I was fourteen but said I was fifteen, which was the legal age to start work. Anyway, dishwashing was not for the faint of heart and my hands suffered from dozens of cuts acquired when retrieving flatware from the basket. The heat of the steam also hurt the hands but you grin and bear it. The only perk to speak of was that I could have all the hot fudge sundaes I wanted. They would feed the staff a designated meal but I could help myself to the sundaes. And for a fourteen-year-old boy whose favorite food was exactly that, I was in a kind of heaven.

I also worked the graveyard shift on that job. So, every morning between around 3:30 in the morning until 5 a.m., the party set would come for the early breakfast they craved after their night out. It was a miracle to see those women. All sorts. Tanned and beautiful. Belly buttons and high heels and gorgeous eyes, I envied the men with them and thought they were unattainable for the likes of me. They were so beautiful and I so inconsequential. Auden wrote a great line I will paraphrase: "At fourteen, gazing in the mirror, all we are not stares back at what we are." That's the general idea, at least. Yeah, that is how I felt, more or less. I would never be with such beautiful people, I thought . . . but I could have a hot fudge sundae. I probably had three or four a night. Especially, around 4 a.m. when the place was buzzing with fabulous people!

To get there, I would take the boat and tie it up at a boatyard that was a block away. At 6 a.m., I would make my way back to the boat and home for a few hours' sleep before starting the day. Three weeks into the job. Looked good for the whole summer. Until I got a tap on the shoulder and the manager was asking me if I had any idea where the filet mignons had gone. A dozen or so were missing. It had just been discovered. So, you understand how the lobster tails had a familiar ring a couple of years later. Anyway, one of the chef's was smiling as I was interrogated and then he made a fist and brandished it in my direction. Ho-hum. Threats never scared me, but I knew my goose was cooked. I did explain that I did not take the steaks, that I would not take the steaks, it was beneath me and besides, and this is where I may have overplayed my hand, "I just like the hot fudge sundaes." Something in my tone or delivery caught the manager's attention.

He cocked his head and then said, "Hey, how old are you anyway?"

I did not lie. "Fourteen."

"I gotta let you go, kid."

I don't think he thought I stole the steaks. I could not legally work at Denny's; he had to let me go. I did get a few hundred dollars which went straight into the bank and then I took a job for cash, digging ditches. This was a funny one. The guy who hired me was a fly-by-night contractor but a decent enough guy. We worked hard. He had an expression, once we were down in a ditch, he would tell us to start digging and then say, "All I wanna see is asses and elbows!" Pretty funny and he went pretty easy on us, honestly, because we only worked six hours with a half-hour lunch in the middle. I made two bucks an hour. He was fair. He was funny. It was honest work. No cause for complaint.

I would borrow that phrase from him years later when I was coaching, "celebrity coaching" the NHL Celebrity All-Star Hockey Team. This was the brainchild of one of the real hockey guys. The 1980 Olympic Team was basically the celebrity team with a few guys from Canada who were actors. I was asked to tag along for games along with a few other actors—George Wendt and John Stamos came for one of the

157

games. We had fun. It was on a trip to Chicago when I was delivering a locker room speech. This was the basic purpose of my being there. I was meant to provide colorful impressions of a professional coach, and the local news crews would be there or some videographer . . . on this occasion, it occurred to me I had the perfect phrase to inspire my boys: "I want to see asses and elbows out on that ice! That's it. Eyes up, but asses and elbows everywhere else. If you have a shot take it. Make no apologies! Asses and elbows. Got it?"

"Got it!" they bellowed.

A moment later, Gordie Howe, one of the greatest hockey players in history, came up to me and said, "That's the best locker room advice I've ever heard."

Not bad. Gordie Howe. A legend. From ditchdigger to coach of legends! Not bad at all.

I am thanking Al for this . . . I think that was his name. But that couple of years, I think every guy I worked with was named Al. "Hey, Al. What's up?" "Yo, Al . . . good to see you, guy!" "What ya got under the hood, Al, a three fitty?" If the name wasn't Al, it was Guy. So, Guy was always a safe bet. Guy. And Al. Yup, they were prolific. The boss at the car wash was Al. He was a funny one too. Folding his arms and talking about us like we were his kids. "Yeah, they're good boys. Good kids!" And then, he would roar a laugh that sounded like it began with a capital "B." Bahahahaha . . . Bahaha! That was it. Al snuck into the *Cheers* set on occasion . . . he may have even made it onto TV . . . at least, that laugh did. John and George and I and a couple of the other guys would fold their arms and bellow that same laugh from the bar. An explosive "B" and several of us, "B . . . aaah!—Hahahaha. All grist for the mill. All harvested from Life. It makes me happy.

I need to complete a picture about my dog Goose. Goose could actually ride on my motorcycle with me. Not on the back . . . that's ridiculous. But she would jump into my arms, and I would arrange her between my legs to lie down across my lap and rest her head on my right

hand while we drove along. It was absolutely safe. We went everywhere in this manner. Another reason she was so extraordinary a
dog. I have to go back a bit in time now to that summer back in Florida.

Goose and I had driven cross country in the Fiat, as I mentioned
earlier. It was 1977. Tucson to Tallahassee in eighteen hours. I think
that's right. A crazy drive. Maybe it took longer. I don't want to exaggerate but it was a straight-through drive. If I got tired, I would wake
Goose and tell her to howl. It was a command we had worked out. Howl!
And she would start right in, just like a wolf howling at the moon. I
would howl along with her to rouse myself and then say, "Okay, Goose,
thanks. You can go back to sleep now." And she would curl back up in a
ball and was instantly back asleep. We stopped in Tallahassee because
I had friends there. Good friends who will be discussed soon. I spent
several weeks in Florida and did some volunteer work at Pine Crest . . .
I am just recapping here. The summer was going nicely. Did some
sailing. A little surfing in my home waters. I was not nervous about
things . . . it was a good break. And I discovered a great value in teaching. It helped me realize I had learned a lot about acting since leaving
school. Teaching was the best exercise for coalescing knowledge—for
acting, for anything. If you can explain it, it means you know it. I think
that's true.

The days whiled away. I think I went fishing a few times with
Stan. I remember his wife's name now . . . Vicky. Great gal. There was
the time Stan and I and a pal of his were out looking for dolphin . . . Mahi-
Mahi is the Hawaiian name and easily avoids the whole trying to catch
a dolphin rather than catch dolphin fish controversy. A dolphin fish is
a good fighter and a good meal . . . some of the best there is. We hooked
something but it was weird and we thought maybe there was a wahoo
on the line . . . wahoos are notorious for being lethargic as they approach
the boat, but once they see it, they run. Well, it was as if we had hooked
a bunch of seaweed until finally a little lemon shark appeared. Seemed
little and a determination was made to haul it into the boat. I manned
the gaff hook . . . grabbed it just below the jaw on the underside of the
fish and tossed it into the boat. It started flopping around on the deck
like the Tasmanian Devil, and two grown men started jumping around

the boat as the third, newly grown man, myself, jumped around with them. A trio of dunces basically running up the ladder to the flying bridge while the shark flailed around on the deck below. Finally, Stan realized he had a little club, a miniature baseball bat stowed above in a locker on the flying bridge, and he produced it forthwith.

"Take this and smack the hell out of it!" said Stan.

His friend just looked at him. I looked at him. Stan gestured the little bat toward me and reiterated his idea, concluding with a more emphatic gesture and the phrase, "You do it." So, I did. I took the bat and descended the ladder toward the jaws of death just feet below. I smacked it as hard as I could. Continued for several more blows. It slowed the shark down a bit. Stan had a go after that. His friend did too. Finally, the shark could withstand no more, and he gave up the ghost.

We were a whimsical boatload of mariners that day! Brave and true and truly ridiculous. At one point, the three of us jumping around actually made me laugh as hard as I have ever laughed. The shark was subdued. Then what to do with it became the issue. Well, I had heard that shark meat was good eating, so we took him home and fileted him, cut the pieces into steaks and bite-size servings, ate some, and froze the rest. It made a great story. Stan and I would repeat it whenever I saw him.

He didn't show up at Karen's funeral. I did see him several months later and he finally told me he just didn't know what to say. I get that. Because of that, though, I always call anyway, try to show up or at least offer a hug. Whenever a friend or even a stranger tells me about a tragic loss, I always say something—even if it's the wrong thing. I remember Wandi. How her call made me feel better than all the rest because she could not really speak. Her grief spoke to mine and as I consoled her, it consoled me. I hope she remembers as I do. I loved her for that call. I still love her.

Later that summer, around late July, I think, Craig Noel called me and asked if I could come out right away and replace Norman Snow who was playing Laertes in *Hamlet*. I told him I could be there in four or five days and he said that would be fine. I am not sure why Norman had to leave the production, but I think it was because his girlfriend, Mary Joe, had to have an operation and he would be leaving the season early. The first thing I asked was: "Does this mean I get my Equity card?" It did mean that. It also meant I would move back into The Alamo. The lesson? Know your worth. Others may take a while to catch up. Be patient. Wait for your reward.

I warmed up the Fiat and grabbed Goose, kissed my mother and grandmother good-bye, and sped off the following day. Vindication!

Somewhere near Ft. Pierce, the water pump in my car gave out, and I had to get the Fiat to a garage for repairs. Turns out the engine was basically blown and would need to be replaced. Luckily, the guy who owned the station had the very same model in his backyard and could sell me the engine for four hundred dollars. Well, I didn't exactly have four hundred dollars at the time, but I called my pal Spencer and asked him to come and get me. His dad, Bob, was willing to loan me some cash to replace the engine.

Spencer's dad, Robert, had always been a positive and supportive influence in my life. I had known Spencer at Rumson Country Day School, sixth grade. The first week of tenth grade at Pine Crest, there was a young man sat two rows from me and the name just came to me. I know this guy, I thought; and then I said, "Spencer, Spencer K...?" He looked over at me and said, "Kelsey?" How about that? Four years after New Jersey, there he was. And he would become my greatest friend. Or one of them, certainly.

Trust me, this will all come together shortly. I am actually quite happy with how things are going. I wasn't sure it would be a book but once I started writing; I thought this was more important than just telling myself. The only way to tell a story is to share it. Write a letter? No. Karen's story is important. And I have the ego or the arrogance to believe I can tell it well. Hopefully, convey a relevance to more people than just me.

So, I continue with Karen. At her behest. To free myself from a nagging self-loathing and regret, to praise her and find the beauty in Karen that lives to this day, to inspire others to live in the moment and be thankful for every day we have here. To comfort some. Those who have been down this same road. Anyone who has lost a loved one. Anyone who has lost a child to murder, or a brother, a sister, a husband, a wife or a dear friend. Or just lost a dear one to whatever circumstance. You will travel your own course through all the emotions and challenges that are now your life. I offer you a hand, a hand to hold for part of this journey. Yours. Mine. Karen's. Hoping to entertain, at least a little. Inspire, perhaps. Console, if possible.

To others who may not share the same grief, you are invited to share her story simply because it deserves to be told. She was an amazing girl. Yes, admittedly, it is my story, too, which is offered as a personal history. Survival. Survivor's guilt. Shame. Love. Unspeakable sadness. Joy. Join us, if you like. I have a had a wonderful life. It has been haunted by an unfathomable sadness and I believe Karen wanted me to unburden myself. To be completely free. To live in the moment as she did. Embrace what life has given me and what has been taken away. Embrace how much fun there has been too. Always easier to embrace the tragic rather than the fond and fancy-free. In comment pages all over the world, gushes of positive response are evident and heartfelt; but, if, within a hundred kindnesses there lurks a single insult, it is the insult we take to heart. Why? Such foolishness. We have to cut that out. That person has no right to rain on our parade. They probably want to inflict some sort of pain because they are in pain themselves. It does not serve us to carry them or their "two cents worth" at all—not even worth a penny.

Wordy. I hope you like the book. I hope it helps. Simple enough.

Karen. I just realized I want to help Karen too. I am still her brother. It is in my heart to help. Karen's heart too.

Okay.

The remarkable thing about writing is I can choose wherever and whenever to go this way or that and as I write, it is as though signals are being sent directly to my fingers to type us in one direction or another. Some of these signals are my invention. Others, and I think a good many of them, are signals from somewhere else. From memory. From Karen. From the history of moments that I had forgotten but are still alive and excavated by this "dig," so to speak. Not quite fossilized, some of them, but damn close. And to find them now has been a pure delight. Well, some are painful, of course. But so many others are joys I had forgotten or had remained hidden because of trauma. They are peeking their heads out now hoping it is safe to come out into the open and shine as they once did. I did not realize how many there were.

People speak of the "inner child." I don't really know much about it except I presume we all have one and most of them are in hiding. I would say that has been true for me and probably true for Karen . . . after we were hurt by life. And nothing hurts in life more than the death of someone precious when we are children. Maybe it's like that analogy about drug abuse or smoking where it is believed that from the fist puff or the first hit, emotional growth ceases at that very moment. I am not sure about any of this but part of it rings true, and when I regressed to that day when Karen showed me the surfboard and then the "water angel" thing, I was first brought to a cave holding the hands of a boy child and a girl child. They were two Asian children who morphed into my sister and me. Described this already, I know. Yes, a Waypoint now. So you know where you are. So I know where I am too. But it occurred to me the other day, when talking with Kayte, that the boy whose hand I held, the boy who guided me with Karen, was that very boy—my inner child. Honestly, it occurred to me because Kayte asked. Was that your inner child? I thought it was possible. I had not seen him in some time. And whenever I saw a picture of him, it was always mingled with a memory of the tragedy that befell him. And his family. Just as when I look at Karen's pictures, I search the smile or eyes for some hint of the future that awaited her . . . the tragic future. Is it baked in there somewhere? I have no answer.

I got off the plane in San Diego. The Fiat was being fixed and Spencer agreed to drive it out with his girlfriend, Debby, once it was ready. Agnes picked me up at the airport. I had reached out to her before I headed back. I was happy to see her. We'd spent a nice winter together. I liked her. I never told her I loved her. I wasn't quite ready for anything close to a commitment to another person. I was good with the dog. Agnes was connected to Goose. We were good together, and that was about as good as I could get, as close to love as I could be. Back then. We would spend the night together and enjoy a morning, sometimes for weeks at a time. And then I would need a little break. It wasn't personal. I needed to be alone a lot then. Still.

There is a beautiful military graveyard on Point Loma. I would grab a crab sandwich from Point Loma Seafoods, a split of white wine or a beer and make my way past the military gates to visit a soldier there. He was born two years before me. Died in Vietnam when I was sixteen. He was eighteen. I would sit beside his gravestone and speak to him. Think about how young he was. How he had gone instead of me. A picnic with him. A couple of hours later, I would drive back home and face the day. He helped me.

I took upon myself an idea. An invitation. If it pleased him, to join me in my life. A way to honor his sacrifice. Pledging to live mine fully. Karen came. Karen and this young soldier and myself. Communing. They were taken so young. I survived. The beautiful San Diego Harbor shining below us. The stretched-out serenity of the Pacific Ocean, reflecting and refracting our time together. I felt close to him. I felt close to Karen. Keeping the company with them I could not find among the living. Prayer. Then I would gather myself. Leave behind a whispered apology. Touch his headstone. And get back to Life.

But Agnes and I shared a wonderful connection. We walked the dogs and went digging for clams. I am not sure it was legal or if the clams were any good, but they looked like little manila clams and tasted great, so the several meals we made of them were good ones. I never checked if it was a horrible environmental crime. Sorry if it was, but that bay provided several meals for us at a time when it seemed natural for the earth to provide and for the wallet to take a break. I remember her standing at the stove frying up bacon and eggs. It was a beautiful time we shared. I probably should have told her. I was as deeply "in" whatever it was, as far as I could be. I was grateful to her. I fear I never made that clear, and I wish I had. I will say no more; I wish to honor Agnes. She was terrific. Unique. I was lucky to know her.

Rehearsal began at the Old Globe Theatre. I was fitted into Norman's costume as best as could be expected. I think we were pretty much the same size. Except for the boots. They had spent a great deal of money on the boots and my feet were substantially larger so a solution that kept most of the boots was desired—in fact, insisted upon. So, Peggy, in the costume shop, chopped off the soles of the boots and had the legs sewn onto some size thirteen sneakers and then tried to match the grey suede to complete what ended up as a pretty unfortunate look. Peggy was a brilliant costume designer and I cast no aspersions about the boot solution, as money so often dictates what can and cannot be done. The result? Not good.

As the rehearsal unfolded before I was put into the show, there was an occasion that suddenly brings these last half dozen pages or so into focus. Goose was sitting in the dressing room. She always did when I was working. She would sit patiently under my spot at the make-up mirrors. When there was a break, she would greet me at the door for a hug and a paw. A great dog.

On this occasion, we were rehearsing the scene where Gertrude describes to Laertes his sister's death. His sister, Ophelia. Hamlet avenges the murder of his father but in the process murders Polonius and destroys the love his life, Ophelia...Laertes's father and sister. His life is devastated by the news of his sister's "suicide." On the heels of his father's murder.

As I rehearsed the scene and allowed myself to listen carefully to what Gertrude was saying, the way she describes the death is brimming with empathy and sympathy and imagery that tears at the heart. I began to sob. Rarely is an actor able to couple his own emotional life with the emotion of the character being played...we loan our emotions to them to authenticate their life on the stage, but it is rare that they will fully coincide. Such was the case for me when I dropped to my knees as Laertes and wept along with him as Kelsey. I saw Karen. Gertrude described Ophelia, but what Goose heard over the intercom was the soul of her man, her possession, her job, whatever best describes the love of a dog for the person who cares for them and who loves them in return, in an agony of loss and sadness. Goose heard that and ran to the theatre. The doors were open from the dressing rooms to backstage, as always. She ran up one of the aisles in the orchestra. Realized I was on stage and ran toward it. She leaped up on the stage, about four feet above her and ran to me, jumped on me and covered me in kisses and whimpers of concern in an attempt to console me. Well, it was a dramatic and beautiful expression of concern. The simplest and possibly the most honest expression of love I had ever known.

So, the statement stands: Goose was the best dog ever.

It just so happens that somewhere in that same theater on that very day was another person connected to the motorcycle. So, my creative conceit about tying events and people to the bike may actually be a credible device for introducing story and characters. That day. If it wasn't that particular day, it was a day very close to that day. It may be it was the day that Elvis died. In fact, I know it was the day Elvis died. I am not sure it was the same day Goose came to comfort me onstage. But I think it was. And as rehearsal ended, a voice came from the audience. It was Stanley. The same Stanley who pointed me toward the entrance to Juilliard a little less than four years earlier. Extraordinary. I do not remember why he was there, but I was glad to see him. It was the first day of a new friendship that had its foundation in a chance meeting years before and would grow out of another chance meeting on the other side of the country four years later. I think Christopher Reeve was in town, as well. Maybe they came together. Maybe not. But Chris and Stanley had become great friends back at Juilliard, and now I would know them both better as a result. I was glad of that. Chris was a lovely man. Stanley too. I believe I introduced him to Goose. My dog. I also believe he stated the dog was clearly my dog. And indeed, she was ... we were one another's.

And what a shame about Elvis. Forty-two years old. A talent that has not come again. Music so fully realized in his voice and performance. His career has not ended. Amazing. Just thought I should acknowledge how extraordinary a man he was and how gifted.

I will offer similar words of praise to Christopher. He was the first of us to really shine. I had known him at school. Not very well. He and Robin Williams entered two groups ahead of me as transfer students and chose to take several classes with Group Six. My bunch. Chris was always as handsome or more handsome than any man has a right to be. Robin was the funniest man of my generation. They were both terrific people. I remain honored to have known them, proud to know them. Their stories have tragic endings, as well; but my, how they did live.

Karen's life was not so full of days as theirs, but hers was the most significant to me. Obviously. It remains the most significant. Hers was the difference. Her life was and is more important to me than any other, save for those of my family, of course. My wife and children.

There is something funny that happens as we go through life. Or, at least, I find it funny. Funny might be the wrong word, actually. Ironic? Perhaps. Seminal. Perhaps. Important? Not so sure. Milestones. Moments that indicate a certain step in our lifetime. A shift. Notable in that it marks a change in how we are perceived. How we perceive ourselves. That sounds about right. It comes down to a word or phrase that we have never spoken or heard about ourselves until it is uttered. A moment that redefines who we are or recognizes who we have become.

Milestone. I am standing in line at the grocery store. I am sixteen. A young mother and her son are behind me in line. I am not sure how it came about but the little boy looked at me and said something about "that man" indicating me. Well, it was the first time anyone had ever called me that, and it landed. My apprehension about myself shifted in that instant. It would never be the same. I was a man.

The same thing happened when my first child was born. Suddenly, I was a "father" who had a "daughter." Two words I had never spoken in connection with myself. Two words that now would forever be different coming from me. When I had my first son, Jude, I said the word with a deeper knowledge and experience than the moment before he was born. When I held him in my arms as a baby, he was my "boy" and

I was a "dad" with a new-born "son." They were always words that had meaning but until now they were not experiences. They are words that grow in depth and resonance as they are experienced. So, when I speak of my family. The family I generated, that I fathered, it is an extraordinary feeling and knowledge. My wife. My children. Words that now embody living people, life experience; and their value grows with every experience as life digs its clay-shaping fingers in and works us.

My sister. Sister is a word that was always attached to a living experience, not a speculation. There is no time I consciously remember that I did not have a sister and so my use of the word was always connected to Karen. She was my only sister and so any subsequent use of the word has only one member to be remembered. Karen, my sister. Still is. Always will be.

There are a few directions we can go right now, so I am a little stuck as to which is the most desirable. I also feel like it's time for a bit of a laugh. Why not enjoy one at my expense? Not the first or the last, certainly.

The boots I mentioned wearing for Laertes in *Hamlet*. Not good. As aforementioned. There was an organic demonstration of this on my first performance. Also, a bit of a lesson about actor loyalty or you might say "actor on actor" crime. I exaggerate for effect.

To the heart of the matter. At one point during *Hamlet*, Laertes returns to avenge his father's death and is leading an uprising that declares with "caps, hands and tongues . . . Laertes shall be king!" Thus, setting the scene for Laertes's entrance. He charges in with quite a head of steam, or at least I did; and he demands of King Claudius, dripping with contempt, "Where is this king?"

Peggy had designed a brilliant set, a flight of stairs at top center stage. Seven steps, if I remember rightly. They had an exaggerated rise and a very narrow set of treads so that the steps were hazardous in the best case. Wearing a pair of refitted suede boots with size thirteen sneakers was a deadly combination for an adrenaline filled twenty-two-year-old actor in his first appearance as a major character in one of the greatest plays ever written. So, as I bellowed down the stairs, I hit the third step of seven, lost my footing, fell spectacularly on my butt and slid down the remaining four. I jumped up in an instant standing red-faced and embarrassed dead-center upstage, hoping I could retrieve some dignity.

It was not to be. Gertrude and Claudius turned to face me, choking back laughter, the only sign of their amusement an irregular, almost imperceptible shaking of their shoulders up and down. Tears streaming down both their faces, Claudius finally managed to speak in a kind of broken guffaw, "What is the cause, Laertes, that thy rebellion look so giant-like?" I learned in that moment that if there was any help to be had onstage after a terrible accident, it was not from my fellow actors. They would be a puddle of dissolved uselessness.

The very same lesson was blindingly clear only one year later. We were performing *The Winter's Tale.* I and a dozen other actors were dancing a forest ritual of marriage between Prince Florizel and the beautiful maiden, Perdita. Perdita is in a spell, asleep until her Prince awakes her and lifts her into his arms. Simple enough. I knelt down, cradled the beautiful Debby in my arms, and as I hoisted up to a standing position . . . I farted. A loud blast that echoed throughout the theatre. And as I looked into the eyes of my fellow thespians, I realized they were teetering on the verge of turning upstage and dissolving. A second later, the telltale shoulder shake was evident and irresistible as I turned upstage myself and shook for a time . . . lost in the hilarity of it. Debby, too, was shaking along with the rest of us as I held her in my arms. The audience itself began to chuckle in universal recognition of something that was clearly not meant to happen. A minute or so later we all calmed down after sharing a communal collapse of the fourth wall. It was cathartic as all theatre is meant to be . . . so they and we had shared a hearty laugh. At my expense. You see? It was okay with me. It remains one of my favorite stories. And it always reminds me the simplest things are often the funniest. In fact, from cradle to the grave, there is almost nothing that so reliably makes us laugh as that simple bodily anomaly.

I've jumped ahead. To remember something that makes me smile. A giggle. Easy enough to jump back. The whole book is leading me in jumps from one time to the next and back again. So, without apology, back in time to the second year at Pine Crest School.

Our second year, Karen's and mine, after our first summer without Gordon—the summer we did the boating safety course, the year we enjoyed so much time together on the water. That second year, we entered school as seventh and eighth graders. Karen ended up with some of my teachers, and I moved on to another raft of educators, some good, some not. It was then, I think I mentioned, when Karen and I started to align along our different paths and drifted apart . . . just a bit. But she with her circle of friends, and I with mine. This delineation would identify us as Karen and Kelsey, brother and sister, but separate and seeking our unique places in the world as newly minted individuals with individual skills and interests, friends unique to each of us, some of whom crossed over from time to time.

We shared a few on occasion. Karen and Momo, always. Gillian, Jan, Betsy, Ronnie, Brian, Spencer and Bob. These we shared to some extent. Ronnie had an older brother. He had an amazing stereo. That stereo was the source of an indelible memory for me. The first time I heard such sound! He poised the needle over the first track of a brand-new album, gently lowered the stylus with the little lever that was part of the mystery and magic, and then I heard . . . lyrics to "California Dreamin'" by The Mamas & The Papas. An amazing song, an amazing sound. You probably know it by heart but it was the first time we had heard The Mamas & The Papas. Craig was his name, and there was Jeff, too, his older brothers. It still surprises me how the memories, once begun, fall into place with increasing detail. And come alive. Remembered. It is nice to see all these faces again. These moments too.

It was at Ronnie's house one weekend that I got drunk for the very first time. Not a good experience, honestly, but a rite of passage, I suppose. Coca-Cola took on a whole new significance in the early morning hours, as I sought to ease my first hangover ever. Later that year, I would become a surfer, adding John, Dave, and Brett to my circle. Karen never seemed very interested in the surfing scene. Not much crossover there.

Dave and John went to our school; Brett lived across the street. Brett was the owner of the fat-tired, ill-fated Cougar that would play its part a couple years later. Great guy. We double-dated a couple of times. He had a few girls he dated and at that time, I was seeing a girl, Pam, who went to Cardinal Gibbons, a school nearby. Never forgot her either. She was a lovely young woman. Pam McM . . . the third Pam. The first girl I kissed on the beach. I remember a night we almost did more, but I was woefully inept and inexperienced. I was afraid. I also never wanted to do anything inappropriate. I probably needed Pam to help me a bit, but it was not to be.

Karen was off with her crowd at that time and doing lots of the same things. Probably, a bit further along than I was with the whole dating/intimacy thing. We all get there in the end, but you remember Karen was far more mature than I in many ways, though I still had a corner on the conventional wisdom brothers are supposed to command. Not so good with girls but pretty good with my sister. There it is again—my sister. Familiar territory.

Our lives unfolded along these separate and not quite parallel paths. There were many times they coincided and many that did not. They were wonderful years, nonetheless. For both of us. Karen needed wheels to get from one place to another, so she, by definition, spent time around older boys—boys who could drive. Brian was a year ahead of me at school . . . a pal of mine but he became friends with Karen too. This is part conjecture now but there was a night that Karen and Brian, with a few other friends went out. I know little more than that. I was at home in my room. One of the great features about my room was that it had its own door in and out of the house. Probably something I should have taken greater advantage of, but I got away with plenty. No regrets except maybe that night with Pam McM. I never really saw her again after that.

On this particular evening, I had stayed home. I would meditate at night after dinner; there was a combined yoga/weight workout that I devised that ended with half an hour of meditation. It was a good time in my life. I think there is more coming up ahead on that subject. Haven't quite decided what, but for the purposes of this tale, it is not necessary to say anything more. I was meditating. At that time. Lights were out, I was ready for bed. I heard a car pull into our driveway. Some shuffling and chatter, doors opening and closing and then a screech of tires and the sound of a car hurtling down the road at a bank-job's pace. An escape. A getaway car. The muffled voices moments before were mixed with panic and juvenile laughter, there was a thud and a couple of, oh shits!—then, "I hope she'll be all right." "She'll be all right." A car door slammed. The clandestine drop complete, they sped off into the night.

I opened my door. There on the lawn just off the driveway was Karen. She had been dumped there unceremoniously after drinking too much that evening. Karen lay motionless for a time as I stood above her. Fine but not so chipper, let's say. The only word she could manage after I asked what was up, was, "Tequilaaaa!" I started to pick her up, and she told me she would rather just stay where she was. I promised her that was not the best idea and carried her into the house through my door. "Tequila, huh?"

I got her into the shower and helped her into bed. Went to the kitchen. Instructed her to drink the whole glass of water I'd brought. It would help her clear the stuff through the night as she slept. "You'll live. Now get some sleep." She thanked me and slipped back into her coma. Tequila. I think they kissed and made up a few years later, as I remember a margarita she made me at her apartment that last Christmas in '74. She was a fun girl who had her share of fun. I am happy for that.

Brian's dad was a liquor distributor and a dinner with his family one night comes to mind. I liked his dad. It may have been just the four of us ... Brian, his mom and dad, and me. I am thinking there may have been a brother. Not sure. The question came up: how would one define a chair? We thought for a while and then Brian's dad said, "A repository for a posterior."

Good answer. My ever-expanding mind expanded just a bit more that day. There are a lot of people out there who might be smarter than I. I never make assumptions about the intelligence of a stranger ... in fact, I assume that they are likely the repository of many an idea and insight I have never gleaned. I look to all for the possible wisdom of the ages, and it was Brian's dad who helped me choose that course.

I am thinking of Danny Eng right now. You remember Danny. Karen's boyfriend. My friend. My mother's friend. It was the summer of 1971. Karen had taken a job with Momo's family at the hotel in Cashiers, North Carolina. She was waiting tables. Danny and I decided to drive up for a visit.

When we left for the mountains, Karen was Danny's girlfriend; when we came back, that wasn't true anymore. Something or someone had happened during her summer up there and when Danny and I arrived, it wasn't very long before a long walk and an explanation that she was moving on in life. I do not remember where we slept or even if we slept but I do remember a fantastic breakfast at a little café in Cashiers that may have been the best breakfast I ever had. It included grits...a southern dish. Grits remain one of my absolute favorites. Not sure why grits are not a national food enjoyed all over the United States. But I do have a theory. And you knew I did, didn't you? I suspect it is a sort of long-held political stupidity about the South. My two cents. Grits! Good food.

Good food should always rise above politics. There is no greater uniter than a terrific meal. Where palates can concur as politics remain starkly at odds. Hopefully, enough kindnesses and a few more meals and some of those walls might come tumbling down. We are not so far apart, you know. Not so far apart as the powerful would have us believe. Dish out a bit more food and a lot less fear and the differences between us seem very small indeed. America is a great place. A nation dedicated to the people. We the people. That's us, by the way. You and me. I would like to invite everyone over for a nice bowl of grits and the beverage of your choice. From a Bloody Mary to a Bloody Bull, from a Mint Julep to a New England Hazy IPA. Let's celebrate our lives together. Let's salute our differences and embrace our likenesses. We truly are one people. Okay, I love America. That may offend you. No offense meant.

Karen's page in her yearbook. It surprised me but I don't know why. Under the heading "H. I." she listed, "Friends, Cooking, Giving Shotguns, Freedom..." The magnificent Karen! Was I completely in line with Karen's interests? Well, shotguns were not and do not carry great interest for me but Freedom—that is the ticket. And so, when I wave the flag a bit, it might be something Karen would support. I don't want to speak for her. I think she would. I was surprised she listed Freedom. And then, I wasn't surprised. We were raised by people who loved this country. Gam, Gordon, and Mom loved this country. And they loved Freedom. They lived the fight for Freedom that gave us the Freedom to even hate this country if we choose. Remarkable.

I am not sure what "H. I." stood for, so I have to find out. Watch carefully as I may insert it somewhere close by or way down the road. In the heat of writing, as things come up, they take precedence and then when the subject exhausts itself or exhausts me, I circle back or forge ahead to discover and share what begs attention in that moment. Moment to moment. I have dreamed parts of this book. I have lived parts. Imagined parts. Above all, Karen. Each have been the journey—life, dreams, imagination. Tools—remembrance and honesty. A picture of Karen. A written memorial. A kiss of the hand to her. Wonderful girl. Majestic woman. Sister. I see you.

Freedom. Since I am in charge here and hopefully in sync with Karen, I wanted to explain the lack of a timeline. I have touched on it, I know. This is as much for my benefit as your investment. Time. If this assignment has done anything it has focused me on the illusion of time. In the last paragraph—"I don't want to speak for her." Well, that was true in context. In the larger context, this is a false statement. In the larger context, I am speaking for her.

"YOU ARE!"

And then; softly, gently, almost approvingly: *"You are . . ."*

Boy, do I hope so. Doubt comes by to ruffle the sheets. There are several blanks. Many days after the time we split off into two concentric circles of friends: Karen's and mine. With overlaps. Gillian and I, Bob and Karen, spent a wonderful weekend together at the house in Pompano Beach. There is an inscription from Gillian to Karen on her page in the yearbook. It is a beautiful, heartfelt statement about how she wouldn't know what to do without her. A year later, we would all have to figure that out.

Bob and I were best friends for a couple of years during high school and a year or so afterward. Bob told me a story once about how strong his dad was. Assuming Bob was pretty much the size as he was when I knew him. As when he told me. He started choking on a piece of food and his dad grabbed him by the ankles, hoisted him in the air, and shook him till the food came out of his mouth. I know this is all a bit odd to remember but I know this is exactly what he said. He was almost six feet tall when we were friends. Weighed somewhere in the neighborhood of 140 pounds.

Clarity. Not clear enough. So, Bob's story was told me close on the heels of the actual event and we both marveled that his dad, who was tall but not particularly muscular or beefy, would have the strength to toss his son about like a doll. At that time, I think his mom and dad were going through divorce, as well. Bob had lived in Caracas as a boy, and I think his dad was a writer. His mom and dad were both very bright people; his mom worked for a well-known nonprofit organization. But it was the first Christmas of our friendship when Bob described his dad dropping off presents for him and his sister, Marian. And his dad cried. I never saw his dad again. I am not sure Bob did either. We made some marvelous memories during our friendship. I will cover some of them in the pages to come.

I spent a couple of days away from writing and spent some time on business.

A conversation with Kayte just now reminded me of Shakespeare. So, a new course.

"Oh, God, I could be bounded in a nutshell and count myself a king of infinite space." *Hamlet.* More books have been written about Hamlet than Jesus Christ. My English teacher told me that forty-odd years ago. It was true then, I think. It is more likely true now, as faith in Jesus has been tirelessly attacked throughout the last decades. This was the same English teacher, in fact, who asked me to join a production of *The Little Foxes* in my junior year at high school. The same teacher who asked if I was in love with Liz. The same teacher who exploded in laughter when I told him our cat's name was Nanci with an "i." The same teacher who was actually a devout Christian who had the simplest, one-word rebuttal to a famous Robert Browning poem entitled "Porphyria's Lover." The poem describes Porphyria and her illicit affair, observed by her husband. The subject sports long braided tresses and they are obviously the source of much desire and attention. Her lover takes her under the watchful jealousy of her husband until he departs. At that point, the husband confronts her and then strangles Porphyria with those very braids. The last line of the poem: "And yet God has not said a word!" I quoted this to Ron, my English teacher. That English teacher. Clearly, he was a substantial figure in my life. It was a parking lot conversation. I quoted the twisted poetry and its final line as we walked to the car. He listened respectfully. "And God has not said one word." A moment. Ron took a moment. I opened my car door and he looked at me. Then, he said—"Yet!"

Which leads to another recollection of the brilliant writing of W. H. Auden: "Perhaps by the time death pounces his stumping question, I shall just be getting to know the difference between daylight and moonlight."

And suddenly, this brace of recollections connects to my friend, Simon Gray. Simon Gray was a terrific playwright. An Englishman. He wrote a series of plays, most famously, *Butley*. Alan Bates created the role on stage and also played it in the film. *Otherwise Engaged* received great acclaim.

I met him auditioning for his play, *Quartermaine's Terms*. The play was about a group of teachers and their room at a school. Their lives turned and angled through the rise and fall of their home lives and academic careers. Quartermaine was a lingering, somewhat doddering permanent fixture of the teachers' lounge, a tenured professor, who witnessed the drama of his colleagues and rendered advice. Some good. But mostly not. And the play ends with a death. It was a wonderful play. Slice of life and a look into the tortured aspirations of a young teacher who fancied himself a writer...that was my part. I think it may have been Simon's part. Simon's autobiographical character.

We first met at the audition. Simon, a tall specimen, bright green, exceedingly English sweater, or jumper, as they like to call it. Grizzled but handsome. Wonderful light in the eyes. I read a scene with him and then we talked a bit. He asked me. Well, he asked me something I had never been asked in an audition. He asked if I was a writer. Or rather, if I wrote. Do you write? I answered, "A little." Simon had a wonderful, laconic delivery in almost everything he said. I am still convinced he was the greatest living playwright I ever knew. Very funny and always at the ready to construct an ironic phrase or two, whether a ribald counterpoint or a serious vanity or an incisive observation based on the unfolding foolishness of a popular social movement. He got things and liked to harpoon them; a mission of protecting us all from too much seriousness, perhaps. I did love him.

So, after I answered that my writing was sparse and a bit tortured, he asked who my favorite writer was. I told him. After Shakespeare, and quite possibly on par with Shakespeare, my favorite writer is Auden. He looked at me and with a kind of sympathetic nod of the head he commiserated that it was quite impossible to write if that was the circumstance. If I was striving to be on the elevated plane of Auden, the odds were very thin indeed that I would enjoy anything but frustration and torture. Just wanting to be a writer? Frustration and Torture! To aim for Auden? Impossible. It was a lovely conversation. I think he told me I had the job.

Now, I had been told that before but did not get the job. Simon was different. He kept his word. I wouldn't see him for the next couple of months. We began rehearsal in New Haven at the Long Wharf Theatre. The very prestigious Long Wharf Theater. The director, Ken F., was a fairly successful director at the time and was married to a very success-ful casting director. A power couple. Donna I. and Ken F. I liked them both. I don't think Donna ever hired me. Ah, well. No respect in your own backyard and all that. Jesus knew. No love in Nazareth. Probably where the whole expression got its start. Most expressions or sayings in English stem from the Bible or from Shakespeare. I'm just saying it without having to prove it because I know it's true. You can ponder it if you like; disprove it if you wish. The effort itself is likely to prove it. That happens a lot too.

But Donna never hired me. Ken had a gentle style as a director . . . always a nice thing to have a gentle director. For my money, very few directors do anything but set their actors on a collision course with the language of the play. If they have talented actors, they just hold on for dear life and watch the play come alive in ways they had never imagined. The bad directors are the ones who try to stop them. The good directors get out of the way and enjoy the results. Once in a very great while, a really good director can manage a little of both. Still not sure I have ever met one. Correction—I have: Jimmy Burrows.

I am a director. I like to think a good one, but I may be delusional. A good actor, however, is the greatest guide into the mind of character and the life of language. It is their gift. Their instincts are tuned to the human experience like no other. I love to watch good actors. And the really good ones make it look like they are doing nothing at all. Probably why there are so many bad ones. The good ones make it look so easy, so effortless, the foolish think anyone can do it. They can't. End of dissertation.

Ken and I had a lovely chat one evening. He was giving me some notes on my performance as Mark Sackling. We were on the verge of our first preview, and I was a bit frustrated about the tone of his notes.

I finally asked, "Ken, do you think the scene should be funny? Or not funny?"

Well, he thought and thought. Awkwardly long ponder. Then, "Funny, I think," said Ken. "Funny I can do," I told him. That was that. It was a funny scene. So funny, in fact, that when Simon was in the audience, I had to ask him not to laugh before the punch line. We became friends—Simon, Ken and I, Donna, too, and the rest of the cast. It was a wonderful experience. The show moved to an off-Broadway house and won the Obie award that year for best play. I was very proud of it. Sadly, I saw Donna a few years later and she told me Ken had died. I don't know how or why. It seemed too soon. I thought he had more to do. I liked him. Sometime later, Simon died. He was mourned and celebrated by the London community. I couldn't go. I was sorry I missed it. I miss him.

And!—I missed the turn. The road was laid out before me, and I missed the turn!

Back on track. Once again, a certain alleyway compelled me down an unintended path, but here we are. Back again where I mean to be.

Simon came to rehearsal one night in New Haven. He had flown in from London. It is late. Earlier, we had suffered a mostly silent ride on the train to Connecticut. He tried a single malt on the way up. Maybe more than a try. Glenlivet. My suggestion. Another round or two on the return trip. And a famous actress riding home with us that evening. A few words exchanged with her. She politely dismissed us with an almost pouty longing for a little shut-eye. A mutual sentiment that she was as beautiful in person as we imagined, Simon and I sat in hushed tones across the aisle as the lovely Miss "S" slipped off to sleep. That is as much indication of her identity I will allow. She was lovely. Completely disinterested. Neither of us were the type to command her attention at the time . . . an unknown actor and a London playwright. Politely and not actually scornful . . . just delightfully unimpressed. She would not remember. I ran into her years later . . . not a glimmer of recognition. Equally unimpressed.

Simon sat across from me. Quite alert now. During the run-through earlier, he had fallen asleep. High praise indeed for our performance. A stupor—he'd been in a stupor! And regained consciousness just as we ended the play. None of us certain how or what to think. Jet lag. That was it. I didn't mention the Glenlivet. But now, sitting across from me. Scotch in hand. Simon was quite perky. The nearness of our famous siren, perhaps. Out cold now. The siren. Out cold. I asked him if he typically passed out while watching his plays. He confessed many drinks along the way, the flight itself, probably put consciousness out of reach for him. But after a two-hour nap in a dark theatre, muffled voices lulling him to sleep, he was right as rain! I mean no disrespect to Simon. He was one of the brightest men I ever knew. I think he would get a kick out of what I have said about him . . . and this.

I also just realized what a cool word "lulling" is. The "L" in all its greatest glory. What is that? Assonance. Onomatopoeia? Who knows, doesn't matter. When a letter sounds like what it sounds like to experience something, it is a really cool sound. So, "lull." Beautiful!

This—to pick up again where I left off. This came up upon a query from Simon. Amid several casual exchanges, across the aisle from our princess, Simon asked me, "Who is your favorite actor?" I thought it was a trick question. After all, he was English, and the English love to invite Americans into an honest moment to be ridiculed instantly because we are frank and innocent, while the English are calculating and caustic. And so, after several moments of wondering if I was being lured into a trap, I finally confessed that I thought John Wayne was a good actor.

I said so. I waited for the noose to tighten. The guillotine to drop. The hatchet to chop me into pieces. Simon was silent. He nodded up and down. He turned his head from side to side. "John Wayne was not a good actor," said Simon. "He was a *great* actor!" Wow! Blindsided by a brilliant Brit. What I had assumed was the body language of dismissal and disgust was actually feigned contempt . . . these were nods and gestures of approbation and agreement. We spent the next hour or so celebrating the performances of John Wayne in almost all of his films. I will spare you the bibliographical nature of our discussion, but several highlights from his most famous films were mimicked and quoted with shared joy. We were fans. We exchanged impressions of our favorite moments. I was better than Simon. You have to trust me on this, but he did a pretty good, "That'll be the day," from *The Searchers*. Not bad. I was in bliss. John Wayne had been my favorite actor since I could remember. He still is. "Put an amen to it, Preacher!" Another of my favorites from *The Searchers*. And "Think back, Pilgrim," from *The Man Who Shot Liberty Valence*. Amazing performances that were at the top of his catalog. But the man, the actor John Wayne, was the most commanding presence in the film world of his time. He remains a commanding presence throughout all film. For all time. My two cents. Simon would agree.

Ironside. Not the battleship. The show. Okay, I am foolish to think anyone would mistake Ironside for *Old Ironsides*, the famous ship; but *Ironside* was a show starring Raymond Burr. The music for it was amazing—Quincy Jones wrote the theme song. Brilliant. As is Quincy Jones. Perhaps, I am foolish to think anyone would remember the show at all. *Ironside*. It was a great show, however. And those who care may actually try to find it. For reference. Assuming you are still with me in this most excellent adventure. Please, do not consider me flippant in this; I am inviting you to a recollection or revelation that may be delightful to you as it is to me. I know it is delightful to my sister. You can catch up if you choose. The internet is marvelous and full of content. Check if you like. Trust me, if you will. I do not lie.

Assuming we are on the same page, there was one episode of *Ironside* that struck me to the core. It is odd that I am relating this to you. It would normally be something no one would remember or even note. At the time. But I did. I was sixteen, maybe seventeen. Well before Karen was killed. I did not remember it until just a few moments ago. Mark was a character in the show. He was Ironside's driver. Please, bear with me as I go through this series of recollections. I realize a TV show from the 1970s is not the normal source for a relevant remembrance of a life taken too soon. As Karen's was. But it is. Anyway, Mark's girlfriend is killed on the show. The police officers Ed and Eve, regulars on the show, tell Ironside to ask Mark to back off and let them do their job. Ironside, also called "Chief," says it is a tough call to ask anyone who loses a loved one that way to back off at all. He says if he lost someone the way Mark did, he would beat down the walls of City Hall until there was an answer. I don't know why it stayed with me. And the quotation is probably not accurate, but the sentiment is. Raymond Burr's performance in the show was always spot-on. And this particular show gripped me as few have, before or since.

I guess I feel there was a blank spot in my reaction to Karen's death. A feeling unearthed by this memory. I let us all down. I didn't tear the town apart until a suspect was arrested. I quietly raged inside myself and let the police do their job. I wanted to do more for Karen. Too late. That show sticks in my head. Funny... it aired maybe three years before Karen died. Before so much went wrong. The police did do their job and I tore plenty of things apart, but mostly myself and the girl who loved me. I know. Spilt milk now. And though there is no use crying over it, I cry just the same. And I have purged so much . . . but, it still pops up. I said it might.

A lateral move now. That same show—*Ironside*. Another episode. Same series. There was a great character on it. A guest actor. The character was that of a Chinese detective posted with the San Francisco police department. He and Ironside squared off as two civil servants from completely different governments, cultures. Ironside, the classic American tough guy with a heart; and the Chinese detective, equally devoted to his job and his country. It made great storytelling, and the character appeared several more times. It was very popular. The whole notion of the two cultures getting along was very appealing. And the show was very well done. My purpose. The actor who played that Chinese detective was a man named Dr. Keigh Dee. It came from him. A lesson I would never forget.

Here is how it happened. My old high school, Pine Crest Preparatory School, had a series of guest lecturers. Dr. Keigh Dee was one of them. L. Ron Hubbard had also been one, who discussed his recent book, *Dianetics*. Columnist and author of *Catch-22*, Joseph Heller, read excerpts of his book to us one morning. It really was an amazing school. The author of *I'm OK, You're OK*. Alan Watts? Was that his name? Nope. That was Thomas Anthony Harris. Alan Watts wrote *The Way of Zen*. He came, too. In fact, they both came. Very popular at the time.

Dr. Keigh Dee was in good company. And he brought a very good message. At least for me. It is simple enough. Basically, the "be patient" lesson. But his had a specific twist about expectation and outcomes. He discussed looking for a parking space in New York City. None available. His answer: drive around the block. Take your time. More often than not, you will find a spot has opened up for you . . . possibly a perfect spot. More likely than not—a perfect spot. If there is a long line at the bank. Rather than worry for the duration of the wait, breathe. And just be. Perhaps, you may gaze at the carpet for a moment. A vision of horsemen riding across a plain. Or the sound of the rainforest. Any number of things might capture your imagination and make the time well spent. Places you might never see. You will see.

The world is a marvelous place. This Life. Its dimensions stand poised to flood an open mind with any number of marvelous things. Filled, as it is, with many mansions. As the Sacrificed told us. This was his message. I have added the Christian resonance. It emanates from my own faith.

Dr. Dee's lecture dealt with his Buddhist faith, but it was striking how many of his observations were in alignment with my own. Goodness reaps goodness; kindness harvests kindness. Always see God's perfect child. His thoughts and words confirmed many of the teachings I had learned in Christian Science. He was not actually Chinese but Japanese, I think. Buddhism was a tradition for him. Christianity, a tradition for me. It was lovely to learn how much common ground there was. And it is lovely to carry him still. And ironic to think that he had no knowledge of the impact he made on a young American boy sitting in an auditorium that particular day. But wasn't that the point? Not to know. To trust that these lessons are their own reward and we are their mouthpiece at best. Hopefully, the good lessons do pass from generation to generation and will continue to do so for a long time to come. A sudden recollection! It was he who asked as he began to speak: "What does *auditorium* mean?" He explained it is a Greek word for a place where people go to hear the bull! Thank you, Doctor.

And I would like to spend another moment on this idea of passing along the gifts we get. A father naturally wants to pass his children and his family the things of his making and his experience, but there is a vast body of knowledge and goodness we take from perfect strangers. It demands to be passed along as well. I have known kindnesses from people I do not know, nor will ever know, save for a brief encounter. I cannot repay them.

I do not mean to be so grand as to say that the Universe and I are in a dance with one and all we meet...but I do mean to say it. We are. We are one. And the goodness I receive at the hands of a stranger is not meant to be repaid to him or her, shekel for shekel. It is meant, and I think demands, to be repaid to someone else or another stranger in kind. It is a covenant of sorts between the giver and receiver that each will become the other in another instance. Clear? I am not speaking about Karma but about common decency. If we want to talk about Karma, I guess it can be said, it may be a bit of a two-way street. And maybe it is a lonely street. I am certain now that Bob, who brought so much misery to my family and to Karen, may not have been an instrument of Karma but a miserable agent of dismay and sadness, his own profound sadness, that challenged us and rocked our family. In fairness, it was rocky enough without him and perhaps his entry into our world was the Universe's way of pushing us to seek happiness elsewhere. Gordon's love had held our family together as long as it could. His will had kept us together. And protected us. That was done.

So, Karen left home. Possibly because of Bob. I left home knowing it was time. Even my mother left home briefly. And then, of course, a criminal band of shadows took her life.

I wonder what the lesson is. I am writing, trying to find out, instructed that Karen's life is not to be remembered as tragic but as light and full of joy. Yes, a conscious waypoint here. Repeating, reclaiming the lesson. We did have such joy together. It has been heartening to feel it so close and fresh as in the days of our childhood. But it is painful still to think of her death and her unkind ending. It is the kindness and the love we knew that I am meant to remember. Brief, yes; yet so vibrant and vivacious. That is what lives. Karen lives.

And I am half-hearted. I am half-hearted in this. In this moment. I am missing her. Right now, the pep talk falling flat. Instead, I am seething with anger.

Still. Still!

My memory of Karen is always bright and brimming with love, but just scratch the surface, and devastation overflows. Is it impossible? Is it impossible to learn the joy we had, however brief, was enough? Is it impossible to hold her in my heart with no trace of the tragedy? I must try; I must not fail. If I fail in this, I do just kill her again and again. Myself.

I am not going to do that. This is just a single step back after so many forward. I remember you, Karen. I do. You stand beside me shining, smiling. I feel you there and I see you there. I am only sad that you had to suffer so and miss the Joy that might have been.

"I didn't miss you. You did!"

That may be so. No event in my lifetime since Karen's death has gone untouched by some measure of grief. Filtered. Every joy filtered by a touch of grief. Yes. Always a little tarnished. By guilt—survivor's guilt? Perhaps.

To let it fill me fully; I am in darkness. Alone. Karen is nearby now but this I must do on my own. Shine a light on Shadow. Give it Love.

But I am not alone. I am surrounded. Immersed in lives I have known. Other lives. Lives past. Other lives here on my behalf. Hands. Hearts. Voices.

"Kelsey, the sadness and grief you have held for decades is human. You need not apologize for it. It is hard to let it go. You have carried so much pain. So brave to strive in a sea of agony . . . to continue through the grim, aching days, when your self-loathing almost killed you. It almost did. And, finally, you know it is time to let it go. We know it's been hard. Let it be."

Truth.

Many voices speaking. Many. The boy on the dock was wrong. I was wrong. I'm not alone, not on my own . . . I feel them. I hear them. In the wee morning hours. In my living room. They are here. Those who guard me and guide me. Who keep me company. They comfort me. Karen too, perhaps, but I do not hear her. I hear many others.

"The happiness is the Truth. The happiness is forever. The tragedy just a bookmark, a single page in Karen's life—a life full of days . . . in a life well lived."

Shadow yields to light. I thank you. Thank you for being here. All of you. My mom among them. Her voice. Her love. I will speak of Mom soon.

Karen is standing on a chair. She is four years old, I think. She is reaching into the candy jar. Her picture snapped in the act! Gam had many a laugh at that photo. It was Karen's way. A taste for candy. She would reach out and take it. She never really changed.

There is a full moon. There is also a bright light from a nearby hotel that lights up the beach. This is important, as the light interrupted a natural rhythm that night. But that light made it important for Bob and me to be there.

It was after dinner. Bob's mom had made us a pretty dangerous chili. And we decided it was fitting to chase the meal with a bit of boosted booze from the family liquor closet. A swig of scotch. Just a nip. We sat on the beach. The moon came up. We nursed the alcohol with great caution. It didn't really taste good but there was something about it that was nice. Warming. It made sense that people enjoyed it. Even if we hadn't really acquired a fondness for it, yet . . . we certainly would in time. We sat in the sand watching the moon climb higher in the sky.

Okay . . . a quick sidebar. I just went to dinner with Kayte and the kids. It occurred to me that the message that came with a thousand voices, could also be barked in a single word or two, a phrase or two, and be equally convincing and righteous: "Knock it off!" "Enough already!" "Drop it!" "Snap out of it!"

Likelier to be persuaded by the more loving tone and words but these brutish entreaties have merit. It's more like being shaken to within an inch of one's life, and bellowed at, but there is surely merit that way, too. Sometimes a person just loses patience. As I have said. And Karen has said. And many others have now added: let it be. Or, "Let It Be!"

Another sip of scotch with Bob on the beach, and suddenly my stomach started to rumble a fearsome rumble; a slight turn of the head and the chili from hell with a peaty finish launched from my body. The combination too toxic for my adolescent constitution to stave off. An expulsion swift and violent. And then, I was just fine. So, Bob and I artfully kicked some sand over my embarrassment. And moved twenty or thirty feet away.

It was just moments later when we saw the beach come alive. A turtle's nest had hatched. A few at first, and then dozens were popping through the sand and making their way toward their new life. Only, the brightest object on the beach that night was that light I mentioned earlier. The little babies were beelining toward it and that way was nothing but desolation and a parking lot. No life. Certain death, instead. We decided we would have to intervene. Handful after handful were gathered and dipped into the ocean. The warm Atlantic Ocean, placid and glasslike that night. It was magnificent. Almost like being immersed in the essence of life itself. And these fledgling charges of ours were meant to be our rescue as well. A couple of aimless teenagers were suddenly enlisted by Life to lend a hand and live in purpose!

The certainty with which the baby turtles marched toward that light was disturbing. The moon did its best to put on a show, but that light was like a magnet to our little ones. Our intercession was of the essence. Had we not been there; scorched by the sun, our span of beach might have been a killing field of baby turtles, a feast for the seagulls by midmorning. A sad sight. Instead, we did not miss a single one. Each was transported to their future, courtesy of our enthusiasm and joy and our human hands. As the night wore on, I think there must have been at least a hundred of them that were shoveled into the lapping waves. And they went on their way. A good night's work. I eased my final handful into the sea and as I did, I looked down for a moment. I saw the most wonderful sight: A little baby turtle surfaced just below me, took a tiny breath and swam back beneath the water. A night to be remembered indeed.

In 1969, Bob and I watched the first steps on the moon. The Moon Landing! Ah, yes, the Moon Landing. Another night to be remembered. I know. If it really happened. I am not going to spend too much time on this. We believed it at the time. Is it possible for the government to stage an elaborate hoax? I would say yes. We have certainly seen a fair share of hoaxes and government deceptions throughout the years. Conspiracy theories that may actually be conspiracies. Not theory. I will not dwell on that either.

Back at that night, watching the moon landing, takes me further back to a similar night. Karen and I watched on a little black-and-white TV the mounting crisis when Russia sent nuclear missiles to Cuba. We sat on Karen's side of our bedroom wing. We each had a room on the second floor, each with a closet, about the same size, though I believe there were two single beds on my side and one in Karen's room. We often slept in the same bed in my room, under the window—the window that was open that Christmas Eve when the snow fell and the reindeer hooves were heard just above us.

To this day, in our upstate home, I like to sleep beneath the window and feel the cool air of winter chill my head as I remain toasty beneath an abundance of covers. It reminds me of the childhood nights when I shared a bed with Karen. There was always magic in the air. I feel that magic again. Whenever I sleep there. I still miss her. Of course, if she were alive, we probably would not be sharing a bed. So, I suppose I'd miss her anyway, wouldn't I? But that night, as the world seemed poised to launch itself toward oblivion, Karen asked me what it meant. It could mean the end of the world, I explained. We were both rapt in the eerie glow from the TV, perched on her little rocking chair and plugged into the wall beneath her desk. It is a lonely image of two youngsters comforting each other in a world where the adults had gone mad. We were close. We were always close. An image that has repeated itself throughout time. A sister and a brother clinging to each other, closer than any two can be.

And into our circle, we invited friends to join us. Karen and Bob were close too. That night with Gillian and the three of us, Bob and Karen became lovers. I never thought more about it until a while back when her old friend, Jan, sent me a picture of them together sitting on the grass. Somewhere. Somewhere in time in a place I did not recognize, and I thought then about how we had our separate lives while sharing an inseparable bond. I guess that bond is still there even though we are separated by such a gulf. Perhaps, no gulf at all. Just a veil. And it takes me back to the idea that Karen has not missed a thing. We are still connected so that every triumph, every joy I have known, Karen has known. It was only my sadness that kept it from me. Karen's joy was fulsome and rapturous. Mine filtered by guilt and doubt and all the other arrows of existence on this side of Life. She is excited, Esther told me. Excited to live again. I am excited at the thought of seeing her again. Whatever that may mean. It is a funny construct. I stumble with this stuff. My last discussion with Esther. I can rewrite my contract. Top on the list: I will recognize and relish every Joy without bound. I will celebrate Life as the sumptuous, amazing gift it is. Warts and all.

It is a hard habit to break. Suffering. I have allowed it to breathe with every breath. To rise and fall . . . a habit in my lungs and my blood.

In my mind. It was not always so. I remember. I do remember. The water angel. Water has always been a path. The vivid memory of the day skiing, the revelation surfing. There were so many other moments. Karen's wish triggered an emergent impulse in me by flooding my mind with her and freeing my mind of impediments. I surrender. I might never have taken this step. The irony that I believed it was my task to always protect her, flipped by circumstance to her always protecting me, is rich indeed. Prodding me, pushing me, freeing me. She is freeing me from something I need no longer carry. She has been with me all this time. Joys I missed that she did not because my grief and guilt abrupted them are now mine to share with her. Enough suffering. Not sure of my words here. Presence. I have been allowed presence in my past. To be present within it. I have earned the joy I would not allow myself to feel. I feel it now. Karen's gift.

The murder killed a corner of my heart, and it froze. I found subconscious and conscious ways to tear at myself and at the pain, but it usually hurt me in the process. She was there through that too. Drinking, cocaine, the stories are varied and numerous. The confusing thing is there was a great deal of fun in the mix that often felt really good. But...

There was a single day, a morning. I drove my little Maverick. It was my mom's car, actually. There was a moment. All things were perfect. The sun. The colors. The breeze. I had just turned right onto one of the east/west roads on my way to school. And time stopped for that second and all things were perfect, as I said. A flood of inexplicable happiness came over me and I felt deep peace...presence. That word. I was present in the abundant life that surrounded me and in harmony with God and His creation. I was at its center. Its heartbeat.

Two years later, Karen's corpse took that feeling away from me, and I believed I would never feel close to God again. That opened the door to many challenging days, but I believe they also led me back in time to God and to Karen and to Love. Slowly. I have said of my wilder days that I was in the midst of a "powerful healing." And though it is a bit flippant, this characterization, at its core, is exactly what was happening. That healing continues to this very moment. There is still more to come. But oh, so much has been lifted. Years and years. I must be very stubborn or very thick as my wife would say. Thick is probably more accurate. I think I mentioned I need more than one try to learn a thing. Sometimes several tries won't do the trick. But that day. When I was a teenager. That drive. I felt as if I was at the very center of the heartbeat of the Universe. And then one day, I couldn't hear it anymore. Silence. Nothing. And so, through the years, I have been climbing my way back. In the midst of a powerful healing! Certainly, a better way of looking at despair than surrendering to it. And I did surrender. But... not completely. Never completely. Because I had heard the Heartbeat. And I remembered it was true. I knew it was true. Just as Buddha (okay, I know I'm not Buddha, but I love this story); just as Buddha sat by the yew tree and heard the earth pronounce, "I bear you witness." I knew the truth. The pain made it hard to hear. The loss was unbearable. But I had heard it. I knew it was there. And I never stopped trying to hear it again.

I am sitting at the kitchen table. Writing. I am a father of seven children. I have had varying degrees of success in that role, but I am as happy today as I have ever been. I pray. Every day. For Love. We are off to breakfast.

I have notes in my head that I want to explore. Hamlet's speech. "There is a special Providence in the fall of a sparrow..." It keeps coming up, as if it has some light to shed, trying to make an appearance. I will explore it. For now, it is a Sunday drive to a breakfast spot and a morning of enjoying the faces of my three youngest. Faith, Gabriel and James. And Kayte. If I stop for just a moment... all I see is Love. It surrounds me. Karen is here. Gordon and Gam and Mom. And more. Two daughters, Spencer and Greer, will join us for the evening on Monday. I am content. I am grateful for all. I hear it. The Heartbeat.

Another of those notes. My buddy, Bob, bought a book about Yoga—Richard Hittleman's *Hatha Yoga*. I think it was called that. We both studied it. Followed some of the exercises or poses. We never did it together, so I am curious as to how I became so devoted. I spent at least a year in an evening ritual doing Yoga, followed by Meditation. Listen to the sound of the inner ear. Like a seashell. My own heartbeat. Pare down the surrounding soundscape and slip into the stream. Silence. Stillness. Spinning. I would float in the air, as if on an axis through my navel, spinning around it, suspended in the center of my room. I never had the nerve to open my eyes to see if I was actually floating in midair. But it sure felt like it.

We had dinner the other night with a lovely woman. Karen. We had met before on *Cheers* and were meeting again through a mutual friend, Bill. It had the ring of something more important than just happenstance. Karen. She had played a girl named Karen. Karen was doing erotic dance on the side to make ends meet and was also a patient of Dr. Frasier Crane. It was one of my more memorable lines: "I hope you're doing this for the money, because this certainly won't square things with your father."

I told her I had been writing for the better part of the last year about my sister.

"What was her name?"

Karen.

And she registered a kind of surprise. It was fun to reminisce with her. Just a coincidence but I will send her a copy of this one day. She has become a friend and I am happy to welcome her to the world of my sister. Kayte and she have become friends. Always nice to welcome another Karen into my life.

Muff Rotella was my first friend's mom. I thought she was beautiful. I remember someone telling me she was named after Princess Mafalda, an Italian princess. I have no idea who that was, but Muff was princess enough for me. I walked into the house one afternoon looking for Little Al. They lived next door to us, and this was customary. Also, I was six. Nothing really nefarious about me or mischievous. This was something we did.

The house was quiet, and I don't know why she was the only one home, but as I rounded the corner toward Al's room, Muff appeared at the entrance to her bedroom in a bra and girdle, stockings and garters pinching at the top of her hose. She was a tall woman and her legs were long and shapely. Beautiful. It was the first, lasting sexual memory I have. She screeched, "Kelsey," and turned on a dime back to her bedroom. Too late. The image was printed on my memory forever. It still brings me delight and a feeling of mystery and wonder at the sheer beauty of the female form. Little Al was my friend. There are a few things to recount when it comes to Little Al and his mom and his sister and even his dad and grandfather. But I did have a crush on his mom. I guess I still do. Now that that is out of the way, there are a few more significant episodes we all shared. Muff's dad, Al's grandfather, was called the Judge. I asked Al once if his grandad was a lawyer . . . he told me no. I asked if he was a judge. He said no. So, even a not too wild imagination needn't work very hard to think the Judge might have been some sort of "higher-up" in the Mafia?—for want of a better word. I do not know. I am simply musing. I liked Muff's father, Al's grandad. He would tell me to relax my jaw and then tap his palm very quickly against the bottom of my mouth to make a chattering sound like a man shivering in a blizzard. It always made me laugh.

Karen and I were invited for dinner sometimes. And it was a little like sitting in a ringside seat. We were spectators at the Italian dinner table. And at this particular table, tempers ran high and the food was plentiful. Big Al sat at the head of the table, Muff to his immediate right. Jeanine sat to his left. Little Al was at the opposite end. Karen and I flanked Little Al. Jeanine was a very sweet girl, a little older than Al. She had some sort of issue. I never knew what. She had a wrist that was bent a little and she walked with an altered gait. Dinner was served. Big Al was a very handsome guy. Made sense that his wife was a fine, attractive woman. She was most certainly as close to an Italian princess as any woman. And New Jersey was filled with them. None like Muff, though. And Big Al was just that: big, strong, and successful. They were lovely together. A power couple. They had the requisite two kids and an ideal life, as far as I could tell.

For Karen and me, a raised voice in our home was rare and frowned upon. We were a couple of died-in-the-wool Waspy kids. So, the spectacle of spaghetti and meatballs served with a healthy dose of vitriol was a little shocking. Once the food hit the table, the family would size up the day's challenges and have at it. I did learn to twirl spaghetti on my fork and neatly shape a nice bite-sized portion. But Karen and I had never really witnessed such turmoil at the dinner table. It was quite entertaining and though it seemed some very hurtful things were being hurled across the table, come time for dessert the tone had settled into a gracious dénouement. An invigorating meal. Wonderful dessert. Some lively dinner conversation. I guess they did this every night and I still feel privileged to have witnessed the phenomenon. They loved each other very much. I was married for a while to a woman who was very vocal about her daily unhappiness ... not my cup of tea, and it was behavior I couldn't handle. She thought nothing of raging in front of the kids or my mom ... very challenging. On one occasion, she really lit into me about something in my mom's presence and then stormed out of the room. I turned to Mom and asked, "What am I supposed to do with that?" Mom responded, "Well, honey ... she's Italian." Of course! I thought back to those nights with Al's family and realized that for all the arguing and carrying on, they loved one another very much. Not me and mine; but them and theirs.

There was a bike ride after school one day. I had ventured a bit farther from home than usual and had designs on some trick riding down a very steep hill ... the steepest in our little community. A couple of years older now. Probably eight years old at the time. I thought it would be very cool to stand on my seat and hold the handlebars while extending a raised leg behind me. My new bike was an English Racer, they called it. Fifteen speed and very swift. And tall. Perhaps, dangerously tall as it did make my distance from the pavement quite a bit higher than my old bike. At the top of the hill, I started down warily and then picking up speed, I lifted my left foot off the pedal and placed it on the top bar of the frame, then took my right foot off the pedal and placed it on the seat, then both feet on the seat as I was holding the handlebars and felt quite stable. So far, so good! I even raised one of my legs. That was okay too.

I am about halfway down the hill now, zooming along. And then, it came to me. Why not try to stand on the handlebars and perch at attention soaring down the hill with my arms outstretched? It would feel like flying. I plotted my move and began to bring my right foot toward the handlebars. It lighted there for a split second and that is the last thing I remember. I do not remember anything. I must have been knocked out. For several minutes, at least. Perhaps. I don't know. I'd landed on my head, as evidenced by the hole in it. No one had happened by, I supposed, as I was alone when I came to.

I took in the scene. Bike, pavement, a dizziness. Moments later, I gathered myself and gathered up my damaged bike. Nothing left but to take the first step of a long push home. Almost there. I passed Al's house and there was a sudden scream—Muff's scream. It was a blood-curdling scream. There was a reason. Blood. I was still wearing my white shirt from school, and it was soaked in blood. I was quite a sight walking up the street when Muff noticed me passing by. I was unaware of the blood. But I realized as she rushed from the house that I was a bit of a catastrophe. I think she wanted to pick me up, but I was a pretty big kid, and I assured her I was fine. So, she ran ahead and warned my mom and Gam about what was walking up the street. I am not sure what I was thinking. I had a concussion and a pretty big wound to my skull along with several scrapes. No serious damage except for the gaping hole. I didn't feel faint. That was good. But I'd lost quite a bit of blood. I convinced my mom that I would be fine. I just wanted to rinse off in the shower and rest awhile. Let my wounds heal. A day or two and that'd be the end of it. I lay in bed with a towel beneath my head and my mom seemed quite calm. I told her I'd be fine, and Mom was fine with that. Little did I know, Gam was on the phone to Gordon, and he was rushing home. Mom and Gam were content to wait for him and confident he would get me to the hospital, whether I was willing or not. That was the point. I was not willing. They calmly told me I could rest for a bit, and we would discuss it again shortly.

Gordon walked in and the discussion went like this. "You're going to the hospital."

"No! No! No!" I insisted, as Gordon grabbed me by the ankles and resolved to drag me from the room if need be. I put up a pretty good fight. My final moments of clutching at the doorjamb left behind a boy's room that had been upended to the threshold. Every piece of furniture, two beds, a rug and several other items had been enlisted by me to slow any progress toward the door. There stood an unholy mess just out of reach as the final pull wrenched me from my grip and Gordon finally held me in his arms, breathing hard, as I continued my protests.

"That's enough now! Stop it!" And I stopped. It was Gordon, after all. And I had been quite valiant. No shame in quitting the field in this manner.

At the hospital, Gordon carried me into the emergency room and they took me right away. I think it was twenty-one or twenty-five stitches to swing a chunk of my scalp back into place and stitch it. Pretty good. Pretty dippy. There was a nice ending, though. The intern stitching me up was very skilled and very young, a young lady, in fact. I barely felt a thing. Another of those times when someone did something wonderful for me whom I can never repay. I will say thank you now.

A point of honor.

My grandfather's eyes had lit up when he saw her. He asked if she was from the Philippines. She was and had come to the US to learn her trade and possibly return home and be the first physician in her family. Gordon's fondness for the Philippine people stemmed from his years in the South Pacific. I touched on this previously. The men who guided him through the jungles of Guadalcanal, whom he had met in New Caledonia, were Philippine and his affection and admiration for them was off the charts. She was lovely and a terrific "stitch man." And it was lovely to see the reverence with which Gordon regarded his comrades of the past and the regard he continued to carry for the Philippine people.

On our way home, Gordon turned to me and said, "Listen, Kelsey... next time I tell you we need to go to the hospital, just go, okay?"

"Okay," I said.

Then, he said with a chuckle, "It's gonna take a couple of days to put that room of yours back together."

195

I saw Al just a while ago. We remain friends. He related a tale his mother used to share about me. We had all gone to visit a cousin or nephew of Muff's, I think. They had a young baby in the home, and we were there to meet the newborn. The baby was beautiful. I looked down upon the child and said one word: "Remarkable." I still feel that way about life and children and I know there are challenges that come along for the ride, but I continue to find babies and newborns and all assortment of others on this Earth, remarkable. They are. We all are. This world. The challenges, the triumphs. The tragedies. All remarkable. And I would never wish them away. Save for a few devastating moments. Those I could have skipped. You know. Overall, though, this has been an amazing ride.

I would not have had a lifetime with Karen by my side. I think I might have preferred that, but as life tends to distance families, the distance of death, the gulf it creates, has an ironic twist. It kept Karen close. I have been told she was there for my mom when she died. I believe that. I mentioned before that Karen was the champion of Love in our family. She drove us all to say out loud what we felt in our hearts. No matter how uptight we may have been. If we love each other, we should say so.

I am not sure if Gam and Mom were able to get there. Theirs was a torrid history. My mom was born in San Francisco, my grandmother in Oakland. This was a symbolic rift that was celebrated with a tongue-in-cheek tradition of pointing out good fortune versus a shabby beginning. No offense meant to the city of Oakland, of course. Both Gam and Mom would agree that San Francisco sounded just that much more glamorous than Oakland.

But Gam was actually born into a family of great accomplishment and station. Her grandfather had been a successful agriculture guy after a walk across the great plains as with many of the early Californians. He developed large tracts of farmland and spearheaded the irrigation projects that ensured there would be fertile, fruitful growing seasons in that part of the state. I believe there were nine daughters and two sons when he decided to move to the newly incorporated city of Oakland. Apparently, his motive was also to put his girls on the market, so to speak. Move them to a place where they might have greater likelihood of finding suitable matches.

There was an announcement printed in the local paper about the arrival of the family and the eligibility of the Geddes girls. Gam's mother, Genevieve, was one of them. Her father, Ellis Dimmick, was the son of a dentist. His grandfather too walked across the country during the great migration and settled with his grandmother, Comfort, in Oregon. They worked a small plot of land, three hundred acres, to claim it as their own but the very next generation had no interest in the rural life.

Ellis's dad moved to Portland and opened his dental practice. His dad then moved his practice and his family to Oakland and at the turn of the century, the lifestyle they enjoyed was vastly different than his parents and certainly his grandparents. The generation of young people in Oakland had a bit more disposable time and also discovered a pastime of drinking.

There was a sad event in the Dimmick family. Ellis's older brother overdosed on a drug that was being used to help sedate dental patients at the time. It was a pretty gruesome death. He died in agony as described in a write up in the local paper and I think Ellis was pretty shaken by it. He turned deeper into drink and met a lovely Genevieve Geddes who came to share his habit and lifestyle.

I am not sure the pioneer family was equipped to watch its children devolve in this way and issues of this sort were swept under the rug rather than addressed. In just two short generations, the adventurous, heroic spirits of westward movement saw its offspring and grandchildren dissipate into a life of leisure and self-destruction. Certainly not all of them, but many were swept up in the new prosperity of a generation that did not have to work to survive or thrive. Not unlike subsequent generations whose forebears did their level best to spare their children hardship. As a result, they often languished in a life without purpose. Now, it is never wise to tar an entire generation with the same brush and I will be specific unto Ellis and Genevieve as they are direct ancestors of mine and Karen, Gam, and Sally.

197

There is a record of Ellis being discharged from the Marine Corps. He did not join the Marines until he was twenty-seven, if I remember rightly. His uncle was a sergeant and helped get him into the Corps. It was a kind of last-ditch effort to straighten him out—at least, that is what it appears to be, by all accounts. Few things had gone his way.

Genevieve and Ellis had married, but Genevieve ended up back at home and even published an article that said he was deceased. That was not so, but I guess her family had enough sway to protect her virtue and the family name by ending things with Ellis, virtually killing him. The Dimmicks were pretty well known because of the death of his older brother and the scandal that came with it.

This was the world Gam was born into . . . Evangeline Lucille Dimmick. It was her fate to be shuttled between aunts and uncles throughout her childhood. I am not sure if Genevieve was ever quite up to being a responsible parent. Her sisters assumed that role. And her sisters were women of great accomplishment and character. Some married, some held prestigious jobs around the turn of the previous century. Exemplary people.

A few of the sisters were very artistic, as well. I still have one of Lela Geddes' still life paintings in our home today. Another of the sisters was the chief buyer for the top department store in San Francisco. She traveled the world buying material and textiles from as far away as China. One of the only records I have of Genevieve is her name on a ship's manifest on a voyage to China she took with her older sister. The only other one I have is her death certificate. She died at the age of forty-one. I do not wish to shame her. It is pretty clear her death was the result of a drinking habit she just could not shake. But I thank her. For my grandmother.

Ellis lived for several more years. After being discharged from the Marines, he ended up in a series of odd jobs, the last of which was doing the laundry at a famous hotel in Oakland. I forget the name but it is the same hotel featured in *Mrs. Doubtfire*. The same hotel I stayed in when I was filming *Down Periscope* years ago. Gam never spoke of her mother and father. I assume she was around town then. She had married Gordon and had a child, Sally. Discovering the history of her

198

parents brought a sadness to me and an admiration for Gam. It could not have been easy. But she did have a family who looked after her. God Bless Them. I wonder if Gam's mother ever saw the baby. Mom. I hope so. I hope she and Ellis had some joy in their love. The succinct discharge record was signed by his captain. He was let go after being discovered drunk on duty. He was meant to be guarding one of the naval installations in San Francisco. The last entry on that document reads: "Character—Bad!"

But Genevieve and Ellis did not spend much of their life together. I imagine after the news of his death was published, they were not encouraged or likely to visit. Gam went from one sister to another. She had some colorful stories of the extended family. Gam was the only child I have ever known who actually received coal in her stocking one Christmas. This apparently because she kept running away when poor Aunt Lela was on duty.

Another of the aunts married into the Worthington family. They owned the Worthington drugstores. I think this was the mother and father that brought Elizabeth and Alex into the world. I am not sure about a great many details here. Elizabeth may have been my mother's cousin. But Alex was definitely Gam's cousin, and she always spoke of how handsome he was. And how brave. Cousin Alex had joined the Merchant Marines before the US entered World War II. They were quite famed for their courage in crossing the Atlantic to supply the Allies, braving the German U-boat Wolf Packs. Alex ended up dealing blackjack in Reno. Gam would always add that tidbit with a flourish and a wink. Colorful. Evangeline also went to a very ritzy girls' school in Oakland: Miss Head's School for Girls. It is apparently still in existence, although it became a coed school some years ago. If it is in keeping with contemporary societal fashion, then the new name is probably something like That Person's School for Them Students. I have no particular interest in insulting people who are truly confused about gender or even want to be confused about it, but I must admit, I like boys and girls, men and women, the Divine Feminine and the Sacred Masculine. That is the kind of hairpin I am. As the old book title imparts: *I'm OK, You're OK.* I think the country could use a bit more of that way of thinking, but this is not the reason for this book or for this paragraph. Natural to stray a bit. After all, I am still breathing and so I am aware of things as they are; and wish many were different. Maybe we could take out some of the "improvements." Or we could just stop hating people we don't agree with on every issue. And vice-versa. Start there? Maybe?

Colorful were many of Gam's tales. For a graduation present from Miss Head's, Gam was invited by her best friend's family to take a cruise to South America. She was seventeen. Her friend's father was a famous actor who had married a young woman half his age. A cause of much scandal. But he was a fun guy and they a fun couple. The trip was fun too. Gam used to say: walked across the isthmus of Panama at the age of seventeen! Now, I always thought she was referring to some contemporary of the Conquistadors, Balboa and Cortez. That sort of thing. But apparently, they ran aground during the voyage and rather than make it through the Panama Canal, they were forced to walk across the isthmus to the other side and transfer to another ship. So, rather than some brave ancestor/explorer, the subject of her boast was Evangeline Lucille Dimmick herself. Descendant of the Dimmicks of Oregon who crossed the country on foot and began a new life a world away from their humble beginnings in New York. Colorful!

Gordon often invoked the Miss Head's School for Girls when he was watching a football game that was not going his way. His team losing in a spectacular fashion, Gordon would say these boys are playing like Miss Head's School for Girls. I thought it was funny at the time but am willing to apologize to any and all who take offense at it now. My grandfather was not a gentleman to cause undue harm to any person or group of people. He was an amiable man and a man in full. He took responsibility for his actions. Most of his actions were polite, deferential, and often heroic. I find it challenging to muster the slightest objection to his behavior at any point in his life. I find it impossible to identify a toxic nature in his personality or in his history. The imprint of his days has nothing that stinks of insult to any but those who tried to wrong him; and with those who did attempt to wrong him, he had a simple rule of thumb. "If you see a bug, step on it or walk around it." It

200

did take me years to decipher what this meant. And I have written of it before, but Gordon was a fair man. He would not dare to snuff any individual but those who made it impossible to do otherwise. Deliberate and decisive. Such would be the end of any who stood in opposition without just cause. Fair-minded and fair. These were the definitive characteristics that clung to him throughout his life.

Into his life came Evangeline. She was fresh out of high school when they met. I don't know the particulars. They were maybe a year or two apart in age. He took considerable ribbing from his fellow fraternity members. But they were in love, and I think Gam had a certain something that Gordon had never encountered. It was on a night drive to Nevada, to witness the marriage of a couple of friends, that Gam and Gordon decided they would marry too. They rode in the rumble seat of a Model T. And they drove home in that same seat as husband and wife.

This set off a storm of outrage. Gordon's father disowned him. Gam's family was resigned, I believe. Let's face it, by this time, her family was quite unmoved by drama in the life of their daughter, niece, granddaughter. She was now Mrs. Cranmer and unwelcomed by the Cranmer family but she had married the president of Sigma Alpha Epsilon and a graduate of UC Berkeley College of Engineering. Not bad. Captain of the Crew too. Back when the Crew meant something at Berkeley. Gordon's father had guided ten wagon trains across the country. He had ridden on horseback. He met his wife, Cora, on one of those voyages. She was French. Her maiden name, Savage. Hence, Gordon was named Gordon Savage Cranmer.

So, Evangeline married Gordon. And the families went crazy. I do not know why, but there it is. Neither family was pleased about it, so I've been told. But Gam and Gordon stuck it out. They had one child, Sally. They had two grandchildren, Karen and Kelsey. Their devotion to the family was without equal. I remain grateful for that.

It was Gordon who told me he was disowned by his father when they married. That must have been difficult. He took a job in a gas station. It was during the '20s . . . The roaring twenties. He also told me stories about bathtub gin, and there is a picture of him and Gam at one of their parties. Gam said she had been a flapper. She was quite a looker. This turned Gordon's head decisively in her direction and away from some of his duties as president of his fraternity. The chapter fell into a bit of a slump, for want of a better word and a threat was issued from the home office that the Berkeley Chapter might just lose its standing. The head of the national board came out to discuss it with him and Gordon challenged him to a round of golf to maintain his title and preserve the status of the house. He won. Not long after, they took that fateful ride in a Model T and tied the knot in Nevada.

Gam described how as a young bride she would slave to make dinner for them. Gordon would walk in the door, sit down to dinner, and five minutes later, he would be finished and fast asleep on the couch before Gam could sit down. She broke down in tears. She also told the story of how one night there was an earthquake. She thought Gordon was snoring, so she reached over and gave him a sock in the mouth and said, "Wake Up!" Gam was feisty. I am not sure how it all came about with her . . . her childhood and being raised by her aunts instead of her mom. Gam was tough. She would say that children should be seen and not heard, and she meant it. Something she was probably told.

She had another expression: "That boy could use a good, swift kick in the pants, and I'm just the girl who can give it to him." That was one of my favorites. Also, Gam never kicked anybody anywhere. She used language as a tool for entertainment, and that phrase was one of her highlights.

She did have an excellent education. She was fluent in French, although she rarely pulled it out. I did come upon one of her French manuals from school that she had kept. She was an excellent card player and could even read the cards. This was a real highlight. It was during a session of cutting cards and shuffling them, laying them, out and shuffling again, that she said a dark man keeps showing up; he is going to suffer a terrible accident or be killed. No one could imagine who it was. A week later, my dad was shot. I will not linger on that. It was one of her aunts who taught her how to read the cards. She had some power. Some strength. She survived so much. She had a tough childhood, but she was cared for as a child by some decent people. That is to their credit. And she loved life. That is to hers. She loved a good time too. "I've seen me some big towns and I've heard me some big talk." That was another of her favorite sayings. Memorable and colorful, my grandmother. I did love her so. She was fun. She was a fighter and a staunch defender of her family.

After Gordon died and as I was growing up, we went head-to-head sometimes. On one occasion, Gam and I had a real dust-up. I finally told her I was tired of kissing her ass. She threw me out of the house. So I stayed with Spencer for a couple of days. Finally, a phone call came Sunday afternoon. Come home. So, I did. Gam was there and she told me a story. While playing Bridge with "the girls" that day, Gam told them what I had said.

One of the girls spoke up in a kind of harumph—"Well, I wouldn't let my daughter go out with a boy like that!"

I am not quoting her because I do not remember exactly, but Gam's response went something like this: "Let me tell you something, sister, Kelsey wouldn't touch your daughter with a ten-foot pole!" I think she started a new Bridge Club after that. Her friend Terry was no longer a member. All Gam had to do was hear her "little man" attacked in any way by someone who had no right to sit in judgment of her family and I was back in her good graces. Pronto!

Bridge. Gordon and Gam were both good at cards and enjoyed Bridge together. They played with friends and Gordon used to play during college and won some money at it. They taught Karen and me to play. Also, gin rummy. I remember Karen and Gam sitting there for hours playing together. Mom too. Gordon occasionally would play some poker and invite us all to join him. "Men have been shot for less!" he would bellow, if you touched your cards while they were being dealt. I suppose someone used to say it to him when he was a boy; or it was common knowledge to him, as the generation just before his would actually shoot people who cheated at cards. Remarkable to think we are just a grandfather away from the Wild West. I miss cards. I'd better pass it along to my kids. It can give hours of time together. Good for the mind. Good for keeping company. My latest batch spends way too much time on their iPads.

That hand of Bridge on the train to Florida! I have never seen a hand like it before or since, and judging from the look on Gordon's face, he never had either.

So, Gordon and Evangeline faced a hard time when they married. Neither family was pleased. I do not really know why. Gordon's dad simply told him he would be on his own from then on. I guess that was okay by him. Gam's family is not on record as far as I know but she rarely spoke of them. Gam never told me about her grandad or grandmother. Perhaps, they regarded her as an embarrassment to the family, and she discarded them as a source of shame in her life. But Evangeline was a proud woman and she had every right to be. She never spoke of her mother. She spoke of her aunts. Aunt Lela being mentioned more than the others. And I think Lela lived with them for a time. Returning the favor, perhaps. Or maybe she helped out with Sally. We did meet Aunt Ernestine once when we were younger. Karen and I drove with my mom to the Newark Airport to welcome Ernestine for a visit. She was colorful in her own right. She had dated Thomas Edison and described him as rather boring. It might have been Ernestine who married into the Worthington family. Grafton Worthington is a name I remember, and it is possible Gam lived with them for a time. I do not really know but I remember that name. Gordon and Gam struggled in their early years, but they had married for love and they stuck with it. Sally was born. Mom.

Mom was wonderful.

Another jump—just because it has popped into my mind a few times over the last day.

Goose! Last night I sang Goose's theme song for Kayte. Her full name was Tintagel, after the castle where King Arthur was born. That morphed into "Tint the Goose" and finally, just "Goose." It may seem odd, at first, that I would jump to Goose after saluting my mom. Well, it's not so strange. They both gave me simple, uncluttered, unconditional Love. They are two of my great loves. There is no question. The song was really just lyrics about my dog that were borrowed from an old cartoon show—*Hercules*. It went like this:

Tint the Goose, hero of fame and story
Tint the Goose, winner of ancient glory
Fighting for the right
Fighting with her might
With the strength of ten
Ordinary men—
Tint the Goose, people are safe when near her
Tint the Goose, only the evil fear her
Kindness in her eyes
Iron in her thighs
Virtue in her heart
Fire in every part
Of the mighty
Tint the Goose!

As it ended in a rising musical flourish, it would invoke a spontaneous howl from Goose that really paid the whole thing off when we had company. I think she knew it too. Goose was aware of her popularity and enjoyed it. Always a little hard on her when she was around a "non-dog" person. She could read someone. Probably better at it than I. Goose always knew how to read a room and make herself scarce when appropriate.

I miss her. But as with all things past, a visit in our mind's eye, presents them fresh and alive as years ago. I am with my dog. Nice.

Ellen was one of those people, the kind of person who did not care for dogs. When we took the production of *A Midsummer Night's Dream* to Scottsdale, Arizona, on tour—okay, I know we are bouncing around again but hang in there—just to clarify, Ellen was the visiting actress to San Diego my final season there with whom I began a life together. As we were leaving for the tour, Ellen made it clear she did not want Goose along for the ride. I conceded that I could send her to Florida to visit with my mom. Gam had died the winter before. Mom liked Goose very much. But a day after she arrived in Florida, she had a little falling out with one of the family dogs and she was on a plane to Scottsdale the next day.

Ellen was very close to uttering the phrase, "It's the dog or me!" Well, my friend, Nathan, who had also been my roommate that summer, advised Ellen that was a very dangerous sentence, indeed. She couldn't help herself, so she raised the idea in conversation that "if" she had said that, what would I have done? Well, I looked at her and said, "Goose, would have won that one." That was that.

She really was an amazing animal. She rode on my motorcycle with me! I know I mentioned it, but I mean she rode on my motorcycle with me! There was a big hill on the way up to work that I would jump every morning. Time the light. Crank up the hill at top speed and "Lift off!" Goose, sitting on the bike with me, loving the flight through the intersection. Yes, it was crazy. Yes, it was illegal, but it was also harmless and we did have such fun together—in midair, on our way to the theatre.

I lived in a small home that summer that I shared with Nathan. Several actors took The Alamo. Ellen one of them, so I still spent quite a bit of time there. The place with Nathan was just down the hill. A one-bedroom affair, so I slept in the garage. I had my little Fiat 124, my motorcycle, a barbecue at the threshold of the garage, a double bed on an oriental rug. Paradise! Nate's mom gave me the rug. I would sleep with the garage door open. Goose was there to protect me. And what's funny is I was there to protect Goose. It was an interesting dynamic. You see, I was clearly the leader of the pack. Goose was the Alpha female, but the idea of security and defending the den was only necessary if I was not around. So, if there were an intrusion or a sound from an unknown source, Goose's first response was to look at me with a kind of, "Well, shouldn't you do something about that?" She knew I was the big dog and best suited to handle a fight. She was happy to go at it with any number of strays or mailmen but the real danger?—that was my responsibility. A responsibility I was glad to shoulder. Glad to shoulder it today. I guess she taught me my place—taught me how things work.

And then, the little hole that is left where she used to be, reveals itself. It is still a hole. Nothing fills it. It is a hole that echoes with her desperate search for me in a strange place too far from home. A construction site. Keeping an old girlfriend company. She ran off but never found her way back. I am confident that she came to a good end. Hopeful a young girl, perhaps, found her and loved her. Until she died. I was meant to do that. Hold her at the end and invite her to stay with me forever in spirit. There are pictures. She is with me. There is a lovely episode of The Twilight Zone. A fella dies and comes across St. Peter, who invites him past the pearly gates but says his dog can't come in. No dogs allowed. Well, the fella thinks about it for a bit and says, "No thanks. Guess we'll just keep walkin'." Some distance down the road, they come upon another saintly presence who claims to be St. Peter who invites them in. "My dog's okay?" asks the fella.

"Of course," says St. Pete.

"So, this is Heaven?"

"Yes, it is."

"Another guy down the road a piece said no dogs allowed in Heaven."

"Oh," says St. Peter. "That was the other place."

Another illustration that sums things up pretty well. James was looking at a picture of me and Goose up in my office. And I am not sure how this all came about but James, when he was four, looked at that picture. Kayte asked him who was in the picture: who is this in the picture? James said, "Daddy and Mommy." Hah! Daddy and Mommy! He told her that. I guess he knows true love when he sees it. A testament. To Goose. And to Mommy. Both.

I am returned to a rhythm of slipping back and forth in time and tale. Mom is in focus again. I think I have been avoiding talking about Mom. A little. There is her relationship with her mother, Gam, that must be explored. Important to know where Gam started and how. We have visited her youth and her early years with Gordon. Then there was the war. World War II. It is important because I believe so much of what we are is baked in another cake. Baked into us by the suffering or successes of our ancestors; and so much of what they experience is in turn baked into our DNA. We inherit any number of emotions and hardships and histories from family that lived generations before us. So, in the name of a complete picture, the women who raised Karen need to be uncovered and traced from the time they shared together, to the time they shared with her.

San Antonio, Texas. I think Gam loved Texas. She used to sing "The Yellow Rose of Texas" and "The Eyes of Texas Are Upon You." She used to say things like: Remember the Alamo. I am not sure how long she lived there but I think it was during that stretch of the war when Gordon was overseas. She and Sally. Mom. It was during this time that Sally became a young woman. Or just became a woman.

I was sitting in the living room with Karen. I noticed that there was red spotting widening at the back of her robe. I pointed it out to her and she went to Mom for some help. I had missed the genesis of this moment but in noticing what was going on, I discovered a young Karen was becoming, or had become, a woman. She was ten years old. So, a little early as these things go, perhaps. Nothing shameful, certainly, though I think she had some sensitivity about it. And I was supportive as a poorly informed twelve-year-old boy could be.

But it was later that evening when my mom called the family, Frank and Wilma, his second wife, and Elisa and announced over the phone that "Karen became a woman today." Oh, my goodness! I felt so bad for her. Surely, a woman can become a woman without having to announce it to the world. I remember offering a sympathetic phrase to her about it and to put it out of her mind. I guess Mom was proud of the fact. Gam was too. It was a mile marker, I suppose.

I can't imagine what they might have said, had they been there the day I had my first erection. But then, I did not know if they discussed it. They probably did. My mom walked into my room one morning well into a season of erections. She respectfully closed the door. It did come up a few days later, though. "I would prefer if you did that in the bathroom," she said.

"I would prefer you to honor the sanctity of a closed door," was my response.

It had begun a few years before, incidentally. And that, too, was a strange and wonderful day. I walked around with a stack of schoolbooks in front of my anatomy for years to come. It was not something I was ready to share with the general public.

My heart went out to Karen on the day of her highly publicized womanhood. She handled it fine. Mom was proud. I never quite comprehended why but I do know the feeling that comes with watching our children grow up. They are good days. Days to be proud. And days that often make us feel just a bit sad. Mixed bag. All this growing up.

So, it was in Texas that Mom did some substantial growing up of her own. Gordon was gone. Sally was ready to spend some time with men; Gam may not have been ready for that. So, Gam, who was probably not wild about having a child in the first place, now had a child who was becoming a woman and that was not an easy hand to play. Judging from her own childhood, who knows what kind of joy or terror she experienced at the thought of being responsible for her own child. Her mom had not really been "all hands on deck," and maybe Gam resented Sally. Oh, I know she loved her. I am just guessing at this. But it makes sense. She did not have a father who fawned on her or loved her as life itself. Gordon loved his little girl. That much is clear and a woman who had experienced such torment in childhood might be a little jealous of a girl adored by the greatest guy she knew. Sad. But true, I think. I loved Gam very much. She was not given an easy life. Neither was Mom. They did not exactly blame each other for the things they thought were missing, but I know there were some difficulties. Not the first time or the last. As things go with Mothers and Daughters. We just hope they can go easier. Nicer. Not always meant to be.

I am projecting a great deal of this from a smattering of comments I heard, and things Mom and Gam told me. Had Gordon lived, I might never have heard any of them. But I was the man of the house. The women of the house were my responsibility; and above all my greatest responsibility was to be an impartial ear for them all. I want to be clear. I write none of this in judgment. I loved them. I loved them with every ounce of my being.

And now, cosmetic dentistry has drifted into my mind. How about that? That's a twisted segue. Don't worry, this won't sidetrack me. At. All.

Okay. Maybe a little.

I spent seventeen years without seeing a dentist. Thankfully, I had pretty good teeth and a not-so-corrupt dentist who addressed the situation when I was thirty-four. Yes, I had not seen a dentist since I was seventeen. I lost two teeth. Not a proud moment. But the first dentist in my life was a bit of a nut. Dr. Brown. I remember Dr. Brown would say I was a brave boy and a strong boy, and I would not need any anesthetic to drill and fill a tiny cavity. So, a promise that he would stop the second I raised my hand convinced me to allow him to torture me. Of course, the second I raised my hand, he would bear down harder on the tooth in question and squeals of pain and pleading would bear no fruit at all. Until the final moment, nothing would stop him. As the filling was completed, the last thing I heard was: "That wasn't so bad now, was it?" It was bad, Dr. Brown. Bad. I should never have trusted you.

Well, that's that. Except, Karen had great teeth. I am not sure she ever had a single cavity. Possibly why we never discussed the evil Dr. Brown and his chamber of horrors. Weird. What was he doing?

Anyway, Karen had a great smile. Some of the folks we both knew, I still know. Many of them were her friends. Many mine. Most of my friends remember her as a girl who always looked like she knew things. The smile to them was enigmatic. They recall she was bright and seemed like a nice girl. A couple of my pals did spend some real time with her. Bob. Spencer. I think they loved her as I did. Maybe they explored a few things as friends that a brother and sister never would. That's okay. We were all growing up and learning how to be with ourselves and with others. They were practicing for adulthood. And Karen was living her days in full. I have said before I am glad she did. Karen's friends. I promised to track them down and I have. That smile! I see it every day. Her picture is in our home. Several, in fact. I see her every day. It was a great smile. Good teeth! That much is certain. Straight. No braces. No cavities. That was certainly not the case with me. I have reached out to Momo, Jan, and to Wandi, my old friend, who attended the same college as Karen for that one semester. A few memories, hopefully. Possibly some insights. Some things I did not know. And some information. Maybe. Who was the boyfriend she went to see in Colorado Springs? I thought it was a guy named Lou, who I'd also known back in Florida. I don't know why I thought so. The picture of that guy on her yearbook page. It would be cool to find out who he was.

And that snowmobile suit. One of Karen's only possessions that were collected by the police and then given to me. She never spoke to me of snowmobiles. Honestly, we didn't really speak a lot after that last Christmas. She didn't tell me she was leaving for Colorado. I don't remember when I found out. Maybe she told me. Maybe she said she was thinking about it. That last Christmas we danced together. Maybe. I only know on that last call, it seemed she was excited to be coming home. I was excited we would have a summer together. "Have a great Fourth of July, Karen." "See you in a bit." I was so happy. I hung up the phone. And that was it. The last time we spoke.

I don't really remember the sound of her voice. That upsets me. I wish I could. I'd like to hear it. I do hear her. She speaks to me. I hear her; but it is a mental thing. Not an aural thing.

I'm going to work on that.

"Okay. Do that. It might surprise you."

I am making a note of it. Now.

"Call them."

Okay, Karen. Calling them. Now.

One of us is aware that I am stalling. One of us. Well . . . both of us. I'm nervous.

When one door closes another door opens. An axiom. A demonstration of that today. I tried to call Momo at High Hampton Inn . . . no luck. I tried to reach Wandi. Disconnected number. I have not quit trying. Just a stall. I am enlisting some help from a few old friends. Donna and Quay. Brian. Spoke to him today. He spent quite a bit of time with Karen and her group after she and I had chosen our individual paths at school. Jan and I are speaking on Saturday morning to get some insights, and I am very excited about that. Jan and I and Karen and Dale and Bob all hung around together. Spencer was in that circle sometimes, as well. Jan lived fairly close to school, and it was effortless to fall into her home for an hour or two after school . . . hang out together. Listen to Hendrix and Led Zeppelin. But my time there was not frequent, save for when I was going out with Dale a little. Just a little. She was a very pretty girl who lived across the street from Jan. Her dad accused me and Bob of being heroin addicts. This was not true. Something to do with rolling up our sleeves. And whatever danger her dad thought Dale might be in, there was certainly none from me. I was still painfully shy. So was she. It was going nowhere . . . one of us would have had to make some sort of move. Neither of us knew how. So . . . nowhere. She was a good girl. Her father should have known better. I was a good boy too. He couldn't know that, but she was lovely and a very nice girl. There was one awkward incident. One afternoon. Dale and I were kissing on the sofa. Karen directed my attention to some rather dramatic anatomical evidence of how much I enjoyed the activity. It was, in fact, evident to everyone in the room. Collectively embarrassing but most embarrassing for me. I was wearing shorts. Where's a stack of books when a boy needs them? Mortifying. I beat a quick retreat.

Today, Quay came to visit. Quay was a couple of years behind me at school. We remained intermittent friends and then in adulthood, became lifetime friends. Our visits are infrequent, but they are always affirmations of a deep love for one another. I love his wife too. And Quay remains a vital, creative person. We are discussing plans to mount a musical about Chagall with the brilliant Jon Andersen, lead singer for the band, Yes. Jon is a serious talent and a remarkable singer . . . a dynamic, lyric tenor . . . amazing voice. It is an insanely good instrument . . . his voice, his voice box. It is an ageless phenomenon. The sound is effortless and unique, as if God's breath is in his lungs. Not an exaggeration.

Anyway, I asked Quay about any friends who may have known Karen. He instantly thought of Brian. I will be speaking with Brian in depth about the days he spent with her. There is a promise of knowing finally why Karen left Pine Crest. And it is a complete surprise to me. A door I never imagined would open. So, I heard Karen say, *"Call."* I ended up calling all sorts of people. Found some I never thought I would. "It might surprise you," said Karen. It probably will.

I spent a lovely evening with my wife tonight.

"Kelsey is happy when everyone around him is happy."

Kayte described a moment when she felt Karen's presence near

212

her. It was as if we were just sitting on the couch together, she told me, as Kayte was wondering what makes me truly happy. This is a good woman, my wife. Kayte explained that there was a kind of conversation with my sister. That is how it felt. She further explained that Karen also mentioned all my kids and my desire to have them all together and happy in my life. This is true. Regrettably, not there, yet . . . but I do not quit. Not when it comes to family. There may be some long gaps, but time does tend to dull some edges and open some doors. So, I wait. Patient. Also, the first statement Kayte heard is true. I would even sacrifice my own happiness if others can be happy; but it is the ideal cocktail, so to speak, to have us all happy. Surrounded by love reflecting and refracting through all the souls present—that is indeed happiness in my book. An orgy of serenity and communion. A group worship. Kind of like church. Scintillating, vibrant, conscious, ecstatic communion with all. Yeah, that'd do it.

And as I rounded the corner into the kitchen, I was trying to remember the word we would use when Karen and I were children of the late '60s. It was almost clear as a bell when the answer came from behind me—"S*paced-out. We would say, 'spaced,' too.*" And it was at this moment, I began to suspect that Karen had been a bit of a pothead. I was kept blissfully ignorant of it, or I was too preoccupied with other stuff to notice. That "separate paths" thing. More to come on that. But last night, it seemed her presence was clearly with us. And it seemed she wanted us to know something. Something that might surprise me. Pothead. Maybe. Not earthshaking or any cause for shame. Makes sense. I see her reaching for that candy.

Karen is coming into our realm. I am not crazy. Perhaps, I am a little foolish or a bit too willing to believe I'm in touch with her, but I have spent a lifetime with Karen and I would know. Haven't quite heard the sound of her voice, as I long to, but she was definitely around last night. It was a warm and enjoyable evening with her and my kids and Kayte. There was love. And there was a bit of mischief. Karen. Yup, that was Karen.

I spoke with Jan. We had a good cry together. I know she had a deep love for Karen and I recounted some of what I've already written. She had sent a picture of Karen and Bob which led me down a funny path for an assumption or two . . . did they have a more significant relationship than I had thought? No. Just a quick one. So, after the night we had all spent together, there was a continuing relationship but not an exclusive or lasting one. I was fine one way or the other with the idea . . . Jan confessed she was a little upset because she had told Karen that she liked Bob. Ah, such is the way of friendship. Obviously, their friendship was more important than the fleeting affections shared with some boy. That is okay.

We also spoke of others who might be able to tell me something I didn't know about Karen . . . about the days of high school after that time we chose our separate lanes. We were still quite close, though. Jan confirmed that. She told me Karen had always been devoted to me. I always felt the same, I told her. I shared my realization with her that these days of writing had shown me Karen was the great love of my life. And how beautiful it has been to spend so much time with her. That started the tears again and Jan cried beside me . . . miles apart but alone together in an almost ancient grief that remains forever fresh. Extraordinary. So much love. We will visit again soon. Jan has had some tough days in her life and our friendship suffered. We are okay now. I am very happy about that.

Again, I pressed Jan if she could think of anyone that might shed a little more light, a little more insight about the few years before Karen's death. The years she and I were in different orbits. Jan suggested I check the funeral book. Surely, one of the many who had signed the book might be able to share a recollection. And suddenly, there was a new path to explore. I had placed the book inside my bag that holds memories of Karen and the documents that track her life and death. There, in the back of the book, several dozen names—many that deserve mention; many that may hold a key. A few who were significant in my life. A door open.

A new rabbit hole!

These morning hours. I spend them drifting in and out of memory, cataloging mentally the connections to Karen and to my own life, before and since she was taken. I was going to write "left," but if I have learned anything, she did not leave. I am solemn in my knowledge. Certain in it. This is new. There is a depth of comfort I hold steadfast.

I am not sure if I mentioned I will load this book with photographs. I always take issue with biographies that are only peppered with pictures. I identify with the pictures and always feel there should be as many as possible. Now, I realize there were very few methods of memorializing people in anything but portraits or historical paintings just a few hundred years ago. That poor wife of the Norman king that did nothing but weave tapestries ... good grief, that was a labor of love. Never would have been finished in the days of television ... I have no doubt. I digress. Not sure why. Musing this morning.

Anyway, you have already noticed by now, this memoir is chock-full of pictures. I like the pictures. In fact, when Esther first directed me to this assignment, I feared there would not be enough. She assured me Karen told her there were. It does still seem a little odd, this gift that Esther undoubtedly has. I do not have it. These words have unlocked so many visions and buried treasure about my sister, perhaps, my "medium" is language. Not a big surprise, but start me talking and things just seem to keep coming. Start me writing and the veils are lifted, one after the other until I've begun to feel I can time travel. I can. It is as easy as stubbing my toe. Although—a good deal more rewarding. Smiling faces warm me. Hands touch me. Goodness and love settle upon me. Karen's gift to her woebegone brother.

Back through the looking glass.

I have opened the register of names who attended Karen's funeral. It sits before me. The little cover depicts a ship under sail. A Spanish Galleon. Ridiculous. This cover reminds me how unsatisfactory I found the whole proceeding. Karen's funeral forgot one thing— Karen! Just read the first little snippet of poetry, and you will see how unconnected it is. Not disconnected. Unconnected. "Sailed away in calm serenity"—that line sent me through the roof at the time. I get it now. But at the time, it hurt me. It seemed a cookie-cutter document of generic platitudes: sentiments meant to comfort, unspecific to any person, name, or lifetime. It does have pertinent information. Born ... passed away ... this and that.

Passed away. That alone was enough to send me spinning. Passed away does not cover it. Murdered would have been better. Accurate, at least. But it is clear to me now, this pamphlet is not meant to be personal or specific. It contains words of solace addressed to no one, in memory of no one in particular. So, the whole affair was not about Karen. It was not personal. Her funeral was not hers. Turn the page and subsequent pages and it is an unrewarding journey. Until ... that last list of names in the back. And there it is! Evidence. People who cared enough to show up that day. People who gave a damn. People who had the courage to look death in the eye, a terrible death, and to embrace a grieving family by grieving with them.

I deeply appreciate the gesture. There were those, of course, who could not be there, who were too devastated to be there. I know. It would have been impossible for them. I love them too. Faith's parents came "on her behalf" ... it is entered so in the book. Faith was a dear friend of Karen's. Especially that last year or two. They shared their last year in high school and continued their friendship until the end. I liked Faith. I didn't know until today that her folks were people of such character. Bless them. I wish her well ... hope she is well.

Others are here I have already mentioned. I was right about Mario Peña—his name is here. Wonderful man. Wanda and Ollie—longtime family friends from Atlantic Highlands. Wanda was Doug's mom. Doug is still a friend. Godfather to my daughter, Spencer. Karen spent a summer with them at their property in Welaka, in central Florida. Jan told me she had gone up there for part of the summer as well. I did not know that. Or I'd forgotten it. The search is bearing some fruit. I think it was the same year I took off for FSU in Tallahassee to study music for six weeks.

The divergent path ... there it is. Karen was working for Ollie on the property, as I remember. Ollie told me Karen was the kind of person who knew the value of a dollar. It is an old expression, even Gordon would have used, that pays respect to anyone who knows how to work

216

hard and take it in stride, without complaint or grandstanding—no whining, no nonsense. An eight-hour day of work. A day that grants a sizeable dose of self-respect and the respect of those around you. That was Karen.

I make a note here to check in with Doug for any thoughts he may have about her. We had all been close through fifth and sixth grade and I remain close with him today. Wanda and Ollie were in attendance. They were good friends. A surprise down the page—Thelma and Lee Bonney. I wrote of them before, and I marvel that they were there. Gam and Gordon's friends. So lovely. I happily state again how much I liked them. Like them even more as they would have driven down from Virginia Beach to be there. The lovely Gillian was there. Jan, Danny and his wife, Marlene. I cannot imagine how painful it was for them... but of course, I can. I hope I can find them. If not to learn more, then at least to tell them what they meant to me. And to thank them. Oddly enough, they have all stayed with me these many years. There was Ron and Diana. Ron, you have met. Diana, you will. She figures significantly in my life. My story. Someone who belongs here as prominently as she inhabits my memory. Mrs. McDaniel and her daughter. They lived two doors up. And a surprise to me—Dwight. I will include his last name. It bears no malice or compromise to mention it in this context. Dwight Snedeker, who had been a friend throughout the years but not one I would have thought would be there to loan support; but he was, and I am deeply grateful for that. I want to him know. Hope he is well and full of fruitful days. The last entry is Leon Bryant. Our art teacher. A fellow of infinite jest, as the saying goes! I still think of him as a great pal. Good skater. To him and to them all I send thanks and best wishes.

And as I am about to close this little book, I think of a man whose name was not among the friends and relatives who had signed it that day. His name is Richard Mitten. He is a man of great importance in my life. But as I was about to stow this part of memory back out of conscience, the book fell open to the floral remembrances page. I have never seen it before. At the very top was Dick Mitten. Richard Mitten, Dick to his friends. Silly, the immature impulse that still finds the nickname so funny. But there it is. And, of course, I number myself among the immature, so I giggle too. But . . . it is at the feet of Dick Mitten where a great deal of my gratitude lies. And a great deal of responsibility for the life I live today, the career I enjoy today.

Sequence.

The word popped into my head this morning. I devoted this project to the idea that sequence had no particular relevance. But in proofing some of what went before, especially the beginning, I said I would be going backward. That was not correct. I started at the end and have bounced from there to the future and to a time well before Karen or me, before any of us were alive. So I am setting the record straight. And I admit I am satisfied with the way the timeline exists or does not exist. I have come to believe that a timeline does not exist at all . . . in life, in our world. We are alive in every moment of history should we choose to be. Nothing is faster than the speed of thought and the imagination gives all things their authenticity. What we think becomes truth if we like. In our minds is all. Thinking makes it so. And that line from *Hamlet* sneaks back into my consciousness. "There is a special Providence in the fall of a sparrow . . ." All things unfold as they are meant to unfold. The tragedies and the continuing beauty of life itself.

Enough. It is enough that we believe we live. It is enough that we love. It is enough that we try. It is enough that we stagger and stand to try once more. Auden said it best: stagger onward rejoicing.

It was the first class of the day in eighth grade. A man stepped into the class and announced that he would be expecting every boy and girl in the class to come and audition for him after school that day. We had never seen this man before and many of the kids did not go, but his energy seemed quite irresistible and, being asked, I thought it was surely something I should do. Come to the music building at 3:15. There were many of us and each would describe what had taken place in the stranger's office. He requested that we choose a song of our liking. And sing it for him. I forget who stepped out before I went in, but the song "Yesterday" by the Beatles was chosen by several of us, and I thought that was good enough.

Richard Mitten sat in a chair in the middle of the room. There was

◀ Mom from her glamour shots.
There is a fun book from her days
as an actress and summer stock.

My dad and mom—I ▶
think this is the 21
Club. The night
they eloped. This is
the look where I was
born. And where
Karen was born.

Mom moved to St. Thomas with Dad and ▼
helped with his business. Not sure she ever
ked the islands. She loved my father, though,
so she went with him to the Caribbean.

▼ And then came Kelsey. Nodding
off in the Virgin Island sun.

Mom brought me back to Colonia to live while she was pregnant with Karen. Here we are at the front of the house.

◀ Gordon as I remember him with the dachshunds. O of them bit my ear when I was young. Gordon was pretty upset about it. The were good dogs.

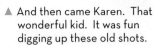

▲ And then came Karen. That wonderful kid. It was fun digging up these old shots.

The only shot of the two families ▶ together. Frank and Wilma. Mom and Dad. Gordon and Gam.

◀ Karen sunning herself on the Maverick.

▲ Danny Eng and the Kawasaki 500. Quick bike.

◀ Danny and me. I do not remember being this skinny. Sixteen years old. This might be after Danny and Karen broke up. We stayed friends.

▲ Karen with Brian.
Prom Night.

With Momo. I will never ▶
see her again, I suppose.
Sad to realize that
about both of them.

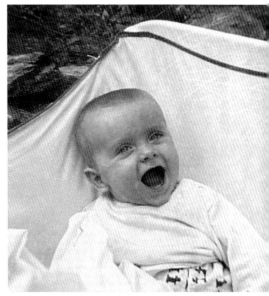

Karen and me. Side by side. I never knew we had the same mouth until I saw these.

▲ Karen's last Christmas.

Gideon, the famous white ▶
rabbit. This used to be
Gam's favorite chair until
the rabbit got to it. You
can see his handywork just
behind his head. Gideon.
I did laugh out loud when
I found this picture.

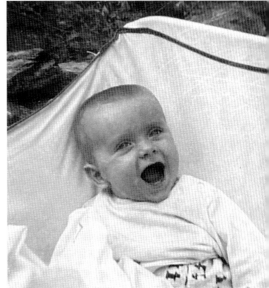

▲ Karen and me. Side by side. I never knew we had the same mouth until I saw these.

Karen - This is the only page that means anything to me so I hope you don't mind if
I sign here - I'll try not to deface it too much,
since it's such a nice page. Don't change too
much because I can't afford to lose you. If
you happen to bump into a memory of me I
hope it brings a smile of pleasure - not annoy-
ance. Love forever and Gillian

Perth Amboy, New Jersey . . . Cancer . . .

F. E. "...!" . . .

P. P. Narrowmindedness . . .

F. P. North Carolina, The Beach, Bed, Space City . . .

H. I. Friends, Cooking, Giving Shotguns, Freedom . . .

Karen Elisa Grammar

Think not that you can direct the
course of love, for love, if it
finds you worthy, directs your course.
Kahil Gibran

I find as I grow older that I love
those most whom I loved first.
Thomas Jefferson

84

▲ Karen's yearbook page. Gillian's inscription beside her picture.

▲ A collage of Karen. A little girl. A ballerina. Graduation day. That's Faith behind the man in the jacket and my mom on the far left. Karen's in there somewhere, white gown and evening gloves. She looked terrific. A wave from her perch in Welaka. Finding a recipe. A tutu. I will always remember.

▲ Karen's last Christmas.

Gideon, the famous white ▶
rabbit. This used to be
Gam's favorite chair until
the rabbit got to it. You
can see his handywork just
behind his head. Gideon.
I did laugh out loud when
I found this picture.

a chair opposite him. I sat down and sang "Yesterday" for him. He thanked me and said he would expect me to show up after school to begin choir practice the next day. I am not sure how it transpired that I was able to play football that year and sing but I think the class time was reserved earlier in the day to accommodate choir practice. So I was able to fulfill both activities. This was the beginning of my individualization in school. I was an okay football player. It turned out I was a better singer. "You are a bass/baritone," he told me. It was a good thing I had played trombone in fifth grade. Because of that I could read the bass clef on our sheet music. It gave me a guideline for the right notes to sing that was more efficient than simply learning by rote. Mr. Mitten was glad to let most of the kids learn the music that way, but he perked up when some of us could dive into a new piece of music sight unseen and make a pretty good stab it.

Things progressed rapidly from there. Different groups were organized. Outfits were chosen. A name was given to the premier group of singers: The Singing Pines. Tours were arranged in the community to sing for luncheons and country clubs and such. It became quite the phenomenon. We got tuxedo costumes with fringy, frilly shirts and bow ties. The girls wore gowns that were attractive enough . . . it was as if we were a uniformed dinner party singing for our supper all over South Florida. We sounded pretty good. There was one major issue to resolve—Gam! This was not really Gam's fault but the idea that her grandson, the grandson she adored and called "Gam's little man"— that grandson was not to be prancing about on a stage in a frilly tuxedo with hair-sprayed girls and evening gowns, waltzing and singing . . . but rather, that grandson, one Allen Kelsey Grammer, was meant to be beating the hell out of his peers on the football field and manning up for the life ahead of him! This was the first of so many disappointments for Gam, but honestly, she took them in stride and arguably yielded the field to the prancing stage version rather than the gridiron-grunting footballer she had hoped I might become.

Okay. I am overdoing it here for effect. Gam always loved me. There was some sincere concern that the path she saw unfolding would not serve me as a man. Simple enough. Gordon had been a man's man—he was good at all sports and good at camaraderie and good at guy stuff and brawling and boozing and whooping it up, as they say. He was handsome and strong and smart, a pillar of masculinity and also a gentleman—polite and cultured and respectful of all women. This was the male role in their society, and I am not sure what has happened to that role today. Toxic? I think not. Inspired. More like it. Exemplary, even more!

But for Gam, no matter what we think of the current role model for the male of the species, my singing, instead of doing something more traditional, caused her great concern. I even sympathize with her. How did the "man of the family" stand a chance of making a life for himself? She underestimated me, yes, but I do not blame her.

So, the scene was set. There would have to be some meeting of the minds, some "come to Jesus" moment for us that would lift the shackles of expectation and celebrate the young man who was emerging from the boy she always adored. Given that we did a lot of singing at ladies' lunches all around town, it was just a matter of time before I would stand before her warbling a Barbara Streisand tune. Oh, dear. What a nightmare!

"Ladies, please, welcome the Singing Pines!"

Gam rose from her table and awkwardly dashed for the cover of the bar. There, as a gin martini landed at her behest, she watched. And grumbled. This is what her grandson was doing instead of playing football! The bartender nodded sympathetically. And then I approached the mike as the introduction to "People" was being played by Joan M., our accompanist. It was rumored she and Richard Mitten were more than colleagues. I don't really know but it was fun imagining it. Richard was not exactly an Adonis. Joan, though, was a real looker . . . I actually envied him. If what I thought was true? Music had brought them together. A great passion. Along with the excitement of having such an impact on the young minds in their charge. I can imagine it was very exciting to have that kind of influence on such a lovely bunch of young people. We were. We were indeed a lovely bunch of young people. Willing and hungry to learn. Amiable. Bright eyed. Easy to fall in love in that kind of atmosphere.

I began to sing some of the words from "People." It was one of Streisand's most famous hits and it was high arrogance indeed that I would be singing it at all. I was singing beautifully, though. Better than ever. Probably because Gam was there. God was kind to me that day. It was during the second verse that the bartender leaned into Gam with another martini and simply said: "Now isn't that better than football?" I know this story because Gam told me. It was a moment of pride for her. As luck would have it, things were going so well that I thought I should jump the octave on the last note. I had never done it before and the surprise on the faces of my fellow Pines was unmistakable and genuine. To Gam's delight, she watched me do something that was good. Something my own. And worthy of her respect. A first.

"Let's get back to Texas. Mom."

Okay, Karen. Back to Texas.

Mom and Gam had a tough time. Gam had always had a tough time and I am not sure if that did not wreck things for her and her daughter. Things for her and her mother had been a shambles. So, not surprising that that difficulty would be passed along. Abilene, Lubbock, San Antonio. These three Texas towns were all mentioned by my grandmother in connection with their time there. I think they lived in all three of them, and it is hard for me to figure it out . . . everything about that time is speculation save for a very few photos and memories I have from Gam's own lips and from Mom's. I know for sure they lived in San "Antone," as Gam would call it. Lubbock and Abilene and . . . Amarillo!— that was the other one she always mentioned. I have no idea about them. I do not know if they are close by or distant from one another. Doesn't make much sense that the Army would have moved them four times in the two and a half years Gordon was overseas. Maybe there is a way to find out. Checking a map of Texas right now!

Well, turns out they are all hundreds of miles apart! No intel coming up on the military and such. So, I am left to just make up a story. I won't do that. I will piece together what I do know and hopefully a tale will evolve that honors them both and sheds some light on what Karen and I knew of them in our day-to-day. From theirs to ours. What continued. What was old, what was new.

Like I said, Gam was tough. She was the sort who didn't spend a great deal of time feeling sorry for herself. She dished out a great deal of drama to those around her and raged a bit. That was not fun. But Gam also had a beautiful generous side. An innocent beautiful girl side. She wanted to be loved, and she was loved. My mom wanted the same but she was quiet about a lot of her wants and her needs. Once in a while she would bewail her fate to us . . . "You treat me like I was dirt under your feet!" That was one of Mom's lines when she felt she wasn't being appreciated or respected. I never connected cause to the phenomenon. Maybe she was just down in the dumps. I asked for an ice cream or something. She couldn't give it to me or wasn't in the mood. Maybe something like that. Or the two of us just overwhelmed her. People are funny. Mom was not exactly sensitive or overly emotional . . . sometimes life just got the better of her. Or her mom did, meaning Gam, and she had nowhere else to vent things or no one else with which to share her frustration. Who knows what sort of life she might have had if things went differently. We used to giggle some and tease her about it too. Once in a while she had to vent, like I said, and we were pretty good listeners even as we would tease her. Nice, though, that we felt safe enough to tease her about it. In fact, I am pretty sure my sense of humor was greatly developed just trying to make Mom crack a smile. Karen and I both got pretty good at it. We didn't spend a lot of time trying because she was a good-natured soul. Just a little sad sometimes. As if having kids took some of her choices from her. Maybe. I know she loved us. I think she loved our dad. That might have been part of it. We were having one of the difficult evenings once when I challenged her: if things were so bad why did she leave Dad? What exactly was so horrible that you had to quit the marriage and move in with your mother? Well, that is the only time Mom hit me. She slapped me right across the face and said, "Stop it! Just stop it!" I hit a nerve. I shot back a look and a snide comment, "Well, did that help anything?" And then Mom cried. I felt terrible about it. She felt terrible. I am pretty certain she told me sometime later, "I just couldn't stay." I think she found out my dad was sleeping with someone else. She never told me that but Karen and I could put two and two together. It was probable and probably had something to do with it.

And so, I came back to the mainland with Mom that wintry night and stayed in Manhattan in The Plaza because of the blizzard. She slept in a luxurious bed for the first time in years and I landed in the lap of luxury quite literally on my very first day in America. Not bad. Easy to figure out why she had come home. And easy to peg why she didn't want to talk about it much. She was hurt. My dad hurt her. Or life did. She never married again. I do not say that with any degree of sadness. I think it suited Mom not to try it again. She was pretty comfortable in her life as it unfolded. She did once tell me she wasn't particularly interested in sharing her space with a man, not anymore. Or no more than an evening or two when the mood struck.

Back in Texas again. Sally is fourteen. And . . . from what I have been told, she enjoyed men. Early. Young men, her peers mostly, and some perhaps a bit older. Gam wasn't happy with it. Sally was young. Not too young. She was a woman early, just like Karen. She got there sooner than her mom expected. Her dad was fighting the war in the South Pacific. And Sally was a woman. There was no shame in it. Maybe that is why Mom was so easygoing about Karen. She never shamed my sister. I think she had felt shame from her mom and would not repeat the pattern. I admire her for that. It takes a great mom to close down a pattern of abuse, stop the cycle. Good job, Mom. And Gam too. Who knows what number of things she would not allow to be passed on to her daughter or to us? They remain the champions of my life—my grandmother, my grandfather and my mom. And Karen. Like I said—the love of my life.

Drifting. There is a distant memory banging around in my brain. It just came up and I stand on the verge of dismissing it, but it is still rattling around in here so why not give it a go? There was a guy who came home with my mom one weekend. I have no idea how they connected but he was, or would have had to be, considerably younger than Mom. She was probably forty or forty-one. He was with a bunch of grad students from up North for the Easter weekend and obviously broke off from his bunch to enjoy some local talent. My mom! She was still quite a looker, so I credit him for his good taste. And his interest in a woman of quality. Though why she chose a dalliance with this young man is hard to figure. Or maybe not. He was a big guy. Handsome. Okay. Not so hard to figure. A weekend of distraction and indulgence. Surrender to a timeless urge. Good for her. The memory that is bubbling up is of a particular drink that was the star of their lost weekend—the Pineapple Smash. Never heard of it before or since. Equal parts of pineapple wine and beer. Awful. And the source of an awful hangover that stretched from Sunday afternoon to Wednesday. If Mom's demeanor was any indication. It was a slow, three-day walk back to her normal self. Pineapple Smash. Good name.

How the hell did that one come up? You know, I think it's because I liked him. That guy. He was funny. And fun. It was also nice to see Mom having fun, too. A nice memory. A silly memory. A welcome intruder here. A break. Pineapple Smash.

Anyway.

Back in Texas, one of Mom's boyfriends had been Kyle Rote. The name came to me the other night and I checked his story and sure enough he was born in San Antonio. Maybe a year before my mom was born in San Francisco. They met in Texas and went the way so many teens go. Natural. Beautiful. Young. Exuberant! That was my mom. That was Karen too. Exuberant. Gam was tough. Life never defeated her. Not until the very end. Karen's death was the straw that broke the camel's back. She surrendered then. No strength left. She died three years later. Inconsolable. That was Gam. Indefatigable until then. Utterly lost afterward. Gam sat in her chair with a brandy and a cigarette until God finally came and took her home. Home was not a clear-cut place for her.

But it was Gam who was the leader of the family in Faith. She shepherded us toward Christian Science and the metaphysical intellect of its founder, Mary Baker Eddy. I believe Aunt Lela had some connection to it in Gam's earlier years and she turned to it by her direction. I am thankful for it in my life. I think Gam may have lost her ability to clear the smoke of the physical world when Karen was taken so brutally. It killed her too. Chalk off another of my family that died at the hands of those feral men. Gam, undefeated, lively, wonderful Gam. That kid who would not quit. She was a fighter until those last few years of unthinkable pain.

Mom managed a dignity that inspired me beyond words. I did not know how she continued. I admired her so much. She had a stoic serenity that defined her during the years after Karen's death. And it may have been her faith that did not fail.

But I have wandered from my thoughts about the years in Texas before I have finished with them. So, Mom was dating a young man, probably fourteen or fifteen years old; Kyle Rote became a very successful professional football player with the New York Giants, my favorite team when I was a boy. Imagine that.

I am trying to get an idea of how things went all those years ago. Gam and Mom were competitive. What I imagine is based upon things I was told years later. Gam liked the attentions of a man. It defined her to be attractive. I think it also defined my mother. I think they liked to pitch a battle or two about who got more attention. Now a young woman, newly ripe, in the full blossom of her physical gifts, and aware of it (as most young women are), Sally set about to get what she wanted. Gam tried to keep her on some sort of track, but I think she also longed for the company of men and some attention as she was a single mother by all practical definition. While her husband was on an island in a vital fight for the future of the world. Not much fun at home in the deserts of Texas. Something I learned by admission from Gam—there were a few men around who would keep company with her sometimes. A double-edged sword, as she had absolutely no respect for the men who had not gone to war. I am not saying she was right or wrong about that, but it was pretty commonly held that the men who ducked service were frowned upon. I know only what Gam told me. She saw a couple of men when Gordon was away. Was she intimate with them? It's something she would never have said. A lot of couples struggled with loneliness and longing during the war. Men were notoriously misbehaved during leave. This was the prevailing notion. Maybe they were, maybe they weren't. It was widely believed that taking comfort in the arms of a woman, any woman who offered a retreat from the darkness of combat, was a forgiven transgression. It was almost axiomatic. Surely, the same can be said for the women who were left behind during war. They certainly weren't making tapestries. And "Rosie the

Riveter" earned the right to look for something more after her shift of building planes and supporting the military machine.

Traditional ideas of fidelity were probably challenged and may have been irreparable when the boys came home. I will not name them now but one couple I knew was rent by it. A man who served but prided himself on remaining faithful to his wife, came home to her and learned she had not done the same. They never got over it. And, honestly, she did nothing wrong. She did something human. Forgiveness must surely have been the right path. But I am afraid it was out of reach. They did stay together but there was a reason he shared the heartache with me. It came with the confession that he had been trying to drink himself to death ever since. Sad. They were lovely people who were dealt a difficult hand. But they stayed together!

Gordon and Gam stayed together. I think I am circling the point I want to make, finally. My grandmother always said two things about her daughter, Sally. "She really threw me for some curves!" That was one. The other, "You'll always have to take care of your mother." Somewhere during those years in Texas, the dynamic between them became one of contention and judgment. Sally had disappointed her mother. Thrown her some "curves." I believe that referred to her appetite for physical, sexual exploration. I think that may also have been accompanied by jealousy. Gam was jealous that Sally could live freely without a care while she had to manage so many things. She had to be an adult. And let's face it, it is not so much fun being an adult. Gam liked fun. Gordon was fun. Gordon was gone. She also had to live with the fact that he might never come back. Not fun. But Sally was up to her ears in fun. And maybe that wore a little thin on a girl who fancied she should be having some fun too.

A moment.

Today is July 1st, 2022. Forty-seven years since the day Karen died. Many July 1sts have come and gone. Finally, something about this one is different. Causes. Beginnings. The events of that day. The legacy of Karen's Life. These all generate habits of speculation and dismay. Sadness and agony revisited. Noting Karen died this day is important. It punctuates her ending, yes, but today, this day marks a new reverie. A new context. For Karen. For me. Generations of us. As far back as we go. Generations of our people. Their suffering, their courage, their blood that runs in our veins. Blood that ran in hers. This is the difference—today, I celebrate her life. Celebrate them. Celebrate Karen. Vibrant. Alive. Charming. Beautiful. Love. Remember.

I want to close the book on Texas now. Offer a last observation that may have echoed into our lives from that time till my mom's final days. As I have said, speculation is all that fuels this idea, but it is based on days I lived with her and Gam. Days that were shared with Karen. Something in those days that could have been passed along. Not in a way I noted at the time but as a generational overlay—part of a cycle that can be overcome, but likely still has some impact.

Here, then, is a Waypoint. Another.

I do not recall Gam ever saying she loved Sally. I do not recall Mom ever saying it to Gam. And, yes, Karen complained that we did not say it as a family. I also do not know if Gam and Gordon were faithful to one another throughout their marriage. I suspect they were not. I have nothing but admiration and gratitude for them, but it feels important to explore this line of thought. I do not recall Gam or Gordon saying it to each other. Those nights when Gam sat with me in Florida, she spoke of their forty-year marriage. She told me tales of how they endured. She spoke of the times she would have to pull out the stops to turn Gordon's attention back to her when there was a new girl around.

Insights. Gordon was a very successful guy and spent a great deal of time in Manhattan—he belonged to the New York Athletic Club and would spend an evening in town from time to time. Mom told me that when she was a young woman in New York, hoping to begin a career as an actress, she was concerned that during a night out or attending a party with a group of girls who were all sent by an "agency," she might actually end up opposite her own father in an arrangement that was "understood" in the circles of successful men and beautiful young women.

So, I am in a conjectural tailspin here. I do not know if my grand-father was unfaithful. He did have a friend named Eleanor who was a Realtor. She drove the first 1966 Lincoln Continental Convertible I ever saw. What a car! Powder blue. And it was also the first time I saw Eleanor. She was a beautiful, leggy blond, tall and irrepressible. She lay across the hood of her car, clowning around in flirtatious gyrations, wearing a pair of short shorts and a little top that did not cover her stomach. I was eleven years old. She certainly turned my head and it would make sense that Gordon had a very similar reaction. It would also make sense that Gam would have a reaction all her own. I never heard a word from any of them that there was something more than real estate involved but Eleanor sure left an impression. She was certainly one of the finest-looking women I have ever seen . . . to this day.

And suddenly, Muff Rotella jumps back to memory. Muff, who had found me walking up the street. Bloody. Confused. After an acrobatic turn with my bicycle. Muff, first to open my eyes to the sheer physical beauty of a woman. And lingerie. Garter belts. Stockings. At no more than six years old. My goodness, my head is still spinning. It did confuse me a bit, but I feel no shame in it. I am not sure if I covered this already. I just checked, for the sake of argument and thoroughness, but there was nothing dirty about it. It was gentle and innocent, an awakening. And I feel the politics that have been attached to this simple human imperative have gotten a little out of hand. The men and women who like men and women and are happy to negotiate terms of intimacy with one another, are certainly entitled to do so as they choose. I salute them and their dedication to sorting out this whole business of love and longing. Relations. And without them, there wouldn't be much chance for the human race—at all.

Please, do not misunderstand me. The world has gotten goofy as heck lately. Do not suspect my advocacy for relations between men and women as some sort of argument for rape or gender bigotry or any number of the other concocted malignancies of modern-day personal interaction. My sister was raped! People of reason know what I am saying. And my sister was murdered. Any suspicion I am advocating for that?

I was heading to St. Thomas with Gam when I took this turn in the writing. As good a time as any to get something off my chest. Merely a cautionary observation, but these days I think we are just making some of this stuff up. No offense.

Back to the Caribbean with Gam.

I have just been born. Gam is heading to St. Thomas to spend some time with her daughter, Sally and Allen, Sally's husband, just after the blessed event. I think Gam was there several weeks to help out with the newborn son. And there were whispers of a handsome man who spent some time with Gam during her trip. Whispers that were mixed with a bit of humor and acknowledged that Gam enjoyed some attention, too. And there were several men in her lifetime, the one or two perhaps back in Texas, who were willing to express it. But . . . one in particular on the island that February, who offered Gam a friendly fortnight of sightseeing and a dinner out. Maybe something more. Maybe nothing more than a kiss. I remember some mention of an embrace and a lovely sunset. Sounds nice to me. People should enjoy being people. I do not blame Gordon and Gam for being human. They were remarkable individuals whose noble bones and blessed hearts still carry me. They are my frame. And my blood.

Sally and Allen. There is a look in their eyes in a picture. They are seated, toasting one another, in a booth at a restaurant. It is the night of their elopement. And in those eyes, I believe we can see the birthplace of Karen and me. It is a lovely look. Also, our blood and bones—their very source, in fact. And in that look is a promise—a promise that they would stick by each other. Sort things out. For better or worse. That didn't happen. But the spark that engendered us has never gone out.

My dad picked Gam up at the airport. She told the story with great flair about the three fistfights my dad had on the way to the hospital. This is how it went. Or how I was told it went. Dad picked her up at the Puerto Rico airport, where they transferred to one of the smaller carriers, much as he had done twelve years later with Karen and me. They flew together to the small airport on St. Thomas. At that point, they transferred to his jeep. An open-air affair. A typical jeep. Now, the fun starts. While driving through town, a local denizen who had disdain for my father and thought he should hurl an epithet as the jeep passed by was surprised by a squeal of brakes and a large man heading his way in a temper. An exchange of blows and Allen jumped back into the jeep and apologized to his passenger. "These guys just

229

think it's okay to swear at people in public and they know if I let it pass just once, they will see me high tail it out of here. I intend to stay. This is my home." I do not actually quote my dad here . . . it is a guess that came from knowing his love of the islands and what he and some of his friends shared with me. This is an approximation of his thinking. I want to acknowledge that. But there was clearly a prejudice at play that wanted to drive my dad and many of his fellow mainland expatriates from the island. And in his day, there really weren't many of him. It had been in play for generations, apparently; sadly, it may be still. It is what killed him. In the end.

These observations may be seen as "politically incorrect," but they are accurate and true. I promised myself there would be no lies in this book. And though it may make some uncomfortable to acknowledge these truths, it will not dissuade me from stating them. I have also sworn to identify any opinion as such—my opinion. I know the difference and I have been faithful to myself and to the reader in both truth and supposition.

The next, "Blankety blank!" that echoed through the streets of Charlotte Amalie brought the same response. Another came with a dash extra for my grandmother, as well. It was met in like manner. I know very little of who or what my dad actually was . . . I have these few stories.

Finally, they arrived at the hospital. Gam also got a kick out of her first time seeing me. There were several babies in the ward that afternoon. I had been born around 11 a.m. There were a dozen of us or so. The very pleasant and lovely attending nurse offered to point me out to her. My grandmother nodded she could already tell. Then Gam pointed at the only white baby in the room, and they shared a bit of a laugh. "Yes. That's him."

Two years later, I was on the floor of a hotel room. On the mainland. Mom told me I wasn't crazy about walking. I liked to swim, she said. I would swim at the beach in St. Thomas. My birthplace. I still think of it as my home. Nothing like that water.

Speaking of water. I am going to dive in here with a sentence I wrote when we started talking about Texas. Here it is: I think my grandmother disapproved of my mother for returning home with us

230

after she discovered her husband had taken a lover. It took me quite a while to build up to this idea. I think the thoughts I had about Texas during the war years, the years that built a wall of sorts between my mom and Gam, can be examined through this idea that she disapproved of Sally because she did not hang in there with my dad. There were many things that led me to the conclusion. Mostly what Gam said to me about her daughter. Mostly what she said about always having to take care of her. I have pictures of that time. Mom, in the heyday of youth and beauty, a young prize of a woman. Gam, a beautiful young woman still, holding up under the weight of single parenthood in a lonely place, while the man she adored was in an even lonelier place. For two years. In a place of war.

Men. Lost in an ancient mystery of the cruel and yet electric pulse of purpose that comes in a time of war. Life. Fighting for Life. That can be exciting. I think. But whatever the truth is about these days for my family, I believe they were days that defined much of their future.

Mom was cast in the role of being a dependent yet rebellious child, wild with appetite and long on irresponsibility. When she married my dad, I believe she saw a chance to prove herself to her mother. She would jump into this love with a man she hoped might prove as stable and worthy as her own father. The man both she and Gam adored. Gordon, the man who clearly played different parts for each of them but who never left them. Even though it felt like that when he was overseas. He came home. He stayed home. He may have strayed sexually, though probably not during the war. He was the commanding officer of a group of engineers on an island where women were not likely to be posted. Gam may have strayed a bit during the loneliness of those vacant days in the Texas desert. But they stayed together. Through it all, their marriage was a place they both occupied, steadfastly, flawed and human, perhaps, but dedicated to one another and to the title of Mr. and Mrs. Gordon Savage Cranmer. It was a banner each carried and each respected, whether or not it was perfect. It was theirs and sacrosanct!

I am not sure my theory about Mom holds. There are a few things yet to consider. Gam and Gordon, Sally and Allen, were from different generations. My dad's mom died in surgery when he was quite young. Gordon's mom died when he was just a baby. Gordon dealt with it in his way, Dad in his. Different men. Different boys. Born into different circumstances and different worlds. They shared an injury but the nuances of damage they suffered were alike in name only.

With Dad, I believe whatever it was that led him to look outside his marriage probably had something to do with his mom. Also, I think his decision to stray was an indication he had already left. I think this may be so with many men. I know I have felt that way in the past. I think Gordon, however, whatever dalliance he may have enjoyed or not, had no interest in leaving his marriage. His devotion to family defined him. His devotion to country did too. And his commitment to his daughter was unshakable.

And as I sum up on the tension between my mother and grandmother that crept into our lives as children, I believe Mom stayed with Gam because she could not look after Karen and me as her mother could. She went back because Gordon and Gam loved her and would care for us as they cared for her. The life with my dad was uncertain and even dangerous on St. Thomas.

And it is here that another idea persists. I believe it persists because it is true. Having seen the kind of life she lived in St. Thomas, Gam told Sally to come home. I am quite certain of it. So many years later. It doesn't mean that the relationship between mother and daughter got any simpler, but it makes sense. She loved her daughter. She saw her in distress. And though she was part of the generation who believed, "You make your bed, you lie in it"; Gam was also a loving mother whose daughter was suffering, and she wanted her to be okay. And something more. Gam was a member of the generation who suffered extraordinary hardships so that their children wouldn't have to, a generation determined to give their children a life they themselves did not know. "Come home," she told her. And Sally came home. Honestly, that saved my life. It made my life. It made Karen's life and my life rich with opportunity and safety. We were fed and clothed and adored. Loved. In real time. I say in real time because the love we enjoyed was always there, always present and always trusted. It had no bound and knew no limits. We were home.

That's pretty nice. What a decade we shared!

"You're getting it."

Maybe I am. I am. Thank you, Karen. If the reader is uncomfortable with these interjections, I am probably ahead of you. I have no other choice. I hear these things, and they are part of the process. A good part. It is enough that I believe. I invite you to join me, though it's not necessary. The information is sound. The relationship is authentic. Karen is real. Her voice unmistakably so. And the lesson for me is almost finished. It was finished the moment it began. I just had to go through a few things to get where I was meant to go. Relive a few, reacquaint myself with another few I may have overlooked or forgotten. It has been challenging, but also easy—sometimes as easy as closing my eyes and breathing the air of childhood. Sometimes not so easy. But I have been led to the ecstatic realization that this life is full of wonder even as it dishes out the unthinkable. Such suffering. Such elation. I am more grateful today than I have ever been.

I am getting it.

"Amen."

Soul contract. Change it. Did I ask for the suffering? Perhaps. May I ask the Universe for a new one? Live in the elation. What was it called? That book? *The Unbearable Lightness of Being.* Great title. Better idea.

Alignment with purpose and Providence. Aligned with God. That's what this is all about. I still miss my sister. But I was never meant to miss my life or curse myself for living. I did that. Not foolish. Human. I know. I've used the word a lot. But Human is the only word. There is no other. So, I have been a human being trapped in loss. I'd like to change that now. I would like to see what it is like to surrender completely to Love. The "big" love. And harmonize my life with God.

Coda. Caesura. A bird's-eye. Terms from music and poetry. Pauses. Pauses allow perspective and relevance in life. Pauses are for taking a breath. And then continuing.

I need a moment. A full measure's rest. To collect my thoughts. Then we'll press on together.

There is something I have to do. I have to formalize Karen's end. For those who get this far, I think there is a need to see what I have seen. Much of this I did not search out until now. I had stowed it in

233

a place as far from memory as I could. Details. For perspective, I now believe these details are important. Some documents and some observations must be included. Including the credible horror of what was done to my sister. Without it, her bravery is questioned and her memory is an obscure personal hurt rather than a towering testament to courage. The reader must know what is known. For Karen's sake.

It is time to submit the record.

Before I do that, I'd like to take a moment to praise Kathy. I want to acknowledge that she has shared how she never got over the death of her young husband. She went on to live a full life. A life of purpose. But with such sadness. An abiding sadness she says is with her every day. I know how she feels. And I hope this may help her as it has helped me. She will be among the first to read it. If she wants to read it. We are connected as we would never wish to be. But . . . we are connected. Kathy is a friend. I wish I could help her as she has helped me. I hope she can remember days of grace and joy in her young life, as she has endured so many days of dissolution and dismay since then. It is a feeble thing—my hope. Powerless. Powerless to help her in any way. I have only this to say—I am grateful for her friendship.

I have spent more than a month away from writing. A longer pause than I'd intended. There were some health concerns in the family and a trip abroad. And I had reached a crossroads. A while back, Jim Bentley, with the prosecutor's office in Colorado Springs, sent me a copy of files about Karen's death. Files from the investigation. The murder scene. This is the record. It was sent with a warning:

> I want to caution you about the details you will learn if you read all
> the material I am sending you. Please consider having someone you
> know and trust to review this information before you decide to read
> it yourself. There is no way to un-ring a bell and perhaps having
> someone else summarize the information might be an alternative to
> reading it yourself.

234

He goes on to identify where to find specific pieces of information that may be more relevant than others. I wanted to thank him for his thoughtfulness and have done so privately. At the same time, I am not sure I would wish the details on anyone other than myself . . . they are something I have pondered and feared for a lifetime. Yet, they are details I have longed to know. I am not sure the horrors of what actually took place can be any worse than those I have imagined. All those years. And so, I will take his advice as intermediary to the reader and will not relay more than a summary of what I learn. But I determined long ago that this is a journey I must take.

I am moments away from knowledge that was kept from me when I was young. I know why. Gentlemen and gentlewomen wished to shelter me from things they believed would harm me. Much the way I hoped to keep my mother from suffering more by sealing Karen's coffin. Will this be a change for me or just a confirmation of what I have believed? There is an alchemy in the written word. Most have experienced it. To see something in writing gives it credibility. Weight. So, there is a dread that has me gently captive. So many things have been said, so many supposed. Now I will know.

This may take some time. Wish me luck.

I have been abrupted in writing for several weeks . . . my last entry was August 26th and this morning it is October 20th. Of the police file, I have read only thirty pages, so far. That has been enough to shift my perspective on a few things and a few of them may be noteworthy. The pages are very clear about what happened to a young woman as yet unidentified. They are very specific about the moments after the attack that killed her. And a few things are different than I had thought.

In my imaginings, the man who found Karen at his doorstep was a "good Samaritan" of sorts. I stand corrected and disappointed that that man did not attempt to help her but simply called the police after leaving her body as it lay . . . eyes vacant, staring at the sky, her legs still on the steps, her head on the ground and a clenched fist above her head with

235

a single finger pointing—somewhere or nowhere—just pointing. She had fallen backward from the trailer door after knocking for help. It was her last hope and disappointment after crawling 400 feet from the place where she had been stabbed. Bloody fingerprints mark the trail of her final moments at exactly 3'6" along the office and walls of the trailer park. She had been on her knees, crawling her way. Seeking help with her last ounce of life. The coroner noted that through a gaping wound in her neck, he could see all the way into Karen's lung. I had been right in saying he almost decapitated her. Freddie Glenn punched holes in my sister's body with unimaginable brutality. There were defensive wounds on her hands.

What I had hoped were a final, few moments of kindness from some stranger, were nothing of the sort, and one couple who were interviewed by the police had heard a young woman scream in the alley behind their bedroom. And did nothing. They just went to bed.

Karen was alone when she died. In reading the first pages, I have been changed. As Jim had warned, there is no way to unsee what has been seen. Jim pointed me the way to a few other places further in the report. I will read them now. These first pages tell the tale of an unknown girl who died a sad and horrific death—the police report is unvarnished and without emotion. Factual. It describes the scene of a young woman's death in the early morning hours of July 1st, 1975, in Colorado Springs, Colorado. A homicide.

Karen.

A visit from my future self. It is a full year since I wrote what you have just read. I will return to October 2022, but today, this moment, it is October 2023. One full year later. I have been wrestling with the final edit of the book. Do I include the actual police report? Or portions of it? Or even just the first page? As I said, I stopped writing for two months after I read the first thirty pages. Honestly, the first words of the report stopped me dead in my tracks. I needed time. It was a graphic, impersonal review of what a police detective found in the early morning hours after Karen was killed. Only she was not Karen; she was a girl without a name. Lifeless. Just a girl who had been desecrated. A body. With a pair of jeans and a blouse I knew. Sandals and an outstretched arm. Smeared blood along a wall. A path of suffering, an enormous pool of blood and from there, the uneasy steps of a hundred yards. Her last steps. Then, the final crawl of her life.

I have decided not to include it. It is not my right to inflict on you the words that dehumanized my dear one. Made her a thing only. A corpse with no life. No breath. No identity. I read in the detective's writing of a someone who was a mystery. A girl. Not a sister. Just a girl with no family. No name. Stains of her final moments marked her trail. The trail. Ebbing moments of a life once vibrant, now limping unsteadily to its end. Unknown. That is what rattled me. She was no one. Just a dead girl no one knew. But me.

I stumbled. I almost fell as I stepped out of the trailer. Shooting a film in Connecticut with my daughter, Spencer. A Christmas movie. We had half an hour for lunch. It was then I determined I must finally open the file on Karen's death. The first sentences struck me like a dagger to my heart. I could not think. Or move. I just sat stilly, bathed in language unbearable to me. Drowning in thoughts and words unthinkable. Then I shook myself back to the surface.

Lunch was over. I stepped from the trailer. Stumbled. As I said. Lost my footing. Spencer saw me. "Are you all right, Dad?"

"Yeah, babe, I'm fine."

I was not.

Later that day, I told her what had happened.

I will return you now to a year ago. The thoughts I had debating whether to share the police report are sorted. And I am content to go back in time now. I start again at her name. And you are back.

Karen.

I will read the police report again now. And again. And after two months, I now find an uneasy comfort in these pages. I have spent so many years playing out these moments in my imagination. Now, I know the truth. There is no smidgen of relief; there is only clarity. It is the end of supposition and conjecture. Horror. Detailed horror. No more imagined fictions of what took place—only imaginings of how she must have felt and thought and suffered during those final hours of her life. Only a few hours from the time they took her till she was dead. What I had I still have—a simple enormous grief.

The report places a new burden on me. An obligation. Some new things must be searched out and some other few must be faced, visited before I close.

I will be gone again for a time. Not so long, I think, this time. Karen calls me and Freddie Glenn has another hearing in two weeks.

There is a paragraph from Jim:

Beginning at page 353 you will find where the police started talking to people who knew what had occurred. From page 540 to 544, there is an interview with Freddie Glenn's sister, Carrie Golden. Ms. Golden describes how Freddie Glenn confessed to the murder.

The supplement where Deputy District Attorney, Charles Heim, interviewed Larry Dunn is at pages 509 to 515. It is a very graphic description from one of the co-defendants and closely fits the physical evidence found at the scene.

I begin there.

Into the unknown.

I jumped off the roof.

I may have been seven years old. Maybe eight. I think seven. I had seen a documentary about paratroopers. I was always fascinated with the Army because of Gordon's time in the South Pacific and how little I knew of it. I was so proud of him and longed to know what he had known but would not share. I mostly wanted to be close to him. Gordon had not jumped out of a plane, to my knowledge. Maybe he did. Army Corps of Engineers. That could have meant anything. He flew or shipped halfway around the world and spoke of trackers and New Caledonia, being stationed at Fort Deal in Florida for a time. And Guadalcanal.

In this documentary, the impact of a parachute jump was stated to be the equivalent of a twenty-foot jump to the ground. A paratrooper must be poised to absorb a landing from twenty feet; he must hit the

238

ground and roll the instant he makes contact with it. So, there I was perched on the roof by the old oak tree in front of our home. I could climb out my bedroom window. I did. I edged along the side of the house. The pitch was exaggerated but manageable and I came to stand directly above the living room window. I had determined to jump off the roof. . . I guessed the distance to be approximately twenty feet.

New imaginings.

New thoughts invade where old ones had been. Larry Dunn's statement is difficult to read. It is now the foundation for my under-standing of Karen's final moments. The chronology. It raises many questions, but it is a step-by-step account of what they did to Karen from the moment they encountered her till the moment they fled the alleyway where Freddie Glenn stabbed her. It was his testimony that gave him immunity from this crime but not from the others he had committed. I believe he gave it to spare his own life. This was a death penalty case. When the death penalty existed; and when it meant something other than it does now. His testimony takes my mind to Karen's once more—how it must have been spinning and searching for a way out. Karen was sitting by a red Volkswagen Beetle around 11:30 p.m. in the parking lot behind the Red Lobster where she worked.

It is my mind spinning now. As I calculate exactly how to relate the next several bits.

The impact was not what I expected. I did not simply launch myself off the roof. A better part of valor led me to at least place my hand on the roof as I vaulted off. Landed. It hurt. But I did roll as the best of soldiers might and jumped to my feet with a new understanding of just how high twenty feet was. What it felt like. I would not repeat it. But I had survived.

Karen did not. She didn't even jump off the roof.

All she did was go to Colorado Springs in the winter of early 1975. She never told me why. I am trying to find the reason for it. Search for clues. The police report. Forensics. The tracking of her friends and final days. It has been helpful and even brought me closer to her. New questions in my head. More questions. Mostly, why my sister? I am still trying to unlock that time. Her time there. Her friends. I will visit

Colorado Springs. Places mentioned in the report. Walk as she walked in her final days and months. And yes, I want to witness the place of her death and her murder and her abduction. Self-torture? Perhaps. I could pretend it's not important to me. But now, after so much time, so much of my life spent wondering, I have an address and a location and the map of Karen's days. I must walk in her footsteps ... and in her fear ... and in her death. Her final days.

And her Ascension.

I pray Gordon came for her. I pray our Dad was there.

And I pray God was there.

I may not learn a thing. I could pretend it's not necessary ... but it is.

I stood on a baseball field just days ago. We had attended a revival called Harvest with Pastor Greg Laurie preaching. The much-anticipated moment came when he called on all of us to invite Christ into our lives. I have always wondered what that moment might be like. I have had a long and challenging relationship with God and Jesus and religion. It was my daughter Faith who said she wanted to go down. Without her I would not have gone. An easy irony—my Faith took me to Faith. And as I stood there, we both watched hundreds of others descend to declare themselves among the willing. To Believe. Also, as I stood there, among the hum of human longing, electrons of worship buzzing, I thought, *Where were you, God? Where were you? For Karen.* And I whispered it under my breath, "Where were you?"

Pages 509 to 515: Larry Dunn. I do not know how they found him, but an arrest in New Orleans led to an interview with him concerning the murders in Colorado Springs that summer. It was his first-hand knowledge that earned his plea deal. They had planned to rob the Red Lobster and pulled up in Freddie's car behind the restaurant. That was when they noticed Karen. I'd always thought she approached them. No. I was wrong. Not the case. With a gun Michael Corbett had given them, McLeod and Dunn approached Karen before they entered the restaurant. Dunn showed her the gun in his belt and told Karen to come with them. "For what?" she asked.

They took her to Freddie's car and left her with him. This is where some of the new questions come. They intended to rob the restaurant, entered but decided against it, and then returned to the parking lot. They found Karen tied up next to Freddie. I do not know what happened during that time in the car with him. No one knows. Except Freddie. I suspect it was riddled with threats to murder her. Dunn stated that Karen asked him not to let the others kill her. He said she repeatedly asked if he would help spare her life. So, after they took her to McLeod's apartment, they left her in a bedroom. Glenn raped her first. Then Dunn. He raped her twice and also stated Karen gave him a blowjob. Then McLeod. Dunn stated that he and McLeod had no interest in taking her life, but Freddie Glenn kept saying he was going to kill her. He wanted to kill her. They both resolved that if Freddie wanted her dead, he would have to do it himself... they would not help him. To clarify, McLeod was a key participant but not the focus of my thoughts because he died. I believe he asked Michael Corbett what it was like to shoot a person and Michael showed him. Shot him. He has not occupied a place in my thoughts throughout the years. I never knew he existed till now. Until I read the report. And now, I only wish he had rotted in jail along with Corbett and Glenn. Rotted in his choice to hurt my sister.

"For what?" It was funny. When I read that it sounded just like Karen. She had a courage, an assertiveness that sounded just like that. I was proud of her when I read it. And I believed Dunn was telling the truth. They told her to come with them, Dunn and McLeod, and Dunn showed her the gun in his belt—the gun given him by Michael Corbett. This is why Corbett had also been charged in Karen's murder—he gave them the gun that played a role in Karen's death. She got in the car with Freddie Glenn. Perhaps, he told her then he might have to murder her... it was his concern she could identify them. Supposedly.

I stood on the baseball field wondering why God had not been there for Karen. "My God, my God, why hast thou forsaken me?" Jesus. I imagined Karen asking the same. I cannot write this in a way that satisfies me. Karen suffered. Jesus suffered. No satisfaction.

There was a boy who loved God. He and his sister would walk hand in hand to Sunday school in New Jersey. Mom would attend the regular service, and they would sit at a table with a lovely woman whose features are past remembrance, save her voice and gentle hand. The

241

boy loved to read from the Bible. It was a special treat when she would call on him and he could battle through the complexities of the King James Version. And he loved it. Speaking the verses out loud helped him understand them—embrace them. And to know God.

Yes, I am speaking in the third person. About myself. But it feels right to see across all these decades and speak of him this way, he who is now so far removed from me. But the same heart unites us, and time does not exist. So, in first person then, I discovered my heart through my love of language and how it connected me to God. As it says in John . . . In the beginning was the word and the word was with God—and the word was God. I think that is how it went with me. I spoke the word, and it brought me understanding. Faith. And God came alive for me. It brought me to my love of language . . . a love that defined my life. And my life's work. Karen sat beside me; Karen was beside me.

God was beside me.

I have tried to read between the lines of the police report. I wanted to find out what had been in Karen's mind. Find out more about that night. More about her life. So I could get closer to her state of mind that night. Closer to her internal thoughts and what took her to Colorado Springs. There were names of men and women who knew her. A store clerk where she used to buy cigarettes. A waitress at a bar who thought she had seen her with a young man having some drinks, enjoying one another's company. Her roommates. Two men and a woman. All quite young. Karen was just eighteen and her circle was close to the same age.

And suddenly in the pages was a name. John. Someone I had known. He and Karen were roommates in Pompano Beach where I attended that party in December 1973. They had been boyfriend and girlfriend. I believe he may be the key to finding out about those last months. John. I don't really remember him. I remember we met and that he was with Karen in a shared apartment, and they were going out. I think he had brown hair and was a pleasant guy. A year younger than I. I have tried to email him at an address that may not be active anymore. People seldom change email addresses; so, I suspect it is he but there is something prompting hesitancy. I have asked that he reach out to me. I am going to keep trying but I will not press him. I hope he has the kindness to empathize with me. Realize he may be the only person who can help me. Perhaps, he feels responsible in some way for Karen's death. I felt responsible too. Maybe he feels to blame but if he knew how I have longed for just a whisp of her in her final days, it would be a blessing to me. I want to know her in that time.

"You do know me."

There again. Beside me. I do know you, Karen. I just want to know how you came to be there that night.

I think I have it. You were lonely. I had concocted some version where you had gone to get your paycheck and spotted them, approaching them, asking what they were doing there. The brief escape was fantasy. I am certain one of the officers suggested it. The report included an incident of a young girl seen fleeing a car. An assumption. The police thought it was relevant and told me they suspected Karen escaped her tormentors for a time. But this was told me before they had Dunn's statement. It was not the case. There was no escape for you, Karen.

Was it beneficial? The truth. I don't know. No, that's not true; I do know. It was beneficial. Not pleasant or comforting in any way but the truth has helped me. The horrors I had imagined were at least equal to what you actually endured. With one small exception. The last words Freddie Glenn spoke to you. That was the final horror I could never have imagined. "Tilt your head back."

Larry Dunn described a sound: "She screamed but it was a low scream like she had a bone stuck in her throat." Then he saw Freddie Glenn stab her repeatedly as she had fallen in some tall weeds. Glenn jumped back into the car. They sped off.

Beneficial.

There is something beneficial in knowing this. It is ammunition to keep Freddie Glenn in jail. I confess as I have tried to put myself inside Karen's thoughts that night; I have also tried to wrap my mind around his. When they brought Karen to the car and sat her beside you, did you tell her you would probably have to kill her? Since she could identify you now? When you tied her hands with the blue scarf, did you whisper you would do with her what you wanted? Was she tied when you raped her or was her willingness to do what you asked enough to leave her hands free for your violation of her body? And for your friends. And on that drive to the alley where you took her, did you blindfold her with the same blue scarf before you got in the car or was it just before you killed her?—before you told her to tilt her head back and punched a four-and-a-half-inch blade so deep into her neck it almost decapitated her. These are the images that have replaced the ones I'd imagined. They have fortified me to fight you. I confess my resolve was weakening. I began to question if you had indeed been in jail long enough, as you have stated in your numerous hearings. My tendency toward compassion confused me in this fight. I actually felt pity for your Soul; now I am not sure if you even have one. The fiendish earthbound magic to which you gave yourself handed you this ending. A kinder ending than the one you gave Karen. I will use everything I know to keep you where you are . . . it is where you belong.

In prison.

My prison too. No escape for either of us—you or me. But no longer do I have doubts or second thoughts about your confinement. Your life was forfeit long ago. I am strong in my knowing. And I can finally forgive myself. You boasted, "I just killed a girl," to your sister as you wiped Karen's blood on the curtains. She washed them. So, the dog and pony show you two put together for that first parole hearing was just that. And the knowledge I have now makes me stronger than ever. I will not allow you to confine me any longer. I have had enough of you!

One last conjecture as I close this up. You wanted to prove what a man you were, how tough, how brutal you could be. You wanted to take your place among filth—really show 'em somethin'!

Congratulations. You're a murderer.

Stay put. You earned it.

And I am free.

Finally.

I am in Palm Springs today. Shooting a film and we have a little place here. We spend much too little time in the desert. A lovely home. The film is a good opportunity to enjoy it a bit. And to do some writing. Digging for her final thoughts, and reading through her final weeks and months, has taken time. Searching for clues and friends who might shed some light. I spoke with Jan and Brian. I still hope to find Wandi for many reasons. Momo too. I hope John calls and there is still a mystery or two to track down—people who knew her then. I will try to find them.

A visit to Colorado Springs. I am wrestling with it. I do wish to walk her final night. I am drawn to it. So, I shall. Not certain it will help. But knowing only part of the picture is not enough. Even if it hurts. Hurting is not really the issue—this has always hurt. Feeling closer to Karen. I feel closer to her. Many doubts are settled and conjecture, what I have imagined, has been harder, more torturous over the years, than the knowing I have now. I mentioned that some of this new knowledge has raised new questions. I turn to them now. I turn to Karen. Her mind. Why was she in that parking lot by the red VW?

Gordon. Karen lost Gordon too. The impact was devastating to us, as much to her as me. Two years later, Dad was killed. I have downplayed that because we did not really know him very well but there was a loss there. Perhaps, it compounded the confusion of our young years . . . we felt pretty rudderless. I did. But I had a job . . . to look after the house and the girls. Woefully unprepared for it but there was a station for me. A set of responsibilities. I replaced Gordon. I could never replace him for Karen. Karen and I had each other. But we were on our way to our separate lives and Karen, I think, liked company. Not loneliness. We both had plenty of that.

I think that is what took her to the Red Lobster that evening. She liked company. I believe she was there to spend a little time with a boy she'd been seeing. Danny. There is mention of him in the pages I have read. A boy who worked with her. Who liked her. She liked him. Karen was happy to have a few boys simultaneously. Maybe it was the time in which we grew up. In the early seventies, we were pretty loose and amorous, you might say. Multiple partners . . . if we were lucky enough to have any.

That was my issue. Very few girls seemed interested. Boys had a harder time of finding companionship. For girls, it seemed pretty easy. For Karen, the added circumstance of the loss she felt may have made it more important to her—friendships and a variety of experience. But, without reading too much into it, Karen liked to spend time with people. We both did. She was good company. That smile. That openness. She was a remarkably intelligent person. Insightful and compassionate. We enjoyed meeting people together, even sharing one another's friends. Some intimately. We made a good life of what we had. I remember driving with her one time and she pointed out, "That girl just checked you out!" It surprised and delighted me, "Where, where?" We took pride in each other. We enjoyed each other. I had to play out the role of big brother from time to time. Rescue. I was meant to rescue and guide her. I will not go back to that . . .

But Karen was anticipating a date with a boy she liked. A few hours later, she was dead. I am not sure Danny knew she was there. I have read no statement from him saying he had seen her that night. Correction, he had taken a swim with her earlier that evening. There is no mention that he was aware she was waiting outside the Red Lobster or that he had seen her after the swim. So, she probably wanted to surprise him. Or maybe she mentioned she might stop by the restaurant later but she was not there when he quit work. We know where she was by then. The police interrogated Danny. Read him his rights, taking him into custody under suspicion of murder. He must have been scared stiff. He was just a kid. I found him, but he does not want to speak with me. I have to respect that. I long to speak with them—any and all who knew her in the final days and hours. I long to see her. In them.

Karen called herself Cassidy sometimes. Her roommates mentioned it. Now, I don't remember this. I don't really know why she called herself Cassidy, but I think she may have liked it as a more "free-wheeling" handle. A bit flirtatious. Not so serious. Karen could seem serious sometimes. Partly because she could barely see, I think. She wore glasses and they gave her an aloof quality, a seriousness that fooled some people. "Like she knew things that others didn't"—that is how an old friend of mine described her. I guess she could be a little intimidating. That intelligence. Maybe she wanted to be more playful. Cassidy was playful.

Karen was sharing an apartment with three others—John, John's friend, and a girl who was in the military. Pam, I think. I am cautious about using names, as I said before. She worked at Fort Carson. It was she who said that Cassidy had taken a little cash out of the drawer . . . twenty dollars. The drawer held the cash for rent and such. Karen wasn't a thief, so my guess is that she planned a little tryst with Danny, maybe a few drinks at the bar where the waitress had seen her with a young man just a week or two before. It does say in the report that Danny asked a friend, "Isn't she cute?" Yeah, she was cute. And she planned to replace the twenty after she got paid.

John and Karen had come to Colorado together in February. He had gotten her the job at the Red Lobster. It was with a friend and several others from the restaurant that John had gone to Arizona that week to help open a new Red Lobster. When they got back, two-and-two had begun to come together, and an identification of Karen's body was made after the roommates contacted the police. Oddly enough, they all had the same difficulty identifying Karen as I'd had. She looked different. In fact, they all said they did not think it was she. It was around that time I visited and confirmed her identity. Our dentist supplied the forensic proof. It was clear she did not look as she had in life. A single entry says her brother came to collect her personal belongings. Such a small phrase for so enormous an event. It seems wrong. Lopsided. It mentions Karen asked John if she could use his truck while he was gone. He said no. And I am sure John spent some time wrestling with that.

Correction!

The future is forcing its way in again. From the days and pages ahead. Something in the preceding is inaccurate. I will address it downstream from here. You have my word.

John. I do hope he gets in touch with me. He is probably a good man and good men damn themselves with what-ifs and if-onlys. I pray he has forgiven himself. If not—John, forgive yourself. Please. It's not easy carrying around a baseless guilt. I should know. I remember you. I thought you were a good guy. God Bless You. I wish I could tell you to your face.

As I stood on that baseball field, where the Angels play, ironically, I asked Jesus where he had been. And his moment of doubt came to me. My God, my God, why hast thou forsaken me? And I knew Karen felt abandoned. Hatred was playing its pernicious role once more ... killing Love. And it swallowed Karen. She suffered so much. They did to her what we did to Christ. Forgive them for they know not what they do. I am trying.

I opened my Bible today to Luke. When I read the Bible, when my eyes land on a page, without fail, there is instruction: in the shadow of death, guide our feet into the way of peace. Oh, how I pray for Karen. And standing on that field, I prayed again. I hugged my daughter, Faith; and she filled my broken heart. I am so grateful for the love I have in my life. For my children and my wife. For the love I have known in my life. And for the love I will know. Throughout my life. I have been blessed. Will be blessed. And I still miss Karen.

A friend of mine was a priest. Ken. Ken is no longer with the church. I offer no reasons for it as it is not my business. But he was an inspirational voice on God's behalf and said something in a homily one Sunday that stuck with me. I paraphrase. As if God were speaking, Ken said, "I am not out to get you; I'm here to help." I am over-simplifying. But that's it. Simple. God is not the architect of woe and tragedy. Life is a gift that comes with many challenges and heartaches, heartbreaks even. God and His Love are there to comfort and sustain. That boy who loved God was so content. He was so happy and saw God in everything. Even after Gordon. Joy was at hand in each day. And God was apparent. Then Karen. And the door slammed shut. I slammed it. But still I cried out to the God of my childhood. In absolute despair. Expecting no answer. Still begging for one. Nonetheless. I have often been moved by the story ... I think it's called "Footsteps in the Sand." The speaker in the piece confides that when he or she was a child, walking the beach, in the sand, there had always been two sets of prints side by side. As the child grew older, only one set of footprints was evident. Where had God gone? The answer came from a still small voice: my child, when you saw only a single set of footprints—that's when I was carrying you.

I turned to the Bible to find the words Jesus said on the cross. There are different accounts of his final moments in the Gospels of Matthew, Mark, Luke and John. This is my history with God . . . I always felt as if I could access God through scripture. So, bear with me. I am not advocating a religion here. I am merely explaining the path I have found in life. I remembered the story of the men who were crucified beside him that day. I went looking for it this morning and found it in Luke. One mocked him saying if Jesus were the son of God, then surely, he could save himself and them in the process. The other spoke of how they deserved to be where they were for the things they had done, but this man (Jesus) had done nothing at all. He asked Jesus to remember him when "thou comest into thy kingdom." And Jesus told him: verily, today shalt thou be with me in paradise.

These were the things that ran through my mind as I stood on the "field of Angels" and pictured Karen on the threshold of destruction. The many times I have been told by mediums that Karen was taken early by God. I want that to be true. And I pray that God indeed did take her from her body. That in her final moments, she was not in the midst of the horror but in the bosom of the Lord. In his comfort and care. And I wrestle with this idea. The scream she made. I can only imagine that though she may have tried to console herself that God was with her, that she would be all right; in that moment when the knife struck, her cry was as the cry of Jesus.

"My God, my God, why hast thou forsaken me?" And I pray that in that moment of doubt and fear and agony, it was then she knew God was with her. Even though her life was ending, she was all right, assured she would be joining Him shortly. In Paradise. I think that is what they must mean when they speak of how God was with her. As his life ebbed from him, Christ entreated, "Forgive them for they know not what they do." I get it now. Hate is powerful. Not as powerful as Love. God is Love. Karen is bathed in Love. Forever.

I need to take a breath.

Jesus promises a safe landing; not a smooth journey. I heard that the other day. Isn't that what I just read? The men who died beside him? It seems apt.

By way of offering a little insight into this "relationship" I have with the Bible, I can relay a few stories. I'm a bit leery starting down this path. I have promised you a book about Karen . . . and me. I did not say I would be preaching the Gospel. And I am not. I am on a journey. Karen is the path.

"I came to bring you Joy."

Esther confirmed it when I quoted Karen. Through Kayte. "Yes," she said. Karen did bring me Joy. I think she may even have come a second time to bring Joy again. You see, I have been shown myself in this. As a boy. As a man. And in this, both have been pointed toward something. I am the boy who loved God. Saw him in all things. It was simple. I am a man who lost God. And lost the boy in him. I am becoming the boy and the man once more through God's Love and the enduring love of my sister . . . the man who loves God. Once more.

So, as the stories go. I do not remember when I first fell on this means of consulting the furies. Or the "sea of troubles" as Hamlet says. It is enough that I found it and not necessary to uncover why. Or how. It is. Something in me. Something I have. Something I have been given. Or I am just insane.

Ooh!—a good sidebar. A digression.

I am not sure if this is still true but forty years ago, I learned that more books had been written about Hamlet than Jesus. Remarkable . . . a character of fiction that has historically captured the hearts of man in like measure to the Son of God. Now, I know not everyone agrees with me about Jesus. This is my personal belief, and I mean no offense. I accept you may not share this belief, but if your measure of another is based on kindness and not assumption, then I beg this simple indulgence. Surely, such generosity of spirit is something we all still have.

Okay, so that was a digression inside a digression. Anyway, it fascinates me that the character of Hamlet would be so powerful . . . it is that good a story. In fact, once asked what books I would want with me on a desert island?—the answer was immediate: The Bible and The Works of Shakespeare. Okay, a bit of a cheat. The volumes of Shakespeare that comprise his "Works" are many and somewhat unwieldy . . . in a pinch I would settle for the Tragedies. If push came to shove, I would

250

There are a bunch of images here. Starting with Goose and concluding with a recent time in my life. They coincide with parts of the story you will recognize. They are here to mark that story and to note the story has not ended.

Outside of Minnesota. This little girl was fascinated with Goose. She would stay with me like that for hours. Goose, I mean.

t summer he
ley's Aunt at
cond time he
time being in
arter. Among
recent years
r Town, The
lomecoming,
rial of the
ominated for
nces in Had-
lot and won
n Enemy of
eeting of the
olia. He ap-
Festival com-
During the

Program from the San Diego Shakespeare Festival. My first job. Actually, my third season there. Goose and I left for NY after that summer. My friend, Russel, did drawings of all the cast and crew that summer. An amazing artist. I was flattered he gave me the orginal of this sketch.

This is the picture of me and Goose. James said was Daddy and Mommy. No question, a great love. Maybe James was on to something.

▲ The day I married Kayte. The love evident, if not exactly what James saw!

▲ The reception.

▲ Our wedding ceremony at the Longacre Theater.

▲ Gam with our poodle, Neveh, sitting beside Becky, Ron's mom.
We were all quite close those years. After Gordon was gone.

COMMUNITY ACTION
☒ ALLEN GRAMMER

▲ Dad ran for office in the islands.
Gunned down. He didn't deserve
that.

▲ Edna Weeks . . . my grandmother. I never
knew her. She died in surgery in her
forties. Maybe that is why Frank said the
family was cursed. So much early death.
Edna, my dad, then Karen. A lot to bear.

▲ A note to Mario Peña's daughter at his passing. He was a remarkable friend. I loved him. He was important to me. I wanted people to know it.

▲ Mom and me. The last year of *Cheers*, 1993. In the first house I ever bought. One of Gam's old dining chairs behind us. I have them to this day.

▲ And Mom. Dressed for a special occasion.

▲ The first season wrap party for *Frasier*, 2023.

All these pictures. Before and since Karen died. All still connected to her—every one.

▲ The Gate of Opportunity. 1870?

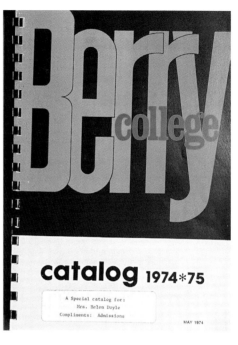

catalog 1974*75

A Special catalog for:
Mrs. Helen Doyle
Compliments: Admissions

MAY 1974

▲ Berry College.

▲ Karen went to Berry College in the fall of
'73 and continued the winter of '74 . . . the
folks at Berry provided this as context.
A look inside. Faces of the hopeful.
Classes to arm them for the fight ahead.

▲ Karen's dorm. I felt her here.

▲ Pictures sent from Karen's friend, Rhonda. Hikes and days in Georgia.

▲ That smile.

I love this picture of her. I did not know of this life, the one she lived after we both left for college. I am extremely grateful to have these images. It is almost as if I am meeting her for the first time myself.

▲ My sister. Gazing at the running water. Surrounded by life. Gazing ahead. Did she know, I wonder? I like her here by the water.

◄ And this final smile.

▲ My brief visit to Colonia. The pond where the older boys played hockey in winter.

▲ Al's old house. Next door to mine. I still remember his phone number. My first friend.

Al died about two days after I took this picture. The giant snow hill was just to the right of his home. The plows had pushed the snow so high. We played King of the Hill. And I pasted a bully with a snowball. All here.

▲ As I left Colonia, I found the old elementary school. #24. Great days there. And behind me, I swear I saw us all. Behind me, but always with me.

▲ The old Colonia house as it looks today.

Pictured on this page are three friends who were alive when I
started writing. Al Rotella, Doug Peterson, and Carl DeGersdorff.
Doug and Carl and I went to sixth grade together and remained
friends for life. Al lived next door in Colonia and was my first
friend. He did live his dream in this production of Chicago! Carl
ran several kitchens from NYC to Miami and was a brilliant chef.
Dougie went into the oil business and did very well . . . a great
athlete and a terrific sailor Good boys. Good men. Good friends.

settle for just *Hamlet*. The line, "Oh, God, methinks I could be bounded in a nutshell and count myself a king of infinite space," is justification enough. The line that came up one day talking with Kayte. It could set me thinking for a lifetime.

Sidebar ended. In Sunday school we learned the Bible could be consulted for its wisdom and instruction. Lessons, identified and studied each Sunday, could inform our daily lives. That is the idea, I think, behind what is called the "living" Bible. It is relevant even in this very day. Our time. Its time. Are one.

Jill. I think the first time I opened the Bible in this manner was for insight into Jill. When we met, she had a boyfriend. I think his name was Chris . . . that's not true, I know his name was Chris. And it was a torment to me that she was so close to home when we were at school. She would slip back to West Hartford for a weekend visit and, of course, to visit Chris. Much torment. Funny how these emotions recalled still have teeth. I feel it now as viscerally as those days. Fondly. Oddly enough. Feeling is a very good thing. Even when the feeling is frustration.

Loneliness. I did long to be with her and even tortured myself a bit when Chris was visiting her in the city. It was just one occasion, but that night I sat in a little pub along Columbus Avenue and gazed at her window on the seventh floor of her 72nd Street apartment building until I couldn't take it anymore. It was sometime during this period that I sat down with my Bible and in meditation on Jill, the book fell open to a spot in Joshua. He was bringing down the walls of Jericho. Something about circling the walls seven times with the Arc and Jericho would fall. I took a moment and conjured up the conceit that in these verses was a clue. Be patient. Circle the walls seven times. Be steadfast and patient and Jill will fall. And she did. Chris became a memory and Jill became my love. Maybe I declared my love for her seven times until the response was no longer, "How sad for you." But . . . finally, "I love you too." Hallelujah!

Spinning a bit of a yarn. It is true I sat torturing myself in that café on Columbus Avenue. And the subsequent message from the Bible is also true . . . it did happen. Just trying to inject a little humor here. To entertain. I realize the last dozen or so pages have been very hard. They were hard for me. The record of Karen's last hours was a very challenging read. I have tried to spare the reader much of what was said but I feel an obligation to convey the horror of her death. It must be noted and respected. And I think people should assume a personal investment in all murder, so that our society spends a bit more time realizing victims deserve as much consideration as those who face judgment for their crimes. Far too many horrors in our day are being overlooked because of the criminal justice reform movement. I concur with much of what they advocate but not to excess. Bail for murderers or manslaughter or violent crimes is unacceptable. And the no bail policies in many of today's cities are crimes themselves. Causing more crime.

I was finishing a film last night. Shooting a film. The one begun in Palm Springs a few weeks back. I was meant to be sleeping in the scene, so my work was idle at best. My mind was not. The character had spent many nights in the desert trying to sleep. For the first time, he was on a couch. A refuge offered by another character in the film. His first night of comfort or warmth in as long as he could remember. I thought it would be a good "touch" to keep one hand clenched a bit as if to suggest the torture in his body could not quite let go. And as I lay there, pretending to sleep, I remembered the first description of Karen's body as she was discovered. On her back. Vacant eyes. A clenched fist above her head and the index finger pointing. Where?

As I lay there, I imagined it was her last conscious effort before she slipped away. She was pointing at the place she was murdered, some four hundred feet from where she expired. It hit me like a ton of bricks. The resolve I had to move back into kinder days was pointed back to that simple moment. An overlap. Forty-seven years ago . . . last night. The same moment. Time means nothing. As promised, the life we shared is still shared and unfolding even as I see her raid the candy jar and reminisce about our moments in the snow or on the hammock. Or driving to a concert. Or reading her poetry. Or watching her

252

graduate . . . top of her class. I was so proud. Still am proud to know her, to have known her. I warned myself this would happen. Why should my life be any different than when I write? So, it is all in there on a master data bank that opens randomly, or at will, to any moment, as if "in" that very moment, at that moment in time. No time.

And I am there again. On a plane in October. In the future. A future that sees me finishing this book. Two years after I began. The future is last night. Karen's last night. My night. My hand as her hand. And now. Like a pulsing rhythmic line of events that stack one on top of the other . . . cards to be played. A deck of endless combinations recalled and shuffled in varying order. Infinite. Yes, there is a linear element. But like a yardstick or a carpenter's measuring tool that folds back in on itself.

There are warnings about using the Bible as a kind of fortune-telling device. Sometimes frivolous, perhaps, but often from a deep need, I ask the Bible for guidance. It is how I pray. On one occasion, in Buffalo, New York, while I was working in the theater there, I wondered out loud how old I would be when I died. As I asked the question, the book naturally opened to a page in Job. Well, not naturally, actually. It fell open which is natural for a book standing on its spine. It will fall open naturally to some page. The page turned out to be quite remarkable. Divine, possibly. Or maybe just a supernatural sense of humor directed it to Job. The very last verse. "And when he died, he was an old man and full of days." Not exactly a number. But definitely an answer. With an ironic twist. Perhaps. Maybe my sister having a little fun with me. I remember thinking so at the time.

I begin with a question or a mystery. I close my eyes and then open the book . . . once open, I run my finger along the page without looking. And stop. Where it stops is the first thing I see. A bit like closing my eyes as Karen instructed me so many years ago. The Bible is a light. I ease my mind into that light, eyes closed, and then open my eyes to the teaching. Fantastical? Possibly. But it is so.

Who is Kayte?

I did the ritual. Opened my eyes. The last chapter of Proverbs. These were the first words I read:

Strength and Honor are her clothing
And she shall rejoice in time to come.
She openeth her mouth with wisdom;
And in her tongue is the law of kindness.
She looketh well to the ways of her household
And eateth not the bread of idleness.
Her children arise up, and call her blessed;
Her husband also, and he praiseth her.

Well . . . I am not sure I have heard higher praise for anyone in my life. Kayte and I married a year later. I will say that we are all human. We all still make mistakes and sometimes our performance falls short of our potential. I am talking about myself here. Kayte has been pretty remarkable. I would say these lines characterize her still. In fact, I would say she has lived up to them in full.

As for me, I have been a disappointment in many ways. To myself. Perhaps I have held an impossibly high standard so that the odds of living up to my dreams are dashed at the get-go. I have a tendency toward self-loathing and probably share this with many people. We need to let it go. Truth is, I have done all right. Why do I constantly dismiss myself? Why do I doubt my worth? I wrestle with it still. Why do I still feel guilt about my sister? Why do I doubt I am going about things in the right way? I often come from want. Confidence is unattractive. Or so I have thought. But I do not believe that is so. Confidence earned is very attractive. And reassuring, inspirational even.

In the book of virtues, I come up short sometimes. Not desperately short. Lacking. My estimation of myself is weak. But I can flip the coin and count myself a good man. A good man—just not as good as I'd hoped to be. Odd. I discount my accomplishments and embrace my shortcomings. What defines me? Self-pity? Bad habit. Certainly. And many, I believe, know how I feel. I know how they feel. But as I rattle on in this manner, comes an ardent: ***"Knock it off! Unattractive. And untrue."***

Okay.

I reread a bit. I guess we can all descend into foolishness.

Presumption. I don't know that. I don't want to write stuff I don't know for sure. So . . . I can descend into foolishness. I know that. I will try to do less of it. And I know, that more than anything, I have tried to be good to others. We all are someone's enemy. I'm sure I am that person to some. I have tried to preserve and project the best version of myself possible. Truthfully, I've done all right, and the beauty of life—is I can do better. Gordon's words are echoing in my ear as they often do. "If you see a bug, step on it or walk around it." Very few bugs out there worth stepping on, honestly. There is only one I can name off the top of my head.

I will edit this book. I am editing this book right now. This is my second review (now third) of the writing here; (oops, fourth) and a suggestion came from a friend that I need not mention I will edit. Five, six, so many edits now, they're past counting! But I explained to him the value of a third level of communication with the reader. The audience. I like including you in the process. I mentioned it earlier. Henry Fielding. *Tom Jones*. One of the great English novels, possibly the greatest. Henry often reminds us as we rise and fall with the fortunes of Mr. Jones that we are likely reading one of the great novels. I believe he insists it may very well be the greatest novel anyone has ever read or ever will. And he does so right smack-dab in the middle of his own book. Speaking directly to the reader as if he were there in the very room with us. I found it delightful. I remember laughing out loud while riding the subway to school. He was in fact riding the subway with me. A young eighteen-year-old on his way to acting school. Burying my nose deeper in the book to mask a belly laugh. Gleeful. A charming convention, Mr. Fielding! Or invention. Commenting on your own work, adding to the enjoyment of it. A window. So, in shameless imitation of Henry Fielding, I have borrowed the trick but without the bluster or brag. I just like the idea of including you, the reader, in the process. So that when I wrote: I am tempted to leave in some of the wrangling passages; I now say, one year later: I am leaving in some of the wrangling passages. And I am editing the book. As we speak. Back to it, then.

A stream of consciousness, a stream of memories, have guided this writing. That stream was a bit halting at times. Other times, it flowed without a single hiccup. Just like life. Leave some blemishes in. Our life together, Karen's and mine, was halting at times and filled with missteps. A few hiccups. Some blemishes, perhaps. Not sure I'd call them mistakes. Leaving them in reflects our life. Exactly. Accuratel y. As it was. My chief observation about myself . . . laziness. Mostly. I believe I could have given just a bit more. I am still working on that. Life with a full try . . . to the fullest.

To the fullest. Yeah, that much is right.

Jumping off the roof. There was nothing lazy about that. Foolish. Maybe. It characterizes many of the choices I have made. It characterized Karen too. We would try things. Step off the edge of the world. Into the unknown. A pitch-black drive on a motorcycle in a thunderstorm. Leaving home. A kiss under a rising moon with a beautiful stranger. Running headlong into the unknown. I wouldn't have it any other way. It's not worth anything if it's not worth everything. I loved her so much. And I am glad she lived the way she did. Brave.

She went to Colorado with John.

I am having drinks with him today.

So, John went first. Karen followed in February. She loved him. He showed me some of the last letters she ever wrote. They were to John. They had hope in them. And they had love in them. Excitement. John opened a very bright door for me yesterday. Filled with light and innocence and images I had never seen. The time that was hardest for me were the months Karen spent in Colorado Springs . . . I had no idea why she went there. I feared she had been escaping someone or something of our old life. I was a little mixed up with my guilt and even feared I was responsible for the something that drove her away. I hadn't protected her from it or from the someone. Even if it was beyond my abilities, there I was blaming myself for it—something unknown. Something nonexistent. The truth?—she left *for* something rather than *because* of something else.

The first time I spoke on the phone with John, I told him I had some holes to fill, some gaps. Why did she go to Colorado? "She came because of me," he said. And he began to cry.

We met at one of my customary watering holes yesterday. John brought some pictures and a couple of letters Karen had written him. He brought me a picture of the day he returned from Arizona. He wore a hat. A picture taken just before he learned Karen had been killed. Moments later he pulled that hat over his eyes and collapsed. He spent three days inconsolable. During that time, he told me he never took the hat off. Not until he came up from the basement and faced what had happened. The police interviewed him.

The promised correction.

John and I spoke yesterday morning for half an hour. There was an entry in the report that Karen had asked John if she could borrow his truck while he was in Arizona. That is not true. Yet it had been entered in the report. There in black in white was a presumption that hurt John. Hurt his feelings. He read the book last week. The final edit had been made. But hadn't. John corrected me. I correct it today. His truck did not run any longer and Karen knew that. She would never have asked to use it. People can get things wrong. Police reports can document moments that never happened and cast aspersions of what never occurred. So, I issue this apology. And this correction. I wrote something that wasn't true. It is good to know that. Good, this chance to correct it. Today, John is a friend.

Back now from the future in which I am presently writing.

It was the police report that led me to John. There were three others living with her. Karen and John were boyfriend and girlfriend, but you could see there was a wider circle of fast friends who loved being young people, idling through nights of partying a bit and working at the Red Lobster.

As John told it, it sounded pretty ideal. There was so much love in the pictures he showed me. They went camping and skiing. It was fun and I was so happy to see her. It was as if time had stood still. I looked at one shot and said to John, "I used to trim that hair." She had such lovely long brown hair. She was radiant in the photos, and I smiled to see her. She did seem happy. John knew nothing of why Karen had moved to her apartment. Nothing of her old friends. Nothing of her high school. I was able to fill in some blanks for him. They had met and a new world was designed solely by their affection for one another. Their world.

There was a terrific New Year's party at her place. I attended that party. John does not remember meeting me. I acknowledged it was a brief meeting at best. He admitted a bit later that he did get pretty drunk. I remember telling Karen I liked him; he seemed like a good guy. And then he told me how she had taken him to bed that night. She was clearly very fond of him. He told me yesterday he never forgot her. That makes two of us. John also told me he visited us, my mom and me, shortly after she was killed. I do not remember that. I will speak of it again in subsequent pages. All that matters now is yesterday. John and I met—met for the first time we can both remember. And it was magic for me.

Karen and John worked at the Fashion Square Mall in Pompano Beach, Florida. He at a shoe store and Karen at the Swiss Colony, a cheese and deli place. I think I went out with the girl whose parents owned that store. No, there I go again. Not quite right—I know I went out with her; I think her parents owned it. Gail was her name. I could have the wrong store. It might have been a Cracker Barrel. Anyway. That would have been a year or two before Karen was there. I do remember seeing her head off to work in that outfit during the summer. I have a picture of it in my head. Maybe she sometimes stayed at the house once I was back home for the break, but Karen still had her own place then. Was it the same place she had the Christmas before?—I think so. John never came to our home. So, whenever it was that they actually met, John knew only of Karen's apartment. The young people who worked at Tom McCann, the shoe store, and the young people from Swiss Colony would mingle after hours and John would sometimes take his lunch hour there to visit Karen. They liked each other. That is how it began. And then one day, Karen asked John if he would like to come over for dinner. That summer. It was 1974.

I remember Cat Stevens and Robert Plant and singing songs I still sing today. I remember lyrics. James Taylor, about a girl named Karin. I sang that when my Karen was alive. I have sung it on both sides of her life. And I have shed a silver tear every time. I loved her. Karen was not saying good-bye to anything or anyone . . . she was eighteen and on her way to an adventure for a few months. Following her heart. She and John were talking about coming back to Florida. They went for a winter romance and to share their newness in life . . . step out onto space and explore the Universe. There was no finality about it. No bitterness. Just Frolic. Love. That was about it.

The pictures are wonderful.

I lay in bed last night half sleeping. Half awake. There was a new home. Beautiful pieces of furniture were waiting to be placed. Where to put them? It was a wonderful space. I felt peaceful and rested. I felt challenged to make sure every part of this home was filled with light and comfort. And it became clear. The home was this book. The Book of Karen. It was my book too. And it belonged to a few others as I made my way through it. It was John's now. Kayte's, my children's. A part of it. And Jan's. It was my mom's and Gam's and Gordon's.

In the dream I was responsible for placing all the pieces. It was our home. It was our life. And it was waiting to be told. There are several elements still in "storage." Actors in the wings. I believe I know most of them now and where they fit, when they will enter. There may still be a few surprises. John has a few that I will share. They are extraordinary. There are a few forgotten friends who will show up unexpectedly. And something else struck me. We will live in these pages forever. Stowed out of conscience, perhaps, as Auden once wrote; but we are here together to tell our story to anyone who wishes to know. Always. This has fallen to me.

Comfort. There are millions of people who have suffered millions of horrors. In writing this, I hope to find words of kindness and consolation. Turn these pages. There are words of woe, surely. Words that remember a wonderful soul. Happily. Words brimming with life toasting the beauty of living life fully. Even if briefly. I am resolved to offer words of solace too. I feel obliged to try. I will try. I promise. I will not forget.

And, God, please save me from sounding like a condescending, self-important twit. I want to help others. I want this book to help others.

Meanwhile . . . we have a few places yet to go.

I got a text from Brad last night. Here it is:

Hi Kels, Merry Christmas to you and your family! I just woke from a dream and had to text. We were driving down some street with the top down singing Leon Russell at the top of our lungs. And of course, we were young and incredibly good looking!!! Miss you.

I miss him too. We will meet up soon and spend a bit of time. Probably, flying down some road singing Leon Russell. Things haven't changed much. Brad and I love each other. I think we loved each other the moment we met. But, we didn't know that then. And I might never have known it if I hadn't met Dale Robertson. So, here I go on another digression. Brad and I have been friends for fifty-some years. He won't mind.

Dale Robertson.

Honestly, I idolized Dale Robertson before I met him. As a boy, I had watched him on a show called *Wells Fargo*. It was about the early days of the wagon train corporation that opened up so much of the country to travel and commerce. They were anthology tales loosely based on historical events from that time in the Old West. He later had some very popular TV movies about Melvin Purves, the famous FBI agent. I think they may have been subtitled—G-man. Government man. Like GI—as in a soldier; it meant Government Issue. Everything a soldier has or needs is provided by the government. Food, wardrobe, weapon. I guess that is how the handle "GI Joe" was born. I am on a funny track here, but it is relevant to Dale. Dale landed on the beaches of Anzio during World War II. He had been a boxer as a young man. Not sure if he was drafted or volunteered for the Army. He was shot in the leg during combat. It left him with a knee that bothered him throughout his life.

To the meat of it. I know what I know of Dale Robertson solely from "the horse's mouth," so to speak: the things he told me after I got to know him. Speaking of horses, he was also an excellent horseman. You can tell when you see him on television. You can just tell . . . the posture and his ease in the saddle. He was an inspirational figure for me and when I was cast in a new show of his; I was excited just to meet him, doubly excited to work with him. It was called *JJ Starbuck*. I was playing a diabolical classical pianist who was plotting to kill his archnemesis, a very critical judge who stood between him and victory in a most prized competition. My character faked his own heart attack, snuck out of the hospital to do the dirty deed, and returned undetected, having rigged his monitor equipment with some rhythmic device to fool the night nurses. I think there were even a few pillows involved to feign a sleeping body in the hospital while he went about his crime. He was, of course, no match for one JJ Starbuck! I arrived on the set the first day and there he was. We smiled and shook hands and he welcomed me to the show. Then we started reading through the first scene we were to shoot that day. The director, Kim Manners, was there. Kim would go on to a very successful career directing several shows of note. He was good guy. Sticking with Dale. The two of us just hit it off. We laughed out loud together and navigated a somewhat tongue in cheek duet of the "heel and the hero." Then one day we were being interviewed for a feature piece in one of the magazines at the time. That was when Dale said, "Kelsey and I met two days ago, and we just fell in love!" It was true. We had fallen in love. The most virile, self-assured man I had ever met just told a perfect stranger that it was love at first sight. Pretty much. With an Oklahoma drawl in a bellowed baritone. Then I echoed the sentiment, "Yes, that pretty much sums it up."

With Dale Robertson in JJ Starbuck.

And that sums up Dale Robertson. A man who wore his heart on his sleeve and bore a heart as big as the sky. We visited from time to time after that. He was my friend. I loved him. We planned an elaborate golf outing that never materialized. I swore I might get out to Oklahoma someday. I never did. Hell, I still haven't been to Oklahoma. But Dale and I would see each other from time to time out in Los Angeles. We would connect on the phone. Always share a laugh. He had a terrific daughter and I think I spoke with his spouse a time or two. Especially, when he got a bit further along.

He called me one day and told me something I have never heard. "Well, Kelsey, I broke my last horse." It didn't mean he was going quit riding. It just meant he wasn't going to outlive the horse he had just broken. And he was right.

Dale stood in my kitchen one evening years ago. I think there were a couple of my other friends around. We got to talking about the world we live in and some of the foolishness we all agreed was foolishness. Other folks might not see it our way but he did say this: "Everybody knows the difference between right and wrong." I still hold with Dale on that. Tidal waves of cultural oppression and popular movements collapse every year or two, imploding on themselves, but they corrode faith in our institutions, in fact, prove corrosive to those very institutions and to the principles we hold dear. They undermine. Why? To control us. Confuse people about what is right and wrong. Confuse them about themselves—who they are. If you don't know who you are, you can be controlled. Once a group of people are in control, they like to keep it that way. I am not going to ask anyone to agree with me. Just keep your eyes open. And your minds.

Dale Robertson lived in Oklahoma. He always knew who he was. A remarkable man. A loyal friend. I have known few like him. A compelling individual. He taught me how a man could love a man . . . no confusion. Stand up, straight out Love. The boy who couldn't tell his own grandad he loved him was taught a great lesson by this "one of a kind": genuine cowboy, genuine hero, genuine man. He was also a hell of an actor. "Movie stars aren't actors," he said one day, "they're personalities." He added, "You're an actor." I am still wrestling with whether he meant that as a compliment. I would rather be an actor than a movie star, but . . . why can't a person be both? Maybe? I think. That movie star thing sounds okay. Doesn't it? Still, I did take it as a compliment. It is, isn't it? I hope so.

So, fifty-plus years after I met Brad, I can tell him I always loved him because I had the good fortune to work with Dale. I have learned a few things in the last few days that support this conclusion—when we met, Brad and I "just fell in love." Just like Dale said.

This morning, I texted Brad.

I just had an epiphany about John (Karen's John) and our home when he visited after Karen died. The life was missing. In the home and in us. The number of people I have spoken to about the refuge our home once was. The fun we all had there. John visited us when there was only shadow. Sorrow. Like Karen, only the husk of our existence remained. The house couldn't even muster a memory of joy. Not then. It never really changed for us. There were still some nice days, but they were always dimmed with mourning.

Brad spent a lot of time in that house. He was there for the days of silliness and sarcasm and love and laughter. We did party there a bit. I was more of a standard alcohol, beer-swilling yahoo. Karen and her pals were into a bit of pot and such, but nothing went on that wasn't fun or exuberant. We were kids. How else could it have been?

I remember when I cut my leg on a barnacle and developed a terrible infection. Had to stay in bed for several days. It meant a private visit form the most beautiful girl in the world. Pam. I, in my delirium. She, a caring Florence Nightingale who thought that maybe a glimpse of her magnificent breasts would help in some way. She was entirely right. Unforgettable. It did make me think I should try to stall my recovery for at least a few more days. She was a true beauty. And a beautiful soul. It was innocent. It was personal . . . not Instagram. We were exploring our sexuality in a youthful, adoring way. I did adore her. She was a kiss in the moonlight. And I never wanted to do anything that might hurt her. She strung a set of beads for me, black and white, for around my neck. I wore them every day until they snapped off in the ocean while surfing. We were good kids. Thank you, Pam. I remember.

The text to Brad was returned and in it was a piece of information that inspired my memory of Dale Robertson. For reasons you already know. I had asked Brad how long we went to camp together. It was a music camp at Florida State University. Brad and I were roommates. We met on the first day of the camp with the other kids. You could say I was musically gifted. I was not a musician. I had been singing for a few years and had some success with it at school. I wasn't bad at sight reading because I did play the trombone for a year in fifth grade. Sight-reading is a way to learn a song by sight rather than by rote. Sing a song. Play a song. I do not intend to speak down to people when I explain the process, but I fear there is far less music education in our schools than when I was a boy. I had the blood of musicians in me ... Mom and Dad were both musicians and had met at music school—David Mannes in New York City. I was not like them, though. I was musical but not a musician. Not yet.

Brad, on the other hand, was a brilliant musician. His dad was a brilliant musician; his uncle was a brilliant musician. He was, hands down, the best musician at camp. And I had the good fortune to be his roommate. I am a little vague on how we got food, but I seem to remember a pink card that was punched for each meal. There was a little fee involved at the dorm check-in. Then our room assignments were handed us, and that is the first time I saw Brad's name. I just texted him again to confirm we were actually in the same room. Something is telling me I managed to get my own room but then we all hung out there a lot. I am awaiting confirmation on that as I continue.

Anyway, check-in was accomplished and we were informed we would be doing a little orientation after lunch. We sat in an auditorium. Very impressive. Florida State is a beautiful school. Our instructors for the term introduced themselves and the projects they would be doing. *Jesus Christ Superstar, Trial by Jury* by Gilbert and Sullivan, and we would be taking composition, conducting, and voice production (vocal coaching), as well.

They got right to it. Moments later, we were handed a piece of paper and were given a test. They asked us to identify the intervals that they would play and then write them down. I turned to someone on my left and said, "What is an interval?" Two notes: one is played and then the next, and the listener tries to hear how far apart they are and identify it—a third, a fourth, a sixth and so on. "My Bonnie Lies Over the Ocean" starts out with a major sixth... "My" and then the first half of "Bonnie" (sung "bah")—that is a sixth. That is what the guy told me after he explained an interval to me. I think I guessed the sixth right. So, one out of twenty was probably pretty poor. Like I said, musical but not a musician. It was an incredibly rewarding experience.

Brad got a girlfriend, Sandy. I was not in a relationship at the time. There was a beautiful girl who was attending camp. We held hands. A lovely walk on a sultry southern night. Shared an innocent kiss. I liked her. Genie, Geanine? It didn't go any further than that. We were hard at it putting the two staged pieces through rehearsal and readying them for performance. Brad played Jesus in *Jesus Christ Superstar*. I luckily snagged the role of Herod. He played the judge in *Trial by Jury*. I played the jury foreman. In the composition class, I finally put to paper a song I had written for Gordon. The lessons in conducting were edifying and challenging. Brad and I were welcome to "jam" in a rehearsal studio that had two pipe organs in it. That was a kick! I learned a couple of songs from my voice coach. Our final performances were smash hits, as the saying goes. Awards were handed out for musicianship... three of them. They went to Brad, of course. The young lady who accompanied most of the productions on piano took the second. I was awarded the third! It was a jaw-dropping achievement for me. This was my first full-fledged experience in a conservatory atmosphere, a full-blown artistic immersion. And I loved it.

We were there for two weeks. Not six, as I had thought. Two weeks, as Brad relayed to me moments later. And that's when I heard Dale Robertson. Brad and I had met and..."we just fell in love." More than fifty years later, we are still friends. It also helped to put that summer in perspective... it was the same summer Karen had gone to North Carolina and worked. The same summer I drove with Danny to visit for a week but then stayed for just one night and turned back around. Driving a wounded Danny back to Lauderdale.

I didn't know at the time, but I had been the recipient of a great boon from an unexpected source. Spencer Lane was one of the more important administrators at high school. Diana was my voice teacher. She worked with the music department and became a true inspiration and influence in my singing. Ron had been the drama coach and English Teacher that year and I had done my first performance in a play. Richard had recruited me years before and started me singing with the rest of the school when we were in eighth grade. It was the summer of my junior year. I was seventeen. Together they had identified the program at FSU and recommended it for me. I couldn't go because of money. Not poor, but we had very little cash lying around to spend on a couple of weeks in Tallahassee. Singing and such! Spencer Lane paid for it. I had forgotten until now. I think Diana told me. My goodness. His generosity bankrolled me to a career. I would never have tried for Juilliard and Carnegie Mellon if it hadn't been for those two weeks in June. I didn't know until it was past decorum to thank him. I will thank him now.

It was Spencer who asked what I had learned that summer . . . "I want to be an artist. Maybe an actor." I loved my time at FSU. And he asked me what plans I had. I told him there were two schools that qualified. To platform from young man to actor. He looked at me and said, "Go get in." He never mentioned his kindness or his generosity. I pray he was proud. I am grateful. I remember hearing him sing one time at the teacher/administrator talent show. Something they tried one year and it was quite a kick. Spencer, it seems, had been a singer. Bass/baritone and may have sung professionally at one time. It was not painful to listen to him. There was something there that smacked of real talent. Yes, he was rusty. I was pretty raw. He still saw potential in me. I saw quality in him. I learned he was a man of character, as well. Remarkable.

As I navigate the latest pages, I find that more and more surprises erupt from connection to connection...influences and inspirations. And the connections are surprising. Unknown till now. I am housing in this book a number of relationships I have not honored in my life. And as I honor Karen, others step forward from my unconscious into this moment. Gratitude. Some who were bad. Some joyous and irreplaceable. My gratitude is new to some. Familiar to others. Unexpressed to many. So, as I said before, our footsteps are taken together. They are Karen's and mine. If she were alive, I wonder if every shadow of my memory would be colored by her. If every joy would be tempered by my dismay at her taking off. I realized not very long ago that I have never allowed myself to be happy. I have been happy but the full blush of joy in life?—no. In every joy, diminishment—a reining in, a sliver of disappointment. There is always a withered leaf or a shriveled edge of remorse and self-loathing. Hitchhikers. Uninvited. Unwelcome. She has grown tired of it. Frankly so have I. Karen put me up to this. Not for her sake. For mine. But... I am resolved to let her shine. She was wonderful. She was soulful and beautiful and wise. And fun. I am grateful I knew her for the time I did and I am grateful I did not let her go. I am grateful it was suffering ungoverned. Unapologetic. It was love. I felt it. Real and forever. Abrupted and ambushed. Indelible, indescribable, inexhaustible. I feel it still and I am grateful for that. And knowing that. As I know it now. I know I can live in Joy. Happiness. I have spent years surrounded by life and children and success and always kept a corner for despair... unwilling, or undeserving I believed, to live so full a life while Karen was deprived of hers. I was wrong. She has asked me to arrive at myself. Oh, God, my God, I miss her so.

"I am with you."

Thank you.

I still miss you.

And I have made a couple of wrong turns. There was a woman in my life who scoffed at me. "Your life hasn't been so hard," she would say. Perhaps not, I explained, but it was enough for me. Maybe empathy just wasn't her strong suit. It doesn't matter. There was a decade there and some kids. I owe her a great debt. I stayed longer than I should've, but she taught me that dying for her was a real waste of time. A waste of Life. So, I thank her for that. I decided to live again. I pray the children will forgive me. I didn't mean to hurt them. But I had actually closed the book on myself. And as a result, I certainly could not help

267

my children or their mother. Or myself. So, I had a heart attack. It felt like the only solution. A little dramatic but as I walked toward the beach that day and whispered to myself it was a good day to die, little did I know that an hour later I would be begging God to show me nothing fancy. No lights, no tunnels. Nothing. Nothing that would take me from this life. I lived. I was given a second chance. I am grateful for that. Karen was along for that ride. I would have loved to see her. She hid.

Now, I do see her. For the past year, I have seen her. In almost everything I do. And thanks to John, I see her in Colorado. As I have never seen her. I see her smiling and laughing. Clowning and loving. "Cassidy" to her Sundance Kid. I had guessed right. She sometimes called herself Cassidy. The police report mentioned it. I connected it to the film. *Butch Cassidy and the Sundance Kid.* I asked John. He said yes. She was Cassidy and I was Butch ... no, the Sundance Kid. I was the Sundance Kid. It was very cute and very heartening. I knew Karen. I knew her very well. It was cute to think they had gone there as a kind of partners in crime. To make their fortune and to make their way together.

Rather extraordinary is the fact that John made his way in time to Florida State University and then to California. Los Angeles in fact ... to be an actor. And on one occasion he booked a job on a very popular sitcom called *Cheers*. Amazing. The man who could offer me insight into my sister's final days was a guest star on the show. Neither of us knew it. Somehow, John did not connect that I was Karen's brother. And I could have had no idea until recently that he had been with her in the winter of '75. And in Colorado Springs. And in her life when she was killed. So, as he tells it, it wasn't until a few years after his appearance on *Cheers* that he read an article in *TV Guide* that spoke of my tragic past and my sister Karen. He finally made the connection. He did not contact me. And I think it is likely that the moment we spoke on the phone ... he had the chance to finally say what he had come to say all those years ago. Remember. He said our home was cold when he visited after Karen's funeral. It was. Maybe he didn't feel safe. Safe enough to explain their connection. And why she had gone there. He probably wanted to explain . . . but couldn't. Maybe he tried. I really do not remember the visit at all. He had a second chance that night on the phone with me—forty-seven years later. I am deeply grateful to him for this . . . if there is something I need to know, I can check with him. And will. I believe we will be friends. Extraordinary that we were so close all these years and never connected. Until now.

"The readiness is all." I knew that statement meant something to me. Something personal and pertinent. It has echoed in my mind since the moment I first heard it. The readiness. It was something I read when I first read *Hamlet*. It was something I heard when I played Laertes in it so many years ago. I had not truly heard it until a second production in Massachusetts. My friend Deveren was performing *Hamlet* and I had agreed to do Laertes again for him. One night before the show, he told me his son had died. Yet, he did the show that night and would return to California for the funeral on Monday. Our day off. The performance that night was the best he ever gave. And when he recited the lines:

> There's a special Providence in the fall of a sparrow.
> If it be now 'tis not to come; if it be not to come
> It will be now; if it be not now
> Yet it will come. The readiness is all.

I finally heard it. And by heard it, I mean, I finally knew it to be true. "The readiness is all."
Am I ready to let her go?
Not quite.
No.

We are in Palm Springs today. James Taylor is playing throughout the house. "Fire and Rain." Years ago, I was on the road. Robert was with me and our two dogs. We were performing in cities around the country in *Othello*. James Earl Jones was the star and Christopher

269

Plummer played Iago. Last names are okay with famous folk. Robert Ousley was my friend's name. He enjoyed a long and fruitful career, so I guess he was famous too. Our tour took us from Boston to Minneapolis, Chicago to Miami and finally to Broadway ... there were other cities; we were on the road for almost a year before the show opened at the Winter Garden. A long drive one night. James Taylor was playing. "Fire and Rain." It broke me. I was singing the line out loud and I just started to weep. Robert was very kind. He didn't know. It was Karen. I was pretty good keeping it bottled up back then, but music can break through anything and that night my heart split. The simple truth. I always thought I would see Karen again. Letting her go. Well ... not sure I ever can.

Not sure I am supposed to. The opening night of *Othello* was as high as I have ever been. Broadway. The show ended. I was greeted backstage by an old friend and a girlfriend from Chicago. Richard and Jeanine. There were hugs and congratulations all around and we made our way over to Sardi's for an opening night party. It was everything a Broadway opening was meant to be.

I am reliving many events as I write. I think there is a reason. To claim the joy of what my life has been. Fully. Nothing kept me from enjoying my success but me. So, I have to go back a bit and teach myself a new set of emotions that more properly align with the events in my life. I had opened in a Broadway play, for Pete's sake! And I sat at the table with a good friend and a lovely woman and was sad. Distant. Richard looked at me and said, "Enjoy this!"

It was hard. Gordon was gone. Gam was gone. Karen was dead. I sat wishing they were there. Sat wishing they knew I'd done what no one thought I could. Not quite right. Karen thought I could. I was determined to prove I could, even though I had my doubts. I did okay. I felt sorry they missed it. And there I sat not allowing myself to enjoy it. I really liked Jeanine too. But I wasn't available really. She was a good person. I was missing my family. My mom had seen the show in Florida and would come up again at some point. The others couldn't be there. Obviously. I am looking back at myself from my kitchen counter in California and allowing him to smile, that young actor, and finally enjoy the good fortune that had befallen him. Befallen. I like that word. It might not be accurate. It implies a level of luck, but it also suggests the recipient is actually there to receive it . . . in the game. "Giving it a go," as they say. I had worked quite hard up until that moment. It wasn't exactly like getting hit on the head with a stroke of luck. More like working very hard and having the good fortune to achieve the desired goal. But at the time, I could not allow myself to relish it. Now, I can. So, I will. I smile today to think of the good fortune that had befallen him, or the good fortune for which he had strived that befell him. I still like "befallen." It's an old-fashioned word. I'm an old-fashioned guy. Yeah. Finally. I really enjoyed that night. My first Broadway play. Wow!

Better late than never.

I still don't know why Karen decided not to stay in college. One semester. That was it. She was a brilliant student. I can't imagine she didn't have ideas about her future and earning a degree of some sort. I will try one last time to reach Wandi. She is the only one I know who may have seen her at school that fall. I remember nothing of why she left, no conversation we may have had. Our old friend, Brian, was able to shed a bit of light on her days the last two years at Pine Crest. He mentioned he had hung out with her one evening when she was waiting for me to finish up some after-school event. I was her ride. Mom told me she wanted to change schools, go somewhere she wouldn't be in my shadow. That made sense.

Brian grew nostalgic when we spoke over the phone and I felt the love he had for her. They had gone to her prom together. It was a picture I never imagined. Karen's prom. She must have been lovely. I wish I remembered how she looked that night. I was probably off doing something with Brad or singing somewhere. If I had known those days were among the last few days I would see her, I might have marked them in a different way.

I imagine many who have lost a loved one do the same second-guessing. If I had done anything differently, maybe it wouldn't have happened? That is probably true. But it has no value. It may be soothing to think there was nothing that could have been done, but I do not believe that. Any one thing that was different might have changed the outcome . . . any one thing, any glance, any gesture. Any cause that might have had a different effect than Karen in Colorado. Anything could have changed it . . . changed the outcome. I believe that! What unfolded unfolded. It was not her destiny. It is just what happened. Nothing more to say.

But I will say more.

Jamie is a friend. A few nights ago, we talked about her brother. He died. We talked about Karen too. And Jamie said something that took me some time to digest. Their circumstances were not the same, but Jamie told me she was wrestling with anger. It was anger directed at her brother. I won't betray her confidence more than that. It is her business. It intersects mine and it triggered something I did not know was there. Anger. Maybe it was, maybe it wasn't. Something to expiate? Something to let go. Something I can let go?

I didn't realize I might be angry with her. Is it worth exploring? She was there all alone. John mentioned Red Lobster did not want employees hanging around inside the restaurant if they weren't working. It does make me wonder what the hell she was thinking. She probably wasn't thinking. She certainly wasn't thinking she was in any danger. Not until she was taken by them. She came to visit a boy she liked. She came for some company. Am I really angry with her? No. Do I want to chastise her for being there, for not running the minute she sensed something was wrong? No. I am not angry with Karen. I'm left only with what I know. Karen came to face destruction. She didn't mean she came looking for it. It came to her, and she was left to face it. Destruction. Could she have stopped it? I think she tried. She could not. Freddie Glenn wanted to join his friends. To prove himself by killing an innocent girl. Now, he wants to pretend he's the innocent one.

No, I am not angry with Karen. I am angry with Freddie Glenn.

I have reached the reason I began this latest edit . . . the place where I used profanity in a way that is unbecoming to me and to the memory of Karen. It is an honest expletive. But it is not necessary. Two words that are beneath me even though they express accurately how I feel

272

about him and his ridiculous entreaties and his amnesia and his protestations that he was a good kid.

That's right. Freddie. You hear me. You know what I'm saying. You know what I mean. I might just say it to your face one day. Your next hearing. Your next scam to get out. Yeah. Maybe I'll be there. In person. Say it then. It's not for this book. Not for Karen.

And God forgive you. I am tired of trying. You consistently surprise me every time you have a chance to own your crime . . . and the latest hearing was classic . . ."I don't remember raping her." I want you to die in prison. God forgive me. Go away, Freddie. Die. If I have to live another lifetime because of this, so be it. I wish you death. Unimaginably cruel death. There.

I love Jesus. He teaches me to forgive and to love my enemy. I have fallen short. How else could it be?—I am not perfect, as he was. I have hoped to be . . . better. I am not. I surrender.

And I apologize for my outburst. I struggle with it. Even as I have grown to a place of greater peace. I can love the young man. The young man whose hopes grew so dim, he could think of no way to empower himself other than to kill an innocent girl. And I am giving him a lot of credit in this characterization. It takes every fiber of my being, but my heart goes out to him. To that boy. To him only. Not the killer he became. The killer he remains. I leave him to God.

My son Gabriel just walked in and told me he has invented his own Devil. "He is very bad," he said. "Do you know why he's bad?"

"No," I replied.

"Because bad is the only thing he's good at." He said it with his unmistakably joyful "devilish" smile. I wanted to write it down. Because it came in the middle of my conflicted mind about the Soul of this man who killed my sister. Maybe "bad" was the only thing he could think of anymore. Maybe there was a good boy in there, as he once said. A boy not unlike myself.

I hold no illusion about who he is today. I believe he is a man trying to bargain with his own death . . . diminish his deed, minimize it somehow. Change his Fate—the one he sealed when he took Karen. What is left of his life was forfeit. Now, the only question is a matter of

273

time. There is no bargain to be made that will free him. There is no way to pretend it didn't happen. Maybe he is hoping I will die and that might shorten his time in prison. Maybe he realizes that for as long as I live, there will be a voice that defends the life of my sister, defends her memory and decries the horror of what Freddie did to her. Karen is forever with me. And with him. She will always be like an albatross around his neck. Karen's murder is with him . . . her death is on him. Forever. He killed her. That is certain. And just as certain, he did not kill her soul. He killed his own.

I have been grappling with those two years of Karen's life I did not really know. There was a great trip to Orlando, Disney World. It was a school trip. It is mentioned by many of her friends in the yearbook. I guess it was a senior class trip—in every sense of the word. From every entry, there is the suggestion that Karen above all could party! It may even have been legendary status she enjoyed. I am thinking now, I should just make a random sampling of some of her classmates. That yearbook is the only document I have that clearly lays out several relationships that I can trace. Hmmm. This is good. Staring me in the face all this time! And there is still the matter of the mystery man on her yearbook page. Nice looking. I will kick myself if I actually knew him. It is possible. I barely recognize myself on the same page. So, it could be he was a mutual friend and a secret love of Karen's. I was this close to letting it go. But she included him on the same page as Momo, me and Mom. The three of us . . . and this guy? Okay. Game on.

You may have noticed that I feel compelled to keep writing even as I discover a new vein of research that must be tapped. So, I will roll down a few more memories and a conjecture or two before the legwork is accomplished. There is some new testimony yet to uncover. I have abandoned the idea that I will speak with Momo. A stroke of luck helped to track her down. An old boyfriend of hers. A writer. But after contacting her, she politely said that she was very fond of the family and certainly of Karen. It was an awkward kind of note, asking if I could tell her the questions I wanted to ask ... truthfully, there are no questions. I am just looking to fill some holes. I would just be guessing at a reason. Gold. I am looking for gold, I guess. I thought she might know where to find some. But I will respect her reticence. I am sad. I always loved Momo. Another lifetime maybe. Jan has been a terrific friend through the years, and I have asked her if she can track down the mystery man on Karen's yearbook page. She has accepted the challenge. Suddenly, a flood of other thoughts and another idea ... Roxanne. I contacted her today and we will speak tomorrow. I am very excited. Also, I reviewed the remembrance book from Karen's funeral ... it may yield some significant information I'd overlooked. I am close. I am certain there is more there.

Brian told me he also had a visit with Karen when she lived in Palatka. That would have been the summer of '73. The summer we graduated. Jan mentioned Palatka too. There I drew a blank. I remember Karen had spent that summer in Welaka, Florida. She did odd jobs with Ollie Clark, longtime friend, husband of Wanda, mother of Doug. The same Ollie and Wanda from Atlantic Highlands where we all met. I visited once too. It was beautiful there. Still, Brian and Jan had both said Palatka ... I did not recall Palatka. Jan said that they had referred to it as Palatka because Welaka was so tiny, so off the map, that the only major town one could call a town at all was—you guessed it, Palatka. Karen had won some tickets on a radio call-in for a concert and invited Brian to join her. I could hear him choke up a bit as he recalled that trip. And, also, as he reminisced about their date on prom night. Clearly, they had been close. Closer than I had known. I didn't want to pry. I was happy to speak with him and respect the bond he had with Karen. I pointed out some time earlier in these pages that Karen and I had divergent paths after that first year in Florida. We both found Brian early on, but he and Karen went beyond that early friendship to something lovely. I am happy for both of them. And it always saddens me to hear someone who misses her as I do. It is a conversation we would rather not have ... to speak of Karen in the past tense. So long ago. Yet, as if she were here again. Breathing and laughing ... making us laugh. As if the friendship still existed. As if Karen hadn't died at all. Forlorn, we both said goodbye. Maybe we will see each other again. Sometime.

Maybe we really will. I always liked him. Even as I felt my shoulder bone fracture while the two of us were wrestling. I was twenty-seven years old. Visiting Florida. I'd been rehearsing a new play. *Plenty*, by the playwright David Hare. Ed Hermann, who starred in the play, gave me a book called *Get Tough*. It was a handbook of sorts for British Special Forces during WWII. I described a few moves. I described them to Brian. And slowly demonstrated a "chokehold" without choking him, of course. This is when Brian decided to sit on me. Try as I could, my left elbow was no match for our combined weight. It was just a hairline fracture. Nothing to do. Just let it heal. It healed.

Brian and I had a remarkable gift for silliness that stuck. Probably would still. I would love to see him.

He also mentioned he thought he'd seen Karen the night she was kicked out of school. Now this was news to me. Something about one evening when she was waiting on campus for the ride home I would give her. I was doing some afterschool event. He said or said he thought someone caught Karen getting high. I heard nothing of it and continue to believe she left the school to change her own story. Not because she had done anything wrong. Is it possible? Maybe. But this is the first I heard of it. Karen was an adventurer. She was also a great kid.

It was a beautiful chat with Brian. It has been a comfort to speak with those who loved Karen as I did. None knew her as long. But they loved her. And that is both painful and joyous. Together.

I am sorry Momo didn't want to speak to me. It's okay.

Every time I connect with someone who loved Karen too, it is as if she lives again. It fills me with warmth. It celebrates her life. Maybe Momo is trying to protect her. Or herself. I mean no harm to her. Nor to Karen, certainly. Moving on.

On our call, Brian mentioned the night Karen was hanging around the campus while I finished off some extracurricular event. I couldn't place it. There were so many of them. But there was one such night in tenth grade. Pam came with me on a date . . . we were seeing each other for a few months by that time. I was announcing at a swim meet. Mom had picked Karen up earlier or she may have been out with some of the older boys at school. I don't know. Afterward, Pam and I went to the beach. A moon path lit our embrace. On a blanket. We kissed. Things progressed as they do with a sixteen-year-old boy and girl. I was a virgin. We both were. We discussed making love. She asked me if I loved her. Not just a question about love. It is an implied question about life. Our life. Did I see a life together ahead for the two us? I wrestled with the bargain I would be making. I told her I really liked her, but I didn't know. I told the truth. I said I would love to know her intimately, but I did not know where we were headed; and I promised I wouldn't be a jerk or hurt her in any way. We fumbled around a bit. Skin on skin. It was exciting and awkward. And then, "Maybe we should wait?" Pam wasn't sure. I had no stomach for breaking her heart if things didn't work out. That was the issue. How could I know? I did know *what* to say. And by now, you know I didn't say it. We left the beach virgins.

She really was a wonderful girl. I thought about her often after that. Obviously. I still remember her and that night after all these years. Who knows what might have been? Summer came and I went off to Rhode Island for a visit with my friend Jay's family. Dan Scott came along. We had a great summer. Pam and I didn't see each other again. Summers have a way of doing that. I owe her an apology. She was a great girl. I hope she had a wonderful life. I hope she has a wonderful life. She is a wonderful memory. Back when we were innocent. Back when innocence was a good thing. For my money, it still is.

The fun of recalling these moments is the discovery of what happened next. I had forgotten the summer after tenth grade. I had a fantastic time with Jay and his dad and mom...his sisters too. The girls were younger. But I loved his family. And Harry, his dad. Remember, I didn't have a mom and dad around, so it was different. I liked it.

Harry said something one morning that stays with me to this day. He bellowed up the staircase. We were waiting to go get some breakfast. Booming through the house, "Where's my Bride?" What a beautiful thing! To have a bride and regard her as such all those years after their wedding. Like I said, it stays with me. Jay's dad had a red Ford pickup with a manual shifter on the steering column. "Three on the tree," I have heard guys call it. It never occurred to me to think of it as anything but a truck with a manual transmission, but men have a way of coining cute little descriptive sayings like this. I don't get it. But I never liked locker rooms or towel snapping either. Not really my thing. I always feel quite distant from conversations with sayings like "kicked out," "under the hood," and "small block three-fitty." The "fitty" is a deliberate misspelling—it reflects the unwritten rule that when discussing mechanical, automotive features, the "f" in the word "fifty" is often silent. So, a small-block, eight-cylinder engine is called a "three fitty" in religious observance of the language men use when huddled together in gangs or groups of two or more. It is also in this configuration that men coin descriptive phrases about their conquests or lack thereof. I was always uncomfortable with any disrespect for the girls, the things that some would say about our young women. I was never the sort to kiss and tell. Never the sort to speak that way. It made me uncomfortable. When a woman has the grace to offer her company to a man, an intimacy, especially, it is not something to be shared with a gathering of men. Never derisively, certainly. So, my descriptions of any encounter with the young women of my generation remain respectful. That is my intention. I remain grateful to any and all of them—women who thought my company worth their time.

That summer in Rhode Island, Jay and Dan and I would do everything we could to arrange a visit with some local girls on an evening. Funny enough, a young man told me several months ago that his grandmother said she went out with me in Rhode Island that summer. I hope she remembers me kindly, speaks of me fondly. I can say with absolute surety that I was a perfect gentleman. Of course, a young man never really knew if his conduct was pleasing . . . too much attention or too little could be equally insulting. A very treacherous balancing game we teenage boys must navigate. But it was magic to be in the presence of these sirens.

And there are a couple who stood out. Let's just say I remember them. The real fun came when the three of us were just hanging out being boys. Jay and Dan and me. Sailing, surfing, eating burgers around the pool. Dan is gone now. Jay is still a pal. They were good days. And, yeah, we were a little preoccupied with girls. That's all.

Such a girl was Carol. Not exactly. We didn't meet that summer in

Rhode Island. But I did see her when I was in Rhode Island. There was a *Sports Illustrated* cover picturing a girl in Miami. She was a "ball girl" for the new basketball team. There was a shot of her in a bikini holding a ball at her side. Fabulous. The perfect shot of the perfect girl in the perfect world of Florida. You know how I loved Florida. Still do. I saw that cover and thought, *Boy, why can't I meet a girl like that?* My senior year, a school chum, Cathy, told me about a beautiful girl she knew who lived near her in Miami. She set us up on a blind date. Maybe it was the law of attraction or just dumb luck, but sure enough, just a bit more than a year later, that very girl was smiling a smile at me that warmed me to the marrow. Carol. I kissed her goodnight at the door, and we went out until we graduated high school.

About six weeks into college, I got a letter from Carol that said she had been dating a guy she met at school. I wrote back saying I was sad about it, but we were miles apart and neither of us had any illusions about a future. I am saying that, but we never discussed it one way or the other. I went off to New York. She went to a university a world away.

Carol. A good memory. A good person. I knew a few in my youth. Laurie, the girl on the dock was one. I was certain she left me because I just wasn't enough for her. She had a relationship with another she wanted to honor. I applauded that but it still hurt. I knew Carol and I were meant to go our separate ways, but that still hurt too. People are funny. I am grateful to these wonderful people. They took a chance on me; shared a part of their lives with me. Maybe I wasn't enough for them. Maybe I was too much. I have been told both. Maybe we wanted different things, but I believe I wouldn't be here if I hadn't been there. Maybe they knew, even if I didn't, that we had gone as far as we could. I always wanted to go farther. Maybe Carol knew that. Maybe Laurie knew, knew that what she wanted and what I wanted were different things. They were willing to hold me and to let me go. They gave me something precious. The refuge of a warm embrace.

You remember my thoughts on refuge. The Impossible Dream. They held me as I looked to the stars. There were others but not so many. Three years ago, performing *Man of La Mancha*, I finally sang that song. And I believe they were all with me, those who held me for a time and let me dream in the safety of their company. Years ago, Claudia and I saw the film, *Man of La Mancha.* Claudia was a good friend. And that night I told her I would sing that song one day. I was completely happy then, in those days, but I wanted more. My mind was on and in the future. I think she knew that. I think they all knew it. I was happy, as I said, but there was this persistent seeking. I could not linger. Not to be confused with contempt for what we have. It is not dissatisfaction with what we know and those we love, but a predisposition toward the unknown, the "undiscovered country."

Keep it fresh. There was a song in the '70s sung by Grand Funk Railroad entitled, "Closer to Home." I would listen to it and weep, wondering where my home would be . . . longing for it. It occurs to me, my home is in the searching, in the yearning for what lies beyond. Familiarity breeds contempt. No. Not contempt. Maybe boredom? Kayte has a saying: you know how you can just go "off" someone? So how do we build a relationship that lasts? When finally comes a someone who makes us wonder if it's time to surrender. I do not mean settle. I mean surrender. Surrender to the idea that it is not an issue to be constantly engaged by life and always asking for more. It is okay. We simply have to construct a lifetime with a like-minded individual. I love children. I love their searching and questioning. They remind me how fascinating this world is. It does not end. So I surround myself with children. Their curiosity. It ignites mine. The journey is its own reward. The growth of it. It is not wise to deny ourselves a new experience, new knowledge, but it can be damning to repeat experiences we have already lived. Learning. Wise to learn once and seek new knowledge; and to recognize a familiar face, the same story in a different mask. That can take a while. I have a tendency to repeat old patterns once or twice before I master them. Then again, Mastery only comes with practice. Hah, hah! So, we slip and slide toward and through our destiny—a willing partner gently holding our hand along the way. The one. The one who matches us. We evolve and grow each day . . . together, so there can never be the dreaded "familiarity" unless we aren't paying attention. We won't "go off" the one as long as we see the "new" in one another; with eyes endlessly fresh, we can greet a new love just about every day. We marry. One. And that "one" challenges us to continue the journey of the self along the path of togetherness. More fun to share the journey. A partner and an adversary. A very special adversary— someone to trust, who will not let us yield to the predictable, the familiar or complacent. To challenge us. Different but equal. Yin to Yang. Male to female. Completion. There may be several stops along the way, but the journey does not end. Nice to linger on a familiar corner from time to time. Nice to enjoy what we have done. Savor what we have achieved. To rest. Celebrate even. Restore. And then resume. Together.

It took me some time to find that. Hell, it took me some time to write it! But I think that's it. If we don't choose to grow, we petrify. If we petrify, the life force drives us elsewhere. A good lover, a good match, won't let that happen.

Dream big. That Impossible Dream. Yeah. A big dream requires the dreamer be willing to work hard. Also, the dreamer will find few people in life who care at all what their dream might be. You must therefore be willing to make your dream known. To yourself. To others. If you don't know, they can't. And once you know, it must be made known. Say it out loud. Enumerate it! Speak it to the Universe. A dream requires action to come alive. A big dream?—talent, intention, tenacity, but mostly—big action! Ask for it. You have a right to ask for it. Then get to work. Once you do, the Universe will do everything it can to help. There is not much else to say.

A dream summons the soul to action.

You take it from there. You play the hand you're dealt. Sometimes. And I also think you can make your own luck. Providence plays a part. Enlisting Divine Providence can really make a difference. How we think about life is how it goes. No matter what, resilience and hard work are essential to success. Success doesn't happen overnight. It can feel easy but only after years of "nose to the grindstone" relentless effort.

And another thing! Things can go against us. That is when we are truly tested. Frame of mind. Optimism. This can help. Are you a glass half full or half empty kind of person? I would rather err on the side of half full, but this observation impresses me:

People who ask if a glass is half full or half empty are missing the point.

The glass ... can be refilled!

There was a time in my life everything was taken—even the glass. I have filled, refilled. Emptied. And filled again ... dozens of times since.

Back to the tale.

I was rereading and have a correction to make. John and I did not meet the winter of '73. He mentioned he did not remember it and he was right. I met someone Karen had been dating at an apartment that Christmas. Maybe by the next Christmas, she was in a different apartment. Not entirely sure at this point. Not sure what she was planning. What she had in mind. Or why she was where she was. Or why she left. Or why she left school. So, I recently reached out to her college in Georgia to check the record of her time there. They confirmed her attendance. Confirmed the record might hold some insights. So, I will visit. I want to see what she saw there. See with my eyes the awakening she must have felt. It is a beautiful place. A beautiful campus.

Wide-eyed. That is how I see her. And with excitement for the future. Her future. It must have been grand. What I know now is she attended a full semester, the fall of '73 and also the winter of '74. I hadn't realized that she went back after that Christmas. The question remains, why did she leave? I am left to guess at a reason. Based on nothing but supposition and ignorance. So, I won't guess. I will visit there and try to assemble something more concrete. I am still reaching out to an old friend who may know. More on that soon, I hope. For now, I am visiting Berry College in March. Next month.

The tale, since I began, has been some eighteen months in the telling. It has been a beautiful discovery at times. Unbearable at others. Heartrending and heartwarming. All at once. To you, the reader, I am grateful for your company. You keep me honest. I have promised you the truth. Your being here makes my suppositions inadequate. So, I must search in the days I did not share with Karen to find as much as I can. And that helps me too. Finding Karen.

Doug is in town. We grew up together. I mentioned him previously. Doug is a waypoint. We had a great talk about our families. They were dear friends from the time we met in Atlantic Highlands, New Jersey. We all were—the grown-ups and the kids of the building. Doug and I, Karen, Bobby and his brother were across the hall, where the magnificent Joanne resided with her lovely sister, Nancy (Nancy with a "y"). From there they cast their spell over us, Doug and me, pathetically lost in our imaginings. And Doug had a sister too. Also Nancy. I always liked Nancy but she was well out of my reach. I think she was a junior in high school. And her friend, Donna, was absolutely devastating to me.

One night they took me to their school for a basketball game. I cannot remember the circumstances of being the boy with two "mature women" on his arm that night, but it was the highlight of my young life. Donna and Nancy bracketing me in the bleachers. Heaven. And they kept saying how cute I was! That young man, the young man I was, surely liked to be liked by girls. The company of women! And that ten-year-old boy in his crisp white shirt and a tie was transported by Donna and Nancy. Things are not much different now. I always thought it a great honor, a privilege to meet a woman . . . young or old. Learn their story. Listen with attentiveness . . . and when granted an intimacy, regard it as the privilege it is.

As Doug and I drove home last night we shared some stories. He waxed on about Gam. How fun she was and how tough. Her words echoed in our hearts. "I've seen me some big towns and I've heard me some big talk!" "That boy could use a good swift kick in the pants and I'm just the girl who can give it to him!" Yeah, that one bears repeating. Gam. Wanda, Doug's mom, Ollie and my mom, Sally, Gam and Gordon would play Bridge for hours or Spite and malice . . . gin too. Gordon also played cribbage. And poker. He taught me and Karen how to play. "Don't count your chips at the table. Men have been shot for less!" And he and Gam did teach us Bridge. I see Karen playing gin with Gam. They were both pretty sharp. And I remember Mom playing Gin for years after they both were gone. It is a nice memory. Seeing

Mom as she would say, "Do you want that card? No? Then I'll take it. Gin!" In this regard, despite their differences, Gam and Mom were pretty much indistinguishable, one from the other. In the world of card games, they were equally vicious and brutal.

So, my son Gabriel just asked me who was the toughest relative in my past... hands down, my grandmother! Gam could handle anything. She was fiercely loyal. Gam was the "Top Kick" as she called herself. The sergeant who ran the whole show for the colonel. She could also be a lot of fun. One time, Gordon headed off to the Indianapolis 500 with a pal of his for a boys' weekend. Gam grabbed the pal's wife and booked tickets on the same train for the two of them and then "surprised" the boys en route to the race. "Boys' Weekend," indeed! Gam wasn't about to let her man get up to no good at the famous race—at least, not without her! Half an hour after leaving the station, the girls ambushed their husbands in the bar car, and they all partied together for the entire weekend. She was able to laugh off a mother who died young, a dad who was a drunk, an economic collapse, a World War and the loss of her man. She was a good person in spite of a tough childhood, being raised by her mother's sisters. And despite being shunned by Gordon's father when they married. She cooked dinner and heaped affection upon her grandchildren. She was generous and wise and an eternal teenager in her heart. I loved that about her. And though we fought quite a bit, I knew she loved me and I knew she was there for me no matter what. Recalling her now, as she had been, the strength and goodness that coursed through her veins, it is clear how complete the descent had been for Gam after Karen was killed. She died just three years later.

Freddie and his pals. Once again, I say he got what he wanted. To prove he was a someone. Murderer. That is where he ended. Not funny but surely ironic. Freddie took a life and lost his own. A few years later, he could chalk off one more. Gam. She actually died with Karen that day. It just took her another three years to finish the job. You didn't get my mom, Freddie. You only broke her heart. And mine. But you didn't get us. Not Mom. Not me. For Gam it was the final straw. Nothing could take her love of life from her until Karen was taken and ended by you. It ended Gam too.

I promised his name would not appear again in the final pages here. I apologize. Certain revelations may yet occur that will wind back to that hated day. A hateful day. When hate ruled over the life of an innocent girl. And hate takes multiple victims as it works its magic. It can engender hatred that lasts for generations. A fire. Burning all. My son asked me yesterday if he can get a gun and kill the man who killed my sister. No. It would not solve anything. I told him hate can be contagious. And it destroys all who become infected by it. Hate is the author of cruelty that has spanned centuries—generation after generation. It is seductive. Hate destroys. In my faith and in its corresponding doctrine, Mary Baker Eddy wrote: "If I should wish to harm my enemy, I would make him hate someone." Hate destroys completely. It can choke the life out of anyone. It almost choked me. And I will not allow it to choke my children. They will not carry it. Though I believe our DNA can actually pass on emotion and the suffering of our past to future generations. The cycle must be broken and only Love can do that. Only Love defeats Hate. Tall order. But Love's returns outlast eternity. So, I recommend it.

I stood on that baseball field. "Where were you?"

"Right there. Right beside her," came the answer.

Simply. Quietly. Clearly.

I heard it. "Right there."

Right there. On that field.

A flood of realization surged through me. Bathed in light. It filled me. All at once: Love is the only way. When things are their very worst, Love is right there. God. Jesus. Close by. Closest when the jaws of death engulf us. Right beside us when fear and loathing seem strongest, and I finally understood what I'd been told was true. God *was* with Karen. Throughout her final heartbeats, her final breaths. And Jesus held her as she died. It was shown me. In the blinking of an eye.

I have Faith. Challenged. Sometimes out of reach. Not that night. Faith. My version of it. Human and flawed. I do not apologize for it. I do not proselytize. I realize many condemn it. Our contemporary culture fears it. Mock the faithful. But the faithful enjoy rights no government can ever grant. Much to the dismay of our elected officials.

Some of them, at least, who imply we can skip God and trust in government instead. Hah! Anyway. Not my job to follow them. From the most "tolerant" bastions of society, the accusations fly, dripping with contempt, that Christians preach Hate. Nothing could be further from the truth. But it is not my mission here to defend my Faith. Nor will I deny it. I have fought too long and hard to find it—too long and hard to find it again. I will not apologize for it now.

"Amen."

The life I am living is walking in the footsteps of the life I lived. Kayte and the family and I are in New York City. There is some business here. The veil between present and past is extremely thin. Here more than anywhere. Now, more acutely than in years past. Because the writing has become a time machine. Widening perception. Any visit to a place in my past and I am transported there in real time.

A turn down 66th Street, I see myself walking into Juilliard for the very first time. At Lincoln Center, I see the boy I was standing beside Karen. We watch the fountain rise and fall for a minute, mesmerized. Then Mom shuttles us inside the New York Philharmonic to hear Leonard Bernstein. The twenty-five-year-old I was walks by the same fountain to play Macbeth in the Vivien Beaumont Theater. I woke Goose asleep in the Fiat, rounding the turn into the Lincoln Tunnel, to see the man-made mountains of New York City. "Look at it, Goose. The greatest city in the world!" I saw us both walking up Sixth Avenue, on our way to move in with Ellen. Goose was howling with alarm as three or four hook and ladder firetrucks roared uptown. I would see it as a warning about that move . . . only, a bit too late. We turned left at 59th Street and made our way to the apartment on 87th and Amsterdam Avenue. It was the most profound cacophony of sirens and horns blaring I had ever heard. They continued on our way, until as we rounded the corner and approached the door, they stopped—I would not be saved. The city and the New York Fire Department had done all they could to turn me around. I wasn't listening. Goose's feeble howls continued as the sirens faded uptown to a fire, the last foreboding of an impending personal disaster. No matter what was to come, however, Goose and I would be together. She was my anchor, my best relationship. Yes, it had been Ellen who stated dogs were second-class citizens. I would have to choose between her and Goose. My old pal, Nate, wisely warned her it was a battle she would not win. I confirmed it. So, Ellen acquiesced. Begrudgingly. There was a détente of sorts and a few months later, we were moving in together, the three of us and a couple of Ellen's roommates. Harry and his sister. Ellen. Goose and I.

I loved Ellen's family. She had two sisters I adored, and I enjoyed her mother and father. In fact, it was with her mom and dad that Goose stayed when I flew out to San Diego to retrieve the motorcycle. As I rumbled up the driveway a few weeks later, Goose stood at attention and ran to me when the bike stopped. She jumped into my arms. Josie approached and confessed she had hoped Goose would not be so keen to see her man again . . . she had grown quite attached to her during my absence. It was a lovely moment. Everybody liked Goose. Except Ellen. Still hard to figure, but why bother? I really liked Alan, their dad. He had been captured by the Germans moments after he parachuted into enemy territory and spent the rest of the war in a prison camp. Just a few years ago, I saw her sister, Betsy, at a film festival. We stay in touch. She married a terrific guy named Stu and had some sons. I lived with her younger sister, Manny, when I was doing a play and nursed a painfully secret crush on her that was surely doomed, but I am glad to note it here. I promised truth in this. That was true.

Ellen was the eldest of the sisters and extremely driven. I admired her for that even as I recognized it was a kind of torture for her. So, how was it we came to be together? An interesting story. Noteworthy. I learned a lot. So.

Ellen.

We were attracted to each other because of the work. I do not remember all the particulars of our breakthrough conversation. We begin at the first day of rehearsal. Ellen and I were introduced. I would be playing Demetrius opposite her Helena. Fine. Somewhere between that and lunch, Ellen made a point of relating how desired she was by men of all ages, perhaps to insinuate there would be no hanky-panky, no summer dalliance between us. Fine. A couple of chats later that day, more of same; and I comfortably decided she was out of my reach. We would enjoy a working relationship and that was that. It was somewhat dizzying as I had honestly not contemplated anything other than that in the first place.

But one night, at a gathering of the cast for some drinks, her roommate Cathy was not ready to leave. I was about to head out and it fell to me to take Ellen home. Her performance as Helena in *A Midsummer Night's Dream* came up as we arrived, and I suggested she might be overlooking a nuance in the text . . . one of her big speeches. Well, it proved a gauntlet I had unintentionally thrown, and she insisted it was not my place to criticize her. I demurred but moments later, as I walked her to the door, she insisted, or challenged me rather, to show her just what I was talking about. Okay. That is how we started. Almost on a dare from Ellen that I prove my statement was sound and justified. I complied. A couple of hours later, we had achieved a professional alignment that grew, in time, into an attraction. Ellen and I came together. For me, I was impressed, truly impressed by her talent and once she trusted me, it was a remarkable collaboration. We returned to New York together. I would coach her from time to time.

On one occasion, she was working on the speech from James Agee's, *All the Way Home*. I suggested that if she stressed the word *this* in "this is a gulf," it would land on her heart and simultaneously on the audience's heart in a powerful way. She took the note. I wept at how absolutely beautiful it was as it fell from her lips. She was as good an actress as any I had known. As I have ever known. And it kept me close to the work I loved. In fact, it probably kept us together for a bit longer than we might otherwise have stayed. For Ellen's part, it was important to her that she be the superior talent. I could not find an acting job. I had a job at O'Neal's as a waiter. Things between us were just fine. I was a good waiter. And for that time in my life, things were as they were meant to be.

A few nights ago, Kayte and I went into the old restaurant. It has changed names since, but it is largely the same. And all those years slammed into today in an instant as we sat at the bar and bought a drink. Nice fella named Charlie beside us who works with Major League Baseball and a lovely bartender, Katerina. It was as it always was.

Suddenly, my old friend, Barry was back behind the bar. Susan, his girlfriend was waiting tables and I saw them all. I even saw the twenty-three-year-old Kelsey, a shiny, young, out-of-work actor, waiting tables. I recounted the tale of my last day of work at O'Neal's. Michael was the manager and I was due to pull the lunch shift. I had a vision about myself: If I want to be an actor, I have to stop being a waiter. I told Michael that. He asked if I could stay for just that shift and I squirmed a bit not wanting to put him in a bad spot . . . Michael then said he could handle it. He let me off the hook. Nice guy. The next day I booked an acting job, and it is the only kind of job I have had since. No pearls of wisdom. Not offering advice. It is just how things went for me. It was time.

Despite this, Ellen found it necessary to reassert her superiority. Not in the relationship per se, but in the context of who had the greater career. She would be rehearsing a play and point out that the actors in it were very good, much better than me . . . I lacked weight and presence. These were her observations. Shared with me on our nights together and it did have an impact. My mother came to visit and asked me in a cab why Ellen found it necessary to run me down all the time. I am not sure she was aware of it, honestly, but Mom found it offensive and also offered she believed I was a very talented young man and Ellen would probably regret the things she was saying. Somewhere in the future. I am not sure that day ever came but we did separate after another year or so and I moved on. I got a job in Minneapolis after I got back from that trip to pick up the motorcycle. The day after I got back, in fact.

This leads me to another sidebar. Barry, my old bartender friend at O'Neal's, was a terrific guy. He was also very connected to the city. Fashion. Society. Restaurants. Barry had his finger on the pulse, as it were. Barry was fun. And funny. He was married to Gail. Nice couple. We did a play together. *Icarus's Mother*. Gail directed. I got my first agent. Jeff. Ellen and I moved on.

Jumping ahead. Jumping back. In the story. Back to before.

I am on a plane to Atlanta. I am flying there to visit Karen's college. Berry College. I did not know it has the largest campus of any college in America. I am anxious about going there. Not sure if I will

289

learn anything more than I could find out on the internet but I wanted to see the place with my own eyes. In Karen's eyes. I know one thing for certain. I will spend the next two days with her. In my heart. In my mind. I am looking forward to it, not knowing what may unfold but to see the world she saw when it was all new and undiscovered is my mission here. I want to look at what she saw. Where she walked. Where she ate. Slept. Dreamed. And then she left. I heard that Wandi does not wish to speak with me. That saddens me. Like Momo, Karen's best friend. Wandi and I were friends. Good friends. She won't speak with me and I'm wondering why. I am left to guess and that is likely a fool's errand, as the saying goes. I love them as I always loved them. Sometimes that is not enough, I guess. From Wandi, I had hoped to learn something of Karen's time at Berry College. But there was more . . . I wanted to tell her how much she always meant to me. Maybe I was alone in it . . . the fondness I felt. But I don't think so. She was wonderful. I will remember her that way. Momo was always in my life when Karen was alive and then briefly, afterward. My mom said she used to keep in touch with her and I always thought she would be glad to speak with me. Again, I wonder what happened. Again, I will allow it to be an ending. I had such hopes. I wish them every benefice and blessing in life. I miss them. Farewell.

And as I fly toward a rendezvous with Karen's days, I wonder if I will find something. I am drawn to this moment in a way that is hard to describe. I sense it may not be necessary, but something is telling me otherwise. So, I am going. Glad to be going. My heart is open. My eyes are filled with anticipation. My thoughts. Anticipation. The unknown. An unknown she met all those years ago with much the same innocence. Maybe that's it. I want to be in her innocence. And mine again. Insert myself into her life and live it with her. A brief walk in the magic of her. The magic she was and the magic she saw in the buildings and the land and the adventure of her youth as it lay ahead. And its promise.

I sip a coffee in a food court of sorts at the school. Chris is meeting me in a few moments. Spring break is on, so not too many students. I imagine it buzzes quite a bit during session. There is a security guard talking with a couple of cashiers. I am sampling some grilled nuggets from Chick-fil-A. First time. Not bad. How was my drive? Easy. An hour and a half. I had turned on the radio as I drove toward Rome, Georgia. Five or ten minutes into it I had the feeling that I should attend more to the journey than the current news. I was, after all, on a journey to the past in a rented truck doubling as a time machine. I dialed my mind to the terrain and the flow of a highway that may or may not have been there the first day Karen made her way to Berry College. A bus ride? Maybe. Probably. I do not know. I will probably never know. Then I think perhaps a friend gave her a ride to the school. But there is no friend to confirm it. Some of those doors are closed. I must respect that. I flash to the memory of a terrible ride on a Greyhound bus from northern Florida to my home in Pompano Beach.

Here I go again! I meant to stick to the drive and of course it takes me to another drive made years before. Wanda and Ollie and I were driving their Bronco from New Jersey to Florida. I do not remember how I came to be on that bus. The circumstances are vague, but I remember it was a miserable experience and when I conjecture that Karen may have arrived at school by bus, my heart shudders and I pray it was some other mode of transportation that delivered her to the dawn of a new life.

I just remembered. Wanda and Ollie lived in Welaka, Florida. They did not want to deliver me another three hundred miles to my home, so they put me on the bus and eighteen hours later, I finally arrived somewhere near my home. Exhausted and dirty and disillusioned. I have never taken a bus ride of any distance more than a block or two since.

And another page in memory pops up—Heidi. We met one night in Minneapolis. She was tending bar and as the night wound down it became clear we were two consenting adults who wanted to continue the conversation after hours. She grabbed a bottle of gin and we drove to my little apartment around the corner and spent an evening together. It was a magical evening. She was a wonderful young woman. The rest will remain unspecific. We talked into the morning hours, and I promised to deliver her to the bus station where she was booked to Los Angeles. The Greyhound symbol convulsed me into trauma. I looked at Heidi and told her I was buying her a plane ticket to Los Angeles. I would not wish that ride on anyone. A couple of hours later, I delivered her to the airport. I never saw her again. She did reach out from time to time. I wish her well. She was hoping to be an actress. She was off to attend the American Academy of Dramatic Art. She was great. I trust her days have passed beautifully. Happily. She deserved it. She was a special and beautiful young woman. It was an honor.

As I drive to Berry College it occurs to me how young Karen was. She was seventeen years old when she arrived on campus. In Rome, Georgia. Was she ready? I know her, so I know she thought she was ready. But is anyone ready to navigate a dorm or a campus or a college curriculum at the ripe age of seventeen? She was an extraordinary young woman, but I have to believe this was not so easy . . . a girl on her own in a foreign place, a mere one among many—all strangers. A bed she had never slept in. In a house that was a dorm. Not a home.

There is no record of a younger freshman that year. It must have been hard for her. But maybe not. She was strong. Loss had made her strong. Though it does beg the question why; why did Karen choose Berry College? They asked me. Almost the first thing they asked me, after we met in the little food court. I still don't know. But I believe I will figure it out. I am not sure I can, but . . . I *believe* I will. The questions that have arisen about Karen have almost always been answered. Not immediately, but in time. A reason presenting itself, unveiling itself. Through circumstance or coincidence. Or patience. In time. So, I am going on trust. Because I begin this particular line of inquiry with more uncertainty than any other. Still, answers have come. I pray for more.

The magic. Karen's magic. The magic of youth. The arrogance of youth. Maybe. Thank God for it. The "set to sea" mentality. The haphazard teenager convinced their time is now. Bless them. Bless us. We have all been there. Perhaps, this was Karen. I am searching. Still.

Clara Hall is where she lived. Clara was Henry Ford's wife. Martha Berry was a woman of means who decided she wanted to help young people advance their futures through education and she established the school which carries her name. Henry Ford visited with her at some point, and I do not want to give history short shrift here, but for whatever reason, he decided to help her build dormitories and classrooms and added acres and acres of land to the Berry College holdings.

I muse he was in a battle with the other industrial giants of his time to give back. And I thank God they were engaged in a contest of sorts about how much they could do for future generations. And I do not think it was guilt, as many of the cancerous detractors of the magnates of old postulate. I believe it was a kind of "one upmanship for billionaires" who had the good fortune to carve an empire from their imagination and vigor and tenacity and wanted to share this lesson—anyone can rise to success in America. They wanted to sprinkle their good fortune like fairy dust into the minds and dreams of the generations that were to come. They were not giving away their wealth; they were donating a legacy of dreams to those whose dreams might dwarf their own.

I was shown Clara Hall. Karen had lived here. I did not sense it at first. I toured the lounge or community room, saw the fireplace where she surely sat. Walked past the laundry room that was probably not such during Karen's time. I imagined her doing laundry there just the same. As we moved from "Clara" to another hall, I saw a banister beside the stairs that led to rooms on the second floor, perhaps rooms in which Karen lived. The wood was old and scarred with many hands of the hopeful. I reached out and touched it. The rising banister to another level. My hand lighting there, a hand touched mine—Karen's.

"I did walk here."

"I was here."

I felt her hand on mine. I was walking in her footsteps. As I'd hoped. I know she has been with me all this time. Here. I was closer to her life when she lived. Her hand on my hand. Hand in hand again. Oh, how I miss her.

My hosts showed me some classrooms and a dorm room in the adjacent hall. A student opened up her room in a welcoming way—a look into her life there. She was probably nineteen or twenty years old. It occurred to me again how young Karen had been. So young. She was mature for her age, certainly, but that didn't mean it was easy. The young lady who stood before me had the look in her eye of a young girl who knew she was doing something good with her life. She liked the school. I imagine Karen with the same look during the first few months there. Excited. Learning. Freedom. Measured freedom. The safest way to strike out on one's own back then. A kind of halfway house. Adulthood thresholded but not quite out the door.

Karen was not one to spend too much time on a threshold, though. She was the pioneer of her life. Willing to brave all kinds of hardship and challenge to find the life that was hers without condition. I am so proud of her. Her bravery. Did she have friends? Did she make some? I imagine she must have but she never really spoke to me of her time there. Seeing this young woman there standing in for Karen in a way . . . it was nice. I got some sense of the optimism that she must have had when she came to Berry College. I looked down the path she would have walked. Stood on the steps at the foot of her dorm, Clara. We peeked into the art building . . . she would have studied there. She took intermediate swimming. Karen was always a good swimmer. The pool was a weight room now. The dining hall was new when she attended. I was where she took her meals. I had my cup of coffee not far from where she must have sat. She was a good kid. So, this student stood before me in Karen's place and gave me a glimpse of her. Grateful. We drove past cabins that were historical buildings from the early days of the school. The "Kissing Cabin" had just been restored. The rumors were a young girl and boy infatuated with one another or just infatuated with the discovery of each other, might sneak off there for a kiss and a cuddle. I pictured Karen there with a young rebel of her liking.

I don't know for certain but I think Karen was the true adventurer of us. I am certain she loved the company of a lover. I am glad she did. And I think she felt no guilt whatsoever in a tryst with a handsome stranger. Good for her. She was an alchemist who harvested gold in all she encountered. Maybe even on that fateful night. I feel wrapped in gold by her as I write. Protected. So, entering the campus through its "Gate of Opportunity," I saw it with her eyes. Went back in time to her time. To her. Nice. It was very nice. I felt the excitement she had felt. My eyes were wide with wonder and possibilities and a little nervous at how large, how great an unknown awaited her . . . us.

There was no picture of her. I painted my own. While touring the science building where she would have attended class, a professor happened up the hall and was introduced. A writer of history books.

Personable. Handsome man. Kind eyes. He mentioned that news of my writing and purpose of my visit had made its way to some of the folks there that day. He asked how it was coming. Why I was writing. Simple. I spent most of my adult life in grief about my sister, I told him. My purpose was given me by Karen. It was time to heal by granting her a small request. Through Esther. I told him what she had said. And told him also that I think it was meant to finally help me release that grief. At least some of it. It no longer served me. And my voice cracked and tears streamed down my face. I apologized. There was no apology necessary but the living grief that still fills me at the slightest mention of Karen, the years and nights and days I have spent in mourning have been endless and forever. There it is. No apology. None necessary. It is . . . forever. Mine and ours. Only now . . . I have equal parts of joy and sorrows . . . side by side. Maybe, a bit more joy than sorrow. Finally.

The president of the school invited me to sit in his office for a time. Leaf through the documents that bore no trace of her. Paged through the yearbook from her year. She wasn't in it. I looked and looked. I sat there and turned each and every page. Pored over them. Nothing. And in a group shot taken on a sunny day, fifty or so students sat in a clearing near the woods, a teacher briefing the bright-eyed on their time ahead; though I did not see her there, I did. I saw her. Felt her with that group, in that group. Warm in the sun. I knew she was among them. She was there. I sat there with her for a time. With all of them. Warm with them. In the sun. With their hopes and dreams.

It felt like home.

Berry College students in a clearing.

One thing that marked our generation was an optimism that was contagious. We all had our own version of it, but it felt like we were destined to change the world. Love. That was the big thing. And I know there were some bad trips during that time for a lot of young people who had dropped out and dropped in, so to speak. For my little bunch and for Karen's, there were few things stopping us from dreaming whatever dream we wished to dream. There wasn't exactly a plan but there was a faith that we would make our way. Drenched in the sun in the middle of that clearing, on a day in September so many years ago, I sat with my sister and her classmates. We were all connected. We were all one. We had confidence and compassion and courage. Looking to the future as a whole generation, convinced ours would be a generation of consequence. I slid back from the clearing into the pages, out of my reverie and back into the little office on a somewhat dreary day two days ago. Back on the trail to understanding why Karen came to Berry and why she left.

Karen's first months at college were marked by fairly good grades. I am looking at the picture in our home of the party I attended at her place in Pompano Beach. So, I am colliding with two stories . . . one that has her living in her own apartment with a pal, possibly a boyfriend, in Florida. And the other a student on campus attending classes in Rome, Georgia. I guess she could have been both. The break during the first quarter. That is a question I am asking the folks at Berry right now. And almost instantly the information is at hand. The break would have been about five weeks long. Plenty of time to arrange to stay in an apartment or even acquire one with a friend. I remember she had a roommate who I thought was her boyfriend at the time. Maybe just friends with benefits, although that saying didn't exist then. But the party I remember that Christmas, the Christmas of '73, was lovely. I remember she seemed happy. We had no discussion about her plans after the break, but she did return to Berry College to finish out the quarter. I had not realized that. I believed she never went back. I was wrong. There is still a mystery though about why she left. I have no idea.

But there was a clue. A subtle clue. In Karen's grades there was a "tell" of sorts. And suddenly, a lifeline. A picture of the clearing was sent to me by the folks at Berry and with it, they told me Karen's roommate from college had seen a post on Facebook about my visit and reached out. I hope to speak with her.

I have learned a lesson. Previously, as each opportunity or lead presents itself, I have paused the writing anticipating, awaiting a new trove of information. Several times now, those leads have proven fruitless, the time wasted. So, rather than wait now for word from Karen's old roommate, I will jump back in time. Or ahead in time from where we are in the book, back in time from where I am now. Back to New York City. Back to Goose. Back to a young artist whose future was uncertain. There was a blurred notion of what lay ahead, a faith that each day was a step toward an undiscerned, as yet undefined best destiny. On a path to a good end. With little victories along the way.

I started running.

Memory is a funny means of transportation. I started running. How I started, I cannot recall. I take a first step toward the memory and slowly other bits fall into place. The path reveals itself. From the deep recesses of my past, images. Moments long forgotten. No longer unconscious; an emergent recollection. Personal archaeology. Archaeology. Yes. Digging for bits of the past. I have been digging for Karen's unknown past. And stumbling upon bits of my own. How our stories intersect revealed as I go.

I started running. I don't remember why or when I started running. Until I write it down. Ah, that's what I'm trying to say! Writing it down is the first step. The next is when the digging starts.

I am standing in Balboa Park in San Diego. Agnes and Goose are there. I decided I should run. I am explaining it. An actor needs to stay in shape, you know. I don't have enough money to join a gym. I am sporting a brand-new pair of sneakers. The sneakers were on sale. Dramatically reduced. I would not have bought them otherwise. But I loved the way they looked. A stranger walks by and says, "Nice blades, man!" Blades? For sprinting, he explained. Ah, so, I'd bought some shoes for sprinting. Damn! I'm no sprinter. Bad feet. But I can't return the shoes, so maybe I can just run a bit and see how it all feels. I began.

Or rather, we began. Goose and me. And we ran for five years. I think that's right. Steps. And more steps.

So, after rounding the bend to the entrance of Lincoln Tunnel, I woke Goose and invoked her to howl—remember?—howl to celebrate her first glimpse of New York City. The concrete landscape of man's imagination gleaming across the river. The greatest city in the world! Then we moved in with Ellen. I got a job at the Magic Pan on 57th Street. A busboy. Walked most days to the East Side near Hammacher Schlemmer, to schlepp bus pans and pour water for patrons. Clean up. Empty garbage. Not many victories there. Not for a boy with a headful of dreams and an empty bank account. We lived on 87th Street and Amsterdam Avenue near the reservoir in Central Park. The reservoir has a track around it where people run. It became my salvation. I don't know the precise moment I became a committed runner, but it had everything to do with Goose. I'm standing in the sunlight along the bridle path that encircles the reservoir. Goose takes off down the trail and I fear I will lose her. I start trotting along after her. Cannot find her; then like a sneak attack she races toward me from the other direction. She had doubled back and flanked me. Ambush! She wanted me to run. So, I rose to the challenge. If I have not mentioned it previously, Goose was the greatest dog. And one of my greatest relationships. Of anyone. On two or four legs. What a wonderful creature she was. I was blessed to know her.

I just flashed back to Jill. I don't know how, but that first week in New York City, Jill and I arranged a visit. We agreed we would meet in the park and just sit and chat. It had been just over two years since that phone call where she confirmed my fears about Michael. She and Michael were still together so, it was her next serious relationship. Goose was with me. I nervously used a game of sprinting and chasing her about to hide my fear. Not fear but rather a host of confused feelings. Jill sat watching me for a time and I finally joined her on the grass at the edge of Sheep's Meadow in Central Park. I was a little winded. Jill asked, "Are you out of breath?" There was a hint of derision in it. I heard a hint of derision whether it was there or not. But it was there. She looked great. I looked okay, too, honestly. Maybe she was looking for the justification of choosing Michael back then, when it was the only choice she could have made. Really. Michael and she were still together, and she made a point of saying he was nervous about our little rendezvous. It reminded me of the night I spent staring at her apartment window while she spent it with her old boyfriend, Chris. Maybe it was something she enjoyed. A kind of torture. Two men wanting her? What the hell. That's okay. Makes a girl feel special. I liked her. I loved her. Still loved her. We chatted for a while. Confessed we had really been in it with our whole hearts . . . at the time. We both knew what went wrong. I smiled and shook her hand. Just a handshake. No hug. A real good-bye. I never saw her again.

What started me running? Goose, for sure, but it might have had something to do with that crack about being winded from Jill. I am such a boy. The girl I liked made fun of me. I determined I would not get out of breath again. I was actually in pretty good shape at the time, but it got my goat. I spent the next several years running. The little victories I secured involved this: lapping another runner as we circled the reservoir.

Okay, I jogged my memory on the drive into work today. It was not when I moved in with Ellen that this occurred. It was the summer before. When Goose was still a puppy. After I had asked Craig to make me an Equity actor. Suddenly had some unexpected extra time. So, I arranged a little trip to New York and a visit to New Jersey for a couple of weeks. And it was in that window, during that visit, that the conversation and closure came with Jill. The good-bye. I must have called her. I guess I needed it.

I'm still convinced, though, that Jill's comment about my shortness of breath had something to do with my eventual passion for logging as many miles in a day as I could. I believe the seed was planted in that moment. Yup. Such a boy! How I came to be as ardent as I did? Well, that was due to the little victories I mentioned. I wasn't getting a lot of feedback from the acting world at the time. I realized I needed something to keep me going. Some daily reinforcement. So, as I stepped up onto the berm around the reservoir and began the day's run, I would spot another runner on the track and decide to pass them at least once before they retired and hopefully pass them once more, "lapping" them.

Goose was always with me, but Goose was having her own adventure. Hers was to log significantly more mileage than I, crisscrossing the park at breakneck speed, careening back to find me just to touch base for a moment and then charging back off to spook some ducks or beg a treat from a picnicker. As I advanced into a more serious runner, Goose developed a different routine. She had discovered a deli on the corner of 87th and Columbus. Somewhere during a day's run, she would excuse herself and beat a path to said corner. It meant she had to cross Central Park West all by herself, dodging traffic, to set up shop outside the deli. It was there I found her. After a run. The first time was a bit of a panic for me but once the ritual had been established, I could comfortably enjoy my dash knowing Goose would be waiting for me, having conned any number of morsels from her kind-hearted victims. A cookie, a crumb, a piece of meat. She would refuse nothing. Visibly larger sometimes. The more successful days.

Through it all, though, Goose remained a physical specimen. By then, I was averaging sixty or seventy miles per week. She matched and almost doubled whatever distance I ran because of her marauder game, charging in and off again, running laterally across my singular course. There was a lot of wolf in her. She could have run all day. And by that time, so could I. I did not have an acting job, so I concocted a daily challenge that could match my ambition. I ran. My victory. And a nice summer. Ellen was working in Stratford. I was in New York. I waited tables. Barry and Gail were stalwart friends. Several others completed a circle of like-minded young people who shared a passion for life. Precious people. I am enjoying all their faces. Their laughter. Gail, Barry, Susan, Katherine, Peter, two Mae's, another Susan, Sal (big guy), Robert and Colby, Ken, Greg, Debbie—they know who they are if they happen to read this book. I remember you all. Lovely people. Thanks.

This was around the time news of Billy and Stephen reached me. They were victims of a shark attack in the Virgin Islands. Impossible. Billy was never found. Stephen had washed up on a shore. He had aspirated into his regulator. John told me he had always had a "big stomach." I didn't know what that meant but Stevie had a tendency to throw up. I guess what he must have witnessed was enough to end him too. I suppose he watched his brother die. I am mystified as to how so much tragedy has latched onto this family through its history. Onto my dad. Onto his dad. And their loved ones. By the time this happened, I remember thinking what next? It did not seem out of "our" ordinary... but, come on! I still think of Skeets, their mother, and what she must have felt. I send her love. Betty and John survived, and I saw Betty a few times in New York. Later in life I would get to know John a bit better and we spent some time in California. Betty died about ten years ago, sadly. John and I had a parting of the ways that was not particularly pleasant. That's sad, too. When Karen died, I didn't really connect with any of them, except our grandfather on my father's side, Frank, who just said, "This family is cursed." I never spoke to him again. I do not really know their story. Just some bullet points along a timeline of fits and starts, fading into obscurity.

The years in New York City were wonderful years but as I write I realize all the beauty and excitement of living there and carving a future were modified, dimmed by seeing them and living them through the lens of Karen and her death. I enjoyed many days but there was always something holding me back. There is a book, *Where Angels Fear to Tread*, by E. M. Forster, one of my favorite writers. He describes the voice of an English tenor. Unable to soar as an Italian singer might, the English voice is lovely but never fully given over to emotion, as if there is a frog in the throat holding it back, a bit of phlegm blocking it, choking it. Just a bit. It's like that. All my life. Since Karen died. Like that.

Our recent visit. When Kayte and I walked together in the footsteps of my younger self. I felt a joy I have never felt before. There has been a change. Kayte. Karen. Writing. My children. Living in each moment of my past and present, hand in hand, as always. With them and even with myself. A joy now. There is a joy. Unfettered.

I love you, Karen.

"I love you."

I want to go back to before. Before her murder. Back to our

childhood. I want to see her smiling again. We are at the beach. Sandy Hook. Gordon's status as a retired colonel gave us privileges at the beach at Fort Hancock. It stretched beyond the public beach out to the very tip of Sandy Hook in New Jersey, a curved finger out into the mouth of New York Harbor. My old window in the apartment building looked out toward the harbor and the New York skyline. Lady Liberty could be spotted in the distance, a solitary sentinel at the gates of freedom.

Karen and I went with Mom one day. We had one of those folding beach chairs and a couple of blankets to lay out. It was a sandy affair. I never really liked the sand . . . too intrusive. A nuisance to clean. And I cleaned all the cars. One of my chores around the house. It was a sunny, autumn day . . . warm still and the ocean was fairly warm, as well. There was a large swell but I do not remember a savage break, so the swells were building up the beach rather than gouging away at it. A sultry day when the sea and the shore gently press each other toward each other as the sun crosses a cloudless sky. Karen and I swam out together. The waves gently bobbed us up and down. Toes tickled the sandy bottom and then we were hoisted upward as the swells must have been ten feet high. Karen swam just a bit farther out than I and as one swell settled me into a trough another behind Karen lifted her high above me and in that moment there she was—the shining smiling child afloat in a massive mountain of water, embraced by it, weightless in its arms, a glowing wonder of a girl. My sister. My beautiful. My wonderful sister.

Ginna was Karen's roommate at college. I spoke to her today. I wasn't sure I would have the good fortune to connect with her. By virtue of her grace and her abiding fondness for Karen's grace and friendship all those years ago, we had a lovely conversation. She was funny. She even reminded me of Karen. They were kindred spirits. Ginna's words. When Ginna and Karen went to school at Berry there were about 1500 students overall. It was a coed school, but the men were not allowed past the flagpole at the heart of the campus and vice-versa for the girls . . . except for class.

I flash back to Brad and our time at FSU. Forward and back. Brad told me in his most recent text that the girls and the boys were on the same floor of the dorm, right across the hall from one another. It shocks me. We were impossibly decent kids. Brad ended up with his afore-mentioned girlfriend, Sandy. But I didn't! Sandy lived off Alton Road in Miami. We all stayed in touch for a while after that summer. I liked her. Brad's mom lived near there. Nice gal. I liked her too. But there was no girl for me that summer. Yeah, there was a kiss one humid night with the preacher's daughter that was pretty darn memorable. But I had a respect for her, a respect for her father, that kept things tame and innocent and I might add, lovely. It occurs to me that the reader might be curious as to why or how I harken back to those times and so often cite a memory of a kiss or the touch of a hand. I think it is because that is the wonder of youth. My youth. My preoccupation then and per-haps a bit beyond. Maybe my entire life. The longing for intimacy, connection. It is fantastic. The stuff of life itself. The simple ecstatic electricity of a single kiss that can lead to who knows where, was always on my mind. Right up to one night on a walk in London. Thirteen years ago. It was a simple kiss on a winter's eve hovering above Hyde Park that led me to the life I live today. That was some kiss.

I offer no apology for celebrating these moments and the lovely women who thought me worth some time on this shared journey. We are drawn to it by Nature's decree. It is meant to be. And I am extremely grateful to them; to those who joined me and invited me to join them. These are blessed memories. And if we are lucky, they live forever. They are reminders of our hopes and our innocence. I loved those early days. They remind us who we were and who we hoped to be. They remind us who we are.

So, I am glad to laugh a bit with Ginna as she recalls her time with Karen. They were a couple of young girls, out of the house for the first time, drawn to rebellion. Apparently, both she and Karen had a loose adherence to the policy of keeping the boys and girls apart. When they met, Karen did not have a roommate; Ginna was looking to dump hers. Her roommate was looking for an "M.R.S." degree. Lost on me at first, I realized she nursed a bit of disdain for the girls at school who came to refine their search for a husband. A "Mrs." degree. This was not Ginna's idea of higher education. Nor was it Karen's. So, the night they met, early in the semester, at a gathering for new students, Karen asked Ginna or Ginna asked Karen, I am not sure whom, but one surely asked the other, "You wanna get high?" A sort of love at first sight! They likely laughed quite a bit and then went in search of food. They determined to share Karen's room, a three-student room on the third floor that Karen had been occupying on her own. Ginna said it was a wonderful relationship. They took many hikes in the hills of the surrounding area. And they stayed friends. She received some letters from Karen after she had gone to Colorado, she recalled. She had not saved them, though.

In one of the letters John showed me, Karen had planned to stop and visit some college friends in Georgia before she joined him in Colorado Springs. I imagine Ginna was numbered among them. She told me they were both T-shirt and jeans kind of girls. Ginna majored in Home Economics. Berry College was renowned for it. I am not sure Karen declared a major. I don't remember asking Ginna. "We met and really hit it off at one of the get-togethers,"—that is what Ginna said. Karen treated everyone nicely. They listened to The Beatles and The Rolling Stones. And they stayed in touch after Karen left school. Exchanged letters. Sadly, it was my mom who told her about Karen when Ginna called looking for her. "I wished it had been me," she said. She wasn't the only one.

Ginna and I spoke for some time as I jotted down some facts and impressions. She mentioned there had been a horse ranch they visited and a camping trip, fifteen of them together. They spent time visiting a lake that is no longer on the campus. There was Berry Academy. It was three miles from the main campus, and I believe it was the satellite campus for the agricultural school that is connected to Berry College to this day.

When I took my tour, the president of the school pointed out a pair of boots outside a dorm room. An indication that the occupant was most likely one of the students who would have to milk the cows in the morning. There is a picture of Karen with a group of girls walking along a path and all of them are wearing a similar looking pair of boots. Another picture has Karen meditating at the bank of a surging stream. I asked Ginna about the boys in Karen's life. Or if there was a certain boy in her life. I had concocted a theory about heartbreak for Karen's grade slide the second half of her semester at college. I speculated the mysterious young man on her high school yearbook page may have been a factor . . . a young love that didn't work out. Ginna shot that theory down. I was happy to hear that Karen had spent time with a couple of guys while at college. There had been no drama in that way.

And I underestimated Karen in my presumption . . . she had always been quite level-headed in her affections and her adventures in love. More than I. Ginna suggested that Karen just lost interest. She reminded me Karen loved Freedom and Adventure. She'd spent the first half of the semester with Ginna "tasting who we would become." Ginna's phrase; I liked it. She enjoyed Berry the first few months but wasn't meant to stay there long. And Karen left, I fancy, to sample the menu elsewhere. That was all. I was relieved. There was no event or sadness that took her from herself. Like I said, I should have known better.

So, it seems her brief chapter at Berry was one of self-discovery and independence, exploration and new friendships. She remained a rebel. Ginna and she were late for curfew several times. They had picnics by the lake. Went camping. Decorated their room together. It was wonderful. They were close and there was another friend, Rhonda. I will try to find her too.

Ginna confessed she was put on academic probation after Karen left school. Probably a wild hair of her own. She did not marry until later in life. She never had kids. She closed the conversation saying she had been aware our dad was killed. And knew about the twin boys, brothers who had died. This was a little strange, but I suppose no more than a muddled memory confused in time. Billy and Stephen. The shark attack happened years after Karen died. It could not have been anything else. We said good-bye. I have reached out to clarify a thing or two since our conversation. A couple of questions. And I think we may have a chance to meet one day. I like seeing those who knew Karen during the days we did not share. I see her in their eyes. I see her.

There are other veins I have yet to open. During this last two years and a bit more, I have been guided by intuition, by a mystery surrounding the days of Karen that have come to life. It has been a mission. A detective, I have been searching for clues and eyewitness accounts. And I have searched the depths of my recollection. Opened. Many openings have presented themselves and many mysteries have been solved. I have loved finding her and her friends. I have loved searching out the people we knew together and many I did not know existed. All leading to Karen. All leading me to freedom from the tragedy. The sheer weight of all I know now almost drowning out the unfathomable sadness. I have found Karen and I have found myself. I am tempted to doubt it all; to think myself deluded, walking a path to an answer that does not exist. But that is not so. What am I doing? Finding Karen.

Doubt haunts my footsteps and insinuates itself into my mind. One foot in front of the other. One question answered and then another. One door closed but another opens. Friends come who want to help. Some have turned their backs. To them I wish my very best. I may not understand their reasons. Reminiscence is surely not an issue but, perhaps, for them it is. Too painful. Perhaps. Too painful for me not to try. I revel in it. This journey. For all its stumbles. For all its fits and starts, it is an affirmation of Karen's life. It "re-members" her. As I said at the outset. And she lives forever. Into her broken body, each remembrance fills her lungs. She is flesh again. Vibrant. The path has led me to her. It has gone down alleyways and friendships. Down hallways and highways. Roads I traveled with her years ago and some I travel with her now. For the very first time. Something else I realize. For my children and for those who did not know her, this leaves a record. They will know Karen. And their father. And their grandmothers, and grandfathers, great-grandparents and ancestors who live in them. Also, it honors Karen and teaches them the death she suffered did not conquer her. She remains the warrior who crawled with her last ounce of courage to fight for her life. To preserve her being. I did not help. I could not. But as I step onto this path again, I realize I still want to save her. This paragraph has led me to an overwhelming hoped for consequence . . . to save Karen. Still. God help me. Just a brother who wants to protect his little sister. A big brother protects his sister.

   "You are."

Brad left yesterday afternoon. I was just polishing a sentence about Brad when I got his message that he would be visiting California in a week or two. So, I put a few ideas aside to await his input in person. Brad is one of the most talented people I know. He is also one of the kindest and wisest. He is a real friend. He gives thoughtful counsel. He listens. And further counsels. He is a magnificent musician with a magnificent musical family that went before him. A father and an uncle of true accomplishment in the music world. More than anything, though, he was a pal in my youth and has remained so. I smile the same smile I smiled when I realized the guy who roomed with me at music camp was someone who was funny and unique and filled with the same kind of sensibilities I possessed. We cared about what we were doing. About the impact we would have in our lives. We wanted to do the world some good and hoped we had enough talent to pull it off. I had no visions of wealth or success but dreams of an artist's life—to sing, to make music, to entertain. That was the dream. To teach. To reach out with my heart and hope the good people of the Universe would receive it with theirs. It didn't really matter how many people. A few would do. Just a few would suffice. If I could make a difference in someone's life. To inspire them or ease them. Give them hope and solace. To know that through my efforts I might make someone else's life more bearable; that having lived, I made another's life better. Just for an instant. I believe Brad shared the same basic wavelength. I believe he still does.

A young boy stood at the stage door of the Winter Garden Theatre. I had just finished playing Casio. The boy was waiting for me. There were some very impressive actors who appeared in that show, more well-known than I, but he was there for me. As I stepped through the door, he presented himself, shook my hand and said, "I saw you play Macbeth, Mr. Grammer. And I just wanted to tell you I have been reading Shakespeare ever since." That young man made my life that night. It was enough. It was more than enough. What he told me is what I lived for. If there had never been another, this would do.

So, Brad and I spent a good few days remembering, reviewing our lives then and since, the days we shared and many of the years we spent apart. The business of life leading us along different paths that led, in time, back to that smiling certainty that we were friends forever. What felt like friendship all those years ago was more than a hunch, more than an inkling. It was a promise. A covenant.

The conversation turned to Karen. Brad had lunch with her just weeks before she went to Colorado. He met her at an apartment in Boca Raton. He thought it was hers but the postmarks on all her letters showed an address in Pompano Beach. And the police noted that her known addresses before Colorado were both in Pompano . . . one our home and the other an apartment she had rented. So, after some thought, we concluded that it must have been a friend's place. Maybe she went there for a week or two after letting her own apartment go. His memories of Karen were as many of our other friends. She was wonderful. Kind. Intelligent. Fun. Brad and she had a nice lunch together. He wished her luck. In that time, they may have even shared an intimacy. It would not have been a surprise. They were friends. Karen was leaving. It was not considered a commitment back then, or a betrayal, for two friends to spend that kind of time together, especially when they might never see each other again. Of course, they never did. Sad. Brad was sad as we revisited his time with Karen. His time. My time. We remembered her together. I didn't think to ask just what kind of good-bye kiss they shared. I wouldn't dare. I'd be happy for them both. Two of my favorite people. She seemed excited to be going. More candy.

And as we reminisced, an old friend, Spencer, enters our orbit. I use different tenses in the same sentence. Sometimes. I do it consciously because what is part of a distant or recent past also has an element of being entirely in the present. So, I write it as it feels. Recollections from the past are present when remembered. Present in the present. So, I do it like that; I did it like that. See? And thanks again, Henry Fielding.

Brad and I steered clear of the subject because, in all honesty, I think we both thought he was dead. I feared he was. I had not heard from him for twenty years, maybe longer. Spence had not been as close to Brad, as they met because of and through me. But they were friends too. Several months ago, I had asked Brad if he had any news of Spence. He had none. But it was Brad's impending visit that got me thinking I should at least try to track him down. The past year and a half have been spent tracking down leads; trying to find people who might have a kernel of Karen to share. A thought, an insight, a memory. Something stowed in their unconscious or even a pristine recollection, one that remains fresh. It was from her closest friends I hoped to find the latter. Alas, they have not spoken to me. I am still trying. Brian though... he came through. Brad even mentioned Brian at one point. We traced our footsteps back to Hendrix, the night we saw him. Amazing. And Brad said he thought Brian had been there. I think so, too, and he chuckled as I chuckle at the thought of Brian. A character, to be certain. We had driven in my Corvair Van. Karen did not come that evening. I think she might have been up in Welaka at the time. But Brian was there. Well... I think he was there. And I believe Spencer came too. A terrible drive. I bought the van for one hundred dollars. Six weeks later, the transmission went and went pretty much as we were driving back from Miami that night, high off Hendrix but sputtering up I-95, limping back to Pompano Beach. It took us three or four hours. A drive that should have been no more than one. We made it home. It reminds me of another night when Spencer and I were walking what we used to call "the strip" just above Las Olas Blvd. Some fella approached us with an offer to buy his convertible for fifteen dollars. Did it run? It did. He really needed that fifteen bucks! We had no idea why. He was clearly desperate. So, we bought it. A nice big green Oldsmobile and drove it for the night. Convertible! Cruised the strip and grabbed a cocktail near Bahia Mar. Sometime later that evening, the car gave up the ghost and Spencer and I had a good laugh, thanking that denizen of debauchery for a night on the town. We had parked the car not far from where we bought it. No longer running. At all. It was not out of gas. We thought of that. It just lurched along in a last gasp and died just as we drifted into an open parking space. Its final resting place, the bottom of a small apartment unit. We had a good laugh about it.

Bahia Mar is in Ft. Lauderdale. It is one of my favorite places in the world. I love boats. I love to sleep on board a boat of almost any size. The slapping of halyards on the masts of sailboats. Aural sleeping potion. For me. It was at a place called Bahia Cabana that I first learned to drink. It was a little bar/hotel on the water at the south end of Bahia Mar by the fire station. It was directly across from The Yankee Clipper, a great hotel where there was a piano bar at the top. Bob, Spencer's dad, took me there for dinner from time to time. Sometimes with the family. Sometimes just the two of us. A terrific pianist played there regularly. And on a nighttime the best view of the rising moon was accompanied by the greatest music of the twentieth century. The standards. The songs my grandfather and grandmother sang during World War ll. The songs Frank sang through the fifties and sixties. My mom's favorites. Honestly, the world's favorites. This was Bob's music too. He told me about the night he said good-bye to Glenn Miller as he boarded the plane that disappeared over the English Channel. He spoke of his time with the Free French in Paris during the war. "Vu qui Passe"—a song they sang in France during the war about the one who passes who might not be alive another day. This is what I remember, though I could be wrong. They lived through days of horror and hope, side by side. The fight. The fight is entrancing and hypnotic. It dictates sacrifices and sacrilege as it magnifies our will to live. To survive. Or die. Bob survived and then came home to die. A tragedy. Gordon survived and came home to live. Different wounds and consequences from the same fight but different men. They would handle them differently. In the end, I think the war killed them both. Or killed a piece of them. Gordon wanted to live. Bob—I'm not sure. Broken hearted. Both of them. For whatever reason. As I have learned. Enough. Enough for them.

My broken heart. Karen. Gordon. Gam. The world. The lies of our generation. The corruption of our dreams. The waste. My mom. Watching her heart break was more than any person should endure. But we do endure. What she endured could break a heart throughout the ages. A human heart. And Mom endured.

The path closes. I can say no more. Not now. For now.

So, when I actually performed in Ft. Lauderdale, as a young actor, it was a marvelous treat for me to stay at the Bahia Cabana. We performed there for three weeks when I was twenty-seven years old. A return to my hometown. A victory lap of sorts. To all the people who warned I would amount to nothing, a rewarding rebuke. Not a gloat. Just a satisfied smile. They'd been proven wrong. Okay, maybe a little gloat.

Forgive me.

Brad also gave me an insight. Something I knew but never fully understood. "Gam wanted to make you tough. She thought she needed to make you tough." This is what Brad said. It was said simply and with the certainty of an eyewitness account. It worked. She did make me tough. If I hadn't been, I would never have made it. Life played a hand. It was tough too. Couldn't think of any reason it should or shouldn't be. Coming back to Jesus. I also had Faith. Do not "become a in the race." These are the words of Mary Baker Eddy. When things are at their very worst, no matter how bad, you do not give up. If we have no Faith, it is that much easier to give in, to lose hope, to lose the will to live. Ironic that Gam, who introduced me to the teachings of Christian Science would finally succumb to grief. I guess some things are too tough. Karen's murder was tough. Karen didn't give up. Till there was no blood left in her, Karen fought to keep her life. I think that helped me. Her strength helped me. There is nothing life can dish out that will defeat me. She gave me that by her example. There is nothing that would make me yield. Christ did not yield. That has helped me too. Even as I did not fully understand. The continuing revelation. Days filled with unfolding, unending knowledge and comfort. In the face of unthinkable pain, indescribable joy. It is a magnificent gift. This life. Confusing, challenging, tough. To lose a child. For a mother to lose a child. Mary did. My mom did. My heart goes out to every woman who has known that sorrow. Kayte has known the pain of losing a child. And every day another mother loses her dear one.

Intelligence.

The word comes to mind here and I am not sure why. So, I will try to work it out.

Hatred.

Another word that springs to mind. To Divine Intelligence hatred is unconscionable. Yet politics and the "seven deadlies" pit us against one another. Whether real or imagined, enemies are made and strategies devised to defeat them. The powerful want us to hate one another.

Why? Control. Again. It's always control. People divided against each other, people separated from God are easy to manipulate and lead. Governments masquerade as God. And try to convince us God has no place, no plan for us. Nor does religion. They lie. And then they promise prosperity and ascendency. One group over another. One group against another. Into the cracks of these contentions, individuals fall. Broken and lost. And they spiral out of control. They want to strike out. And often do. They choose violence or self-harm. Sometimes they choose both. Sometimes they choose the unthinkable. Render unto Caesar what is Caesar's. Render unto God what is God's. Things have not changed. And to those who suffer under Caesar's hatred (and they're all Caesar) I wish the unifying truth of brotherhood and kinship in God's embrace. God does not teach hatred. Men do. Beware of them. Those who teach hatred. Beware how powerful hatred can be. And how cunning.

It is the same singular devil who teaches hatred to both sides. It was hate that killed my sister. Hate. Freddie Glenn who bore the knife.

Spiraled a bit myself there. This comes off the back of a conversation I had with a group of people recently who were quick to point out the dangers of algorithms and such that target one way of thinking and magnify it against others. The point being to cultivate silos in society that generate hatred between people. Evil. Agreed. Dangerous. We all nodded assent. Then they went on to repeat a series of claims about people they didn't know. People who had been targets of algorithms designed solely for this bunch to embrace. I just shake my head. Two sides of the same coin. And once we allow ourselves to hate or be led to hate people we do not know, that is where the real danger lurks. Once we hate, we become smug, self-satisfied, ignorant, dismissive, loathing, intolerant, destructive people. And the very things we hate, we become. It is tempting, though. Humans are easily drawn to things that villainize others, different people than themselves. Drawn to things that feed their self-satisfaction and sense of superiority.

Lead us not into Temptation but deliver us from Evil.

Does this mean temptation can lead us to evil? Evil against one another? Honestly, I never really connected the two until this moment. Till I wrote them down in the same sentence. Didn't realize it was a sentence. Temptation can lead us to Evil. I see, said the blind man. And drop your voice.

I am human; I am not innocent in this. I will try to do better.

When I started this book, I had no idea it might make me a better man, a bigger man. Dear sister. Dear sweet Karen.

Truth.

I did not want to assume Spencer was dead. Not without checking. I had no idea how to find him but then it occurred to me, Spencer has a son. I did not recall his first name but I remembered MacPherson was one of his names. It was a name from Spencer's ancestry and I know he held it in high esteem. It was a nod to that esteem that would live in the name of his son. And I remembered that. I remembered how Bob would speak the name with great reverence. His carriage would enlarge. His height increase. A proud name.

And it led me to Arthur. Spencer's son. Last week, we met. It was a good meeting. There was contention, as there is between different generations and different schools of thought. His bride, Rachel, joined him. And his mother. It was wonderful to see her again. Cindy. The content of what we exchanged was not so important as it was to connect. I am resolved to know him better. Perhaps, we can find accord on a few things and grow together. I will leave it at that. I did feel an overwhelming desire to acquaint him with his family beyond what his dad might have told him. I sensed there were some blanks. Arthur told me Spence didn't really share a great deal with him. Cindy confessed she hadn't really known much. So, maybe I can help a bit. More than anything, the hopeful product of a pleasant dinner in Atlanta was that I might actually see Spence again. Arthur said he would reach out to his dad's current wife. A good gal, he said. God willing, I will speak with her soon and she can help. I would like to see him. I am not sure what to expect but Spencer was the one I called first, the one who came instantly when I told him Karen is dead. I did tell Arthur that. I wanted him to know the depth of character from which he springs. The young man I knew was a man to be admired. His dad.

By the way, Spencer is not dead. Brad and I kicked off instantly into

313

memories that came alive at the mere mention of his name; and that young man lived again. Spencer and I met at school in Rumson, New Jersey. For all I knew, Spencer had been there since kindergarten. He seemed like one of the cool kids. I was not. So, we did not become friends during sixth grade. I remembered him, though. I remembered he was a pretty good athlete and a deadly dodgeball thrower. He had a good aim and was spry enough to avoid any but the most accurate of counterattacks. That may have been the moment I saw him. Really saw him. There was a kind of glee and a bit of mischief in him. There was also a depth I didn't know was depth at the time, and a bit of mystery. As if he had something going on I did not realize, I could not realize, except that what I saw was not the complete picture. Never thought much about it till now, actually. And I never thought of Spencer again until that day in tenth-grade history class. A new kid at school. Like I had once been at Rumson. Two aisles over from me, toward the back of the class he sat. I looked over and I think I mentioned out loud to no one in particular, "That kid looks like Spencer K . . . !" He turned and said, "Kelsey?" How 'bout that? He remembered me.

It was a fun couple of years, the last two grades at Pine Crest. Well, three. Tenth, eleventh, and twelfth. There was Jay, Glen, Dan, Karen, Jan, Momo, Gillian. Wandi, Susan, Roxanne. Holly, Lynn, Luann. Debbie, Nini and her brother, Jay. Pam and Liz. Brett, Brian, Brad and Faith, Bob and others. Ray. Ray knew Spencer. I have a different memory attached to every one of the names. Too many to include here. Names and memories, dozens more, that I retain but didn't realize until now.

Ray.

Ray deserves a little love. We didn't go to school together. I met Ray at Driver's Ed class. I have never really written about him. We were not bad boys, exactly. But we were determined to do things like get the VW up to third gear on the back stretch of the driving course. There was a Plymouth Fury in the collection of cars donated for the classes. It was pretty quick and didn't handle very well, so we would race too deep into a turn and then oversteer trying to make the rear end come loose. Make the tires squeal. An Oldsmobile Le Mans that we would drop into first gear to get a "patch." I realize these are all expressions from another time. Boys with too much time on our hands, I suppose. Miraculously, we both graduated. The whole purpose of the class was to get a lower insurance rate when we finally got our licenses at age sixteen. So, we clearly couldn't have been that bad. Come the middle of tenth grade, we all turned sixteen and spent the rest of the school year driving to the beach, or down to Miami whenever we had the chance. Just to drive. We loved it. I think I have a blank spot here. I do not remember Karen getting her license. I'm sure she did. The following year. I just don't remember. The truth is she didn't have to drive. I would take her any number of places. She had boyfriends or girlfriends with boyfriends who were happy to drive. We rode to school together or when she went to Palm Cove, I think my mom took her. Again, these were the days when we aligned with our own group of friends yet still enjoyed the occasional crossover. I enjoyed her friends a great deal. She enjoyed mine. Karen was like the air I breathed. We were here together always, even when we weren't together. She was a constant. We revolved around each other. In our different orbits, yes, but I never missed her because I knew she would always be there. Kelsey and Karen were brother and sister; you never got one without at least a little piece of the other. Some days, I wasn't particularly sure of myself. Karen would do her best to be a cheerleader of sorts. I would run interference for Karen when Gam or Mom were at her about something. I had trouble seeing the good in me sometimes, but Karen always could. I was tough on her sometimes. Trying to fill the shoes of a father we didn't have. Once in a while I did okay. We fought sometimes. But rarely. She understood me, understood I loved her more than anything. She was a great sister. I am lucky and grateful she was in my life. She was beautiful and smart. We enjoyed each other. I know I've said this before. There is so much I miss. It's nice to remember. Right to remember. The Book of Karen . . . times we lived together. Times gone by.

Ray was around a lot in those days. Ray went to Pompano High. His dad was a builder; I only met him once. We were playing golf. An unlikely lesson, courtesy of Ray's dad. A plane had landed on that

315

very golf course a few weeks before. It made the news. An emergency landing. Two men on board. No one was hurt. Ray's dad was one of them. A mechanic had just done a tune-up and full service on his plane for him. Its first time back in the air, he invited or rather insisted the mechanic join him. To "guarantee" his work. There was a look exchanged as the engine sputtered and failed. "I had a feeling" kind of look, Ray's dad flashed at the mechanic. They landed in a glide. On the golf course. The mechanic was handed the bill for getting the plane back to the hangar. The unlikely lesson. Do your job. Someone's life may depend on it. Maybe even your own.

I am tempted to launch into a rant about our world today. Why? I will leave it to you. Yeah, probably has something to do with the number of people who have been hurt these days by people not doing their job. People in charge; asleep at the wheel. But like I said, I will leave it to you.

Back to Ray. Ray liked to wrestle and throw sand. Laugh if someone fell down, that sort of thing. Kind of mean. Kind of juvenile. I once told him I expected better of my friends. And to his credit, Ray thanked me and said he would do better. No one had ever asked him before. Or cared enough to ask, I suspect. I did. And what's funny is, I didn't like Ray, at first. When I first saw him in Drivers Ed—the classroom portion before we got out on the track, I pegged him as kind of an asshole. I chuckle as I write this because I think he pegged me the same. But a few weeks later, after all our shenanigans out on the track, Ray and I were pretty tight. He was all right. Still a little angry. It seemed that way. Angry that his dad wasn't around a lot. Maybe. I only met him that one time. Or maybe his dad was too tough on him. At least he had a dad, I remember thinking. Maybe Ray's dad was tough for a reason. He'd been right about that mechanic, after all.

Anyway, he had a nickname for Ray..."Butch!" Butch was a word we used back then for a tough guy. Maybe Ray feared he wasn't tough enough. Tough enough for his dad's liking. I read a world of hurt into that. Maybe I was wrong. I think his dad loved him, but I wasn't sure he knew how to show it. So, I was impressed with Ray when he had the grace and guts to thank me for asking him to be a better friend. That was really something. His dad would have been proud. I was proud to know him. And Ray was as good as his word. He and I grew closer the next couple of years. I remember a night I was just playing the piano. Ray sat in the living room listening. "You play beautifully," he told me. "That was beautiful." Two years after we met, Ray was the kind of friend who could praise a friend. Honest and open and kind. A great guy.

So, on Ray's eighteenth birthday, his dad gave him a .38 pistol. He showed it to me. I didn't have a problem with guns. I grew up with them. Ray swore his dad had given him the gun to honor the fact that he was a man now. Seemed reasonable enough. But there was something going on with Ray. That night, Ray was out cruising around shooting at stop signs. I have no idea why. Cops pulled him over. He had a bunch of pills on him. Again . . . no idea why. Something was wrong. The cops kept asking him if there was someone after him. There wasn't. But . . . maybe there was. Maybe Ray. An angry streak, something in him, something that didn't like himself . . . *was* after him. Something that didn't feel loved. I'm honestly just grasping at straws here.

Ray ended up in jail. In prison for a couple of years. It wasn't until after Karen had died, after I was working in San Diego, that Ray called and said he wanted me to come to his wedding. He was living in Gainesville, Florida. I believe he was on probation, but he had a job in a grocery store and it was there he met an angel. She was really an angel. Beautiful and kind. She was a checkout girl. I think back to the days when the checkout girl was always cute. I don't know why. The girl at the register in almost every grocery store or supermarket was a cute high school girl who had to fend off the admiring glances of every boy from town. Just a smile from her set a boy's heart racing. That's how I felt about it. I don't have a specific girl in mind here, but I remember thinking this way a few times as I watched the numbers run up on the register. I am down this rabbit hole and trying to figure out how I got here. Why is this thing a thing for me? With the checkout girls of the world. Why?

Got it.

I think it was a moment to simply be in the presence of a perfect stranger. The tempo controlled entirely by her. Item after item, fingered, flipped and examined. Then pushed along toward the bagging area. It gave me time to wonder about them. Who were they? Where did they live? What kind of life did they have? I suppose this is the mind of an actor. What motivates a person? What do they think behind the mask of their public life? Maybe we all do this. I don't know. I do it to this day with any number of assorted people—men and women alike. "Others" as well, just to stay current. But with the checkout girl it was just the two of us. Briefly.

I wondered what her world was like outside the store and the position that put her on display. On display. That is part of it. She had a public persona that was correct and efficient and lured me into thoughts of a private life, a secret life lived far from the penetrating eyes of her customers. She always had a nice manicure. Nice hands. Glasses. A pair of glasses added to the allure. A cool demeanor. Aloof. Yes, the checkout girl was always a bit aloof. Maybe because of the job, the focus it required. There was often a flash of a smile but then the back to business stoicism . . . warm and charming but businesslike and distant. Yeah, this really was a thing for me. I still muse about the secret life of a working girl. What makes them tick? Who are they? What are their dreams and aspirations? Who will they be one day? That might be part of it. The job is temporary. Maybe that's it. A summer job. A stop along the way. Not a final destination. Maybe that is what I find intriguing. Where are they heading? Who will they be?

My goodness! I just realized this is what happened to me when Kayte and I met. I wondered about her. We were on a flight to London. She was working. A public life. On display. The subject of my searching eyes and curiosity and musings about her. Musings about her away from the trappings of a glamorous profession. I thought she was glamorous. In her job. Charming and distant at the same time. Outgoing but with perfect restraint. Coy and aloof. She occupied my imagination. I wanted to know her. I wanted to know more about her. Both things remain true today.

I climbed off the plane and Ray introduced the most charming young woman as his fiancé. She was warm and beautiful, and they were clearly in love. I saw in Ray the kind of love I dreamed of, and I saw the same in her. Ray and the checkout girl! Not aloof. Not clinical in any way. Gracious and outgoing. She had the look of an angel as I said before. And it was clear she was for Ray. It was fantastic. Ray was glowing. We spent the night at his apartment. There was a pool. We all went swimming. The next night, Ray had his bachelor party. Some giant club. I had never seen anything like it. Teeming. There was a wet T-shirt contest. I had never seen anything like that either. Some eye-popping moments, to be sure. Several of the girls seemed almost professional. Funny how some images just stay with a person. We had a fun night. Finished early. Nothing more. Ray had a wedding in the morning, after all. I had never seen him so happy. The wedding was lovely. The reception simple and filled with jubilation. This portion of the world was right with itself. At least for these two. These two who had found heaven on earth.

I have always believed we should celebrate the good fortune of a friend. From turmoil and angst, Ray emerged on cloud nine. I boarded my flight home. San Diego. I never thought of it as home really, but I guess it was. My home. Where my dog was waiting. Where I had found my creative voice. Where I began to make a living, start a career. Where on cool nights I would sit by the fire with Goose. She sat so close her fur would be warm to the touch. My time in San Diego was a time of healing. It was the winter season. Just before the Shakespeare Festival would begin. My final season there before I would return to New York. There was a sense of peace in my life. I missed Karen. But it was almost three years since she had died and a part of me had begun to feel my life calling. Still, there was a sense of guilt that my life should call at all. My grief shifting to self-loathing at times. Whenever I felt good about where my life was, I felt it was not my right. That my life couldn't and shouldn't feel right ever again.

Two days after Ray married, his young bride was killed in a car accident. I do not remember her name and I apologize to her and her family for that. She was a terrific young woman. I cannot imagine the grief they must have felt. I knew what Ray would do. His sister called me with the news and then I spent the next two days trying to reach him. My memory is dim about leaving him a message. Did we have answering machines then? I think we did. It was 1978. Maybe not. But I remember begging him not to do anything rash. Doubting if it would help at all. Now I remember! I pictured him sitting by his phone not answering. I was begging him to pick up. I could see him sitting there. Knowing I was ringing. Knowing I would try to talk him out of it. What he was planning to do. Something violent. Something against himself. I tried to call him every hour on the hour. He knew it was me. Two days later, his sister rang. Ray slammed his car into a tree. The Highway Patrol said he must have been driving at a very high speed. He died on impact. The car burst into flames. Ray was burned beyond recognition.

A moment of silence, please. A little love for Ray. And for his bride. Of all the senseless stories I have known, theirs is the saddest. God Bless Them.

I want to honor a few other people before I button things up and make a final salute to Karen. Ron, Richard, and Diana. And as I write this, I realize I do not want to make a final salute to her. Nothing final; rather a lasting, living one. I have enjoyed writing this book because it has been a daily devotion to my sister. Karen. I will miss it. The active search for the best way today to salute her and see her. Her life has been feverishly within me as I have searched for words. Searched for her. Memories have burst upon my consciousness in the least expected, surprising ways. Delightful ways. At times. Terrifying, sad discoveries too. At times.

The purpose has always been to help others. Help the ones left behind who face a loss they cannot fathom. To help me face a loss I never could. And to free her. Free Karen from a prison of my sadness. Of the memories I hold today, the good far outweigh the bad. I remember Karen as she lived. Not completely. A few more discoveries are out there—I know it. And still a few more in my memory yet to unlock. Memory. Amazing. So much life in there. So much of it good. Some pages ahead are marked for us. Blanks now, but ready for a visit from this wonderful life. Pages that will capture it and hold it forever. There we will meet and remember together.

Brad. As he left, he made a departing observation about my youth. He shared that Gam had tried to make me tough. Yes, I mentioned that already. Then he said that in the early years we shared he had never known anyone work as hard as I did. I was serious about it. Frankly, I had forgotten that. Or maybe I never realized it. Karen knew. Karen realized it and that fueled her predictions for me. Predictions that I have tried to honor. To honor her. Brad also added something that surprised me. "Everyone knew," he said. "Everyone knew you were going to go far. Maybe you were the only one who didn't know. And maybe that's why you did okay." Honestly, I was never sure I would do anything. What I did do, all I did was do what came to me. Almost as if there really was no thought at all. No sense of a future but a discovery that lurched from one lesson to another. One means of expression to another. I knew I loved people. I knew I loved feeling I was part of something important. I knew that making someone laugh or cry was important. To me. It unified my heart and mind with the hearts and minds of others. Ministry. Connection. I am just writing words as they come to me. In the Book of Matthew there is a line. Do what is given unto you. I am not sure when I first read it. Not sure when I absorbed it. But I did indeed absorb it. And I took it as instruction. The pages of this book exist by virtue of the same instruction. Do what is given unto you! This was given me. And as I approach the end, I will not rest until the story is complete. So, I am sensing the end is near but not quite. It is closer now than when I began. That's all. And there is a part of me saddened by that. I have loved walking with Karen. You see, the active hand in hand, as once we were in life, has been this book. I will never let go. Now that I hold her as I never thought I could, I will hold on forever.

This is what I wish to give.

To all those who have lost the hand of him or her they loved. For whatever reason, but certainly for those who have had the hand ripped from their grip and the soul torn from their heart. Whether by cruelty or war, circumstance or fate, murder or the seemingly senseless conundrum of life on earth; for all who have wept in despair, I hope this can give some solace. Remember them. And they live again. Hold them in your heart. And see them. And see God. For it is with God they dwell. In God's arms. And in His arms, we are one with them forever. If there was a single piece of advice I would give, it would be that in these trying times, step toward God rather than away. I stepped away. I do not regret it. I just realize it was a mistake. I spent a long time in the wilderness. This book brought me home. I am home again with Karen. It takes me some time, as a rule, more time than most, to sort things out. I am a slow learner. I am stubborn. I held on to my pain thinking it was an affront to my sister to let it go. Once I get it right, though, I am steadfast. I will always mourn Karen, but I will never lose her again. She is with God. And I'm with Him.

You know that recently, I flew to Atlanta to meet Spencer's son. His wife. Him. And see his mom again. I honor their privacy. But it was a lovely visit. Maybe I will get to know them. I did know his mom in the early days. We recounted there had been a great deal of fun. And now, as hoped, I have a way to contact Spencer. Finally. What I may learn, who knows? But I will have the chance to tell an old friend he stood for something in my life. Something rare and authentic. Individual. Unequaled. More to come.

But as I flew that day, sitting in my seat, drifting in and out, on the way back from Atlanta, my mind settled into a conversation. With Jesus. Yes, Jesus. The Christ. Your doubt is welcome. Even God welcomes doubt. Remember Thomas? But there Christ was. In my head, surely; but then, where else would He be? Unless He chose to stand in the cabin before me and make a real show of it. For me, this would do. This was enough . . . just enough. To get my attention. I slip back in time to the baseball field.

"Where were you?"

Right there, I know, but I still doubt. *But* . . . there He was! On the plane. As I said, right beside me.

In the simplest way, I murmured an apology, "I am sorry I didn't believe You could do it. I'm sorry I doubted You. I'm sorry."

"Okay," He said. "It's okay. Time for you to stop now. I got this, Kels. You can let it go."

A phrase from the Bible haunts me: Take my yoke upon you. I didn't get it. I heard a sermon recently, one of the sermons that populate the radio; this was the topic. I always thought it meant that I was to take Christ's yoke upon me to carry Him and His pain. The preacher explained just the opposite: By taking his yoke upon me, I was handing the burden of my life to Jesus. Like a pair of oxen, we would share His yoke. When I could not carry the weight, Christ would take it. He would do the pulling. He would carry me.

"Let it go."

Again, "Let it go, Kelsey. I've got this."

And again.

Quiet. I sat, quiet. A tear slid down my cheek. There on the plane. It all slipped away.

"But it's heavy," I protested once more. "I should handle this. I can take it. I can. Please? This is mine. You already carry so much."

Then Jesus said, "Because I can. It's why I came. Why our Father sent me. Rest now. It never was yours to carry. It's mine."

Yeah. I finally found Jesus.

He'd been there all along.

Right there.

I'm thinking of that Kipling line: A teardrop slips into the ocean. I felt washed clean. How many teardrops in the sea? All unique. All one. No! It's "dewdrop." The dewdrop slips into the ocean. When east meets west. Teardrop works better for me here, though. Maybe the dewdrop was always a teardrop that slipped into an ocean of other tears and washed the shores clean with their passion, their sadness. Or their Joy. Remember. We can cry tears of Joy too. I like that. An ocean of tears. All oceans all tears. All sorts of tears.

Gordon came to mind last night as I drifted off to sleep with my son, James. Whenever I carry him to bed, I think of the last time Gordon carried me up the stairs. I pretended I was still asleep as we started up. I wanted to remember the feeling. I do. I remember it.

Cocktail onions! I remember them too. It was Gordon's cocktail onions in his Beefeater Gibson at the Fort Monmouth Officer's Club that started my love affair with all things pickled. Starting there and spending a lifetime finding the oddest, most exotic pickles from around the world. Lime pickle, pickled cauliflower (preferably hot), Giardiniera, pepperoncini, pickled jalapeños, cherry peppers, Calabrian chili paste, pickled asparagus, the classic dill and any number of others. A basic rule of thumb for me is sugar is not welcome. I have no love for a butter pickle. The sweetness eludes me. In my first love, the cocktail onion, sugar is the enemy. If I see sugar in the ingredients of a jar of cocktail onions, or pearl onions as they are sometimes called, that jar will remain on the shelf. As my tastes matured, I found another remarkable offering—the pickled okra. Nothing makes me happier than a pickled okra... a good one. They are not all good because some companies cook them a bit too long, which means they are not crisp. A pickled okra that is not crisp may just as well be a rotten egg. Come to think of it, I have no love for a pickled egg: seems the best way to make a perfectly good egg taste like a rotten one. Not my cup of tea and I am not all that crazy about tea. There were scallions and carrot sticks, celery and cucumber. I always liked a traditional crudités. Hot stuffed cherry peppers—a complete winner! Once I found them, I thought I had found a piece of heaven on earth. I am not capitalizing heaven in this instance because I do not really think of them as Heaven but as a wonderful taste that makes life seem just a bit more sublime. I recall a scene in *Frasier*. Niles said something about a certain dish being "to die for!" Martin stated, "Niles, food is not to die for; your family is to die for, your country is to die for." I concur. Sublime is still high praise though, and it does accurately describe how I feel about the hot stuffed cherry pepper. Second favorite is the mild stuffed cherry pepper. The difficulty throughout the years has been maintaining a reliable supply. The companies to offer them have come and gone. And the new ones that offer them are rarely up to my standards. Until very recently I had pretty much given up. Then one day in a deli on Long Island, I found a jar that looked very promising. The mortadella sandwich from this deli was a poem. When I got back to the house we were kindly given for a week or so out on Montauk, I opened them. I picked one that had a nice color, somewhere between the green of a young pepper and the red of a riper one. Sliced it into quarters as is my wont, and then popped one into my mouth. Magnificent. I subsequently contacted the Cosmo's Food Company in Connecticut and secured a supply. I am about to eat one now. It is secretly my intention to ensure they never go out of business by keeping up a steady demand for them. All by myself.

How does this connect to my sister? I was wondering that myself as I started down this path. Food. Karen and I shared a love of "picking." We loved leftovers. And we loved Mexican food. There was a little place up the road from us in Pompano. Smitty's. There was a cute neon sign with the name outside the restaurant. He was just an American guy who married a woman from Mexico—he loved her and she loved him and they both loved Mexican food. So did Gam. Sally loved it too. I think because they had lived in Texas and would cross the border for an adventure and a meal sometimes. And Karen and I became fans of the cuisine because it is just so damn perfect. Healthy and flavorful. Colorful. We went there at least twice a month, and it was a staple in our lives. Smitty would come and sit with us for a while. He offered a refuge to us at a hard time. That's it. Refuge. Again. Still reeling from the loss of our captain, Smitty took Gordon's chair for an hour or two. Family. Yeah, Smitty felt like family. A respite from a sad season.

Comfort. Conversation. Communion. Friendship. These all come up when we think of food. These are the values enhanced by a gathering at the dinner table. Phrases like "comfort food" come to mind. I find certain of these foods comforting because they connect me to the past, comforting because it was a better time. If not better, then it was at least a time when my family was alive. When Karen was. Karen made the greatest chocolate chip cookies. Gam made an amazing leg of lamb. The mere mention of leg of lamb transports me back to the dining table, all of us gathered round and talking to each other, smiling, laughing. Food. A time machine. What am I craving when I crave a certain food? The past? I don't know. But like a favorite song, a raft of feelings hitchhike with a favorite meal. Steak is Gordon. Karen is chocolate chip cookies. My mom cooked an amazing pork chop. Gam was potatoes au gratin and that lamb. And I? I am popcorn. It is my gift. Popcorn and escargot. And Karen also invented a remarkable treat. If you take an Oreo cookie and dip it in an iced Coca-Cola, dip it long enough to harden the inside because of the cold, and long enough to soften the cookie part with the liquid, it is like a piece of fizzy chocolate cake surrounding a frozen vanilla cream treat. An amazing flavor. My goodness, I see the two of us sitting there watching Bugs Bunny, dipping away and savoring this elegant creation. I highly recommend it to anyone, young or old. Make sure you keep the cookie submerged long enough to soften the outside and harden the inner core. Plenty of ice is essential.

There is a dish, however, that is not such a fond memory. Fish sticks. Mom is also fish sticks. When my mother announced we would be having fish sticks it was code for, "The adults are going out tonight and the children are staying home." Fish sticks is Babysitter. Why did we never eat fish sticks when the adults were home? I have no idea. Could it be we lived in a two-tiered system of nutrition, robbing us of dietary justice? Good enough for the children but nothing the parents would touch? Surely not the greatest affront but I regard it as culinary torture to this day. Nope—I don't much care for fish sticks. Sorry, Mrs. Paul. Sorry, Mr. Morton. Sorry, Mom.

But I do love fish and chips. Huh? Go figure. Well, I married a girl from England. I must have warmed to the idea of battered fish and French fries. Kayte. Kayte is curry, by the way.

Richard, Ron, and Diana.

I really must tip my hat to them. They were the first to put their faith in me. The first to recognize and then champion my potential. They each took a piece of their lives and offered it to me. They gave me their time. They didn't have to. And I am forever in their debt. Richard was the music guy. Ron was the acting teacher. Diana was my voice coach. It was Diana's idea to send me off to Florida State for that summer music camp where I would meet one of the great friends of my life. Richard got me singing every day and even secured a spot in several churches every Sunday where I would get fifty bucks just for singing with the choir and doing a solo or two. And Ron sealed the deal with my love of the spoken word. English is an amazing language and it gave me my ticket. My, how I did love reading from the Bible in Sunday school. It is delicious to speak in the English language, delicious to send the words of the poets spinning through my mind and lips and lungs. It may be Ron did not teach me this love, merely unlocked it. Pointed me in the right direction. Nevertheless, I am deeply grateful to him and to the three of them. Because once unlocked, my freedom, my life, my everything would be built on my love of performance and the search for truth; not true things but hypertruth, supernatural truth—the authentic expression of universal connection between us, all mankind, our maker and the worlds we build. And the words that define us. Expression is my Heaven. It is my connection to God. And my connection to all. Hyperbolic?

Maybe.

I have to confess it took me thirty years to even scratch the surface. I remember thinking just a while ago that I had begun to crack this thing . . . just begun. That was about five years ago. Imagine that.

The first night I sat down for a meal at Diana's home, she put on Aaron Copland's *Fanfare for the Common Man*. I heard God! In that music. I would fall asleep every night to Leonard Bernstein conducting Copland's *Appalachian Spring*. How extraordinary that just a few years later, I would be sitting in Alice Tulley Hall in New York City listening to Aaron Copland talk about his music. And how Bernstein conducted it better than he could himself. He actually confessed that. Bernstein found things in his music he didn't know were there. Copland's own words. Transcendent!

Bernstein. The man I watched conduct when I was just a boy at the New York Philharmonic. Twenty years later, I would say hello to him after performing *Sunday in the Park with George*, by Stephen Sondheim. The blessings I have known!

Richard taught me how to take the work seriously. To show up. Gordon did that too. Different context, same lesson. Do your best. Each and every day. And only you know if you have. You are the sole judge of your integrity, of your effort. Only you know if you have given it your all. We can lie to ourselves, if we wish. But why would anyone do that? Con themselves? Come on! And yet. You know what I'm trying to say.

The truth is I have never held anyone to a higher standard than myself. That is probably okay. And that leads me to Ron. The day I careened off the highway in Brett's Cougar with Liz in the back seat was also the day of my first rehearsal for *The Little Foxes*, by Lillian Hellman. I was late, obviously. I was an hour late. When I walked into rehearsal, Ron began a shaming litany about how people must be on time. I mentioned that there had been an accident that morning. He stopped in his tracks and asked if everyone was all right, but not before he finished his chastisement: for every minute a person is late, each minute must be multiplied by the number of people who have been inconvenienced. Thus, a five-minute delay, if fifteen people are waiting, amounts to seventy-five minutes of wasted time. An hour late for twenty people is twenty hours lost. It is a somewhat tortured calculation, but it does carry some weight. A lesson. Be on time. Be reliable. When you are, everyone benefits. When you are not, you waste more than just yourself. Punctuality is almost as important as productivity. The latter suffers without the former. Can't do the job if you're late for it.

Ron moved past the indictment that day and we developed a working respect for one another. Three weeks later, I took a timid bow and received my first standing ovation. I was hooked. I loved surfing. But this I could do for the rest of my life. Bless Ron for this gift. Or for seeing the gift in me. And cracking the egg.

One parting piece of praise for Diana. After a voice recital, an audience member, another student probably, told me how much she had enjoyed my singing. I returned the compliment with excuses about how I didn't really sound that good and how I was not happy with what I had done. Diana pulled me aside and told me never do that! Never tell someone who is offering praise that they are doing so foolishly or contradict them . . . it is basically spitting a compliment back into their face. Be gracious. Be grateful. And say thank you. That is all. Never belittle a person who has taken the time to tell you what you have done is extraordinary or special. It may not cost them anything to say that, but it does cost them when they are told their praise is unearned. Be a gentleman. I have never done anything like that again. I have Diana to thank for it. In the years I have continued in the spotlight, I have always thanked people from the bottom of my heart for taking the time to tell me they were moved or entertained by my work. It is a special gesture. It is the most valuable of compliments. Time. Time taken from their life to offer thanks. Never disrespect it.

Bless them. Ron, Diana, and Richard. I would not be here without them.

And Mom. I certainly would not be here if not for Mom. "Swallow your burps," she said. I was six or seven, sitting at the breakfast nook with Karen. I had discharged a formidable belch.

"Chew before you swallow," was my retort. Karen and I convulsed with laughter. I have often said or thought that my mom was responsible for cultivating my sense of humor and comic timing. Karen identified a certain look our mom would make which became known as "the pucker." It was a look that could go either way. A stage. She could be poised on the edge of laughter or rage, and it was Karen who realized calling it to her attention would more likely encourage a laugh than a tirade. "Uh oh, there it is—the pucker!" Thus, our campaign to diffuse any tension would begin. The pucker would usually surrender to a smile. Crisis averted.

On this particular morning, Mom was in a pretty good mood. She joined in the laughter. It lasted for several minutes, rising and falling from crescendo to dribble and we finally got back to breakfast. Swallow. That was the trick. I had stumbled upon the ironic use of two phrases linked by the same word. One was meant to save our lives. Too big a bite, you could choke. And the other was meant to save our reputations. A burp out loud was forbidden. The ultimate embarrassment at table. A burp must be swallowed. But suddenly, there it was, "Chew..." with a slight upward inflection, followed by a pause and then finished in descending bass, "before you swallow!" Well, the best bass I could muster as a seven-year-old. Introducing the concept of chewing a burp was a brilliant turn, if I must say so myself. And the phrasing, as good as any quip uttered by Frasier Crane. It all started with Mom. "I did a button on that French toast, if I must say so myself." That was a

Mom phrase: "If I must say so myself." She would follow any number of pronouncements with it. I get it from her. I can hear her saying it right now. As if she were sitting here beside me.

Maybe she is.

I have made many suppositions about the inner life of my mother. I know she was a bit of a wild child. At least that is what my grandmother said. To say anything more would be indecorous and Kayte told me I must honor my mother. Keep it respectful. And so I have. And shall. I had hoped my mom would get around to documenting the family from her point of view, but she never did. I will make a deeper dive into some of the papers I have from her. But as a definitive history, I have nothing specific. I have some pieces. Mom told me I swam before I walked. People arrive at things at different times and in different ways. Maybe I had a soul-level awareness that my feet would be an issue in my lifetime, and I was putting off the nightmare that was to come. I stand firmly on them now—in constant pain. Not complaining. I learned of a study or a survey, at least, that asked, "If you could trade your affliction for someone else's would that be of interest?" Almost without exception, people preferred to keep the one they had.

I and my feet have had a torrid history since the day I saw my feet literally drop at the age of eight. Possibly, a complication from the polio vaccine. I have lumbered through life since. I often think maybe it was God's way of slowing me down just enough to stay on track. Who knows if I might have spun completely off onto a different tangent and run myself off this plane entirely. But I love my feet. I got them from Mom. Mom's feet carried her with dignity throughout her lifetime . . . and they carried me. *She* carried me—to the beach at least. Where I would swim instead of walk. Most people, when they stumble upon old pictures of their parents, are surprised how young they look. I see my mom's photos as a snapshot into a life I did not know. She was a beautiful young woman. She enjoyed the attentions of men and knew she was nice to look at. She enjoyed the company of men to a point. One of her best friends was a friend of the family, as well. Ron. Very handsome fellow. He adored my mom. He and Sally dated and he often dated others—Richard comes to mind. The suppositions people make about our society and the lack of tolerance

330

mystify me. We grew up in a world of diverse opinions, races, and friendships. Gordon taught us to judge no one by their exterior but by their character and humanity. Never by their sexuality or sexual preference; after all, it was none of our business. Karen and I were taught to allow all people the dignity of friendship without conditions, save one: Hurt the ones we love, hurt our family—you're out!

My mom was like that too. She brought a man home for a visit once. Karen and I liked him. We were sitting with him at the breakfast nook, the very same nook. The house in New Jersey. This man pulled a load of change out of his pocket. A lot, we thought. Karen and I were wide-eyed and impressed that he had so much money. He offered to give us some. It seemed innocent enough. Mom blew her top. She asked him to leave. Even I am surprised that I have unearthed this memory . . . it was so long ago, so buried in the past. I am seeing a quarter in my hand. My mom tells me to give it back. Maybe Karen too. Yes, we both handed him back a quarter. The man protested that he meant nothing by it, but Mom was steadfast. She was even crying, I think. She insisted he go. We never saw him again. I am left to wonder what was going on. Maybe I missed something in his energy or maybe Mom was offended that he would try to win us over with money. She only introduced us to a few men in her life. I guess he flunked. Ron. Ron would be a friend of the family throughout my life. This guy? No name to remember but I think Mom liked him enough to introduce us, and in that moment, he made a fatal error in judgment. He bribed us. Maybe that's it. I was impressed with her at the time, and I was baffled at the same time. Mom could be tough. She came from tough stock. Gam. Gordon. They didn't survive the War and the Depression without being tough. Gordon grew up without a mom. Gam grew up with Mom and Dad on the periphery of her childhood. She was tough. Gordon was. Mom was tough too. She survived her daughter with a quiet devastation, broken but stoic. She sustained in life still trying, never giving up. Tough. Broken and still striving.

She bounced around a lot as a girl. Born in San Francisco, moved to Texas, back to California after the war. Attended Hollywood High, I think tenth grade. Moved to New Jersey where she graduated high school from Vail-Deane. It was a private girls' school, and Mom was one of a dozen who graduated that year. I believe it is still in business. Probably co-ed by now. She went from there to working at Chevron with my granddad. She tried to do the rounds in Manhattan as an actress. Did act in some Summer Stock productions under the stage name, Sally Sullivan. I have a picture of her in a long grass skirt doing the Hula. Very racy. Sally was fun. She deserved some fun. She gave up a lot for us. She was a good mom. Mom did a play at our school in Florida. We both saw it. She was great. *The Torchbearers*! That was the name. It is amazing how the mind surrenders these tidbits as one page flips to another.

I never thought this before but maybe Mom's desire to be in the acting world, the singing world, fueled my interest without even knowing it. I fulfilled a dream of my mother's. It was clearly the right dream for me. Or maybe her dream and mine were the same in another life. We both came to nurse it in the other. There I go. Drifting into other realms that might not be real. Or might be more real than this one. This one came crashing down around us when they took Karen. Hasn't been right since. We had to make do.

Mom became a real estate broker in Florida. When Gam died she sold the house and moved to Lighthouse Point. She stayed there a few years and migrated north to Welaka, Florida. Another few years there. That is when I finally got the job on *Cheers*. In a late-night phone call, my mom confessed she was having an issue. She didn't know what to do about the show. *Cheers* was on opposite *Simon and Simon*. Her favorite show. What would she do? What should she do? What could she possibly do? "Mother," I said, "Watch *Cheers* and tape *Simon and Simon*! Honestly!" I added. "You can't be serious!" I still think she watched the other show first. We were a funny family in that way. I remember the time my mom was making breakfast and stopped in her tracks, saying, "Oh, honey, I'm sorry. You had a birthday last week." And then, "I completely forgot."

It was okay. I'd forgotten too. But that's the way it was. Sometimes things would slip our minds but there was never a deliberate slight. Just a little forgetfulness.

I remember another fun phone conversation we had. It was during a bit of trial in my personal life. Some nasty articles were written about me, but I never really paid any attention. Sticks and stones ... you know. But a few times, Mom called me and said she was having some difficulty. Some of her "friends" would call repeating things they'd read. *How are you, Sally? How awful for you! How are you coping with a son like that?* You get it. Mom asked what she should say when her friends called.

"Those aren't friends, Mom."

That's all I said.

I was going to say that Mom saw the light after that. I do not know. I am writing the truth here. So, the truth is I have no idea if she stopped talking with them. I know she never mentioned it again. My hope is she connected the dots and stuck with the friends who respected her. The friends who would do anything for her. There were plenty. Friends who wouldn't call to gloat over a tabloid article about her son. Her real friends.

After *Cheers*, I asked my mom to look for a property in Northern Florida. A lake property or along the St. John River. Looked at a couple of things and almost pulled the trigger. But it seemed I would be stuck in Los Angeles for a while yet. I abandoned the idea of a nice waterfront property in Florida and focused on the work. After several months, Mom decided to pick up her life and move back to California, land of her birth. She called one evening to let me know.

"Where do you intend to live, Mom?" That was my question.

"Well, I thought I would live with you."

I rolled my eyes at the other end of the phone. Mom sensed there might be something different than she'd planned after her flight touched down in Southern Cal. I heard the doorbell ring and the creak of a door as it opened tentatively. I was lying in bed with a friend of the season and heard what was surely Mom's voice. I sprang to my feet and dashed into the living room.

There stood my mother. She indicated a young man who had greeted her outside the gate saying he needed to see me. "He's outside, he needs to see you," she instructed. I looked out the door. Just some guy who knew I lived in the house and wanted to party. Yes, he had been helpful showing my mom how ringing the house and saying nothing would probably work. That much was true. I had opened the gate without asking who it was. Hence my surprise at hearing my mother's voice. I sent him away with a dose of praise, thanking him for conning my mother. So, not exactly praise. Then I turned to my mother and explained she was going to have to make a few adjustments about who was whom and who could be taken at their word. Basically, nobody. No one could or should be trusted. Let no one in, Mom. That was my directive. Trust no one.

"I can't take much more of this" she said.

"More? Of what exactly?"

"This is too much, and it will have to stop!" she insisted.

I looked at my mom with great affection and told her we'd be finding her a place of her own.

This was to everyone's liking. Mom had decided she was coming back to California. Where would she live? She thought she could live with me. That idea was pretty much shot on this very first visit.

Mom was around a good deal of the time. All Christmases, Thanksgivings. Birthdays and trips to Hawaii. Everything I could give my mom and share with her was a pleasure. We just wouldn't be living together anymore. Those days were behind us.

I want to take a moment to praise my mother. Sally. She placed a great many of her dreams aside to raise her children. It was also those dreams or interests that shepherded us to Broadway shows and to the New York Philharmonic, the circus and museums, tennis lessons, piano and church. She was a good mom. I began to regard her as a "little Buddha." Calm and stoic. She set an example of dignity and character that inspired me and many of her friends.

It was an article in the *National Enquirer* that first revealed Karen had been raped. The police had told me she had not been and I wondered why. To spare my feelings. I told my mom the same thing so when we learned in the tabloid press that Karen had been raped, it was distressing. But, surely, I had made the same decision in keeping her casket closed. To spare my mom the sight of Karen's corpse. So altered and spent. There were tragic signs of a violent end in her face. She was almost unrecognizable. So, I guess their motive was to spare us more suffering. How could rape be any worse than murder? As I think back to the time, though, it was probably an effort to spare us the details of just how horribly she had been treated that night. Details that would wrangle and torture our imaginations. We make so many mistakes. All of us do.

I apologized to Mom when we both learned about the hours before she was killed. I hadn't meant to keep anything from her. It was just a few months ago I learned from the police report that Freddie blindfolded Karen that night with a blue scarf. Why didn't they tell me more of these details when I went to bring her home? Maybe it was an ongoing investigation . . . that might have been part of it. John told me when the police interrogated him, they actually accused him of hiring someone to kill her. I think they were pretty stumped for a while. They were throwing out all kinds of ideas to shake some truth out the people who knew her.

But . . . back to Mom. She handled it all with the same characteristic dignity. Like the little Buddha she had become. So, Mom continued in her life. I think she was proud of me. She came every show night to the filming of *Frasier*. I believe she actually watched the show on television. After all, *Simon and Simon* was off the air by then; the field had been narrowed considerably for her. Mom worked, sold several homes. We rarely spoke of Karen. Mom's ability to go on after the loss of her child was an inspiration. She continued. I cursed myself with too much drinking and drug abuse. And some fairly exotic sexual behavior. Started out being a lot of fun and then the fun ran out. It was my way of burying myself along with Karen, until the only option was to deal with it and live my life. To mourn my sister without destroying myself.

To resolve grief does not end it. Resolving it is a balancing act. Living with grief while not undermining Life. To abide with it. Not surrender to it. It did almost kill me.

How did I survive? Well, I just wouldn't quit; I didn't want to let Karen down. I didn't want to let any of them down. I wallowed for a time thinking myself a victim. And I hated myself just a bit more with every taste of success. Drinking didn't help. I guess you could say I tried to drown my sorrow. But I had a foundational belief: I am obligated to fulfill the life I was given. Anything less would have been an affront to my family and to God. They gave me life. I owed it to them and to myself not to quit. Owed it to Karen. And to God.

I love life. I love it so. Loved it even as it seemed unbearable.

In time, I managed bit by bit to become an actor of note, a man with a sizable dose of success, and in time, I also managed to build my family. To rebuild a world that reflected the one I had known as a child. I was fortunate to find a career I loved. One that occupies me to this day with fascination and a sense of purpose. Purpose. I had a job. And my job in large part saved me. In my work, I was always healthy. I always wanted to help people. And I found in acting the means to reach perfect strangers with laughter and pathos. And to entertain them. That is about it. And I wanted to fulfill Karen's vision to "do it all." So, one foot in front of the other. I really like Churchill's statement: If you're going through Hell, keep going! It is not my intent to minimize the challenges that came up. Even in the sumpter of a successful career, my self-loathing got the better of me. Oh, I did have some fun. I was a fun guy. But I'd always feel bad about it. Guilty. I searched for love. I searched for relief. Often where there was none in sight. But through it all, I didn't quit. Gordon didn't. Gam didn't. Neither did Karen. Quitting would dishonor them. And truth be told, I still believed in God. Even when I cursed Him. I begged for help. And finally, in whispers I began to hear, "Hang on." I hung on. "Get up." I got up. And then . . . began a little Joy. Joy that weaved a touch of gold into my days. In the midst of fissures and fiascos, triumphs and tabloids, an indescribable Joy would shine through and sustain me. And "Forgive yourself." Yeah, the tallest order. Not quite there. Witness this book. But I am close. I am bathed in gratitude for all the love I have known. For all the love I have today. Gold. I thought I lost my sister. My family. I didn't.

Also . . . Mom set a good example. She carried on. She was my inspiration. And she never abandoned me. She lived her life as she held her grief. She grew deeper in Faith and once gave me a Bible with the simple inscription: "The Lord does provide—Love, Mom." I think she was offering me a lifeline. She inspired me with her gift to abide in the face of all life took from her. She survived. In style. Magnificent. Unbowed, unbeaten. I certainly couldn't let her down, could I?

Sally enjoyed her social membership at the club. I like calling her Sally. Her home was in a community within Sherwood Country Club where Kayte and I lived for a while. We came to live in California because I wanted to be close to my children, Jude and Mason. So, Kayte and I set up housekeeping as we began a family of our own. These were some trying times. The dynamic of starting a new life while being in a fight for parts of the old one, had some impact. One night Kayte and I were having a tiff. It got a little heated and we climbed into bed with some remnant anger. A bad feeling... and a bad thing to fall asleep angry. After several minutes of staring at the darkness, we heard a loud bang from the other room. I grabbed a golf club by the bedroom door. Kayte volunteered to confront the danger. She always does.

"Don't get carried away," I said, "I'll get this one, okay? You stay here. I will be right back!"

As I enter the living room, I hear the sound of the TV. A moment looking around and I realize there is no one there. I know the TV wasn't on before. What was that bang? I turn off the TV. Stand for a moment. And wonder. Was that my mom? Did my mother intervene? A loud warning? Never go to bed mad with each other! I said a little thank you to her. Out loud. "Thanks, Mom." I smiled. And turned back toward the bedroom.

"What did your mom smell like?" Kayte asked. "I had the most beautiful scent of flowers waft by me when you were in the other room." And then we both thanked her. Mom had been there. And she wanted us to stop. Mom had seen anger destroy any number of relationships in her life and in mine. I think she wanted this one to last. Some gal, my mom. She intervened. I believe it in my soul.

I saw Spencer yesterday. My old friend. He lives in Cape May,

New Jersey. Years ago, we had visited there when he was overseeing the refit on a boat he captained. Spencer was good with boats. He always had been. We mumbled through the years we had shared. A few clear spikes of recall enunciated themselves into the conversation. I have missed you. You too. *Good to see you. You too. Wanna drink? Sure. Everyone is gone. I know.* Then again. *Everyone is gone. Mary. My dad. They're all gone. Chris just died in March. Leslie went years ago. Sad.* Spencer was sad. I was sad to see it. I wished I could cheer him up. Not much there to brighten our chat. Karen. We talked about her death and how we moved on, or didn't, after that. Recalled the day in history class when I spotted him and pronounced his name under my breath. A friendship neither of us had contemplated would blossom that day. Spencer was my best friend from that day forward. For a long time. And then we wouldn't see each other at all for forty years. His son, Arthur, sent me his information after our dinner in Atlanta. He had to clear it with his dad. But the news came that Spencer would be happy to see me. And there was a phone number. I texted first—I will be East in a couple of days. I would love to see you. I will call before I come. Okay. We spoke the day before my friend Anthony drove me down to Spencer's home in Cape May. Really looking forward to seeing you. Me too.

I am the last one left. That was Spencer's lament as we nursed a rum and tonic. It was good to see him. We don't look the same. He is still in there, though. I recognized him. I know his soul. It's a good one. *He* is good one. And it was indeed good to see him as I gazed into his eyes and told him I loved him. I did see him.

Yep, the way they talk about in Hollywood. "I see you." As if we see people as never before. We take ourselves so seriously. As if no one ever knew anything in the past. Tempted to preach here but then I'd be just like the rest of them. Pulling myself back in the nick of time. See? Bottom line, the simple act of seeing someone we love after not seeing them for many years has always been pretty special. So. I saw Spencer. Saw him as he was on the gym floor back in Rumson. Saw him as he laughed and slipped a wink into the conversation that only I would appreciate. He did it just two days ago. It was indeed good to see him. A great face. A wounded face. Doe-eyed. A bit bewildered, slamming into what we all must face in time—the loss of everything we have known. I did see him. We touched on sadness and Karen and the days we shared. Caught up on his family. The days I shared with them. Spencer drove me to the Alabama state line when I left for California. Drove alongside me, rather, as we both had motorcycles back then. Epic. Kind of. And now, so many we both loved . . . gone. Then a customary snort, a familiar chuckle and a drag on a cigarette. Spencer.

Kayte told me she smelled that smell, my mom's smell, many times since that night. Many times. She was on bedrest with our daughter, Faith. And Faith's twin brother. Perhaps she was there for him too. At thirteen weeks, his sack ruptured. We prayed it would seal itself up and he would be allowed to reach full term. The flowers wafted by. Doctors advised us his continued growth without the safety of his amniotic fluid would surely kill him and probably take Faith too. It did not repair. We begged God to spare us this tragic choice. But sometimes we are asked to play God. So, a needle through Kayte's belly into his heart killed him. We killed him. Our son. We killed our son so Faith might live. We wept as we watched his heart stop. Saw it. It is the greatest pain I have known. Kayte's scream was enough to make a man mourn a lifetime. Another lifetime. Mom's scream when she learned of Karen's murder. A mother's scream. And the flowers came again. Just to let Kayte know that she was there . . . watching over her. Watching over her granddaughter. Holding her grandson. Perhaps. Mom knew we needed that child. We both did. Kayte and me. As never before. We needed Faith.

Mom died in that house. Karen came for her, the psychics say. Many friends who stayed in the house said they saw her there. Kayte sensed her there. I did. Mom.

A pal of mine was driving up Federal Highway and saw her "rocking out" as he put it, listening to "Stairway to Heaven." Led Zeppelin.

Blasting on the radio. Stopped at a light. She didn't notice him. I was still in high school so I cringed a bit, but I knew it was the kind of thing my mom might do. She loved music. All kinds of music. Rocking out! Faith was born. July 13th, 2012. As they prepared Kayte, the question was asked about what kind of music she liked. Lynyrd Skynyrd. A playlist started and the baby came in time. Just as Faith arrived, a track from Bad Company came on. Not Lynyrd Skynyrd but Lynyrd Skynyrd adjacent; they actually open for them these days. Paul Rogers, singing "Shooting Star." Yeah, we thought that was pretty great. Our shooting star. She sure was. Is! And then came . . . of all things . . ."Stairway to Heaven." Mom. It seemed like more than a coincidence.

Well, it is more than a coincidence. I was in the Hamptons. The home I had bought in Bridgehampton, in fact. I loved that home. It was a month after my heart attack. A call came: Sally is dead. She was found fully dressed on top of her bed. As if she had readied herself for the day, possibly a viewing of a home, she was nicely dressed. Her blood flow was not very good. Because she died at home, there had to be an autopsy, but her heart just stopped. It was her time. I thought she would be with us for some time to come but I was wrong. So, it was a surprise. But not like the sudden death of someone walking out the door and never seeing them again. Mom's life had been full, even if shorter than I would have liked. Full. Full of suffering too. But many joys. Lots of heartbreak. Like most lives, I suppose. Very few see their children slaughtered. That was not like most.

I wanted to spend a bit of time alone with the news of her death and with her in my heart. A reverie. She was my mom. A good mom. I took a drive. As I started the car, the radio came on. I did not turn it on. It came on. What was playing? Yeah. "Stairway to Heaven." Rocking out, Mom. I will never forget you. I know you have not forgotten me. Or your little girl. Thanks for bringing me life. And thanks for living with such grace throughout yours. I carry you now. I always will. I am your son. Karen is my sister. I carry her. I live for you and her and Gordon and Gam and Kayte and the children, the life I was given. For my family. And for the children we have lost, I trust they

340

are in your care and in the loving arms of the Father. I am grateful to you forever.

I drove through my old neighborhood. Amy's house. Diane's. Charlie and Mabel's. Little Al. Virginia's. There was Paul and Carol. Jack and May Todd's house. Five Chimneys. The Colonia Country Club. I had not thought it necessary.

On a recent trip to New Jersey, I was close enough that a visit to my earliest days of memory would be easy enough. Newark Airport is a short drive from there. My flight didn't take off for a couple of hours. So there I stood. In front of our old home. And it was nice to see us all again. The family and the neighborhood children. And to retrace the steps of my youth with the friends of my youth. And Karen.

There had been two large pine trees on the front corner by the driveway. Not there anymore. But I saw Gordon and me. We were watering the lawn, some newly seeded patches in the spring. Nat King Cole. Gordon had a little transistor radio we would listen to as we watered the lawn, and the news said that Nat King Cole had died. I remember it because I really liked him. The world had lost one of its greatest voices that day. I am happy to remember that boy who marked a great man's passing, silhouetted against the frame of his grandad, tiny rainbows all around us. Refracted sunlight in the mist. Reflecting on life. Watering our piece of lawn. Our piece of paradise. I saw Karen's head sticking out the window, urging me to come in off the roof.

As I drove down the street it was as if I traveled further back in memory. Carl's house on the left. We played football on the front lawn. The giant snow hill the plows had made stood there beside Al's house. It was there I pasted a bully with an ice ball after he hurt Karen. Driving down the hill where I skinned my knee riding my first skateboard, I turned down the road and saw the creek that ran through my memory and still ran behind the homes along Stafford Road. It was a nice neighborhood. There was some new building going on. A few big homes. New money. Revitalization. I guess I was doing my own version. Revitalizing a life lived long ago. Haunted by ghosts of children I knew in childhood. The love I had for them teasing them back to life.

Al told me Patty had died. Raymond, who lived one street over from me came backstage a few years ago. We keep in touch. Virginia was my first kiss by the creek. Amy's dad died in his sleep one night. We didn't know what to say. We just played along the street that day. More subdued than usual. I remember feeling sad for her, wondering how she must feel. The woodpile behind our old house. Gordon taught me how to use an axe and a hatchet out there. The backyard where we all played baseball and "war" in the woods. Karen's "pixie" haircut. Easter outfits and Super 8 movies. St. Bernard puppies at Diane's house. Mrs. White's lawn was no longer there. "She'll skin you alive if you go on that lawn," Gam warned. I always wondered how that would work. I took Gam's words as literal. Almost all the time. Wild imaginings of Mrs. White chasing us down the street, jaundice in her eye. *Get those damn kids off my lawn.* We never did venture onto her property. My grandmother's warning sufficient to scare me to this day. I reveled in the memory as I took a walk upon the ruined splendor of a long-gone green expanse. A bare ruined choir now, as Shakespeare's. Where late the sweet birds sang. Us. All of us.

My child's eyes saw home. My boyhood home where there were a dozen children of an age who ran along the streets, played baseball, had a few fights, rode bikes, stole a kiss and grew together in nature and in the nurture of parents who thought they made the right decisions and lived a proper life. Carol's dad bought a new Cadillac every season. He just liked the feel of it—a new car each year. His home was no more spectacular than any other. Just across the street from ours. Gordon had built the first home on the street. It was humble but lovely. An addition was put on when Karen and I came to live with them. Mom took the upstairs bedroom, Gordon and Gam moved to their new digs behind the den, and Karen and I took the remaining bedrooms on the top floor. Three of us upstairs. Gordon and Gam in their private wing on the ground floor. I thought it was very fancy, their wing. Magical. Reeking of accomplishment and history. Respect. We

342

were to respect their room. Their privacy was sacrosanct. We were also taught to respect the privacy of others. If there was gossip it was under the breath. No unkindness, as I recall. Not like today. Any trouble was accompanied by a whispered prayer on behalf of those whose struggles had become a public matter. America was a nicer place back then. We wished each other well.

Tempted to preach, but no, the expression speaks for itself. The expression speaks for itself and for a time long gone. We wished each other well.

As I turn on to New Dover Road, in the rearview mirror a dozen children, little Karen, too, wave good-bye. A nap later on the plane took me back. Back there. Back where we never left our lovely street. Our lovely friends. Still together. Still innocent. Still dreaming in joyful anticipation of the life to come. Still dreaming today of the life lived then and dreaming still of the life yet to be. Only now, all one.

Our trip to Florida. The first trip when we took the train. I flashed upon it when I visited with Spencer. We stayed in a small motel with a pool in Hollywood. The first day, Karen and I swam for hours. We loved to swim. And the sun! Gosh, it was amazing to feel that sun on a winter's day just after Christmas. We were in Heaven. A few hours later, we finally went inside. The pinkness of our skin gave way to a stinging rose, bright red. On fire. That is how it felt and then the shakes. I shivered in bed as I tried not to move. My skin felt every wrinkle in the sheets as an affront. It was very painful. I imagine Karen felt the same. So, we skipped the next day by the pool. Another day later though, we were back at it, full bore. Never gave it a second thought. The pain was only temporary. The joy of Florida, warm in winter, was eternal, happy.

A memory we would relive again and again. Till we moved there. Our wildest dreams come true.

Then Gordon. You know the rest.

The other day in Jersey. In the old neighborhood, I wandered farther from our customary haunts and drifted toward the places less familiar. Just as when I was a boy. And I found the spot. The spot where I smelled death. The first time I smelled death. There. It was below the pond where kids would skate during the winter. Below the dam that created it. An unfamiliar scent caught my attention as I pedaled my bike. I passed, then turned back to where the scent was strongest.

My tree is gone! The tree I used to climb is gone! Dancing along with one memory and another cuts in with blinding clarity. Again. Waypoints. My mind is full of them. You may have spotted one or two in the last few paragraphs. Waypoints. Timeless. Indelible.

There she stands. Smack-dab in the mid-retina of my mind's eye. My tree. That tree that stood before my childhood home. My tree is gone. And it is fitting to remember her. The house is changed, remodeled. But turn a page to the days of my youth and it remains untouched. There in front of the living room window. To those of us who knew it. Who learned to climb upon its branches. Who grew strong with climbing them. That tree remains. She is still there. To be honored here by a grateful boy. Her branches held me aloft. Embraced me. Took me closer to the sky. And in her arms, I learned to dream of days ahead. But never dreamed a day so far removed would take me back to her. Her majestic trunk. Her strength. Leaves so green. Bark so dark against the winter snow. Still alive. The queen of our front yard. Today.

I leave Colonia behind and realize I never will. But as I drive, the scent that abrupted my bike ride half a century ago pulls me back. Just as it did that day. I have described this moment to my son Gabriel. I stopped beside the railing of a little overpass above the creek. There, alongside it, was the rotting carcass of what seemed to be a Scotty. I guessed. A pet. Rotting but recognizable as someone's dog. I don't know how the dog had died. I imagined it may have been hit by a passing car and crawled there below the roadway. Or maybe someone threw the body down after hitting it. I don't know. But. It was my first encounter with death. The decay. The stench. Mortality. My first glimpse of mortality.

Our early days together are alive again. Karen and me. She is alive again. That wave in the rearview mirror was not good-bye but a reminder of where I can always find her. That beautiful little girl. I had a lovely visit with her in the branches of our tree. A lovely visit with the neighborhood. I did ring the doorbell of the old home in hopes of saying hello to its occupants. I hope it will be a good home for them. There is a lot of love there.

I had not known that an actual visit to Colonia would be so vital to me.

There is one more place I must visit. One left before I close. Colorado Springs.

I will not go there to relive her murder. I have done that every day since. I want to see what made her happy there. See where she lived. I will take her final breaths with her. I have to go there. See the place where she expired. Yes. I have to. But I am still searching for the Karen she was in the days before. I learned a lot from John. And there are two more friends, one I knew and one I did not. We have spoken and both are keys to finding Karen. The Karen whose days I did not share. I want to know those days or find some insight into them and into her. The days she lived without me. I want to know them, if I can.

I am surrounded by life.

Why did I say that? The kids were putting a little video together on their iPads. This morning. Kids laughing. Beautiful. And I was having a dream or a half-waking dream as I lay in bed. There were little pig stickers. Some sort of time-telling decals teaching kids how to tell time. The am hours were marked with a little sunrise and the p.m. with the phases of the moon. This doesn't make much sense on the face of it. Dreams. You know. But on the pig faces from 12 a.m. until noon, were written the words "Hooray! It's a brand-new day!"

Yeah. A brand-new day.

You may recall my mom had the pucker. One particular time that just sprang to mind: Karen and I were being driven by our mom. Perhaps, we were out shopping. I don't recall. But Karen and I did not know the word *fart*. Never heard it, in fact. We said "poop" for that particular bodily function. For the more common use of the word poop, we instead said "grunty." Because of the sound one makes while…you know what I mean. Somehow, we decided to press my mom on the proper name for a "poop." I think Mom said that some people call it a fart. "Not that kind of word, Mom," we replied. "The proper word." We wanted the more scientific name, the proper name. She paused and said, as she often said in these instances; "Well, if you must know," prefacing her pronouncement as was her custom. The pucker grew more evident. "If you must know. It is called passing gas."

"Passing gas?!"

And we dissolved in tears of laughter. Explosive foolishness. And such fun.

So, on this brand-new day, my children's laughter echoing through the house, I begin with the silly side of our childhood together. Our mom was fun. Funny. Funny to us. As mentioned, I have often credited Mom with helping to develop my sense of humor. Sense of timing. If I could make her laugh! That was the greatest feeling. Karen and I laughed together. She was fun and funny. Just like Mom. I was sad sometimes. Karen too. And Mom sometimes. Especially when the day overwhelmed or the kids got just a bit more unruly than she could handle. She was a great mom, though. And she could be silly. Silly when we were sad. A great mom. As a boy I had psoriasis. That made me sad sometimes. My mom would put cream on the rough parts of my skin. She substituted the word leprosy to the tune of a song called "Jealousy." "Leprosy, oh my God, you've got leprosy!" Dah, da, da, daaah, dum; da, da, da, daaah, dum! It made me laugh. It helped. She made me smile. I was pretty hurt by the skin thing. No one wanted to touch me. I learned the word "communicable" at a very early age—such a big word for a little boy. "Don't worry," I would say, "it's not communicable." Mostly to little girls who would pull away from me when they saw the rough patches. I have not thought of that in a very long time. I wanted to be liked but felt I was repulsive. There's an eye opener!

Karen never pulled away. And throughout my life there have been any number of people who did not. But there is something deep within me still convinced that I am indeed repulsive. Is it my dad not wanting me? His mom dying when he was a boy? Gordon's mom dying when

346

he was still an infant? There's an angst salad for you. If we do indeed carry the lives of our forebears. Exhausting! Let it go, already. It is surely time and it no longer serves me. At all. So. Adiós! Buenas noches! Arrivederci! And the horse you rode in on!

That should do it.

I spoke with Karen's friend, Faith. Faith was at Palm Cove in Karen's senior year. She remembered I was upset that suddenly Karen and I were graduating the same year. I did think it ironic and kind of funny that we celebrated the same senior year. It was her yearbook that guided me to Faith again. Was I upset? Didn't see it that way. I was proud of Karen. But then, recollection and perception are unique to each of us. I always liked Faith. The register from Karen's funeral was signed by her family on Faith's behalf. She could not attend. It was nice to speak with her. She is in possession of information I couldn't have. Also, as I said, I had always liked Faith. It was nice to speak with her. And to offer an apology if I did anything untoward in our youthful days. I am deeply conscious that some of my behavior as a teen might have been thoughtless and hurtful and I am forever sorry for that. It wasn't on purpose. Still, it torments me. More than you might think. I actually forgot to ask her why she wasn't at the funeral, but she reminded me she came by the house in August a few weeks later.

The funeral was held three days before Karen's nineteenth birthday on July 12th. Faith says she met my girlfriend then—Jill. I didn't remember Faith dropping by, but I was truly living in a fog. She said my mom gave her Karen's prom dress. I don't remember that either. But I do remember so many wonderful things. The party at Karen's apartment the Christmas of our first year at college. I am talking to someone in the picture. It may have been Faith. In speaking with her recently, I wished we had remained close. I guess we weren't close but it felt like that; I always remembered her. Good memories. Faith gave me some valuable information. On two pages in the yearbook, there appeared to be an acid wash. I was curious why it was there. Faith told me it was because the school had not liked the content on those two pages and blocked them out. Narrow, twisted, so and sos—canceling those boys in that way. Thank God that sort of thing doesn't happen today!

Anyway, Faith told me many of the students decided to try nail polish remover to clear the black ink. Obviously, Karen had too. It left a strange effect that I interpreted as an attempt to scratch them from her own memory. I constructed a scenario with a tortured narrative about a boy she must have liked who hurt her; she wanted to scratch him from existence. I even concocted the idea that he was at Berry with her. As if they had decided to attend the same college to be together and then they broke up. I thought it possible he was a bully or some such. She was a new kid at the school; maybe there were a few of her peers who were not nice. I was relieved to learn that that was not the case. Faith explained the young man in the picture was a great guy who had recently passed away. I am sorry to hear it. Her impression of him was a good one.

I was also glad to learn a bit more about the epic trip to Orlando and Disney World. It is mentioned by almost every schoolmate who signed the yearbook. I guess there was a small contingent who tried acid on that trip. A "good trip" was had by all, judging from the testimonials I have read. No surprise. Once more, I am reminded Karen always was a bit more adventurous than I when it came to the counterculture. She enjoyed herself. I know she enjoyed marijuana. It seems pretty silly now to attach such a stigma to it. But having expanded my thoughts on it, I still think young people should be encouraged to avoid it until adulthood. My understanding is THC is deleterious to developing brain function in young people. I have not made a personal study of it but the reading I have done leads me to believe an abundance of caution is prudent. I probably would have said the same thing to Karen at the time. And I am sure she would have leveled a dismissive "What a square!" at me.

I was a square as a big brother. I was supposed to look out for her. And that would have been within my job description. Square. I didn't really mind. Also, when I would feign anger, it was accompanied by a wink of conspiratorial comradeship. We were just two years apart, after all. And I did dabble a few times myself in the world of pot. Just made me stupid, though. So, it wasn't for me. I didn't like feeling stupid. Boys are stupid enough as it is throughout adolescence. Stupid even into young adulthood and beyond. On second thought, boys are not really stupid. They are simple, honestly. Simple and impulsive and meant to rush in sometimes where angels fear to tread. They are human. And there is nothing wrong with that. Why take it any further?

When I was speaking with Faith, my daughter of the same name was sitting opposite me at the breakfast table. I mentioned the fact that they shared the same name. Faith said, yes, she had heard. And though we did not name our daughter after her, it does bring me joy. The name Faith reminds me of Karen. It is a lovely name that fits our little girl beautifully. And it is reminiscent of a time when Karen was alive. We also gave Faith Karen's middle name, Elisa. Faith Evangeline (after my grandmother, Gam) Elisa Grammer. Elisa was my dad's half sister. So, she carries family names except for "Faith." She is the first Faith of our family. Faith Evangeline Elisa Grammer.

Your children are not your children.
They are the sons and daughters of Life's longing for
      itself.
They come through you but not from you,
And though they are with you yet they belong not
      to you.
You may give them your love but not your thoughts,
For they have their own thoughts.
You may house their bodies but not their souls,
For their souls dwell in the house of tomorrow,
which you cannot visit, not even in your dreams.
You may strive to be like them,
but seek not to make them like you.
For life goes not backward nor tarries with
      yesterday.
You are the bows from which your children
as living arrows are sent forth.

The archer sees the mark upon the path of the
    infinite,
and He bends you with His might
that His arrows may go swift and far.
Let your bending in the archer's hand be for
    gladness;
For even as He loves the arrow that flies,
so He loves also the bow that is stable.

This poem was written by Kahlil Gibran. On the occasion of Esther's reading, the second one, she asked me who Karen's favorite poet was. I thought for a moment and remembered Karen liked Kahlil Gibran. I was pleasantly reminded of it when I looked at her yearbook page in search of clues for this book. I have the remembrance book with me, the one I mentioned of her funeral. Inside it is the envelope I used to jot down the messages from Karen delivered through Esther that session. "Speak to me about children," is written in my hurried scrawl. Below it is the word, "Pictures." This I wrote as she relayed that Karen said there were many pictures to help tell her story. And below that is what Karen said when, according to Esther, they had visited my home together one night. "There lies my brother." It was the morning after that night, Kayte woke and said she saw Esther in her dream. The session was some time later but Esther mentioned Kayte had "caught" her. Kayte had said she saw Esther hovering above her. Did I mention Kayte's dream to Esther? First? Is that when she said she had been caught? Or why she said it? Because I told her? Who knows. I am amazed by all this stuff. Nonplussed. I doubt it on an intellectual level but believe it on another. Remarkable. Either way. I am writing, aren't I?

I finally went and read his poem. It carries a nice lesson. I agree, in principle. Why did Karen want me to read it? I have come to learn the past, present and future are all stacked upon one another, and any number of worlds or realms are simply a page turn apart, separated only by perception. When our perception shifts we see another layer of reality. Things are not as they seem and are exactly as they seem.

I really enjoyed the film, *Ready Player One*. "Reality—it's the only thing that's real." I like that. It's just that Reality is far more complex than just its image through a single lens. But we do know what is real. Karen is dead. Karen is alive forever. Both true. Real. Pain is temporary but forever. When the wind is right. When a certain song is playing. Pain. Fresh. Pain surges through our being, indistinguishable from the moment of its inception. Gibran says life does not move backward. Maybe. I have had visits from my future self. Did they come from a life already lived but not in my consciousness at the time? Is my past informing everything I am today? Yes, I believe it is.

Your children are not your children. Well, I get the point but if we do not enjoy them as our children, how will we ever understand how God sees us? We are His children. We are all His children. Surely, the way we look upon our sons and daughters is teaching us the eyes of God.

I am happy to be the "bow" from which my little arrows are launched . . . I like that. But once again, what is Karen trying to show me? Let my bending be for gladness. Gladness. Maybe that's it. Maybe Karen is telling me I was not meant to save her or carry her. Wanting to is fine. Cursing myself for failing? No.

"Forgive yourself."

There she is. Again. So, I thought I would set an intention and meditate for a time. Meditate on hearing Karen. Focus on hearing her. Seek a dialogue with her.

My son, Gabriel, does not feel well today. He is a wonderful boy. He insists he is fifty years old and not a boy. Which makes him an even more wonderful boy. When I call him, "my boy," he corrects me and says he is not my boy. He will answer to "Mr. Fancy Pants." That's okay, apparently, but he is not "my boy." And, yes, I get that. But! I am his "Dad." This time around, at least . . . this layer of being. And proud to be of service as such.

"You served me well, Kels."

And there she is. Karen. How 'bout that! Is Karen saying I did okay trying to be a replacement for a dad? A replacement for Gordon? I remain deeply confused.

"You were a good brother."

Was I? I know her life was not my job. I know her death was not my fault. But it felt like it was.

"You were a good brother. You did everything you were meant to do."

Am I really hearing this stuff? Well, clearly, no, I am not actually hearing it. What am I hearing? My imagination? No. I know it's Karen. At least, I think I know. When Kayte fell pregnant after Faith had been born, I asked her what she thought we were having. "If it is not a boy," she said, "then everything I believe is a lie." Gabriel came. A boy. A most wonderful boy.

And so, if I am not hearing Karen, then everything I believe is a lie.

"It's not!"

As I matured, it was my conviction that many of the things I knew with certainty became less certain. I stand corrected. This work has reassured me that most of the things I knew have grown more certain than ever. The clutter of adulthood piles any number of misconceptions upon a perfectly good human antenna and scrambles the signals. The simple signals of God. The truths remain true. Our ability to see can be clouded by tragedies and longings and loss and broken hearts and material possessions and even Satan's seductive magic. A spiritual detox. Once in a while, we need a spiritual detox. Clean the plumbing. Clear the clogs. I know I said it before but there comes a time when we just have to let Jesus take it. And many of the things I have written here might send the self-appointed armies of Christ running. But not Christ. Not Jesus. I know that too.

When Gabe was just two-and-a-half, maybe three years old, he looked at his mom and said, "You killed me." He pointed at his heart. "Here," he said. Right where the needle had entered the chest of Faith's twin brother. Once again, I am confused by this. But the truth of what has happened speaks to a truth we are more comfortable denying than believing. Still, I choose to believe amazing things can happen, especially when we love so much. Was Gabriel allowed to come right back? Is he the ultimate gentleman? Who stepped aside for his sister. Ladies first. It is not necessary that he is. Do I love him more or less if he is not? No. But it is rational to believe that Gabe gave his life so that his sister could live. It is also rational to believe he came close behind because he was meant to live the life of her brother. And so he is. It was written in stone. We just didn't know it at the time. Is it rational to believe a loving God would deny us our loved ones after death? No. It is not rational to think the love we have planted in the earth would be taken from us when our time is done. You can choose to believe as I do or not. If you wish to disprove it, you are welcome to try. Not sure that's possible. God created us in Love, and we live in Love. Before, during and after our visit here, Love encompasses us. This I know. Hate is an illusion. A powerful one. But Love is truth. Love is God.

Can I prove it? No. I can only live it. I believe it. I can tell you how much I doubted it; and tell you I do not doubt it now. God Bless My Children. God Bless Them. I am so grateful.

I have noticed lately that it is in fashion to post outside a store or commercial establishment: Hate is not welcome here. Well, if you put the word "Hate" on your front door, surely you have hate on the other side. "Love is welcome." "Forgiveness practiced here." Post a message like that on your doorstep. Seems like a better idea. If you talk about how much you hate Hate, then surely you are its disciple and advocate, a child of hate. You are in its clutches. It is posted on your door! You get it. Open the door to love, instead.

I realize there are no real chapters in this book. Rather a stream of remembrances without headings and titles. Remembrances that range from my first bursts of recall to the unfolding reflections of the writing itself.

I love doing this. A friend suggested I might want to structure the book with at least a few chapter headings. I agreed. Right now, I am trying to figure out just what they should be. I have an idea based on an old film script my pal, Richard, and I were trying to write years ago. We called it *Between Then and Now*. What happens from where we were, to where we are. "Between then and now" is the Webster's

Dictionary definition for the word "since." Simple. And it occurred to me it was a good setting or concept for the book. Where we were; where we are. What has happened since.

A stream of remembrances. Memories, each with a kind of ending that is not a finale. I don't want this to be like a bad movie that doesn't know when to finish. It won't be. I realize it's been a little hard to follow sometimes, this jumping back and forth in time, from one place to another, seemingly without connection. I hope you know by now I will make the connection for you.

And I want my sister to rest assured that this has done some good. I introduce Karen to you as only I have known her. I invite you to love her as I did. And at the same time, ease the pain of anyone who may have lost a loved one. A life's love. Too soon. Taken by violence, disease or tragedy. So soon. Let Karen show you how they do not die, the ones we love. How they live on each day. And may she teach a simple truth. The precious moments, no matter how fleeting will always endure in our hearts. As long as we flood with good the place where anguish lives. Does the pain end? No. But it will not conquer the irreplaceable spark that was Karen. Her memory is not tragic. Her memory is full of joy and discovery and striving and excitement. In her eyes I still see the magic of her future. The past was so rich and beautiful and the final pictures I have attest to the beauty she was and the love she created. There are friends like me who miss her every day. There are those who never knew her who know her now. And I hope in knowing her, you will number her in your hearts. Embrace her as I do. And your loved ones too. We can hold them together. Embraced by Love. Love. Home. Alive!

There is an animal rage as pure and righteous as the day it seized me, but it does not occupy Karen's place. Not anymore. It lurks in the shadows and in my nightmares. It finds its way into my sad moments or when I fear for the safety of my children. It inhabits a place of woe that is kept at bay by the good I remember. The last year and a half of writing and discovery has tipped the scale. I have joy within me that will not yield to the raging animal ranging through my being. It exists in me on a cellular level. This is why it will never disappear, I suppose. But now, almost as quickly as it claws its way through a weakness, it retreats into the shadows. No longer crushing me. No longer able to. Thanks to Karen. I am happy.

I saw the Roman Coliseum in my dreams. As it stands today. The stop signs outside along the street, the traffic lights and directional placards along the old Appian Way. And I saw the standards that were borne two thousand years ago, the throngs of Romans there to celebrate Caesar or watch the entertainment, human slaughter on the grandest scale. State sanctioned murder. A mere one among many, among so many we felt like one. And behaved as one. One murdering, barbaric beast set against the innocent. The more innocent, the more entertaining. The Christians were great sport indeed as it seemed the Roman Empire took particular delight in reenacting the murder of Christ, over and over again. Not so different from today.

Something else. My life, as it has been lived until now, was filled with people and experiences I cherish. I feel however that I owe them all an apology. Or at least an explanation. I am sorry I could not give you my all. There was always a little something held back. Grief kept me from living. As I told John, Karen's John, I have never allowed myself to be happy. I feel now that I stole many things from myself. And stole some of what was possible for others. From others. Happiness. I have never been fully happy. To those who may care, I apologize with the regret of a half century lived partway. I look back on you now and I am grateful that you had the effrontery to offer me love and I am sorry I couldn't take it. Thank you. Blessed people. I carry you forever in my heart and in my prayers. I feel such love for you. Even for those who hurt me. I lived at 95 percent. I apologize for holding back. It wasn't really my fault. I chased the frivolous at times that counterfeited happiness. Chased it with my whole heart but found it quickly fell short. The only place I felt safe enough to give it my all was behind the mask of an acting role. A character. I have lived fully there. In the world of my imagination. Acting is where I conduct an honest and truthful life. Losing Karen led to losing so much more. Now I am not saying I am the only one guilty of wrongdoing; it does take two to Tango. And to tangle. So, some of the issues might have been more than just mine alone. But in my dedication to Karen, missing Karen, I did miss some fun. And I may have seemed aloof. Distant. I was. For that, I am sorry. I would also like to offer that in most cases, I did give it my best. And 95 percent is not all that bad. I just wish I'd done better. And I hope you can accept why I did not. I am not saying I want to go back or still be in love with my first girlfriend. Maybe there were a few that deserved a better shot. Of course, there were. Some pretty great people, men and women. But I was not ready. I really did care in the moment. It was true and genuine. Even if short-lived. I couldn't be happy. Until now.

I'll say this. I never deliberately hurt anyone. Well, past the time I was a neighborhood boy looking after my sister. Or defending a boy that was being picked on. Nothing serious. Nothing vengeful. Even when I participate in the hearings for Freddie Glenn, it is not vengeful. It is just.

This happiness thing is sticking in my mind. I was happy. Just not fully. I have friends to whom I am loyal and grateful. Brad. Richard. One I knew before Karen was killed. The other afterward. I love them with my whole heart. And the happiness I feel when I see them or just reach out in a text or a call is absolutely joyful. That I have had. There are a few gone. Friends who died. Their passing makes the world just a little less bright because each was a singular, unique member of my affection without equal. So, I hope it is clear, I have been happy. There were just moments that pulled me back, a melancholy injecting a lull in the conversation, infecting a sunset with a flash of sadness. Missing Karen. Wonder interrupted, wondering what life might have been had she lived. And there has been—comfort. What do I mean by this? There is comfort in knowing I loved Karen so completely; allowed myself to care so deeply it could destroy me—100 percent. Maybe there is comfort in that. To love with every ounce of my being. To prove such a thing is possible. Love without end. Without apology. Comforting. The pain that comes with it? Natural. When it is lost or taken? Agony. To those who know what I have known, I wish you a powerful healing. To share with you my own. And to share this comfort: There may be tragic days behind us; a few ahead that are bound to hurt, but, oh, the love we have known. Such luck!

Al died yesterday. His name was Alfred but very few knew that. His friends contacted me in the afternoon saying Alex had died. He had changed his name at some point in his life. Maybe for acting. I know he did some work on Broadway. He got where he had always wanted. That's amazing. But he couldn't stay. Life got the better of him. He drank to excess and to extinction. We spoke on the phone just a few weeks ago. I told him he would have to stop drinking if I were going to keep believing he was worth helping. Tough language. But I meant it. I knew he would die if he did not stop. He did not. And now I see him with that band of kids in the rearview mirror. Waving good-bye. Or maybe just waving from a happier time. When we were all fresh and brand new. Life ahead of us. So full of promise. I like remembering him that way.

I awoke.

After ten hours at the dentist. It began in the morning with a discussion. Years of compressing my front teeth have led to a collapsed bite and we were there to build it up. Remove bacteria lurking beneath old dental work, crowns and such. The anesthesiologist recommended a two-part sedation that began with a drug that peels away perceptions and prepares a road for the mind to wander a bit. Or not wander but discard dead concerns and focus on a simple stream of information. It is almost as if the walls of the world drop away. And the stars and the sky open up. Back through time. No time. A sense of the eternal.

As before but wanting more; I wanted to talk to Karen.

It sounded like I was being shouted at. "Kelsey, wake up! Wake up!"

The dentist and the anesthesiologist were basically screaming through a fog. My little boat finally nosing its way through, back into consciousness.

No Karen.

Except, I felt as if I had been somewhere that was important. Closer to her. I felt good. I was in pain; my shoulders were aching from lying on such a narrow bench for so long. But I felt that something good had happened. I just couldn't say what.

Two days ago, I received the key to the city in Atlantic City, New Jersey. It was the highlight of my life. This is funny stuff. To stand in almost the exact spot where sixty-two years ago I said, "Gam, I love Atlantic City!" I looked over the crowd and saw me there, that young boy in a blazer and gray flannel slacks, oxblood penny loafers. We were looking right at each other, both of us smiling ear to ear. Here I go. Back to the Dennis Hotel, a couple hundred yards down the Boardwalk and 20,000 days ago. Karen and I in a giant bathtub, splashing about. Two kids stepping squeaky clean from the water and wrapped in giant fresh-smelling towels. Then down to a beautiful dinner. White linen, silver, steak, dessert and from the bottom of Gordon's coffee, a single sugar cube absorbing the last drops, the final sips for us before we went up to bed and brushed our teeth. The next morning ahead of us, the long walks and swimming at the pool, the sun, the smell of the ocean. We thought it was Heaven. It was. And on May 26th, 2023, it still is. I felt them with me. Gordon, Gam, Mom, and Karen. My family of origin. Smiling a collective smile. Back in one another's arms.

At dinner that night, Spencer and Julie, his bride, joined some of my new Atlantic City friends. Soft-shell crab, oysters. People stepped up for a quick picture. Do you mind? Of course not. Back to chatting and dinner. A little beer business. A cocktail or two. Sharon was there. Joe. Anthony and Shane. We talked about the Steel Pier. The summer ahead. A nice visit. It had been a long day. Spencer was annoyed with the people coming up. He had always been a bit like that. A quiet man who liked one-on-one time and small gatherings instead of crowds. A decent man. An old friend. I was happy he had been able to join me in the celebration after so long a time apart. We had lived our separate lives. And there was nothing tragic about that. Nice to find time though for this page in an ancient friendship that was more of a memory now. But as we rose, it was Joe, one of my newest friends, a gem of a man, who asked why Spencer was there. I explained the importance of connecting to every memory I could muster to complete the tale of

Karen's life. I had honestly believed Spence might be dead. I had to be sure. Not just to close a chapter but complete one in the interest of giving a 100 percent honest telling of what had gone before, and the remaining threads of life that still connect to Karen's. Joe, who knows about the book and why I am writing, took a minute. He looked at me and said, "You know why."

I nodded tentatively, not sure exactly what he meant. Joe leveled his gaze at me. "You weren't there."

I am in bed. Just after the dental surgery. The fog cleared now. Karen is here. My intention was muted by the drugs. As they recede, she intercedes. And I am with her. I know I could not stop what happened. I could not stop her murder. I was not there. But why am I writing? I do know why I started. But now the why of it is something more elusive and deeply sad. I know I could not stop what was to take place that night. My sadness now is that I was not there to hold her as she died. To see her on her way. To whisper to her that she would be all right; it would be all right. I've got you. Whispered as her life left her body, knowing she was dying. And as the tears ran down my face, I realized how much it would have meant if only I could've been there. Just to hold her. Let her die in my arms. Kiss her good-bye. Been there. To thank her. Comfort her. See her off.

I lay in bed. Holding her. As I have held her so many times in my mind. Never quite knowing why. I have stood in my living room imagining Karen in my arms. I have felt her with me in a thousand dreams. I have stood near our old home and in the places we visited as children, the places we loved. And finally, it was the simple enormous grief that I could not kiss her, kiss her good-bye, that taught me why— why I have grieved my entire lifetime. She should not have died like that. Even though I could not stop it. She should not have died alone. I should have been there for that, at least. Just to hold my baby sister as she died. As she took her last breath. In my arms. Tears ran down my face like a gentle rain. As they might have done that night. As her life slipped away in the arms of her brother. To catch the dewdrop as it slips into the ocean. I wasn't there. Joe was right. But there was more. More than he knew. More than I knew till just a few days ago. I could not save her. But even more, I could not hold her.

I am at peace with that now. This book—Karen's idea. It is my way of seeing her off. And something else. The shame I'd always felt. It's gone.

Thank you, Karen.

"Don't mention it."

Funny. She was always funny. She spoke to me of other things. And she continued with me through the night.

"Remember me. And remember you. You were a great brother. You were a great kid. You were the fastest runner in the neighborhood. The tallest boy. You looked after me. You stood up to bullies. You protected other kids all the time. You were a great guy! Forgive yourself. Please."

It was nice visiting with her. Joyful. She took me back to Colonia and to Florida. To the boat. The skiing. She showed me her friends. And all the love she had known. The day I drove around New Jersey, she had been there, too. Even in the rearview mirror. I slipped by our old school, Middlesex County #24, just blocks away from where we lived. Where Miss Scherer sang "Goldfinger" to me when I wore a trench coat to school one rainy day. Where I had lunch every day at Patty's house. We would watch an episode of *Dick Van Dyke* together and we even tried a kiss one afternoon on the couch. Between bites. Kids. Karen was always beside me; sat beside me, the two of us riding the school bus. Walking to the bus stop. Walking home, too. Every day. We were in the yard. Playing.

There was happiness in my heart, as she continued. It was like we were sitting with each other, just talking.

"And love your life! Look what you've done!"

I wondered about my children. The Gibran poem . . . your children are not your children. My children come and go in my life. The older ones. It is the source of some frustration. Sometimes sadness.

"Their lives are their own. Joy. Live in Joy. Love your children. Enjoy your life. Invite your children to enjoy it with you. If they're not ready, they're not ready."

That's what she told me. The readiness is all. How about that! Been there all along. It was an upbeat conversation. Full of wisdom and humor and love.

"Be happy. Come on, Kels, don't you think it's time?"

Yeah. I'm ready.

Rhonda. It is time to speak with Rhonda.

When Karen wrote to John, she spoke of a few friends she would visit in Atlanta before she joined him in Colorado Springs. I had guessed Rhonda was one of them. I was wrong. I had meant to call her earlier, but the writing insisted it wait until now. Maybe a funny expression but truth. I wrote a dozen times that I should get in touch with Rhonda but I waited. Waited until now. It is the perfect time to speak with her. She loved Karen. We all did. So, somewhere after my sedation had obscured the lines between here and the past. After I had spent the better part of an evening chatting with my sister. Freely. Unedited. Flowing. I called Rhonda.

The things she said. I will preface with what she exchanged about the traffic of her life. The business of the decades between then and now. See what I did there? But . . . in the end, Rhonda told me what Karen told me. And what I have heard from her myself.

Wheaton, Illinois. Rhonda grew up there. Stayed in Georgia through college and beyond. Berry College, where she met Karen. We spoke on the phone. She had returned to Wheaton after living in Georgia another twenty years after school. She also told me her husband had died recently. I expressed my sorrow. Conveyed my sympathies. We discussed a few things about the time they had known each other. She and Karen. Rhonda thought I had actually come to pick up Karen's chest from school as she left. I had never been there until just a few months ago. This sent me into a tailspin about who might have retrieved her chest after she left school. Or helped her retrieve her chest. But it was not I. So, some things may never be known. Though I hope I might still find the truth, a name.

A boy had come to pick her up and take her chest home. The chest was a talisman in our lives. It was the chest Gordon had with him in Guadalcanal. It was the chest that would house our toys as children. It was the chest that would cradle Karen's belongings and her memories in the years after Gordon died. Her chest. It was also the chest that split my head open after I was jumping on the bed one night on the Jersey Shore. My head and "injury" are attracted to one another like . . . well, I have run out of analogies; suffice to say, my head and I have had several encounters with hard surfaces that consistently prove my head is no match for concrete or marble or pavement. Or wood. It was a wooden chest. So. Just under a hundred stitches in my skull will testify to my talent for collision with the intractable. Rhonda said she had tried to call me. Years ago. After a *TV Guide* article had identified the guy on *Cheers* was the brother of Karen. She had reached out to the publisher in hopes they would connect us. They did not. It was the same article John had read when he finally realized Karen was my sister. We lived just a few miles from each other, worked in the same industry and had even been on the same show once. And he had never made the connection. I think John wished he'd reached out then but he never did. Perhaps, because of what he felt was a cold reception at our home after Karen died. We are friendly now. And I am grateful to know him. Healing. It was healing for me to speak with him. I suspect it has been for him too. Rhonda shared the news about her husband's death, and then without prompting, she launched into a monologue about Karen. I include it now just as I typed it, doing my best to catch every word as she spoke:

> Never said a bad thing about anyone. She was amazing. I never
> knew anyone like her. Once, she jumped up and down on her
> bed completely naked. In her and Ginna's dorm room. Playing
> Leon Russell. She was one in a million. Ginna told me Kar-
> en had been murdered. We never spoke of her again. I still
> think about her. I miss her. It was so unfair. She was such a
> free spirit. We would go camping. She was a really great per-
> son. She would be over the moon at your success. I am so glad

▲ This is a picture taken by John. He showed me these images when we met.

Karen, in her Swiss Colony uniform, climbing a ladder at Tom McCann.

▲ And John.

▲ I had never seen these pictures. I am glad there was this time for John and Karen.

▲ I saw her here and said to John: "I used to trim that hair."

She was lovely. And she loved that hat! The same hat she wore that last Christmas in front of the tree.

▲ Karen skiing.

◀ And not skiing.

▼ Fun in the kitchen at Red Lobster.
A costume party? That's Karen
with the cigar in a fedora.

▲ Yes, they worked at the Red Lobster.

▲ Her gang of friends. I loved seeing
these. A glimpse of her days.
And her joy with these people.

▲ And apparently someone in
the apartment liked beer.

▲ Looks like someone is about to pounce.

▲ Yes, indeed. She pounced.

▲ No idea here. *Butch Cassidy and the Sundance Kid?* Maybe.

▲ Adventure in the high country. In a yellow Vega. Fun.

▲ Campfire.

▲ Again, I am grateful to John for these pictures and grateful for the smile they bring me. I have never smiled before; now, I can a little, when I think of her in Colorado.

▲ Karen's place. 123. The apartment she shared with John and two others.

▲ The Red Lobster. A pawn shop now.

▲ The kitchen entrance. Karen prepped salads and probably walked out here for a smoke on her break. Opposite is the dumpster.

◀ The dumpster shed where she would have been seated as she waited for whomever she came to see. Staff not working were not allowed inside the restaurant. I still don't know why.

Just behind here, I found Mac.

▲ The parking lot behind the Red Lobster where she was kept tied up in the car. In Freddie's car.

▲ The 7-Eleven where she was seen buying cigarettes on her walk to work. It looks just like it did fifty years ago. The police report mentioned a store clerk who thought she was a nice girl.

▲ The field where she was taken and stabbed. It was a trailer park then. Now, the frontage off a freeway that wasn't built at the time.

▲ Across the street. The address in bold numbers where two people stated they heard a woman scream and went back to sleep. It is the very house she saw. She was right there, and they did nothing.

▲ The street. She crossed this street on her hands and knees.

▲ A stump of a tree by the curb. Cut down as she was. It just made me sad to see it—a melancholy irony is all.

▲ And she came to this address. The mailbox is likely the same. The numbers are obscured to protect the owner. I believe it is the same owner who found her body. The wooden fence where I broke down unable to reach her. Just steps away from where she died. Where I wanted to sit with her for a time.

▲ Just above the mailbox.

▲ I moved along the fence and finally saw the stoop where she fell back and died. Finally.
I am here. With her as she lay dying. With my sister, Karen. As it should have been.

you are doing this. People deserve to know about her. She is always with you. She is watching over you. I can see her smiling that beautiful smile. She made a big impression on me as a person. The way she treated people. I should be as good as she was.

Leon Russell. We did love Leon Russell. Jumping up and down naked! That brought a smile. We were always a kind of nudist family. Karen and I were not particularly embarrassed to be naked in front of one another. We didn't live like barbarians. It was Florida. The clothing was skimpy and sometimes just not there. Nothing remarkable. Nothing weird. Just relaxed. Freedom. Freedom of Expression! Yeah, that was us. She was the best person I knew. My sister. And from what I have learned from others who knew her, they thought so too.

I forgot to ask Rhonda if she knew why Karen never went back to school. Ginna told me it was because she didn't really see any point in it. She did well in her classes before Christmas that year but never really enjoyed it when she returned. Rhonda said something insightful about how young she still was. Seventeen. She missed the ocean. And Florida. We did love Florida. So, Karen went back home that spring. Not back to our house. But home to South Florida. She got an apartment and worked at the Fashion Square Mall. Where Mom had worked all those years off and on. Fashion Square, Sears, where I bought the ski that took me to water angel status that ecstatic day in our youth. She got the job at Swiss Colony.

A big smile on my face as I remember a night spent with Brett and his girlfriend, Vicki, and her girlfriend, Gail. Gail's parents owned Swiss Colony. At least, I think they did. I told you this already. But on this particular night, after driving in the backseat of the Cougar with Gail, we stopped at Vicki's apartment. Brett and Vicki had done the dance already, so they wasted very little time in excusing themselves and retiring to the next room. Gail and I sat on the couch. Facing a wall with an amateur landscape painting hanging there. A few minutes later, there were all assorted grunts and groans that finally set the picture banging on the wall. A rhythmic forward and back, forward and back; bouncing toward us, then back. Rhythm increasing. Crescendo. Then ... an awkward smile of recognition between us. We had never met before.

"So," I said, "this is fun."

"Nice to meet you," said Gail.

"Nice to meet you, too," I said.

Gail. She was a nice kid. We stared at the carpet for five minutes or so before Brett and Vicky emerged somewhat disheveled from the bedroom, and we all went for a drive to the beach and a bite of food. We actually saw each other a couple of times after that. Nice girl. And I am pretty sure I saw her one time at the Swiss Colony and met her parents. Anyway, nothing more than a nice memory came of it, but it reminds me we lived in a pretty friendly time. At least, I thought we did. The record tells a different story, I suppose. But we were nice people. Nice kids. And Karen met John, who worked at Thom McAn near Swiss Colony. The following spring, she would go to Georgia, visit some friends (I still don't know who) and then fly to Colorado Springs. She would work in the Red Lobster. She lived with John and two others in an apartment there, not too far from where she worked. She bought Marlboro Lights at a store near work. People saw her walk there some days. One night, she took that walk for the last time.

Neither of us knew our dad very well. But he deserves to be respected in these pages. He was Karen's father. Karen is the subject of this book. For whatever reason, we did not spend much time with him. It is not important now. The way he died needs to be discussed. He was murdered too. I think hate is the reason people do these things.

The man who killed Dad was a taxi driver. He drove around the island in a taxi that had some very dark things written all over it. He lit a fire beneath the house and shot my dad when he came down to investigate. Arthur Niles was acquitted for insanity but years later in NYC, a friend of mine met a bartender from St. Thomas. He was excited to tell him we were friends. Kelsey Grammer, the son of Allen

Grammer. The man from St. Thomas responded, "He's getting nothing out of me." My friend pressed the man a bit. Finally, he revealed that a group of men had drawn straws to see who would assassinate my dad. Hate. A different kind of insanity.

And the man who killed Karen surely projected his hatred onto her. Lives are easily taken under the influence of hate. Karen was a young girl who became a subject of contempt and a target of loathing. Dad fit the same description for the man, or men who killed him. These are not easy things to say, nor are they easy to comprehend. But with the taste of hate in our mouths we can all do extraordinary things. And it does seem hatred's vein runs deep in this world. Making us all likely tributaries. Evil acts can woo us to greater evils. Every single one of us. Shop owners, restaurant owners, let's be careful with those Hate signs. Please. God save us from Hate. Lead us not into temptation. Deliver us from evil. Yeah, me too. Amen. God Bless My Dad. I am grateful to him for his part in my life. I am grateful to him for Karen. May he prosper evermore and find Peace.

New Jersey played a big part in the family. On my father's side, at least. The Grammers date back to before the Revolutionary War. The Cranmers came from California. My mom came east with Gordon and Gam for work and moved to Colonia, where they built the first house on Surrey Lane. Mom went to Vail-Deane and graduated high school. Then attended the David Mannes School of Music where she met my dad. There is a long wormhole of generations that takes both families back to Europe and centuries of heritage. Not to be documented now. Just to be noted. Karen and I were a product of that heritage. Educators, businessmen, warriors, men and women of faith, victims of religious hatred and persecution. They were all a part of the soup that was our blood, That soup was full of courage and sacrifice. In Karen, courage was abundant.

Knowing her. Knowing her was to know one of the great people. She was full of light and kindness. She was fun. I spoke with Esther the other day and she shared more of what she thinks Karen and I were to one another. It goes back lifetimes. Karen was a very old soul, she said. You were close. You were many things to one another. In several lives. Lucky to be brother and sister in this life. Lucky to find each other right off the bat this time. To start together. Unlucky that it ended so soon. I am torn about offering the past lives narrative here, but it is the currency of what Esther does. I believe it. But I do not need it to believe that Karen and I were connected. In the most extraordinary way. We were one of a kind. Perhaps, a repeat one of a kind. Now and possibly forever an authentic "one-off" that casts a shadow through our singular and many lives.

I have experienced a few stalls while writing. I am in one now. Briefly. I know the next words will find me. There are a few trips to take. I leave for Sandy Hook next week. Where we used to swim when we were kids. I may see her there. I will visit Colorado Springs soon. I still have a few feelers out to those who knew her. I have not yet spoken with them. I would like to include them. They have insight and knowledge of us both during the time we were apart. And when we were together. A perspective. A point of view I will not have. And there is one I hope to reach who may have been the last of her friends to speak with her.

Then I will begin poring over the many pictures we have so I can share them with you. I have a sad heart as I realize the story is drawing to a close. At least, the telling of it. I have felt her with me. I have held her. Hard to let that go. But I don't have to let it go; I know that now. The story will never end. Yet, a book needs an ending. We'll see what comes up. The thing that is essential. To introduce you to Karen. And to ease the pain of anyone who may have loved as deeply as I. And lost that love. It is in these pages. It has brought me to a new place. A new life.

I had a dream. What do I want people to know? I want them to know there is Joy. In all of this there is still Joy. I wrestled with guilt about it. But the guilt is gone. I have had Joy in my life, and nothing can take that away. Except myself. I've stopped doing that. But! We must never stop fighting. We must always fight to stop the cruelty that happened to Karen. There is nothing good that came of it. Such cruelty. I can come to terms with it by virtue of knowing how close she remains. How alive in my life even after her death. But! Like I said. We must never abandon the fight to stop anything like that happening to anyone ever again. Maybe it is beyond our power. But we must not stop fighting it.

Fight. Rage against the dying of the light. Dylan Thomas. Rage against human cruelty. Evil has no right to expect anything but a battle. And only good can defeat it. If our cause is just and God stands with us. Evil can win a battle or two. But we cannot quit. We will not quit. Ever. Fight.

That is all I meant. And to that end, I want to say one more thing about Karen. Not my sister, but the name. A Karen. That's how they put it. Not sure when this became all the rage. And as rages go, I take comfort knowing it will go away. But it merits mention here. That is my sister you're talking about. My sister's name. She was one of the kindest, bravest, most decent people I ever knew. What you have done to her name is unacceptable. I know we love to pick on people and make assumptions. But it is assumptions that let us plunge the knife into one another. A heady combination of ignorance and arrogance. I am asking it to stop. Out of respect for Karen and hopefully what you have learned about her, you know her name is not one to be ridiculed. My two cents. I take special joy in meeting those who share her name. It is always a blessing to meet them. For their sake, if not for Karen's, I ask better of us. Respect.

This nonsense is not likely to stop. I know that. But wouldn't it be nice?

Kindness.

I have fostered some and there are those to whom I have been unkind. I did not mean to be. I probably had a choice, but I can't say I was aware of that at the time. I did not choose to hurt anyone. I hurt my kids. I did not mean to hurt them. Said some things they took as gospel when I was just fooling around. Kids do that. They look up to us until they decide we don't deserve it. We have to be careful. Mind what we say. I've heard many people say someone needs to "earn" their respect before they give it. I see it differently. I respect everyone until I "learn" I should not. Then I stop listening. I don't stop caring, necessarily. I just don't count on them. I don't condemn them. I no longer hold them in high esteem. That's all. Grain of salt. Forgive them and all that. And there He is again. Jesus. Forgive them. But in this case, even though they know what they do. People can disappoint us. We parents all disappoint our kids. If we don't someone else will.

Life has a way of kicking us in the teeth. My grandmother echoes in my ear. That boy could use a good swift kick in the pants. Somewhere along the way, of course, kids need to learn how to deal with a bit of adversity and disappointment. Can't learn to pick ourselves up if we're never allowed to fall. How else do we train for the truly life shaking events that visit us all? Live deliberately. Make amends when possible. Hopefully, our kids will forgive us. Live. Live fully. We are going to face some consequences. Face them bravely.

I do not say this lightly. If you have been paying attention, you already know that. This has been hard. Much harder than I could have imagined. What happened to Karen is still mind-numbing. But I know more now than I did. Because of what happened to Karen I am highly tuned to any cruelty I may have perpetrated. I have wrestled with this in the writing. I know I have brought it up many times. Perhaps, to beg forgiveness. Perhaps, because of the cruelty I have known, I am seeking redemption for any cruelty I have inflicted. Whether I meant to or not.

I am hearing Dale Robertson in my head. "Everybody knows the difference between right and wrong, Kelsey." And when we choose "wrong" knowing it's wrong; and choose to do it anyway, that is a problem of conscience. And character. And Soul. I have not done that. But I have been careless sometimes. I have overlooked the emotions of a dear one. For any pain I have caused, I am truly sorry. That has to be enough. Has to be enough for me too. This is the end of it.

Respect. Self-respect. Give and get.

The kingdom of heaven is at hand. This is simple. Touch it.

I looked up at Gordon. He was as tall as a mast. I was walking beside him. The docks in Atlantic Highlands. But this time, a walk beside him as a man myself. I pitched my head to mimic the angle I looked up to him when I was a boy. I could see his head up by the second story of the yacht club. And I thought for a moment what it must have felt like to look down on an adoring face. *My* face. It was last night as I lay in bed that I remembered the perspective of seeing him above me. Still there. And I began to wonder where Karen had been on those many nights we walked the docks and regarded the various sailing yachts tethered there. I loved those walks. Was Karen along? I think she was sometimes. But mostly we would complete a loop from the seawall to the end of a pier, turn and make our way back, ambling toward the destination. That wonderful bar filled with friends and like-minded people where I would shoot a few racks of pool before we lumbered back to the apartment for dinner. Karen was there occasionally, yes, but this was a time that seemed reserved for Gordon and his grandson, Kelsey.

So, I told my wife and family that I would be back after a brief walk. I retraced the steps out one pier and then another. That was when I looked up at Gordon and longed to see one of my own boys, or girls, in a mirrored duplicate of my stance with him. Only now, I would look down upon the adoring face of a child. My son or daughter. As Gordon did. As Gordon had looked upon mine. Last week, I climbed the stairs of the old yacht club and very little had changed. The bar was still there looking out on the water. I stood where the pool table had been. And I brought a host of voices. Ghosts of Gordon's friends came into view. Like looking through them and out upon the sea that lured so many of us into imaginings of other lives and pasts and paths not taken. The cocktail hour. This was nice. And again, the image of Gordon high above me. The tower of my childhood, the man I hoped to be one day. I awoke last night after seeing him. And asked about Karen. Where was she? Ah, yes! Of course. Karen was probably playing with Bobby from across the hall. I remember we were friends, but Karen and Bobby had a real bond. They spent hours together. Laughing. She and Bobby were playing with Poochie!

Poochie was a tiny stuffed bear. Brown. About three inches tall. Karen had imbued him with a personality. He was a very entertaining bear! He charmed all who met him. There was always a chance that Poochie would take exception to something said in conversation and a sudden headbutt to the solar plexus would ensue. His was a high-pitched voice who was very charming, then suddenly strident and fierce as punishment was administered. One never knew what the offending comment might be, but without warning, Poochie would launch himself into the abdomen and ignite gales of laughter.

Karen was funny. Her timing was impeccable and Poochie was one of our first indications that she had a remarkable sense of humor. Karen and Bobby would laugh and laugh and laugh with this little bear. Karen painted his portrait. And now that he has remembered himself into the equation, I must hunt for him. Some years ago, Mom found him in a forgotten box in her possession and it was with great joy I opened a birthday gift that year with a card from Poochie. "I'm back!" In Mom's handwriting. I shook with laughter. She had found our long-lost family friend. Unearthed a piece of Karen. A welcome reminder of something joyful. So many changes in my life and so many moves have sent him back into the abyss of storage. I must find him. If I do not, it serves me, nonetheless. He is alive again. She with him. Karen. She was so much fun.

This is the same thing John said about her. John who had gone with her to Colorado Springs. How much fun they had together. How she played. The Garden of the Gods. Colorado Springs. There John and Karen nicknamed each other Cassidy and Sundance. Playing out the roles of Butch Cassidy and the Sundance Kid. They had seen the film. And spent a day running over rock faces, hiding in crags and fancying themselves on the run together. It holds special meaning for John. He asked me to be sure I mentioned it. Several times. I am honored to do so. I am grateful to him for this story and grateful for his help in finding Karen. In that time. In their time. Now ours. How willing she was to explore life and love with John. I am happy she found that. Karen was always open to a new adventure. She loved people as I love them. Lusty in her loves and lusty in her thirst for life. I admire that. I admired her. I am happy to know about her life spent without me. Happy to know there was joy. And happy to hold her final days in a better light than I have all these years. It was just a mystery till now. Overshadowed by the horror of her final night.

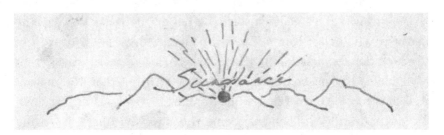

Karen's sketch of her day at Garden of the Gods with John.

June 30th. Next week. Colorado Springs. I planned to go on the anniversary of her murder. I have tortured myself enough. Enough. I will make the journey the following week. Its impact will be the same. There is nothing poetic about forcing myself into direct reflected history. Masochistic, perhaps. Not poetic. Walking in her footsteps is sufficient without the added measure of heartache and irony. July 9th. Avoid the first. Makes sense. Then I realize that is the day of her funeral. No, I checked. That was the twelfth. I flew to identify her body on the ninth. So, no way to sidestep a bit of irony here. I will fly on the sixth. But it doesn't really matter. No way to avoid this trip or put it off. Because it is time. Time to go to Colorado.

The first sign I saw was Bijou Street. I have flown here before. When she died and when I came for Freddie's parole hearing. This time, though, I have the knowledge of what I've read in the police report. All the names and places where Karen had lived are familiar to me now. I see a sign and it jogs a memory. A memory from the sterile record of an investigation that was just "ongoing" for hundreds of pages. The *Gazette* building is two blocks from the Antlers Hotel, where we are staying the night. It was in the *Gazette Telegraph* where Karen's picture was run by the police hoping to identify her. A copy was found in the garbage at Danny's home, his grandmother's home. Anna's home. Where he lived. There was a pair of glasses sketched on her lifeless face. Did it animate her features for him? Jog his memory? He doubted it was Karen when he viewed her body. Just as the others had. It was Pam, one of Karen's roommates who thought the same but realized it had to be Karen. A latent fingerprint on a ramen noodle soup container matched her corpse and that sealed the deal.

Danny was arrested for suspicion of her murder, but it was clear he had no ill will toward Karen. Cuffed and terrified, the police drove him to the station for questioning. He liked her. He had been with her that night but had driven home after they took a swim together. Karen went back out around 11 p.m. I think. She went to the Red Lobster. Sat down beside that red VW. Then they came. I don't know what I'm writing right now. I don't know if it's necessary to share any of this. But it is pouring from me. And I follow. Where? Where. I mean to write it not as a question. I follow from "where" I am, to the place I am meant to go. Karen. Just a teardrop falling. She was sitting on the first step of the pool. Karen loved the water. They went for a swim that night. I see her, saw her. Sitting there. Standing where I had never stood. And following. From there to the next. To the 7-Eleven where she would buy cigarettes—Marlboro Lights. To the Red Lobster where she worked. To the parking lot where she was spotted. To the place where she was stabbed and crawled where she would die. I stood where I could not be so many years ago. And I cried out like a child whose hope had died. My hands where the gate was. Barbed wire separating me from where she took her last breath. Where I was meant to be. Finally there. Beside her. Karen, I'm here. Crawled. Crawled an impossible distance to the stoop where she was found. And pointing to where, I do not know, she surrendered. And I stood silent. My head pressed against the fence. All I wanted was to sit there beside her for a time . . . where she fell back. Where I was not there to catch her. Or hold her.

I am here, Karen! I'm here now. I'm here! I will never leave. I am finally here. And you are in my arms. And I will hold you until God stops me. My sister. My love. I will be where I was meant to be. Beside you. It is agony. To see you die. It is agony. But I am here at last. I'm here. Your big brother. Who did nothing until now. Your brother.

I want to hold you forever.

"No, Kelsey. I'm glad you came. Thank you. Love me forever. That'll do."

He's got this. Jesus Christ. God. You know, I never quite bought all that "Praise, Jesus!" stuff. Hard lesson for me. After decades of an abiding, but limping, faith, Jesus came and took me by the hand. I was just as surprised as anybody. And I never believed He had been there for her. Till this book. Faith had always fallen a little short. Life had thrown a shadow across its face, dimmed it. I held on as best I could. Then Jesus came and told me He would carry this; He's got it. It wasn't my job; it was His. He was there. And He was. Is. Shining right beside me. And I believed. I believe. Praise Jesus! I am reborn. With Karen. Still, I will stay for a time with her in my arms. I will stroke her hair. Comfort her. Do what I was not allowed to do. And then get up. Hand her back to Jesus. And move back through time to life.

The day in Colorado Springs was full. Kayte was with me. John and I spoke on the phone as we traveled along the past. Pathways. Moments. Friendships they had known. Where they lived. Timberland Apartments. Now, The Grove. Remodeled and renamed. Apartment 123. We couldn't find it at first. I called John to ask where the apartment was within the complex. I stood by the pool and thought about how much she would have liked having it. Karen and I loved that little motel in Hollywood, Florida, with the tiny pool. We loved a pool. It was easy to imagine her swimming there. We didn't have a pool at our home in Pompano Beach, but the guy next door did and said we could use it. He was rarely there. So, it was ideal for a skinny-dip on a moonlit night. Yeah, when you grow up in South Florida, an evening skinny-dip is an essential pastime. Or was. We both explored many a friendship in that pool. It sat just ten yards from the hammock that hung between the branches of our rubber tree and the large mango. The hammock where we mourned Gordon together that night so many years ago.

These were the images that ran through my mind as I spoke with John, trying to enlist his help in finding the apartment they had shared. The pool was in plain view of the many apartments there, right in the center, so that would explain why she wore cutoffs and a bikini top when she would take a swim. She took a swim that night with Danny. And as I said, I saw her there. Sitting there in the shallow end. Talking with him in whispered conversation. We did love a pool. And as John confirmed I had the right place; Kayte came around the corner and pointed in the direction of 123. She had found it on the end of one of the units. Ground floor. You couldn't see it from the pool. It was tucked on the opposite side. I walked to the door and saw the numbers. Her last home.

John had been doing some research on his own. I had told him we were going to Colorado Springs. He had been searching old addresses and was aware the Timberland Apartments had a name change to The Grove. Yes, he confirmed, we were in the right place. I knew from reading about her final hours that Karen would often walk to work so that was our next place to visit. John said he had just discovered it wasn't a Red Lobster anymore. "It still looks like a Red Lobster," he told me. "But it's a pawn shop now." We asked Jack, our driver, to take us to the address on Academy.

And just under a mile away, we found it.

I was close to the moment I had dreaded. One of several.

The parking lot. The same one where Karen had been taken.

It was bigger than I imagined. The building sat squarely in the middle of a very large parking lot with dozens of places in front of and behind it. Kayte and I stepped out tentatively and began circling to the right of the building. I didn't think Karen would have been sitting out front. Red Lobster had a rule that if you were an employee, you could not go inside the restaurant. I don't get it. Having a drink at the bar, waiting for a friend to get off work? Or friends at work? The kitchen crew liked to pal around. What's the big deal? Maybe they rescinded it after Karen's murder. Nobody should die for a rule like that. A silly rule. Not saying she did . . . just saying.

So, she had taken up a position by a friend's car. Out back. By the dumpster. I scanned the parking lot for the place her attackers would have spotted her. Kayte was behind me and said she wondered if perhaps we would find some kind of a sign. In these sorts of situations, she suggested, that even years later, signs can be found that point to what happened. That was when I rounded the back of the building and saw the old dumpster shed that sat right behind the back entrance. Possibly where the kitchen staff would exit after work. I imagined she may have been sitting there when they spotted her. I approached the shed and looked for a place to sit. I noticed a high curb that ran behind it. A likely place. I approached for a closer look. Kayte lingered some distance behind. I told her I was going to check it out. "Some kind of sign," she repeated. I turned back and there, sitting behind the shed was a young man. No shoes. He did not look homeless. He had a somewhat pleasant demeanor, almost a smile, a friendly disposition. I turned back to Kayte and said, "Come check this out." She approached me, tentatively. And then she saw him too. We were still some distance from him, and I decided to ask him if this was indeed the old Red Lobster. I came closer and he regarded me kindly, I think. A moment's pause. He said, "Yes. My uncle used to work here years ago."

"Was this where they would keep the dumpster?" I asked. He said it was. I turned to Kayte. Looked back to him. On the odd chance it was forty-eight years ago, I asked him when his uncle had worked there.

"Maybe twenty years ago. "Why?"

"My sister used to work here. A long time ago." Then I volunteered she had been sitting nearby when she had been abducted and killed. I was thinking maybe he'd have heard about it. Nothing.

"Sorry, man," he said.

I turned and headed back with Kayte, nodding a thank you toward him as I did.

It was amazing he was sitting right there. And strange. I hoped he was all right. He looked healthy and suspicions about him being there using drugs didn't really ring true. Homeless? I didn't think so. He just looked like he was taking refuge there for a while and rubbing his feet. I suddenly wanted to know his name, so I hopped back a step and asked him. He said his name was Matt.

"Matt," I said. "Nice to meet you."

"No. Mac!" Mac. I repeated it back to be sure. He nodded. Mac.

I took a few pictures of the parking lot and the rear entrance. I imagine Karen and her friends working in the kitchen. Seems like they were a fun bunch. They all enjoyed each other. Enjoyed exploring relationships at work and socially. Four roommates living together, working at Red Lobster and a pool to swim in. A romance or two. Nice. Times were very open then. People too. Or at least a great many of our generation. A generation marked by openness and optimism. Karen was a true child of the sixties. She enjoyed people and if the mood seemed right, an intimacy was welcome. No strings attached, necessarily. A chance to be taken. To be enjoyed and possibly lead to something more if it seemed right. If not, that was okay, too. It was a lovely time. I am glad Karen lived as she lived. It was what took her to Colorado. That spirit of discovery and freedom. And it was to bring her home for her nineteenth birthday. Back to Florida. John was coming too.

Our trip to Colorado Springs was meant to mark her final days. To mark her happiness there. And to mark the final moments of her life. There. Where she had taken her last breath. I'd planned to stand outside the place where they had raped her. But something happened. Moments before leaving for the airport, a last-minute review of the police report gave me a name I hadn't noticed before—a name I did not know. Skip. Skip who lived in Wyoming. On July 6th, Pam had called my mom and asked if she knew where Karen was. She was worried about her and thought maybe she had gone to Wyoming to visit Skip for Fourth of July. My mom had said she would call Skip and ask. The kicker is I have no idea who Skip was, no recollection at all. I never met him. Not to my knowledge. I searched through the next several pages and realized there was no further mention of him. Those few frenzied searches for some further knowledge of Skip took up whatever time I had to find the additional addresses I wanted. I resolved to let them go. There was nothing I could learn from them beyond the multiple horrors I had already imagined. Could I have learned something of their mindset, of their surroundings, that would justify or at least explain what they did? The best man in me cannot muster the slightest interest in justifying their actions. It is the best man in me who would try. I have tried already. None exists. There is a common decency these men jettisoned. What I do know? These men did what they did because they wanted to. They enjoyed it. Enough of them.

I checked in with Faith and Jan. Was the mystery guy in Karen's yearbook actually Skip? They both had a vague memory of a Skip. Something. Something perhaps? Maybe. They would get back to me. For my part, I had carried the notion that an old boyfriend in Wyoming figured into Karen's visit to Colorado. Maybe my mom had told me that. Pam, her roommate, told the police that Skip had visited for a couple of days. I thought it might be time to track down Pam. Maybe she had some insights. A last name would have been a real blessing. But it was not to be. Pam had died some years ago. On the phone with John, I told him I had looked for her but discovered a page about her passing. John said he had just discovered the same thing. A moment of sadness that another possible line into the time of Karen was lost. I thought how fortunate it was that John and I had connected. And that we shared a passion to know more. To button up so many mysteries. John would like to see the police report. I will share it with him with the same warning Jim Bentley had given me. The nightmare in words is startling and heartbreaking, but the knowledge it holds is a benefit. At least it was for me. No matter what. I will wait a bit to see if anyone can help find him, but it seems Skip is gone. At least, from this story. He may be the young man on Karen's yearbook page. That is about it. He visited her in Colorado. Pam said for two days. My mom knew him but never really spoke of him. Karen did not see him again. I guess it wasn't much in the end. His last visit with her was probably a good-bye. After all, she was coming home. With John. So, Skip was just a trap door that opened and closed without much fanfare. Bless him. He spared me some suffering. Suffering that was not necessary on the last leg of this journey.

In the moments before I dashed from our home, I didn't have time to write down the address where she had been taken. I did not need to see it. I could skip it. A constructed avoidance by me for effect? Maybe. But I am grateful I did not go there. Skip was a distraction. His time with Karen had not been one of consequence. But the distraction of Skip saved me from images that would just add clutter to an already teeming brain. There was plenty to discover on that final search for Karen. Plenty that was far more consequential. Karen's courage. Her bravery. Her beauty. To witness her joys and her final surrender to malevolence; I had all I needed.

Her death. Her final breath. I saw them both. I saw weeds in a field near a freeway. Weeds similar to the high grass where she'd fallen and been stabbed again and again. Where her blood was found. I saw the apartments where the police had questioned people who thought they heard a scream and then did nothing. She was so close. Why hadn't they opened a door? Helped her? That poor girl. So, she staggered across the street and fell a few hundred feet from where she was stabbed. And died. And I came here as a witness. To fulfill my promise. To Karen. To bear witness to her life. From start to finish. Karen.

She was an Oreo cookie dipped in an ice-cold Coca-Cola. She was a poem. A light. Fun. Innocent and wise. Brave. A Warrior. A sister. The best sister. I remember, Karen. I remember. I always will. Thank you for bringing me back to the days of our youth. Our time together. Our family. I have remembered things that make me smile. Old friends and some I never met. We have celebrated you together. Laughed together. And cried. My kids know you now. They know Gordon and Gam. And Mom. Gam is alive in the imagination of my son, Gabriel. He calls her Gam-Gam. "What would Gam-Gam do if she were here?" he asks; usually, when they're up to no good. "Well," I tell him, "she would hit the roof!" I tell them all to look up and sure enough they squeal with delight at the sight of Gam hovering above them about to swoop down and terrorize them. Gabriel loves Gam. Gam-Gam! His eyes light up whenever he speaks of her. She would love him. She is vibrant in our lives today because of Gabe and because of you. You would love him, Karen. You'd love all of them. They have learned of my respect for Gordon and my love for Mom. Because of you. They know of Gordon's sacrifice and strength. Mom's patient, stalwart devotion to her children. Her dignity in the loss of her baby. They have seen me weep for you and roar with laughter at the same time. You're writing about your sister? Yes, I tell them. They know you now. Hold you now as I do.

Karen. Sumptuous. Rich. And alive.

Kayte and I went for a bite of food. Shared a bottle of wine. We talked. Reviewed. I had never felt what I felt at the wooden fence just feet from where Karen left her body. It had broken me. Again. Just when I thought nothing else ever could. Kayte asked, almost as an afterthought: what was Mac doing there? Behind the dumpster shed. Why was he there?

And then a moment later, she suddenly said, "I wonder what his name means."

She grabbed her phone and looked it up. Mac means "son of."

The "Son of..." was there. Right there!

You can take that as you wish.

This is your story, Karen. I hope you like it.

It holds you.

It holds me.

It holds our love.

Forever yours,

Kelsey

ACKNOWLEDGMENTS

I would like to acknowledge a few people. I will strike a preemptive apology to anyone I may forget or overlook. I have been overlooked in the past and have not liked it one bit! I shall do my best.

I enjoyed a variety of support throughout the writing of this book. A small army of old friends who helped. Some did detective work to find friends of Karen. Roxanne, Donna helped track down a couple of loose ends. Sadly, some people did not wish to be reached. I am still befuddled by that but not going to make any suppositions about it. I wish them all well. Faith and Jan, old friends of Karen's, were instrumental in helping me with some of the details of her high school days. We remain friends, too. I am happy for that. Brian shared some details I had forgotten. I am grateful to find him in the periphery of my life today. And anticipate a time to bring him back into a continuing friendship. A lovely man. Rhonda helped. And there was John. Wonderful John, who filled in so many blanks for me about the last year of her life. Doug and Al, Bradley, all shared insights about the family and the early years of our friendship before we were lifetime friends. Spencer.

Joe from Atlantic City. And Anita. Paul from Idaho and a lasting friend from my Juilliard days. They honored me by reading the book and offering insights. They continue to honor me. We remain friends to this day. I thank them.

Kayte, of course. Kayte offered me insights and perspective as I worked my way through the book. It was two-and-a-half years of writing. There were times I would not be present for her or my family. Kayte would gently nudge me when I stalled and bring me back to them. I did disappear a few times down a sadness I could not shake. I am so grateful to her for her patience and understanding even when it seemed the writing was a gulf that distanced us more than she might have liked. If I needed a demonstration of her love for me, there couldn't have been a better or more loving one. In one of her more opaque encouragements, Kayte said she was very excited to read it . . . once I recorded it. A mysterious, lovely woman. A sense of humor! I am grateful for that, too.

I would also like to thank my kids, Mason and Jude. They both helped with the book while working in my office this year. They pored over hundreds of pictures, and in the process I hope they learned a bit about their family and the aunt they never knew. I am grateful to them for their assistance. Terrific young people.

My friend Richard cried with me a lifetime over Karen. And we cried together as I read passages aloud in the early days of writing. What a friend!

I had tireless support from my agents and manager, Jordan and Adam. Much appreciated. Adam being the first to say he felt as if he knew Karen. That made my day. I am grateful to my publishers and to the team that tailored the manuscript with care and respect for my voice and ultimately, respect for Karen. That was essential. I want to thank Nicole for coming on board in releasing the book. Through Nicole I learned that the book has had an impact in ways I had hoped but never imagined. Ultimately, it leads me to Karen. To thank her for her love and beauty, her intelligence and patience with me. My goodness, she was a wonderful sister!

There is one last name to enter here without whom this book would never have come together. Jordan McMahon. A tireless advisor throughout this process, he has represented my wishes to the publishers and facilitated many of the final touches necessary to complete this journey. I am eternally grateful to him for his dedication and professionalism. He is also a great friend.

KELSEY GRAMMER

ABOUT THE AUTHOR

Kelsey Grammer is a six-time Emmy-winning actor, best known for his work in *Cheers, Frasier, The Simpsons,* and others.